Brian —
Happy Birthday
With Much [Love?]
Helen
(+ help from Clyde!)
Blair creek 1999

THE BIG-GAME RIFLE

The Big-Game Rifle

by JACK O'CONNOR

SAFARI PRESS, Inc.

PO BOX 3095 LONG BEACH, CA 90803

THE BIG-GAME RIFLE by JACK O'CONNOR

Copyright © 1952 and subsequent renewal by Jack O'Connor, published by arrangement with Alfred A. Knopf, Inc. All rights reserved. No part of this book may be used or reproduced in any manner whatsoever without prior written permission from the publisher. All inquiries should be addressed to: Safari Press, Inc., PO Box 3095, Long Beach, CA 90803, U.S.A.

O'Connor, Jack.

ISBN 1-57157-000-4

1994, Long Beach, California, U.S.A.

10 9 8 7 6 5 4 3 2 1

Readers wishing to receive the Safari Press catalog featuring many fine books on big-game hunting, wingshooting, and firearms, should contact the publisher at the address given above.

This is the 46th title published by Safari Press.

For

the grand old timers who have had a hand in developing the modern American big-game rifle, its stock and its equipment: Charles Newton, Adolph Neidner, Sir Charles Ross, Frank Hoffman, John Dubiel, Townsend Whelen, Ned Crossman, Bob Owen, Seymour Griffin, Rudolph Noske, Bill Sukalle, Alvin Linden, Tom Shelhamer, Charles Askins, Sr.

WARNING!

This book contains data on handloading and firearms that reflect the particular experiences of the author. The author used specific firearms, ammunition, and reloading equipment under conditions not necessarily reported in the book. Under no circumstances should the reader try to duplicate the loads mentioned in this book. The handloading of ammunition and the discharge of a firearm should never be attempted without the supervision of an adult experienced in both handloading and firearms. The publishers can not accept responsibility for the firearms and handloading data in this book.

Introduction

MANY THINGS which sound very logical simply are not so. One of the most logical things I can think of is that because they are shot less and used less than some other types of firearms there would be less interest in big-game rifles than in .22 rim-fire rifles and in shotguns. As far as logic alone goes there is not a flaw in the idea. The only thing that is wrong with the assumption is that it isn't so.

More shots are undoubtedly fired at cottontail rabbits in a year than are fired at deer in ten, and more shots are fired at tin cans than at cottontails. Most men have far more opportunity to shoot a shotgun at game than they have to fire a rifle.

In spite of all this, though, the big-game rifle is the romantic and glamorous weapon of the average man's battery. He may use it only on his annual deer hunt, but he plays with it, dreams about it, talks about it, reads about it.

Without looking up the definite figures, I would guess that at least 60 per cent of my fan mail as an arms and ammunition editor has to do with big-game rifles. The other 40 per cent is divided between shotguns, varmint rifles, .22 rim-fires, and handguns. That is curious but true, no matter how illogical it may sound!

The big-game rifle is the weapon of romance and, when a man picks one up, he becomes for the moment a pioneer, an explorer, a wilderness hunter, a present-day Daniel Boone. His annual deer hunt is the event which he plans for three months and talks about the remaining nine. If he hits his buck it becomes history, something he will never forget. If he misses a deer, it is a mystery that he must solve. One would think (also more logic) that the gun editor would get more letters about rifles and equipment *before* the hunting season. Actually he gets far more mail after the season is over (in December, January, and February), as it is then

INTRODUCTION

that the hunters are brooding over and evaluating their experiences of the past season.

It would also seem logical to assume that civilization and the hunting of big game were not compatible and that big-game hunting was destined to vanish from the land. Actually this is not so at all. More people hunt big game right now than at any other time in the history of the world.

In most of Europe, big-game hunting has been the prerogative of the rich—or at least the well-to-do—and a few have done a lot of hunting, as it has generally been considered in the Old World that to the land owner belongs the game. If the owner of a Scotch deer forest so wishes he can shoot 25 or 30 stags a season, just as he can also (as has actually happened) kill 1200 grouse or pheasants in a day.

In the United States the game is presumed to belong to the State—to the people. The take of game is spread thin but fairly evenly. Most states have a limit of one deer annually. This makes for more hunters and more hunting, but a much smaller individual kill.

The increase of certain kinds of big game has been fantastic. It is true that the buffalo herds of the Western plains are no more. It is also true that some game animals such as bighorn sheep and grizzly bear have decreased in the United States to a tiny fraction of their former numbers; but there are undoubtedly more whitetail deer, more black bear, and probably more mule deer in the United States now than there were when Columbus discovered America. Thickly populated and highly industrialized Pennsylvania has more deer hunters than any other state and an enormous herd of whitetail deer, a herd so large that it has increased beyond the carrying capacity of the range. Wisconsin and Michigan are great deer states, and so is New York. I have seen many deer near Westport, Conn., and in Westchester county, almost in the shadows of the towers of Manhattan. Heavily populated California supports both hordes of mule and blacktail deer and tens of thousands of hunters.

INTRODUCTION

The total elk range has shrunk, but on what is left the animals have increased to such an extent that it is difficult to keep them down to the numbers their winter range will support, and many states have large herds of elk that had few or none forty years ago. Antelope, which thirty years ago were almost a thing of the past, have increased so much that most Western states now have open seasons. In the fall of 1950 I hunted antelope with some friends near Gilette, Wyoming, and in one day I believe we must have seen around 1,000 head. We were in sight of antelope almost every moment of the entire day.

Many millions of Americans live close enough to deer hunting so that now, with the 40-hour work week practically universal, it takes no great amount of time or money to go on a big-game hunt. Actually, the majority of the deer I have killed in the United States have been on week-end hunts, and many times I have slept in my own bed, eaten breakfast at my own table, and have returned for dinner in my own home with a buck. Hundreds of thousands of other Americans live close enough to big-game hunting to be able to do the same thing.

Modern transportation has brought the rarer types of big game close to many who not long ago could not possibly have taken the time. In the United States there are few stretches of wilderness which are not close to automobile roads and often to places where airplanes can land. Once I left Tucson, Arizona, after lunch by automobile and the next morning I got a shot at a desert bighorn ram in the San Francisco mountains of northern Sonora. In the fall of 1950, I watched a herd of elk as I stood on a landing strip back in the Selway wilderness of Idaho while a companion and I loaded a cargo of elk meat into a small plane. A little over an hour later I was home.

It is now possible to hunt easily in areas that once required elaborate expeditions and months of time, and as a consequence, more Americans are hunting in foreign countries than ever before. Each fall sees literally hundreds of Americans after game in Canada. The first time I hunted in the Yukon I went by train

INTRODUCTION

from Tucson, Arizona, to Vancouver, B. C., (two days) then from Vancouver to Skagway, Alaska, by boat (four days), from Skagway to Whitehorse, Yukon Territory, by train (one day). The last time I went, I flew from Seattle to Whitehorse between morning and midafternoon. On that same trip, one of my companions, Herb Klein, of Dallas, Texas, was delayed. He flew from Seattle, spent the night in Whitehorse, then chartered a plane, landed on a lake to meet us, ate breakfast, and rode out to climb a mountain and kill a great Dall ram with a curl of over 47 inches, a ram which is in the very top class of the world's sheep trophies.

Not many years ago a hunt in Africa to secure representative specimens of a good number of species took the better part of a year and consumed so much time and money that only the rich and the leisured could afford it. The hunter had to go by steamship from New York to London, then through the Mediterranean into the Red Sea by way of the Suez and down the coast of Africa. He required a host of porters. Travel was by foot-power and slow. Now he can fly from New York to Nairobi in a couple of days and by motorized safari he can travel fast and do in six weeks what used to take six months. Once the man of moderate means could no more think of an African expedition than he could think of owning a yacht or maintaining a harem. Now such a trip is a possibility to anyone with a good upper middle class income who is willing to save for it.

I presume I have made the point that more big-game hunting is available to more people than ever before in history and also that big-game hunting is a democratic business open to Joe Doaks, the bookkeeper, as well as to Jack van Kale, the millionaire. Interest in big-game rifles is just as widespread and just as democratic. As an arms editor, I get letters from trappers in the Alaska bush, from farmers on the Nebraska plains, from Pennsylvania steel workers, and I also get them from Indian Maharajahs, General Motors vice-presidents, admirals, and generals. A look

INTRODUCTION

at a scope sight or a shiny cartridge, and the feel of a satin-smooth rifle stock, makes the whole world kin!

My own big-game hunting experience has been limited to North America. I have done more big-game hunting than most, much less than some, and where personal experience is lacking I have in this book drawn on the experience of others. I have never shot an Alaskan brown bear, a polar bear, a Mexican jaguar, a musk ox, or a tapir. Like most American hunters I have killed more deer than anything else; and I have hunted deer in South Carolina, Pennsylvania, northern Mexico and many Western states. I have hunted elk in Arizona, Wyoming, and Idaho; antelope in Sonora, Chihuahua, Texas, Arizona, and Wyoming. I have shot my share of grizzlies, moose, caribou, and goat, and I have hunted all species of North American sheep—Dall, Stone, bighorn, and desert. I have hunted desert *javelinas* in the hot, sandy, cactus-covered wastes of Sonora and the snow-white Dall sheep in the ice-sheathed sub-arctic mountains of the Yukon-Alaska border. Some of my hunting has been done as a dude with pack string, guide, cook and horse-wrangler, but most of it has been done on a shoestring on trips where I was my own guide, my own cook, and my own packer. I have hunted like a well-to-do man, and I have also hunted like one that was broke. I remember one trip where the objective was a good Canadian bighorn. My companion and I had two guides, a horse-wrangler, cook, cook's helper, and thirty-five head of saddle and pack stock. For two men the trip cost over $3,000. I also remember the trip for my first Mexican bighorn, which is one of the rarest of all North American trophies and one of the most difficult to obtain. My total outlay on that expedition was about $15!

It seems to be the fashion for those presumptive enough to write a book on big-game rifles to list the total of the game they've shot. I am not going to try it. I could tell how many mountain sheep I have shot and how many grizzlies, because I have shot fewer than 20 rams and less than 10 grizzlies, but I do

INTRODUCTION

not know how many deer I have taken and consider this box-score business unimportant anyway. Far more important is the fact that thousands of American hunters have shared their experience with me through correspondence, and that the eyes of many see more than the eyes of one.

Most of my hunting has been in western North America from the Alaska border to northern Mexico, some in the brush, some in plains, but most in the mountains, and if my enthusiasm seems to run toward the mountain rifles and flat-shooting cartridges it is because most of my experience has been in that direction.

I have shot more big game with .270 and .30/06 rifles than with any others, but I have also used the following: .25/20, .25 Remington, .250/3000, .257, 7 x 57, 7 mm. Magnum, .30/30, .30/40, .300 Weatherby Magnum, .35 Remington, .35 Whelen. In addition I have owned, shot, and experimented with rifles for most of the common American big-game cartridges and a fair number of European cartridges.

Contents

CHAPTER		PAGE
I.	Big Game and Big-Game Country	3
II.	Black Powder to Smokeless	19
III.	The Quest for Higher Velocity	33
IV.	Factory Big-Game Rifles	50
V.	Custom Rifle Making	74
VI.	Planning the Custom Rifle	85
VII.	Rifles and Cartridges for Forest Game	110
VIII.	Rifles and Cartridges for Mountain Game	136
IX.	Problems of the Saddle Rifle	173
X.	Rifles and Cartridges for Heavy, Soft-Skinned Game	186
XI.	Rifles and Cartridges for Thick-Skinned, Dangerous Game	210
XII.	The Construction of Hunting Bullets	225
XIII.	Iron and Glass Sights for the Big-Game Rifle	235
XIV.	Sight Adjustment for Big-Game Hunting	258
XV.	Becoming a Good Game Shot	270
XVI.	The Rifle in the Field	297
XVII.	Killing Power	323
XVIII.	Reloading Ammunition for Big-Game Rifles	337
XIX.	Slings, Scabbards, Cleaning Kits	347
XX.	The Selection of the Battery	359
	Index *follows page*	371

CHAPTER I

Big Game and Big-Game Country

ONCE I met a mining engineer who had just returned to the United States after spending five years in British East Africa. Since I have always dreamed of hunting there, I wanted to pump him about his experiences.

"Did you do any big-game hunting while you were there?" I asked.

"Oh, no," he told me. "I never got around to it."

I was floored. He was a fellow Arizonan, an outdoorsman, a man who was interested in rifles. He had been in the dreamland of the big-game hunter and yet he told me he had hunted no big game. But my mining engineer went on talking. Presently he was telling about shooting a bull eland, the largest of the antelope and an animal that will weigh a ton on the hoof.

"I thought you said you didn't shoot any big game over there," I said.

"I didn't," he insisted, "but I did shoot a lot of buck!"

He went on to explain to me then that in Africa, "big game" means dangerous game—lion, Cape buffalo, rhino, and elephant. The various antelope, which range in size from the tiny dik-dik, which is about the size of a jackrabbit, to the gigantic eland, which is larger than a moose, are all lumped under one classification—*buck*.

To an American, who is used to thinking of a 150-pound whitetail as "big game" and a 200-pound black bear as "dangerous game," this classification comes as a shock. Actually, according to the African classification, most Americans are not big-game hunters at all, and the only game animals on this continent which would be rated as big game would be the grizzly and the Alaskan brown bear. In truth, North America is pretty shy on animals that can be classed as "big" or "dangerous" in the African or Asiatic sense. Both the grizzly and the brown will ordinarily rather run than fight, and although many people have been mauled or killed by the big bears, such happenings usually come through bad luck or bad management or both. The Mexican *tigre*, or jaguar, although under certain circumstances he can be a fairly rough customer, is not a great deal larger, and probably much less dangerous, than the African leopard. On very rare occasions human beings have been killed and even devoured by mountain lions, but the average lion is desperately afraid of man and has about as much fight in him as a mouse.

Let us grant then that, in the Old World sense, most of us are not big-game hunters, as we shoot at relatively small, shy, herbivorous beasts whose instinct is to leave the country at the first whiff of man. Nevertheless, this is a book for North American hunters written by a North American, and as a consequence we'll use a North American classification.

What, then, is a big-game animal?

For our purposes, big game means any herbivorous or carnivorous animal usually thought of as "game," rather than vermin, and protected by game laws. This classification would include the little Southwestern pig-like animal called the *javelina*, or peccary, even though he weighs only about 50 pounds on the hoof. It will also include the big moose, the polar bear, and the Alaskan brown, some of which may have a live weight of 1,500 or even 1,800 pounds. The big northern wolf will weigh more than a javelina, and indeed he will weigh more than some varieties of American deer, but he is not under the protection of the game laws and hence will be classed as "vermin."

BIG GAME AND BIG-GAME COUNTRY

Actually, there are three ways game can be classified—by weight, by the country it inhabits, and by whether it is dangerous or non-dangerous—and upon these classifications depends the choice of rifles and cartridges. Obviously, the hunter needs a more powerful rifle for a moose than he does for a whitetail deer because the moose is larger and harder to kill. He needs a rifle with higher velocity and flatter trajectory for plains and mountain game than he does for forest game because the shots average much longer. Likewise the hunter needs a more powerful and deadly rifle for dangerous game than for non-dangerous game.

But first let's classify game according to weight:

CLASS I (*50 to 350 pounds*).

NORTH AMERICAN SPECIES	APPROXIMATE WEIGHT	WHERE FOUND
Javelina	40 to 50 pounds	Southwestern U. S., Mexico, South America
Whitetail deer	80 to 300 pounds	Eastern U. S., Northwestern U. S., Southern Canada, Mexico
Mule deer	100 to 350 pounds	Western U. S., Canada, Northwestern Mexico
Pronghorn antelope	80 to 125 pounds	Western U. S., South-central Canada, Northwest Mexico
Black bear	150 to 300 pounds	Most of North America
Mountain lion (*puma or cougar*)	125 to 200 pounds	Western U. S., Southwestern Canada, Mexico, South America

THE BIG-GAME RIFLE

Class I (50 to 350 pounds).

NORTH AMERICAN SPECIES	APPROXIMATE WEIGHT	WHERE FOUND
Jaguar (tigre)	150 to 250 pounds	Mexico to South America
Mountain sheep (Rocky Mountain Bighorn, Desert sheep, Stone, and Dall)	175 to 350 pounds	Western Canada, Western U. S., Alaska, Northwest Mexico
Rocky Mountain goat	200 to 400 pounds	Northwestern U. S., Western Canada, Alaska

OLD WORLD SPECIES

Old World sheep and goats (large Asiatic sheep of Argali type including Ovis Poli)	200 to 450 pounds	Mountains of Central Asia
Small Asiatic sheep (Kamchatka sheep related to the American Ovis Dalli, Urial, Asiatic Mouflon)	70 to 200 pounds	Mountains of Asia
Mouflon	60 to 70 pounds	Sardinia and Corsica, and transplanted to the Bavarian Alps
Barbary Sheep	150 to 250 pounds	Mountains of North and Northeast Africa
Bharal (Blue Sheep)	125 to 150 pounds	Central Asia
Ibex, Markhor, Tahr, Takin, Serows, and related goats and goat-like animals	125 to 250 pounds	Mountains of Central Asia, Italian Alps, Persia, Arabia, North Africa, Spain

BIG GAME AND BIG-GAME COUNTRY

Class I (*50 to 350 pounds*).

OLD WORLD SPECIES	APPROXIMATE WEIGHT	WHERE FOUND
Chamois	65 to 100 pounds	Mountains of Central and Southern Europe from Pyrenees to Caucasus and to Asia Minor
Small to medium-sized Asiatic and African antelope	40 to 450 pounds	Africa and Asia
European and Asiatic deer (Roe and Fallow deer)	65 to 200 pounds	Europe and Africa
Leopards	80 to 150 pounds	Africa and Asia
Various small Asiatic bears	100 to 250 pounds	Asia

Class II (*350 to 2000 pounds*)

Elk (American Wapiti)	350 to 1000 pounds	Western U. S., Southwestern Canada
Moose	700 to 1400 pounds	Northwestern U. S., Canada, Alaska
Caribou	350 to 500 pounds	Northern Canada, Alaska
Grizzly bear	400 to 900 pounds	Western U. S., Western Canada, Alaska
Musk ox	400 to 1000 pounds	Arctic North America
Alaska brown bear	700 to 1400 pounds	Western Alaska and adjacent islands
Polar bear	700 to 1800 pounds	Arctic regions
OLD WORLD SPECIES		
Lion	400 to 600 pounds	Africa, rarely in Asia
Tiger	400 to 700 pounds	Asia
Large African antelope	250 to 2000 pounds	Africa
European Red deer	350 to 500 pounds	British Isles, most of Europe

THE BIG-GAME RIFLE

Class II (*350 to 2000 pounds*)

OLD WORLD SPECIES	APPROXIMATE WEIGHT	WHERE FOUND
Old World elk (closely related to North American moose)	700 to 1200 pounds	Northern Europe
Zebra	500 to 1000 pounds	Africa

Class III (*2000 pounds and up*)

Wild bovines like the Cape buffalo of Africa, Gaur, Tisne, and Yuyal of Asia	2000 pounds and up	Asia and Africa
Giraffe	2000 to 3000 pounds	Africa
Rhinoceros	up to 3000 pounds	Africa
Hippopotamus	up to 8000 pounds	Africa
Elephant	up to 12000 pounds	Africa and Asia

Dangerous and Non-Dangerous Game

By far the most dangerous animal that walks the face of the earth is a human being with a good rifle in his hands, and pitted against him, few other mammals have the slightest chance. Potentially, one of the few dangerous North American game animals is the big Alaska brown bear, but I have read that there has never been an instance of a guided sportsman getting mauled while hunting brownies. Even under circumstances that are favorable to the bear, when ranges are short and going is heavy, the big animals don't have much chance against an armed sportsman and an armed guide. People have, in a good many instances, been killed by brown bears, but they have been resident Alaskans who have blundered on to them and who have usually been underarmed or unarmed.

Actually, from what I have seen and from what I have read, I'd make a guess that the grizzly is a more dangerous animal than the larger Alaska brown and has mauled, maimed, and killed many more people. Whether this is because the grizzly is an ornerier customer than the brown, or whether it is because the grizzly comes in contact with more people, I cannot say. I would make an offhand guess, though, that every year about ten people are mauled or killed by grizzlies in Canada alone, from the United States border to Alaska.

Almost always, these maulings and killings come either from blundering into a sow with cubs, from encountering at close range a grizzly that has made a kill, or from following a wounded grizzly into brush. My friend, Dr. John Hammett, of New York City, followed a wounded grizzly into the brush in 1949 and was attacked. Fortunately for him, a shot had broken the grizzly's jaw. Otherwise he would have been dead or maimed for life. Another friend of mine, a Champagne, Yukon Territory, Indian named Field Johnson, who guided me on two trips in the Yukon, was set upon by a short-tempered grizzly in the spring of 1950, and was badly mauled and buried. He escaped with his life only by feigning death; something which, he said, was quite easy to do after he had been dragged for a half mile, beaten, chewed on, and covered up with soil and brush.

The fact that both the grizzly and the brown bear are potentially dangerous lends spice to hunting them, but neither is very formidable if the hunter has any luck at all and practices any decent management. The hunter who stalks the grizzly above timberline in some great open basin, who has an adequately powerful rifle, who can shoot, and who keeps cool, is in about as much danger as he is in his living room sitting before the fireplace reading a book. He is in probably far less danger than he is when he packs the family car, herds his wife and young into it, and departs for his Sunday picnic.

The last grizzly I shot was in an open empty basin in the Pelly Range of the Yukon. My guide and I saw the bear about a mile away, striding purposefully along the side of a hill, bare except for a smooth carpet of grass, moss, and lichens, and an occasional patch of stunted arctic willow. We watched the bear for a moment and it soon became apparent to us that he was traveling and that he would come through a pass below us. We ran down the steep hillside and sat down so we could waylay the bear when he came through. I had a .300 Weatherby Magnum loaded to give the 180-grain Remington bronze point bullet about 3,200 f.p.s. velocity. I fed a cartridge into the chamber, laid the rifle over my knees, picked up my binoculars, and watched the bear. On it came, striding swiftly and purposefully, like a man who has just got off the 7:46 at Grand Central and has to step right along to get to the office.

Then I turned to my guide.

"When he gets on the other side of the willow patch, I'll bust him!"

On came the bear. We were in plain sight but he never saw us. He walked through the willows and when he came out on the other side I had the safety off. I put the crosshairs in the scope low behind bruin's shoulder, followed him along with a moving rifle for an instant, and squeezed the trigger. As the rifle recoiled I saw the bear plunge forward on his nose, struggle convulsively for an instant and lie still. The combination of a powerful rifle and a well-placed shot made the grizzly about as dangerous as a chipmunk. In that case circumstances were so favorable that it would have taken a genius to have got into trouble.

Under the right circumstances almost any animal can be dangerous. Once when my wife and I were hunting in Sonora, she wounded a boar javelina that might have weighed 50 pounds on the hoof. She tracked it down, cornered it, and it charged. She dropped it at her feet, but if she hadn't, it might have cut her up pretty badly.

As bad a scare as I ever had came from a buck mule deer. I had taken a shot at it at about 300 yards. It went down at the forequarters, then got to its feet, and ran into some piñon trees before I could shoot again. A friend and I took out after it, tracked it through the narrow belt of trees, and found it lying out in the open and apparently about dead. I felt around on its neck while I held one antler, then found a big artery and cut it. Instantly my buck was very much alive and for the next few minutes he scared me half to death.

Probably the world's most dangerous game animals are the African elephant, the Cape buffalo, the rhino, and the lion—all found in Africa. Many hunters have been mauled and killed by all of these animals. Just which one of them is the most dangerous, I cannot say, as various hunters put various values on them. I'd make a guess, from what I have read, that most experienced African hunters would put the elephant first, the buffalo second, and the lion and rhino in a poor third and fourth.

The reason the elephant is so dangerous is that he is so enormously large and that he is so often hunted in heavy cover where the hunter may be within a few feet of him and not know it. Under those circumstances, a shot, from the most powerful rifle that can be fired from the shoulder, unless it is perfectly placed in the brain or spine, can do no more than halt one of the great animals momentarily. The Cape buffalo is also a tough customer, big and with enormous vitality. He is also, I understand, the most cunning and vindictive of opponents once he is wounded, and will, figuratively, grind a victim to a pulp. Like the elephant, he is also hunted much of the time in brush and jungle, where visibility is poor and where the hunter can be almost on top of the game without being aware of it.

The African lion has killed many hunters, but from my reading it has struck me that those who got into a mix-up with lions did so from very bad luck, poor shooting, poor judgment, panic, or a combination of them. Today, the lion is most often baited and shot from a boma. He is a plains animal that should afford good shots, and he isn't a very large animal, since he weighs only about 400 pounds. I can see no reason why he should be any harder to kill or any more dangerous to hunt than a grizzly.

THE BIG-GAME RIFLE

The rhino is dangerous largely because of his bone-headed truculence. He is apt to charge at the slightest provocation and, because he is a big beast with a thick hide, he is often difficult to stop.

The tiger is a larger animal than the lion. A big Bengal tiger, I understand, will weigh up to 600 pounds and the great long-haired Manchurian and Korean tigers will weigh more than that. In parts of China and India, tigers habitually prey on the unarmed, ill-fed, and timorous natives. It is rare, though, that one mauls a white hunter, since the beasts are usually shot from a machan perched in the trees over a bait or are shot from the backs of hunting elephants.

BIG-GAME COUNTRY

The choice of the big-game rifle is conditioned, first, by the size, vitality, and possible bad temper of the animal to be hunted; second, by the type of country in which the game is found. Naturally, one would not hunt moose with a .25/35. It has been done, but it is not a good idea, since the moose is much larger, tougher, and harder to kill than the whitetail deer for which the .25/35 is designed. Likewise the hunter who goes after mountain sheep—the hunting of which often necessitates long shots—with a 38/55 is making a poor choice of weapons.

Actually, the country in which the game is to be hunted is of enormous importance in the choice of a rifle and cartridge. In thick brush and woods, there is no need for high velocity and flat trajectory, as a 150-yard shot is a long one. In plains hunting for antelope, on the other hand, shots are usually long and the best rifle is one of very high velocity, very flat trajectory. The weight of the rifle does not matter much on the antelope plains, since even if a man hunts on foot, the going is easy, and the hunter most often moves around in a light truck or a jeep and doesn't have to carry his rifle far. In such a case he can take a 14-pound rifle shooting a super-accurate high velocity cartridge,

BIG GAME AND BIG-GAME COUNTRY

and he can have it equipped with a high-powered scope with a field so small that it would be useless for hunting whitetails in heavy cover.

The sheep or goat hunter in North America, Europe, or Asia, needs a flat-shooting long-range rifle built as light as it can possibly be built and still retain accuracy, as nothing can *seem* heavier than an overweight rifle in genuinely rough country. I learned my lesson and learned it well once in the Coast Range of northern British Columbia when I hunted goats with an 11-pound .300 Magnum on a Magnum Mauser action. It was a grand rifle. It would keep five shots in a group the size of a dollar at 200 yards. It had a very flat trajectory and enough power to knock a grizzly flat in its tracks. I could shoot it as well as any rifle I ever had; but it weighed about 3½ pounds too much, and those extra 3½ seemed at the end of the day like 35! When I got back from the trip I was offered a nice sum for the rifle. I sold it down the river and replaced it with a lighter .300 Magnum rifle.

The more open the country is and the longer the average shot is, the more important flat trajectory and great accuracy become. The rougher the country, the more energy it takes to get around, the greater burden a heavy rifle becomes. The rougher the going, the more tendency there is for the hunter to demand a light, short, compact rifle. The Model 1903 Mannlicher-Schoenauer carbine with the 18-inch barrel chambered for the 6.5 x 54 rimless Mannlicher-Schoenauer cartridge was a European answer to the demand for a rifle to be used on a small, easily killed animal (chamois, largely, but also roe deer) and to be carried by the hunter himself in very rough country at high altitudes.

It is interesting to note that the British, who hunted in the high mountains of Asia, turned the chore of carrying the rifle over to the *shikari*, or guide, and as a consequence, used much heavier rifles.

A more or less logical division of big game country itself would be about as follows:

Open Plains. The antelope country of Wyoming is, for the

THE BIG-GAME RIFLE

most part, typical open plains country and so, to a somewhat lesser extent, is the antelope country of Arizona, Chihuahua, New Mexico, and Sonora. Some plains areas are gently rolling, but some are almost as flat as a billiard table. There are vast areas of plains country in Africa, where all plains game from the tiny dik-dik through the various larger antelope, and the lions that prey upon them, are hunted. Many plains areas are found in Asia where the various types of Arabian, Indian, and Tibetan antelope are shot.

Plains conditions can be found on tops of high mountains. Fannin sheep have been shot in northwest British Columbia, in such areas as Table Mountain, when they were out on flat-topped plateaus or "mesas" and the conditions of shooting and stalking were exactly the same as in the Red Desert country of Wyoming, even though the game were wild sheep instead of antelope. I once hunted sheep in Wyoming where the bighorn rams bedded down in the heads of rough, steep canyons, but came out to graze on high, flat plateaus. From pictures I have seen of the hunting of Ovis Poli in the Russian and Chinese Pamirs, these great long-legged but lightly built sheep, with their wonderful flaring horns, are often hunted under what might be called plains conditions, even though the lofty plateaus on which they are found may be at 16,000 and 17,000 feet above sea level.

The incredible herds of buffalo that were shot off in the United States during the last half of the nineteenth century were hunted under plains conditions. The great barren grounds that stretch to the Arctic Ocean beyond the limit of trees, all through northern North America, Asia, and northern Europe, are simply arctic plains or prairies, and the conditions that apply in the Wyoming antelope country or on a desert playa down in Sonora also apply there—not only to the caribou, but to the barren ground grizzly, the occasional polar bear that wanders in, and the musk ox. All plains hunting is marked by ease of getting around, by difficulty of finding cover for successful stalks, by long shots.

BIG GAME AND BIG-GAME COUNTRY

Rugged Open Mountains. Typical of rugged, open mountain country is the sheep country of the world, wherever it is found, from the Atlas Mountains of North Africa, through the great wild sheep and goat ranges of Asia, to our own sheep country above timberline running from the Brooks Range in arctic Alaska down through the Colorado Rockies. Barren open mountains are sometimes produced by country that is too rocky and sterile to grow trees or even large bushes, but usually it is produced by aridity or by altitude that puts it above timberline. The Barbary sheep and ibex country of North Africa is open and barren because of aridity and so is the desert sheep country in Arizona, Nevada, California, Lower California, and Sonora. The great Asiatic sheep ranges are mostly very high and also very arid. The American wild sheep are mostly hunted in country that is made open and barren by the fact that it goes above timberline, which may be at only 3,500 feet above sea level in Alaska and parts of the Yukon, but at 11,000 in Wyoming.

Conditions favorable for sheep are furnished by sterility of soil in many areas—notably in canyon country, where there is so little good soil that few trees and shrubs grow and the sheep has what he demands for existence—great vistas where he can see his enemies a long way off, rough and steep country that will enable him to outclimb them.

Open mountain country puts a great strain on the hunter. Usually is is too rough for horses and the sheep or goat hunter has to transport himself, his rifle, and his equipment. Shots average long, but not as long as in the plains because often intervening ridges give cover for a stalk. I have shot Dall, desert, Stone, and bighorn sheep, for instance, at less than 100 yards because intervening ridges enabled me to stay out of sight and to stalk close. It is infinitely more difficult to get around in rough mountain country, but shots are much less difficult as a rule than in plains hunting.

Thinly Wooded Mountains. Much deer hunting in the western United States is done in perfectly delightful country which is steep, but not steep and rough enough to preclude the use of horses. Often one can see game at from 200 to 1,000 yards across great, thinly wooded basins and canyons. One runs into spots of such country from Canada to northern Mexico. Such country is often arid and semi-arid. I have hunted mule deer in such country from southern British Columbia, through the Salmon River country of Idaho, to the mountains of Arizona and northern Chihuahua and Sonora. One of the finest deer hunts I ever had was about 50 miles south of the American border in Sonora in the foothills of a mountain called Sierra Azul (the blue mountain). It went up to about 8,000 or 9,000 feet and was heavily wooded by yellow pine, oak, and manzanita; but the lower ridges were carpeted with yellow, frost-cured gramma grass and spotted thinly with evergreen oaks. In the heads of the canyons and in the draws, the oaks and brush grew thick, but these areas were small and it was easy to push deer out of them. In a five-day hunt I was off my horse only to shoot or to lead him around a particularly steep place. The beautiful little blue-gray whitetail deer with their handsome antlers and great white fans came booming out of the little thickets onto the open grassy ridges, and cutting them down took a lot of doing. I know of no greater sport than hunting such country if it is well supplied with game. A horse furnishes the muscle and the wind, and all the hunter has to do is to think, to look, and to shoot.

But the man who hunts on a horse in such country has to know how to shoot, since a high proportion of his shots are running shots and many of them are at fairly long range. Shots do not average as long as they do in the plains, but they average longer than they do in very rough mountains, and far more of them are running than in either plains country or rough mountains. In such country a 150-yard shot is a very short one and a 250-yard shot is, I believe, about average.

Heavily Wooded Mountains. Alas and alack, much hunting over the world has to be done on heavily wooded mountains, the most difficult of all types of country to hunt. I, for one, do not mind climbing, nor do I mind hunting in heavy woods. When the two types are combined, the hunting is grim. Getting around in such country is laborious, difficult, and exhausting. Usually such country is so noisy to hunt in and the visibility is so poor that the only shots offered are on opposite hillsides, sometimes at ranges of 400 yards or more. Shorter shots are usually at very close range. Much of the Selway and Lochsa elk country in Idaho is of this type, and so is elk country in Montana. The heavily brushed, steep mountains of the Coast Range of California are a variation of this type of country.

Forest. A high proportion of the world's deer hunting is done in level or rolling forest country where shots are short, mostly within 100 yards and many within 50 yards. Almost all big-game hunting in the United States east of the Mississippi is forest hunting. So is the blacktail hunting in the Pacific Coast rain forests, much of the brown bear hunting in southeast Alaska, and most of the moose hunting in Canada east of the Rockies. Many shots must be taken through brush, and since the game can be out of sight in an instant, bullets should be of sufficient weight and construction so that they will drive through the game on a broadside shot and leave a good blood trail.

Open Brush. For many years I did a lot of hunting in level semi-open country on the lowland deserts not far from the Gulf of California in the Mexican state of Sonora. Shots would range from 25 to 200 yards on desert mule deer and occasionally on whitetail. Now and then even desert bighorn sheep traveling from one range to another are caught down in this open brush country. Conditions are similar, although the vegetation is entirely different, on the high plateaus at 7,000 feet elevation and above in the Sierra Madres of Sonora and Chihuahua and in Arizona and New Mexico, where one runs into the Rocky Mountain mule deer, elk, and wild turkey. Hunting in such country is a combination of still-hunting and stalking. The hunter moves slowly and quietly upwind and crosswind, keeping his eye peeled for game and never having to exert himself unduly. Similar hunting conditions are also found over much of the high African plains country.

Jungle. True jungle is tropical, but some of the country on the Pacific Coast of North America from Washington north into Alaska doesn't miss being jungle by much. Jungle is incredibly thick. It is difficult to move fast in and visibility is poor. Elephant hunters write, for example, of getting within 20 feet of an enormous bull elephant and of being unable to see well enough to place a shot, so thick is the growth. Much jungle game is dangerous—elephants, tiger, Cape buffalo, various Asiatic wild oxen. Flat trajectory and hair splitting accuracy either of cartridge or sights are out of place in jungle hunting; what is needed is very heavy bullets at moderate velocity, bullets that if they do not strike a vital place will yet knock down a large heavy animal or make him pause for an instant so a better shot can be driven in.

The choice of the rifle, the cartridge, and the sights for hunting depend, then, on the size of the game animal being hunted, its disposition (dangerous or non-dangerous), and the type of country in which it is found. No one in his right mind would hunt chamois in the Swiss Alps with a .465 Nitro Express double rifle weighing 11½ pounds and fitted with crude non-adjustable open rear sights with a large ivory bead front sight—a weapon for jungle shooting of the heaviest game. Nor would one hunt Cape buffalo with a .270 W.C.F. equipped with a 4-x scope.

These are extreme examples, but in the field one often sees choices almost as bad. In the Idaho elk country I saw a chap hunting 600-pound elk with a .32/20, a cartridge which would do for 50-pound javelinas in the open brush of Arizona and Sonora. A .30/30 carbine is just as miscast for antelope on open plains, in spite of the fact that it is a good deer rifle for forest country and a fair one for open brush country.

CHAPTER II

Black Powder to Smokeless

THE REAL popularity of big-game hunting began with the enormous spread of the Western European peoples into the new and undeveloped sections of the world, mostly in the eighteenth and in the early nineteenth centuries. The British emigrants to North America found themselves in a wilderness teeming with big game and with savage Indians. Those who pushed into the wilderness had to have rifles to exist. With them they hunted wild turkey, whitetail deer, black bear, and elk; and with them they defended themselves and their homes against the Indians. The American frontiersman had, of necessity, to be a crack shot and a good hunter. Because the rifle was as much a tool of survival as his axe and his plow he treated it almost like a living thing and gave it fanciful names such as Old Betsy, Old Meat In The Pot, or Old Reliable. Among his principle recreations were the turkey shoot and other contests with the rifle. In terms of purchasing power of the dollar, the muzzle-loading "Kentucky" rifle was enormously expensive. It was a hand-made proposition from start to finish and often cost around $100. In terms of present dollars such a rifle would be worth today at least $500 and possibly $1,000. No wonder the young pioneer considered that he had made a good start on his life's working capital if he had a rifle, an axe, a plow, and a couple of horses. With those tools, and a bride to turn the raw materials of the forest into victuals, he could set out into the wilderness, make a clearing, build a cabin, put in a crop, kill game for the larder, and protect himself from the Indians.

The conquering British in India also found themselves in a great game country which was thickly populated by ill-fed, degenerate human beings without the arms and the inclination to protect themselves from marauding tiger and leopard or from the raids on their crops of the herbivorous animals like the wild boar, the black buck, and the swamp deer. These men, too, became big-game hunters but more for sport and recreation than the Americans, who had to hunt big game to live.

All through the nineteenth century the British, whether they were pioneering in Asia or in Africa, or whether they were rich men hunting as a hobby, were the world's greatest sport hunters. They occupied a position similar to that occupied by the Americans today. Some of the British hunted ivory for the money that was in it. Some, like the Americans, hunted for meat and to protect themselves on their African farms. Great numbers of British, though, hunted purely for sport. They were the world's first trophy-hunters in a modern sense. England was full of wealthy and leisured people in the nineteenth century, people with a tradition of sport and a zest for adventure. They organized elaborate expeditions and hunted all over the world—for sheep and goats in the high mountains and plateaus of central Asia, for mixed game in Africa, for tiger in India. Wealthy British came in great numbers to North America to hunt. A high proportion of the world record elk heads shot in Wyoming in the past century were killed by Englishmen and are still in England. They hunted in such outlandish places as Crete, Arabia, and Persia. They were the first hunters to bring out the great wild sheep of Central Asia—Ovis Poli, Argali, Littledale's sheep, etc. These moneyed, leisured, adventurous Englishmen were a highly literate group, whether they were army officers or civil servants in India, or whether they were simply wealthy men with the love of wild places in their hearts. They wrote many books, and anyone who has read these books can have only the greatest admiration for them, and can read them with wistful nostalgia for a day when a gentleman was a gentleman and we lived in easier and less troubled times.

More than a hundred years ago there was a great difference in the weapons used by the British and by the Americans. The British hunter was usually a wealthy man. He was a sports hunter who killed for trophies rather than for meat. He traveled with a large retinue. He usually had a flunky to carry his weapon for him. Because the British pound was the world's standard of monetary value in those days, and its purchasing power was high all over the world, our Englishmen could travel with an astounding amount of impedimenta and carry with him, wherever he went, his high standard of living. Forty-five years ago a party of wealthy Englishmen went into the desert sheep mountains of northern Mexico. They assembled their outfit around the desert mining town of Ajo, Arizona, and I can remember when the old-timers there still talked about it with awe and wonder. The British had portable bathtubs with them and even though water was scarce they had their nightly tubs or knew the reason why. They insisted on tables to eat on, and folding canvas chairs. The tables had white tablecloths and the border Mexicans and the American desert rats who served them had to dish up in courses the grub they had cooked in Dutch ovens on mesquite or ironwood coals. One member of the party was a titled Englishwoman and to protect her fair complexion from the hot desert sun she always wore white gloves and traveled on her cayuse carrying a white umbrella with a green lining. An old Papago Indian, who is now dead, went along as a sheep guide and a horse-wrangler, and whenever he told me about the English he always shook his head and muttered: "What a people, those English!"

The German, Swiss and Austrians have always been hunters and riflemen, more than most other continental Europeans. As American soldiers, who were in those countries after the war, can testify, rifle shooting and big-game hunting were widely practiced and not merely a prerogative of the rich and noble as

THE BIG-GAME RIFLE

in other European countries. The sturdy Swiss and Bavarian mountaineers had communal grazing lands where they hunted or where they rented out the hunting rights to city dwellers. Here they shot roe deer, chamois, the European red deer, or *Hirsch*. Prior to the war German business and professional men would rent fields and wood lots from land owners or from the German government. They would hire game keepers to keep poachers out and to protect the game from predators. As a consequence, interest in hunting and in rifles is widespread in Central Europe and the Central European gun nut or rifle nut is much more akin to the American than the American is akin to the British.

As a matter of fact, the first genuinely successful hunting rifle used in America was a direct descendant of the German "Jaeger" rifle. It was built in Pennsylvania by German emigrant gunsmiths. The German hunting rifle of the early eighteenth century was a heavy, rather short-barreled rifle of large bore—from .75 to .90 caliber. It was adapted by the German gunsmiths who came to this country as the famous "Kentucky," following the specifications of the American frontiersmen. Lead was hard to get and so was powder. American pioneer hunters wanted a small bore rifle of relatively high velocity which was adequate in killing power for the rather small whitetail deer and black bear ordinarily encountered, and for the Indians that had to be shot in the course of events—and who were probably no more difficult to kill than deer. They wanted also a rifle which was economical in its use of those scarce commodities, powder and lead. European rifles had been slow and difficult to load since the lead ball had to be pounded down on the powder charge with a ramrod and mallet. Then some unknown genius, some pioneer American rifleman, discovered that he could use an undersize ball patched with greased linen or buckskin and driven down on the powder charge with a smooth push of the ramrod. As the greased patch went down the bore the fouling was cleaned out. Because of the patch the bullet was tight against the rifling. The bullet was given its rotational spin and then the patch fell away when bullet and patch left the muzzle. This was a genuinely epoch-making discovery—a discovery which made the rifle practical for hunting and for war because it enormously speeded up loading without impairing accuracy or velocity.

A typical German Jaeger rifle would have about a .75 bore, use a ball weighing around 640 grains at a velocity of about 800 f.p.s. Energy would be 910 foot-pounds. A typical Kentucky rifle, on the other hand, would be .38 caliber using a 78-grain bullet at a velocity of around 2,000 f.p.s., with 690 foot-pounds of muzzle energy. The Jaeger was about a 100-yard rifle, the Kentucky a 200-yard rifle and often skillful shots with it could reach out and kill an Indian at 300 yards or more. It was a real precision instrument and even today those old Kentuckies, when properly loaded and handled, will give accuracy comparable with the best modern rifles used with iron sights. In a modern sense, the old Kentucky rifles were not very powerful. Actually they struck a blow about like that of the modern .32/20. However, these rifles were used by skillful shots who were fine hunters. The shots they got were usually at short range and at standing game. When they hunted they placed their bullets and they placed them right. A man who is as good a shot as they were, and who is as good a hunter, can kill all the deer he wants with the .32/20 even today.

Barrels of those old Kentuckies were made of soft iron and gradually they wore out, even with soft bullets of pure lead, and with relatively cool-burning black powder. Then they were taken to the gunsmith who "freshed them out" or rerifled them. A rifle might start out as a .35 caliber and end up as a .40 or even .45 caliber. All a man had to do when he got his rifle refreshed was to buy himself a new bullet mold of the proper caliber and he was set.

When the American hunters crossed the Mississippi and drove west, they encountered longer ranges, heavier and more dangerous game. They hunted the big buffalo, which often takes a good deal of killing. They ran into very tough and unfriendly

THE BIG-GAME RIFLE

Indians like the Sioux. They also encountered the large and ferocious plains grizzly which was rough, truculent, and aggressive because he had associated all his life with bow-and-arrow Indians who were afraid of him. Consequently, the American plains rifle was developed. In a way it was sort of a reversion to the short-barreled German Jaeger rifle of larger caliber. These rifles were cut off in their prime by the advent of the breech loader; but they were made by such famous gunsmiths as the Hawken Brothers of St. Louis, and carried west by the beaver trappers and the mountain men who hunted the great Rockies even before the Louisiana Purchase and the Mexican War, men who poached beaver in Mexican Territory and who often became better Indians than the Indians themselves. The famous Kit Carson was one of them.

Kentucky and Jaeger rifles were flintlocks, of course. So were the early plains rifles. Most of them were changed to caplocks after a Scotchman named Forsythe had developed a percussion cap which was the first step in profound changes which developed the modern rifle.

The first successful breechloaders came in just prior to the American Civil War and the breechloader is simply a step to the repeater. Except for some Sharps rifles and carbines, and for some Henry and Spencer repeating rifles, the Civil War was largely fought with muzzle-loading rifles and indeed even with some muzzle-loading smooth-bore muskets. After the Civil War the old muzzle-loading army rifle was redesigned as a breechloader—the first of the trapdoor Springfields. It was a .50/70 caliber. In 1873 the same makeshift action was retained, but the caliber dropped down to .45/70. Some of these old trapdoor black-powder rifles were used as late as during the Spanish-American War, in spite of the fact that they had been replaced as the official U. S. Army rifle by the .30/40 Krag in 1893.

The hey-day of the black-powder breechloading rifle lasted only around twenty to twenty-five years—from about 1870 to 1890 or 1895. Actually black powder was on its way out by

1890, and by 1895 it was very definitely on the run, not only for sporting use but also for military use.

The era of the latter part of the nineteenth century was a romantic one from the standpoint of the hunter-rifleman. It saw British big-game hunters going all over the world. It saw the buffalo exterminated in the western United States with these breechloading black-powder rifles, the antelope and deer thinned out, grizzlies and sheep driven into the highest mountains. This period is one which is strongly entrenched into American folklore. It was the day of the old black-powder Frontier Model Colt revolvers, the big, powerful single-shot Sharps buffalo rifles, Winchester Model 1873 lever-action rifles for the .44/40 cartridge. It was the time of Wild Bill Hickock and Billy The Kid, the time when a handful of American trappers and cowboys could stand off a horde of Indians at Adobe Walls, and it was also the time when General Custer and his command were wiped out on the Little Bighorn by the Sioux.

Many are the marvelous tales that are told of the shooting in those days and many of them have grown with the telling. A trapper is supposed to have knocked off an Indian who was standing on a cliff, making insulting gestures toward him, three-quarters of a mile away. Buffalo hunters were supposed to be able to lie down, take their shooting sticks, and polish off a whole herd of buffalo one by one at 800 yards.

All of this may have happened and it may not have happened. The .44/40 Model 1873 was the most widely used rifle by the ordinary cowboy and Western hunter. It used a 200-grain bullet with a muzzle velocity of about 1,250 f.p.s. and only 688 foot-pounds of muzzle energy. In traveling over 200 yards the bullet rose about 15½ inches. It doesn't sound like more than about a 125-yard rifle to me.

The famous .40/90 Sharps straight cartridge used a 370-grain bullet at a muzzle velocity of about 1,350 with about 1,500 foot-pounds of muzzle energy. Over 200 yards the bullet rose 10½ inches and over 300 yards the trajectory height at 150 yards was

THE BIG-GAME RIFLE

about 26½ inches. The famous Winchester .50/100 black-powder cartridge used a 450-grain bullet at a muzzle velocity of 1,383 and 1,719 foot-pounds of muzzle energy. Over a 200-yard range the bullet rose 12 inches and it rose over 30 inches in traveling 300 yards. With any of those great old black-powder cartridges, and at a range of 400 to 500 yards, the shooter would have to know within a few yards exactly how far the game was away in order to hit, because the angle of fall of the bullet was so sharp.

The .40/72 Winchester for the Model 1895 was one of the ultimate developments of black-powder center-fire cartridges. It used a 330-grain bullet at a muzzle velocity of 1,359 with 1,386 foot-pounds of muzzle energy. Over 200 yards the mid-range trajectory was over 12 inches.

Because the British did a great deal of jungle hunting on large and dangerous game the old black-powder cartridges were considerably more powerful than similar American cartridges. As an example, in double-barrel big black-powder rifles, the famous old .577 cartridge used a 480-grain bullet at a muzzle velocity of 1,680 f.p.s. with 3,050 foot-pounds of muzzle energy; the .500 caliber used a 505-grain bullet at 1,500 f.p.s. velocity and 2,520 foot-pounds of muzzle energy; and the .450 used a 480-grain bullet at 1,550 f.p.s. velocity and 2,560 foot-pounds muzzle energy.

The British also used ponderous 8, 10, and 12 bore double-barrel rifles. The 8 bore bullet weighed 862 grains and with its velocity of about 1,450 it turned up over 4,000 foot-pounds of muzzle energy; the 10 bore used a bullet weighing 670 grains and at a similar velocity it turned up over 3,000 foot-pounds of muzzle energy.

Steps in the development of the hunting rifle were, as we have seen, the development of rifling itself, in the use of the patch by American frontiersmen. The percussion cap was an enormous step forward in the development of the breechloader, single-shot like the military Springfield, the Sharps and the Winchester

BLACK POWDER TO SMOKELESS

Model 1879 or Remington Rider rolling block and repeaters like Winchester and Marlin lever-actions.

The development of fixed ammunition with brass cases and center-fire primers was a tremendous step forward.

One of the most revolutionary of all steps was, however, the development of smokeless powder. It had advantages over black powder both for hunting and for war. Black powder is bulky. The mass of soot and clinkers which it throws out of the bore increases recoil, gives away the position of the rifleman, and keeps him from determining the effect of his bullet. It burns dirty. For good accuracy the bore of a black-powder rifle has to be wiped out often. It is an inflexible powder which burns at the same rate, confined or unconfined. Black powder is a mixture of about 75 parts by weight of saltpeter, 10 parts of sulphur and 15 parts of charcoal. Its speed is controlled by the size of the granulation. It is designated in sizes as Fg, FFg, FFFg. Fg is a slow-burning rifle powder and FFFg a relatively quick-burning pistol powder. At the time of the invention of smokeless powder the composition and manufacture of black powder had not changed essentially for centuries. Whereas basically black powder could be varied only in grain size, the varieties of smokeless powder are almost endless. Smokeless powder is highly specialized and different kinds vary in composition, in coating, in grain size, and in perforation. Some smokeless powder is made in rods, some in perforated disks, some in balls, some in square flakes, some in flat strips, and some in irregular clusters. Most is black, some is white and some has been orange and yellow.

Smokeless powder was based on the discovery of nitroglycerine (an oily liquid formed from the action of nitric and sulphuric acids on glycerine), and on that of gun cotton (which is formed by the action of the same acids on any kind of cellulose, including cotton). When nitro-glycerine and gun cotton are mixed, a so-called double-base powder is formed. An early and famous example is cordite, which is still used extensively in Great Britain and is so-called because the powder is in the form

THE BIG-GAME RIFLE

of cords, or long strings, which are loaded into the cartridge case before it is necked down. Another very famous double-base powder is excellent American Hi-Vel No. 2 made by the Hercules Powder Company. Bullseye is a double-base pistol powder. Single-base powders are straight nitro-cellulose and contain no nitro-glycerine. They are made by dissolving gun cotton in a mixture of ether and alcohol. The resulting "colloid" is a gluey paste which is squeezed out in strings like macaroni. Diameter of the strings is controlled, of course, by the size of the holes through which the mass is pushed. Length is controlled by cutting. One powder may be the same as another in composition, coating, and grain size but be of different cut.

Smokeless powders were developed in the 1880's. The first successful one was evolved in France, but at the time similar experiments were under way in England.

The advantages of smokeless powder over black powder are many. First and most obvious, of course, is the absence of the clouds of smoke which used to pour out of the muzzle of a black-powder rifle. Position of the rifleman is not revealed to a possible enemy. The rifleman can see the result of his shot. Smokeless powder is far more efficient in that for its bulk it creates a much greater volume of gas and hence, bulk for bulk, it can give far more push on the bullet. It is clean burning. Because of the greater efficiency much higher velocities can be developed with it.

However, with barrel steels in use at the time early smokeless powders also had their disadvantages. They burned at much higher temperatures and pressures than black powder. They were much more erosive and shortened barrel life considerably. In some of their early forms they were less stable. Nevertheless, invention of smokeless powder in its various kinds was a tremendous revolution, and almost over night the fine old black-powder cartridges were on their way to obsolescence.

The first center-fire smokeless powder cartridge was the 8 mm. French Lebel, which was developed in 1886. In Germany the

BLACK POWDER TO SMOKELESS

8 mm. Mauser, or 8 x 57, cartridge replaced the old 11 mm. Mauser black-powder cartridge as the official German army cartridge in 1888. The .303 British service cartridge, which was originally designed for compressed pellets of black powder, was quickly adapted to smokeless. The United States army dropped the .45/70 black-powder cartridge for the new smokeless powder .30/40 Krag cartridge in 1893. The famous 7 x 57 mm., or "Spanish" Mauser, cartridge came along in the early 1900's, and at about the same time the 6.5 rimmed cartridge for the Dutch and Rumanian Mannlichers, Model 1893, came into being.

All of these cartridges quickly became favorites for hunting rifles. The .303 British cartridge was widely used in Africa by sportsmen hunters and settlers, and the users were delighted by the flatness of trajectory, the excellent killing power, the absence of smoke, and the lessened recoil. British hunters carried many 6.5 Mannlichers over the world and so did the Germans and Austrians.

Very quickly, sporting cartridges for smokeless powder were evolved. The Winchester Model 1894 rifle was brought out for the .38/55 black-powder cartridge, but it was adapted to a new smokeless powder sporting cartridge known as the .30 Winchester center-fire or .30/30, which, as it was first loaded used a 165-grain bullet at a muzzle velocity of about 1,900 f.p.s. As far as sporting cartridges go this is the most revolutionary cartridge ever developed in the United States. It became the standard American hunting cartridge almost immediately, and in the hunting fields displaced the great old black-powder repeating cartridges used in the Models 1876 and 1886 Winchesters and in the repeating Marlins and Ballards.

With one jump muzzle velocities of sporting cartridges went from around 1,400 f.p.s. to around 2,000 f.p.s. This great increase in velocity flattened trajectory out and made range judgment less critical. The use of these smokeless powder cartridges was a revelation to hunters all over the world. For the most part they found the killing power ample, and were absolutely astonished

THE BIG-GAME RIFLE

at the ease with which they could hit. Today, it is fashionable for certain nostalgic individuals to hark back to the black-powder cartridges and to say that they were superior in killing power to the smokeless powder cartridges which succeeded them. Lads who were using them did not think so. I have talked to many hunters, including my own grandfather, who were brought up on the black-powder cartridges, who had the latest black-powder rifles, but who dropped them like hot potatoes as soon as they saw the new smokeless powder cartridges perform. Actually, they were infinitely superior in every way, in range, in power, and in practical accuracy. Practical hunters found they could kill game farther and deader with the .30/30 than they could with the .45/70, with a .33 Winchester than they could with a .50/110.

Many cartridges in military and sporting use today came from this era. The 7mm. Mauser cartridge has, for example, kept up its popularity. It is still a military cartridge in many countries and it is still an excellent all-around sporting cartridge; yet, except for newer powders and better bullets, it is exactly the same cartridge that was developed in the early Nineties. The old .30/40 Krag cartridge is still a good seller in spite of the fact that no rifles have been made for it since the manufacture of the Model 1895 was discontinued in 1931. The 8 mm. Mauser cartridge, developed in 1888, and only slightly changed, was the German military cartridge of World War II.

Higher velocities made possible by smokeless powder made jacketed bullets a necessity, as pure lead would not take the higher velocities. Smokeless powder also made alloy barrel steels necessary and the greater range and flatter trajectory encouraged the development of better sights, such as the Lyman-type aperture sights and telescopic sights. Higher velocity and flatter trajectory resulted in greatly increased shock power and, for the first time, made real long-range shooting a possibility.

Smokeless powder also meant that most cartridges were of bottleneck shape, and the development of the excellent Mauser

BLACK POWDER TO SMOKELESS

and Mauser-type actions during the 1890's and early 1900's, meant that most cartridges would be rimless.

The first smokeless powder cartridges were, for the most part, designed for military use. Calibers ran up around .30. Bullets were relatively long and heavy. Velocities averaged around 2,000–2,200 f.p.s.

Some of the early smokeless powder sporting cartridges that followed the lead of military cartridges were designed from scratch. The .30/30 Winchester, the .303 Savage, the .33, .35, and .405 W.C.F. cartridges are examples of this. Some were merely smokeless powder adaptations of old black-powder cartridges—of which many of the British Nitro Express cartridges for double-barrel rifles and single-shot rifles were an example. The .577 was a highly favored old black-powder cartridge, and a straight case .577 Nitro Express is a very powerful British cartridge for the largest game. The old .45 black-powder Express rifles were the direct ancestors of the modern .45 Nitro rifles loaded with cordite powder.

By the middle 1890's most armies had adopted smokeless powder cartridges and new bolt-action rifles to handle them. Smokeless powder cartridges had the old black-powder cartridges on the run for the world's hunting. How quickly the smokeless powder cartridges killed off the old black-powder jobs can be shown by quoting from the Winchester catalog of 1896. Then we see cartridges listed like the .38/56, .38/70, .40/110 Express; .38/72, .40/50, .40/70, .40/60, .40/65, .40/70 Ballard; .40/70 Bullard; .40/82, .40/75, .40/85, .40/90, .40/90 Sharps straight; .42 Russian; .43 Spanish; .43 Egyptian; .44/60, .44/105, .45/75, .45 Martini-Henry; .45 Danish; .45 Rumanian; .50/110, etc. Within a few years most of these black-powder cartridges were obsolete, and only a few survived to the outbreak of World War II. When the war was over the cartridge companies discontinued loading almost all of them. About the only black-powder survivors (and these are now loaded with smokeless) are the .44/40, the .32/40, the .38/55, and the .45/70.

THE BIG-GAME RIFLE

The next step in the development of smokeless powder military and sporting cartridges got under way about 1905 when the German army substituted a sharp-pointed 154-grain Spitzer bullet at a velocity of about 2,900 f.p.s. for the old 236-grain bullet in the 7.9 German military cartridge. This step had repercussions all over the world. The United States had been designing a new military rimless cartridge to be used in a Mauser-type rifle known as the 1903 Springfield or the "New" Springfield. The .30/1903 cartridge was to be used with a 220-grain bullet at a velocity of about 2,200 f.p.s. When American ordnance experts became aware of the German experiments they dropped the 1903 cartridge and in 1906 brought out the famous .30/06 cartridge which was originally loaded with a 150-grain bullet at a muzzle velocity of about 2,700 f.p.s. Americans who used the new cartridge were astounded by its flat trajectory, its terrific velocity, and the strange things that bullets driven at the then unheard of velocity of 2,700 f.p.s. did. Similarly, the famous 7 x 57 mm. Mauser cartridge was later given goat glands by the substitution of a 139-grain bullet at a velocity of about 2,900 f.p.s. for the old 175-grain bullet. The good old .30/40 Krag cartridge which was originally loaded with a 220-grain bullet at a muzzle velocity of 2,000 f.p.s. was stepped up to give a 180-grain bullet 2,500 f.p.s. or the 150-grain bullet about 2,700 f.p.s.

CHAPTER III

The Quest for Higher Velocity

THE DEVELOPMENT of smokeless powder resulted in velocities being jumped from 1,300–1,500 f.p.s. up to around 2,000–2,200 f.p.s. with the resulting flatter trajectory, lessened recoil, increased ease of making hits at longer ranges, and probably increased killing power, although there might be some argument as to that. Another result, of course, was the reduction in bore size and in bullet weight and diameter, since the same results as far as killing power went could be obtained with a lighter but usually relatively longer bullet of smaller diameter. High velocities simply were not practical with black powder, so before the more efficient propellant came along the only way killing power could be greatly increased was to load a heavier bullet of larger diameter.

The discovery that sharp-pointed or "Spitzer" bullets retained velocity better, and the resultant introduction of the German 7.9 military cartridge, Model 1905, with its 154-grain spitzer bullet at a velocity in the neighborhood of 2,900 f.p.s. was probably the thing which touched off the quest for still higher velocities. When the United States army followed the lead of the Germans in 1906 and designed the .30/06 cartridge with its 150-grain sharp-pointed bullet at a muzzle velocity of 2,700, this lesson was brought home to this country. For a time only military full-metal cased bullets were available for the new 1906 cartridge. Just who first tried this ammunition on game I cannot say. It would seem logical to assume that, when struck with one of those relatively light, full-metal cased, sharp-pointed bullets, game would not be greatly damaged because the bullet would drill a small hole straight through unless a bone were struck. It was found, however, that in many instances the bullets upset and inflicted damaging wounds because the bullets were relatively unstable. The shank of the bullet was short, the point was long. At 2,700 f.p.s., after being shot in a 1–10 twist, which was actually designed for the 220-grain Krag bullet at a muzzle velocity of 2,000 f.p.s., these light, short bullets were greatly over-stabilized. More often than not, they turned sidewise when they struck game, tumbled through and mutilated the flesh, and gave a very high percentage of one-shot kills. Hunters began to notice that in many instances the game seemed to be paralyzed by this high velocity effect. The results of this then rather astonishing velocity of 2,700 f.p.s. was noted and written up in the sporting magazines. It attracted a lot of attention and inspired a controversy as to the relative effectiveness of heavy, large caliber bullets traveling slowly as compared to that of lighter bullets traveling fast. The arguments have gone on ever since.

Theodore Roosevelt took a Model 1903 Springfield with him on his extended African trip in 1908. He used regular military full-metal cased bullets and enjoyed a lot of success with them. His rifle, I believe, was not remodeled into a sporter but was simply a military rifle equipped with sporting sights. About 1910, the late Stewart Edward White, novelist and outdoor writer, the late Capt. E. C. Crossman, gun writer, and a couple of other hunters obtained Model 1903 Springfield rifles and had them remodeled into sporters and fitted with well-designed sporting stocks. These were the first sporting Springfields and they gave rise to what practically amounts to an industry—this business of rebuilding military rifles into sporters. White took his Springfield sporter with him on a long African hunt and used it with the old .30/06 ammunition as well as with some sporting

THE QUEST FOR HIGHER VELOCITY

ammunition which had by that time been developed. He considered it very effective.

Conscious of the interest in the new army cartridge, the Winchester Repeating Arms Company found that they could adapt their Model 1895 box magazine lever-action rifle to it. They brought out a Model 95 for the .30/03 cartridge in 1905 and one for the .30/06 cartridge in March, 1908. The only difference between the .30/03 and the .30/06 is that the .30/03 case has a neck about 1/10 inch longer. It was, of course, loaded with the 220-grain bullet. Ammunition of the .30/06 variety could always be used in rifles marked .30/03 but not vice versa.

In North America, anyway, the next step in the quest for higher velocity was the .280 Ross cartridge which made its appearance in 1910 for the Model 1910 Ross rifle. Rifle and cartridge were developed by Sir Charles Ross and manufactured in Quebec, Canada. As originally loaded, the .280 Ross cartridge used a 145-grain bullet at a muzzle velocity of 3,050, which was terrific at the time. The .280 Ross case is a large, semi-rimmed case with the head slightly larger than that of the H. & H. Magnum series of cartridges. The Model 1910 Ross had a straight pull action. When the bolt is correctly assembled and adjusted the action is a very strong one. However, the bolt can be improperly adjusted and when it is the bolt can fire the cartridge, and because it is unlocked it will fly back in the shooter's face. It was this defect in the rifle, and no fault of the cartridge, that caused the .280 to become obsolete in this country. A long series of bloody accidents gave the Ross a bad reputation and the company ceased production.

The .280 Ross cartridge itself was a powerhouse and killed most big game as if it had been struck by dynamite. According to contemporary tests, though, the .280 Ross sporting rifle with factory ammunition was not accurate. Townsend Whelen in his book, "The American Rifle," published in 1920, writes as follows:

"The .280 Ross rifle does not seem to handle this cartridge (the 145-grain sporting load) very well. The accuracy is not good. I have heard of a few rifles that would give 8-inch groups with this cartridge at 200 yards, but I have never personally seen one. Two rifles of this caliber which I have owned would give about 12-inch groups at 200 yards when shot from my concrete base muzzle and elbow rest or prone with either target sights or telescope sights. Also Dr. Mann obtained two selected .280 sporting barrels for testing and upon placing them in his V rest found the best groups that they would give averaged 7 inches at 100 yards. The trouble seems to be in the neck of the chamber and the groove diameter of the barrel."

A special match cartridge was made for the .280 giving a 180-grain bullet 2,700 f.p.s. Like the 145-grain bullet, the 180-grain bullet was also undersize by about .002 inch, but the inertia of the long, heavy bullets seemed to cause prompt upsetting and accuracy was good. It became very popular in England for long-range match shooting.

The .280 was manufactured in the Model 1910 Ross rifle for only about four or five years. It became rather popular in England and after the Ross Company had folded up in Canada, .280 Ross rifles were made on Magnum Mauser actions by various British custom rifle makers. Waffenfabrik Mauser also brought out .280 rifles on Magnum Mauser actions. Ammunition is still loaded in .280 Ross caliber in England.

The rifles were, for a short time, very popular among a very limited section of the hunting population in the United States prior to the first World War, and wealthy men often took them on long hunting trips into the Canadian Rockies. The cartridge was very advanced for its day. Forty years later it is still excellent and cartridge design today is just beginning to catch up with it.

Probably the next step in ultra high velocity, as far as the

THE QUEST FOR HIGHER VELOCITY

United States went, anyway, was developed of the .22 Savage High Power cartridge, which came out about 1912, loaded with a 70-grain bullet at a muzzle velocity of 2,800 f.p.s. It was a fairly accurate cartridge—the first commercial hot-shot centerfire .22 ever developed. Recoil was light and it was easy to hit with. As is the case with practically every new cartridge, the .22 Savage High Power was greatly over-praised. It was boosted as being adequate for any North American big game. However, further use in the hands of many hunters proved that although it might kill deer like lightning one time, it might inflict only a superficial wound the next. In fact it got such a bad reputation on deer in Arizona that arms regulations written by the Arizona State Game Commission were so worded as specifically to outlaw it. For years it has been illegal to use a bullet weighing less than 87 grains on any Arizona big game and the intent was to stop the use of the 70-grain bullet of the .22 High Power.

The .22 High Power cartridge was designed by the late Charles Newton of whom we shall hear more later. He had another high velocity cartridge under his belt to sell to the Savage people. Just as he had used the .25/35 case necked down to form the .22 High Power, he used a .30/06 case shortened and necked down for the .250/3000. Because the .22 High Power with the 70-grain bullet had been criticized as being too light, Newton wanted to bring out the .250 with the 100-grain bullet at about 2,800 f.p.s. However, the Savage advertising department had been conscious of the interest in ultra high velocity so they insisted on a lighter bullet which could reach the then stratospheric velocity of 3,000 f.p.s. With then existing powders that could not be done with a bullet weighing more than 87 grains. The .250/3000 was brought out then with an 87-grain bullet at 3,000 f.p.s.

The .250/3000 cartridge was and is a most excellent one. It was the first of the sharp-shouldered cartridges. Its shoulder with a 26 degrees–30 minutes angle has been shown to be exceedingly efficient for burning modern smokeless powder. The relationship of case capacity to bore diameter is very good and the .250/3000 has always given top accuracy even in fairly light rifles. The 87-grain bullet, particularly for open country shooting, was adequate for animals the size of deer, antelope, and sheep and that little bullet in the .250/3000 was even advertised as being deadly on grizzly, moose, etc. The late Gene Jacquot, sourdough who outfitted hunting parties for many years in the Yukon, used a .250/3000 and killed many grizzlies with it.

To inject a personal note into this, I have used a .250/3000 off and on since 1917. I have never killed anything larger than a deer with the .250/3000 but I can testify that it is a grand cartridge. I killed a lot of whitetails with the old 87-grain soft-point bullet, and when I hit them in the chest they were almost always killed instantly in their tracks. Later, the factories brought out the 100-grain bullet at something over 2,800 f.p.s., and it is probably a better deer bullet, particularly in brush, where the 100-grain bullet is somewhat less deflected than the 87-grain.

The next step in the development of ultra high velocity in this country came when Charles Newton, who had designed both the .22 High Power and the .250/3000 Savage cartridges, started his own company and developed an entirely new line of cartridges. Like the .280 Ross, the Newton cartridges were many years ahead of their time, and they were on the market before general acceptance of ultra high velocity came into being.

Newton was a Buffalo, New York, lawyer and gun nut. He was also what might be called a semi-pro ballistician. He was a pioneer in amateur cartridge designing. Today practically every other hole-in-the-wall gunsmith has designed a cartridge by taking an existing case and necking it down, blowing it out, shortening it, changing the slope of the shoulder or something of the sort. There are so many wildcat cartridges made like this in existence that it would take fifteen detectives and five statisticians to keep up with them. Newton is the guy who started it all. Like many such rifle enthusiasts, he was a woodchuck hunter. As we

THE QUEST FOR HIGHER VELOCITY

have seen, he developed the .22 High Power Savage cartridge by necking down the .25/35 Winchester cartridge, and the .250/3000 Savage cartridge by shortening and necking down the .30/06 cartridge. Sometime or other he developed a high velocity .30 caliber wildcat cartridge for a gunsmith called Fred Adolph. It was called the .30 Adolph Express, and I believe it was the .405 Winchester case necked to .30, but I am not sure.

Newton then decided to develop his own line of cartridges and name them for himself. His first step was the .256 Newton, which is simply the .30/06 case necked to take a 6.5 mm. bullet. Early Newton literature gave ballistics of the .256 as follows: a 123-grain bullet at a muzzle velocity of 3,103 f.p.s., with a muzzle energy of 2,632 foot-pounds. Velocity at 100 yards was listed as 2,891 f.p.s., velocity at 200 yards, 2,689 f.p.s.; and velocity at 300 yards, 2,495 f.p.s.

It is rather doubtful whether Newton ever reached those velocities. He may have, with then existing powders, but if he did pressures were high. His velocities were taken in 30-inch barrels whereas the Newton rifles were furnished with 24-inch barrels.

Chronograph and pressure dope taken independently at the time the .256 came out and printed in Townsend Whelen's "The American Rifle" gives with the 129-grain Newton bullet and 48 grains of DuPont No. 10 a muzzle velocity of 2,863 f.p.s., with 54,260 pounds per square inch pressure. The same bullet with 54 grains of DuPont No. 13 gives a muzzle velocity of 2,975 with 56,200 pounds pressure. With 48.5 grains of No. 15 a muzzle velocity of 2,875 and pressure was approximately 55,000. Those pressures are pretty high, and in later years when the Newton line of cartridges was loaded by the Western Cartridge Company the .256 with the 129-grain bullet was given a muzzle velocity of only 2,760 f.p.s.

Another Newton cartridge and a more powerful one than the .256 was the .30 Newton which was brought out with the 172-grain bullet at a claimed muzzle velocity of 3,000 f.p.s., which

THE BIG-GAME RIFLE

seems to have been the McCoy because with 79 grains of DuPont No. 13 powder Whelen records 3,000 f.p.s. with 50,740 pounds per square inch pressures.

Newton also brought out the .35 Newton. The case it used was the same as that used by the .30 Newton, a large, rather fat case with a fairly sharp shoulder and a headsize about like that of the .300 and .375 H. & H. Magnum. Newton claimed 3,000 f.p.s., velocity with the 250-grain bullet, but when the cartridge was loaded by the Western Cartridge Co., velocity of the 250-grain bullet was listed as 2,660 and a muzzle energy of 3,930 foot-pounds—surely no pop gun at that! Newton also intended to manufacture a .22 Newton and a .280 Newton, a .33 Newton, and a .40 Newton. The .22 Newton was based on a shortened and necked down .30/06 case and the .40 Newton on the .35 and .30 Newton case. It is exceedingly doubtful if more than a few pilot rifles were made in any of those calibers.

In getting into production, Newton ran into many difficulties. In the first place he apparently originally intended to import Waffenfabrik Mauser actions from Germany and to barrel them and stock them in this country. He did not intend to load his own ammunition. However, World War I came along and shut off his source for actions. Then as the American arms manufacturers went into war work, obtaining barrels, cartridges, components, etc., became very difficult. He designed and tooled up to make his own rifles, lock, stock, and barrel. He was forced also to manufacture his own bullets and his own cartridge cases. All of this took money and know-how. He was a lawyer, a gun nut, an amateur ballistician, and a promoter; *not* a financier and production manager. Furthermore, the country was not ready for his advanced cartridges. It had not been so many years since the average American hunter had shifted from some old black-powder job to a .30/30. He was quite pleased with it. When someone came along and told him in advertisements that his .30/30 was obsolete it made him mad. More advanced gun nuts were playing with the .30/06 and gun editors were beginning, in

THE QUEST FOR HIGHER VELOCITY

a timid way, to promote it. The run-of-the-mine American hunters weren't ready for the .30/06, much less for the .30 Newton. Furthermore, they had been using lever-action rifles almost exclusively for a couple of generations and no bolt-action rifle looked to them like a hunting rifle.

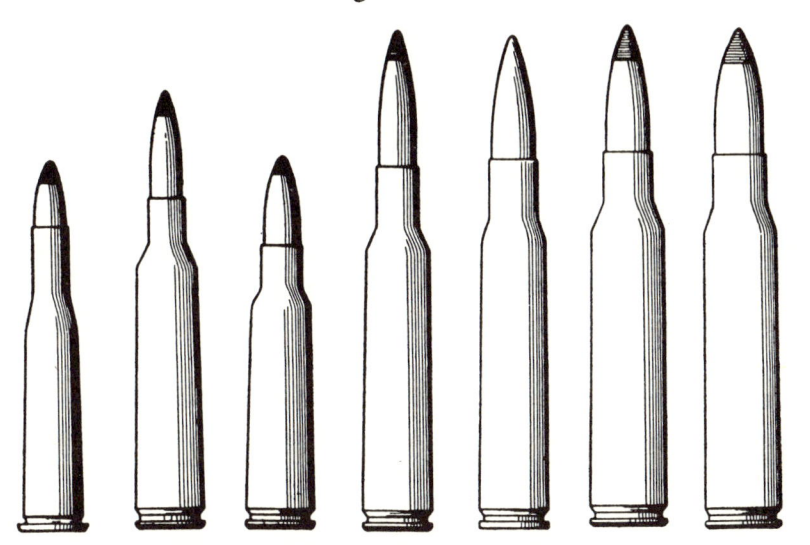

The cartridges designed prior to the first World War by the late Charles Newton. Left to right: .22 Savage, 70 gr.; .22 Newton, 90 gr., .250 Savage, 87 gr.; .256 Newton, 140 gr.; .30 U.S.S., 150 gr.; .30 Newton, 172 gr.; .35 Newton, 250 gr. The .22 Savage High Power and the .250/3000 were brought out for the Model 99 Savage lever-action rifles, but the others were for Newton's bolt action rifle. These Newton cartridges are still good, though obsolete, and enjoy a considerable esoteric reputation.

The Newton Company had a rough time. It went through various receiverships and finally one of the receivers sold off rejected barrels and parts which were assembled and peddled by mail as "Meeker" rifles. This, the last gasp, came around 1927–28.

In spite of the fact that the whole story of Charles Newton and the various Newton arms companies is one of frustration and gloom, Newton earned a place in the history of the American big-game rifle. The man was an innovator in many different ways. At a time when cupro-nickel was the universal jacket ma-

THE BIG-GAME RIFLE

terial and caused a tremendous amount of metal fouling in rifle barrels, Newton used pure copper jackets for his bullets and thus avoided metal fouling. He designed interesting and novel bullets and the one he called the "Bearcat" was practically a dead ringer for the present day Remington Core-Lokt. His rifles had what were, for that day, excellent stocks and his actions employed hinged floor plates for quick emptying—practically the same system that is used with the present-day Winchester Model 70 action. He was the first bullet maker to employ paper insulation between the core of the bullet and the jacket.

Newton died broke and discouraged. At the time of his death he was also generally discredited. However, with modern powders the excellence of his cases is just being realized. With such powders as DuPont No. 4350, even higher velocities than Newton claimed are being obtained. No factory rifles for the Newton cartridges have been made for almost thirty years, but the demand for the cases is great enough so that a small concern finds it profitable to manufacture them.

Possibly, though, Newton's greatest contribution to the development of big-game cartridges was that he made many people conscious of the virtues of high velocity, flat trajectory, and great shock power. He founded sort of a cult, largely composed of men who are now middle-aged and even elderly who were in their hey-day of interest and enthusiasm back just before the first World War. Newton got out a most excellent catalog filled with fine articles and interesting data which caused many new converts to high velocity to come rushing down to the mourner's bench shouting Hosannas and jumping for joy. It was these Newton enthusiasts who later paved the way for the acceptance of such cartridges as the .270 W.C.F.

The next step in the development of the high velocity big-game cartridge in the United States was the design of the .270 Winchester cartridge. Upon taking a peek at the .256 Newton and the .270 W.C.F., one might naturally conclude that the Winchester ballistic engineers who designed the .270 had once seen a

THE QUEST FOR HIGHER VELOCITY

.256 Newton cartridge. Both cartridges are based on the .30/06 case. Both get their efficiency by substituting velocity for bullet weight. The dope I get is that Winchester designed the cartridge some years before it came out as an experimental military cartridge, then dropped it, but later decided to add it to their line when they brought out the bolt-action Model 54 Winchester rifle in 1925. As a youth I had owned a .250/3000 Savage and a .256 Newton. I was pretty much bitten by the high velocity bug and so when I saw the first advertisement of the New Model 54 Winchester rifle for the spectacular new .270 Winchester cartridge I obtained a rifle and 100 rounds of ammunition loaded with the excellent 130 grain expanding bullets at a velocity of 3,160—higher than Newton had ever reached with his .256. I liked the .270 cartridge from the start and I still like it. I have owned many .270 rifles, both factory and custom made, and I have three in my gun rack right now. Since 1925 I have done a good deal of my hunting with the .270. I have shot everything with .270 rifles from 40-pound javelinas to 1,500-pound Alaska moose and large grizzlies. In a good rifle the .270 is very accurate. Trajectory is very flat and recoil and muzzle blast are somewhat less than that of the .30/06.

When the cartridge first came out there was considerable controversy as to whether or not it was really a big-game cartridge. Many people were suspicious of the light bullet because they were still used to thinking in black-powder terms, as in those days the only way to increase the power of a rifle was to increase the weight and diameter of the bullet. As far as I can discover the .270 with the 130-grain bullet would kill moose and grizzly just as well as the .30/06 and it is somewhat easier to hit with at long and uncertain ranges.

In the years prior to World War II, the .270 sold only fairly well. The only factory rifle made for it was the Model 54 and later the Model 70 Winchester. It played a poor second fiddle to the .30/06. Some custom rifles were made in .270 by Hoffman, Neidner, and small custom gunmakers like W. A. Sukalle of

THE BIG-GAME RIFLE

Tucson, and later Phoenix, Arizona, but in 1927, two years after it came out, the famous and conservative New York gunsmithing firm of Griffin & Howe did not even list the .270 cartridge in their catalog.

By 1940 the popular acceptance of the .270 had grown to the extent that when Remington Arms Company revised their Model 30 bolt-action rifle and called it the Model 720 they brought it out in .270 as well as .30/06. Since World War II has been over the .270 has been in great demand. It is available not only in the Model 70 Winchester but also in the new Remington Model 721. It is also available in the Mauser rifles made by Fabrique Nationale of Belgium, and imported into this country, and in the Swedish Husqvarna. Birmingham Small Arms Company of England, has sent a great number of .270 rifles built on Pattern 14 Enfield actions into Canada. In the Model 70 Winchester the .270 and .30/06 sell about fifty-fifty. I understand that in the Model 721 Remington that the .30/06 outsells the .270. However, all the custom makers with whom I have talked tell me the .270 is in much greater demand than the .30/06. Seymour Griffin of Griffin & Howe, a firm which did not even list or make a .270 rifle in 1927, tells me that prior to the war they made more .30/06 rifles than all other calibers put together and now they make more .270 rifles than all other calibers put together.

The .270 cashed in on the pioneering work done by Newton. It sustained the interest in high velocity and flat trajectory. It proved to many people that velocity can be substituted for bullet weight and killing power maintained or increased. Today .270 factory ammunition is furnished with the 150-grain bullet at 2,770 f.p.s. and with the 100-grain bullet at 3,540 f.p.s., as well as with the original 130-grain. The 150-grain load is intended for brush and forest use at medium ranges and is hence loaded down so as not to destroy too much meat on a deer. The 100-grain bullet is strictly a varmint bullet although it should do very well for lighter game like antelope and deer shot in open country. For

THE QUEST FOR HIGHER VELOCITY

all-around use the 130-grain load is still the best factory load, but 150-grain spitzer bullets can be loaded to 2,960 f.p.s. in the .270. With their great sectional density and high retained velocity at longer ranges these 150-grain handloads may well be as good for all-around use on all North American big game as the 130-grain bullets. Possibly they are even better.

While Americans were beginning to get used to the .270 Winchester cartridge with its velocity of well over 3,000 f.p.s., many experiments were going on in other parts of the world. Some of the best known in this country were those of an American-born German ballistic engineer named H. Gerlich who manufactured the Halger rifles and cartridges at Keil, Germany, who exported some to the United States at a very high price, and who wrote some articles for American sporting and technical magazines that stirred up a great deal of interest.

Halger rifles were based on specially heat-treated Mauser Magnum actions. I had one in .280 and it was beautifully made but fearfully long and heavy.

The .280 Halger-Gerlich simply took the old .280 Ross cartridge and loaded it with the most advanced German nitrocellulose flake powder. Apparently it was very progressive burning, because many German cartridges, including the Halger, were loaded with so much of it that the stuff was compressed and yet nobody seemed to get blown up.

Gerlich claimed a muzzle velocity of 3,900 f.p.s., with the 100-grain bullet in his .280, 3,500 f.p.s. with his 145-grain bullet, and 3,043 with his 180-grain bullet. With the 145-grain bullet and at 328 yards, he claimed retained velocity of 2,900 f.p.s., and at the same distance and with the 180-grain bullet retained velocity of 2,700 f.p.s., or about that of the 180-grain .30/06 bullet at the muzzle.

Gerlich also brought out a .335 Halger cartridge which used a belted Magnum case like that of the .375 H. & H. Magnum and which gave a 240-grain bullet a muzzle velocity of 3,125 f.p.s., and a retained velocity at 300 meters of 2,482. Foot pounds of

THE BIG-GAME RIFLE

energy at the muzzle were 5,220, or about that of many of the big British Nitro Express elephant rifles.

Very few Halger rifles ever came to the United States, as both rifles and ammunition were fabulously expensive. One New York firm imported a few Halgers and listed them at 1,000 depression dollars each and ammunition at about $1 a shot. However, the Halger cartridges had a very definite influence in the United States since many rifle enthusiasts read about them and thought about the superiority of their performance.

Actually, the .280 Halger inspired the development of the .280 Dubiel cartridge, a wildcat which saw some play in the 1930's. It was simply the .300 H. & H. Magnum case necked to take a .288 bullet. Ballistics equal approximately to those of the .280 Halger were achieved. A fair number of rifles made up on German Mauser-Magnum actions in .280 caliber were sold and the cartridge had its day in the sun. Various other wildcats based on the big .30 Newton and .300 Magnum cases in 7 mm. and .270 have been developed.

Interest in high velocity was given considerable impetus in the United States with the development of the .220 Swift, which was brought out back around 1935 by the Winchester Repeating Arms Company in the Model 54 Winchester rifle. With its 48-grain bullet at a muzzle velocity of 4,140 f.p.s., and muzzle energy of 1,825 foot-pounds, the .220 Swift is not and was not supposed to be a big game cartridge. It is rather an ultra high velocity long-range varmint cartridge and an exceedingly accurate one. The boys were not happy, though, until they had shot big game with the Swift and they found that under the right circumstances the Swift would kill big game like dynamite. The performance of the tiny bullet at its very high velocity caused many to long for a heavier bullet of somewhat larger caliber at comparable velocities. They felt that then they would have an all-around big-game rifle with astonishingly flat trajectory and great killing power yet coupled with mild recoil.

Ultra high velocity long-range super duper Magnum car-

THE QUEST FOR HIGHER VELOCITY

tridges in .270, 7 mm., and .30 calibers are myriad. Ralph Waldo Miller of California, pioneered blowing out the .300 H. & H. Magnum cartridge to increase the powder capacity and give the 180-grain bullet up around 3,400–3,500 f.p.s. He also did extensive experimenting with the Magnum and .30/06 cases variously necked down and blown out. He was joined in the experiments by E. Baden Powell, a California engineer, who named the series of cartridges, the P.M.V.F. which stands for Powell-Miller-Venturii-Freebore, just in case you are curious. The line of cartridges was taken over by the Hollywood Gun Shop but at the present time not a great deal is being done with them.

As this is written, the torch of ultra high velocity is being carried by Roy E. Weatherby who operates Weatherby's, Inc., 2793 Firestone Blvd., South Gate, California. Weatherby has a complete line of cartridges beginning with the .220 Weatherby Rocket, which is a blown out .220 Swift case, and going through the .257 Magnum, .270 Magnum, 7 mm. Magnum, and .300 Weatherby Magnum. The .257, .270, and 7 mm. Magnum cartridges are based on the shortened and blown out .300 Magnum case, but the .300 Weatherby Magnum, like the .300 P.M.V.F., is simply the regular .300 H. & H. case blown out. Weatherby cartridges are at least part of the way out of the wildcat class at this time, since Weatherby is, at this writing, prepared to furnish loaded ammunition. He has cases made for him by Speer Products of Lewiston, Idaho, and primes them and loads them at his South Gate, California plant. Cartridges and ballistics are, therefore, standardized. Weatherby also manufactures rifles bearing his name on remodelled and especially heat-treated F. N. Mauser actions. All other parts, except sights, are made in the Weatherby plant at South Gate—barrels, stocks, etc.

Ballistics and loading data for the Weatherby Magnum cartridges are published elsewhere, but Weatherby claims 3,300 f.p.s. with the 180-grain bullet, and reasonable pressures in the .300 Weatherby Magnum, and very high velocities with lighter bullets in the smaller calibers.

THE BIG-GAME RIFLE

The Weatherby cartridges have been used to a surprising extent in the big-game fields of the world and particularly the .300 Weatherby Magnum cartridge has made a most excellent reputation for spectacular killing power and long-range accuracy. Recoil is rather heavy, not much less than that of the .375 Magnum, but in the two rifles that I have played with accuracy has been excellent and flatness of trajectory remarkable. More will be said about these cartridges later.

Roy Weatherby is sort of the Charles Newton of today, and like Charles Newton he has been having his headaches. Components have not been easy for him to get and he has run into plenty of production problems. However, he is finding that the other experimenters in ultra high velocity have, to some extent, paved the way for him.

Elsewhere in the world, cartridge design and experimentation were going on. The British firm of Holland & Holland brought out the great .375 Magnum cartridge, a big modern large bore high velocity cartridge designed for heavy bullets. It came out well before World War I. Holland & Holland followed it with their Super .30 or, as we have always called it, the .300 H. & H. Magnum. The same firm also brought out the .275 Magnum which, as loaded in England, uses a 160-grain bullet at a muzzle velocity of 2,675 but which can be loaded with American powders to much higher velocity. British and Germans both made rifles for the Savage .22 High Power, .250/3000 Savage and small bore high velocity rifles were developed in both countries. The interesting .240 Holland & Holland Nitro Express cartridge, for example, uses the 100-grain bullet at around 2,800 f.p.s., the .242 rimless Nitro Express Vickers cartridge uses the 100-grain bullet at 3,000, and the .246 Purdey uses a 100-grain bullet at 2,950, almost all identical in ballistics to our own .257 Roberts.

The German 7 x 64 cartridge developed by Brenneke was a sort of forerunner of the American .270 Winchester and the cases are quite similar except that the body of the 7 x 64 case is smaller toward the head than the .270. The 7 x 64 also has a

THE QUEST FOR HIGHER VELOCITY

sharper shoulder. Loaded with that excellent Rottweil flake powder and the 173-grain spitzer bullet the 7 x 64 gives a muzzle velocity of around 2,900 f.p.s.

In not much over sixty years velocities have jumped from around 1,400 f.p.s. to 2,000 f.p.s., from 2,000 to 3,000, and from 3,000 to 3,500 and in some cases 4,000. Cartridge design is by no means over.

Curiously enough, though, we find that some of the most popular and useful cartridges were designed right at the beginning of smokeless powder. Within its limits there is still no better cartridge than the 7 x 57 Mauser and it is difficult to find a better all-around cartridge than the .30/06. Many of those old-timers have been changed somewhat by the use of different bullets and more efficient powders but basically they remain the same.

Possibly in thirty or forty years we may be using for all game .23 caliber rifles driving special bullets from a taper bore at a velocity at from 7,000–10,000 f.p.s. Such cartridges may make the currently popular .270 and .30/06 become as obsolete as they in turn make the .45/70 seem obsolete. Those velocities would make as yet undeveloped barrel steels mandatory and probably new systems of rifling. At least they are something to think about.

BALLISTICS DATA ON EARLY HIGH VELOCITY CARTRIDGES

CARTRIDGE	BULLET WEIGHT	MUZZLE VELOCITY	MUZZLE ENERGY
.22 *Newton*	90	3103	1921
.250/3000	87	3000	1740
.256 *Newton*	123	3103	2632
.256 *Newton*	140	3000	2800
.280 Ross	145	3050	3002
.30/06	150	2700	2445
.30 *Newton*	150	3208	3445
.30 *Newton*	172	3000	3440
.35 *Newton*	250	2975	4925

CHAPTER IV

Factory Big-Game Rifles

Big-GAME rifles are manufactured in relatively few countries of the world in bolt-actions, lever-actions, slide- or pump-actions, in double-barrel non-repeating actions similar to those used on double-barrel shotguns, and in a few instances, on falling block single-shot actions.

Each of these types of actions has its advantages and disadvantages. Of them all the most popular, by far, is the Mauser-type bolt-action, the best-known example of which is the Model 98 type Mauser action, as made prior to the war in Germany, and made now in Belgium, Czechoslovakia, and possibly in other countries. Widely used actions inspired by the Mauser are the Model 70 Winchester, the 1903 Springfield, the British Pattern 14 and U. S. Model 1917. The Remington Model 721 and 722 action is a Mauser-type action with some rather important differences.

The Mannlicher action as used in the Austrian Mannlicher-Schoenauer rifle is also of the turn-bolt type but in other respects it differs greatly from the Mauser. With the turn-bolt action the operator lifts the bolt handle up, pulls it back, pushes it forward again, then turns it down so that the lugs at the head of the bolt lock in the recesses of the receiver ring. At various times straight pull bolt-actions have been manufactured, among them the Model 1910 Ross, the Lee, and the Model 1895 Mannlicher straight pull which was the official Austrian army rifle. All lacked the camming power of the turn-bolt actions and none are now being manufactured.

For use in a big-game rifle the Mauser-type bolt-action has many advantages. It is exceedingly strong and very rigid, since the bolt locks close to the head with massive lugs turned into recesses in a rugged receiver ring. It will hold pressures to the limits of brass cases and the rigidity of the action keeps the cases from stretching. Since high velocity and great power go with high pressures, the overwhelming majority of the newer big-game cartridges have been designed for bolt-action rifles. Another great advantage of the Mauser-type bolt-action is its ability to eject swelled or dirty cases because of its powerful cam action. Likewise it can also seat dirty and oversize cases, something which is of the utmost importance, not only to the combat infantryman, but also to the wilderness hunter, and to the handloader, who will use the same cartridge case over and over again. A Mauser-type bolt-action is a very simple one. The bolt mechanism can be dismounted, cleaned, and dried without the aid of tools—something which cannot be said of most other types of actions. The Mauser-type bolt-action also results in a more rigid and a more accurate rifle. The one-piece stock holds action and barrel together firmly and the cartridge is backed up rigidly at the time of firing. A properly made and adjusted bolt-action rifle is the most accurate of all rifles.

On the other hand, an action of the turn-bolt type also has its disadvantages. It is not the fastest of actions by any means, although if a man is willing to practice it he can work up a very respectable rate of speed in rapid fire. Operating the bolt between shots makes considerable noise and in some cases this may enable game which has been confused by the first shot to locate the hunter and run before he can get off the second.

The mechanism of the bolt-action adds considerable length to the weapon as compared to a double-barrel or single-shot rifle of similar barrel length. Another criticism of the bolt-action rifle is that for saddle use it is too thick and bulky, particularly if the

THE BIG-GAME RIFLE

bolt handle has not been turned down closer to the stock or made into what is sometimes called the "butter-knife" variety.

Lever-action rifles are faster to operate than bolt-actions. They are also thinner and are better adapted to saddle use. Lever-action rifles are favorites of Western cattle ranchers who carry rifles in saddle scabbards for long periods of time, in case a shot at a coyote or some other varmint should present itself. Since the breech blocks or breech bolts of lever-action rifles do not lock at the head, they are not particularly suitable for handloaders because the cases stretch upon firing and it is often difficult to seat them again as the lever-action lacks the camming power of the bolt. Because the design of the lever-action demands a two-piece stock, the lever actions are not as accurate on the average as good bolt-actions. The lever-action is exceedingly complicated. Whereas the Mauser-type bolt-action can be dismounted with the fingers, the man who dismounts the lever-action needs a special set of tools, a blanket to spread the parts out on, and a few hours of leisure. In strength and ruggedness, for the toughest of wilderness use, or in war, the lever-action cannot compare to the bolt-action.

In spite of all of this, the lever-action is an entirely satisfactory action for most hunting. It is the traditional American action and in spite of its drawbacks it has served satisfactorily for over three-quarters of a century. It is not the strongest of actions, but it is strong enough for cartridges of the deer class.

Winchester and Marlin lever-action rifles which use the hammer at half cock as a safety are very convenient for the left-handed man, who will often find another type of safety slow and clumsy. The Savage and Marlin lever-action rifles eject the fired cases to the side and are suitable for scope mounting. The Winchester lever-actions, on the other hand, eject the fired cases straight up and a scope, to be mounted on them, has to be offset —a clumsy business at best.

Actions for double-barrel rifles are simply the familiar side-lock and box-lock shotgun actions. A double rifle has the great advantage of two very quick shots in case of an emergency in the hunting of dangerous game. What happens after those two shots are fired I wouldn't know, since I am not a jungle hunter of dangerous game. A good double rifle also has a very low line of sight and points as naturally as a shotgun. Presumably, therefore, a double of good weight and balance is very fast to use in an emergency.

Double-barrel rifles are still made by the great British firms which specialize in their manufacture. They are also made in Belgium and possibly still in Germany and Austria. They are very expensive, prices for a first rate double starting at around $1,000. Since they are made, though, for the most powerful cartridges in the world they probably pay off in life insurance, and a man planning to hunt in Africa probably should have one in his battery—one that he owns or has rented.

Admirers of the double rifle cite as an advantage the fact that if the mechanism for one barrel goes bad, the user has another barrel and is still in possession of a single-shot breech loading rifle —far better than nothing at all. I would not consider a double as fool-proof as the bolt-action, however. Often a twig or a leaf that has fallen in the action can keep a double from closing and a broken firing pin which has pierced the primer can prevent a double from being opened. As compared to the simple bolt-action, the double is as intricate as a watch, and the average owner of a double has no more business trying to strip the locks of his double than he has in trying to repair his own watch or to fill his own teeth.

The double-barreled rifle is very difficult to "regulate" as the British say—or to get the two barrels to shoot together. And when this is done the barrel alignment is good for only one particular bullet weight and powder charge, and probably at only one particular temperature. If one changes powder, bullet weight, etc., the barrels will not shoot together.

It seems to me that the only field for the double is close-range shooting at dangerous game. Even at best the double is not par-

THE BIG-GAME RIFLE

ticularly accurate. Because of the fact that it has two barrels, rather than one, it is heavy for its caliber. Because of its construction, it cannot be fitted with a receiver peep sight. Although the British fit many doubles with tang peeps I would consider them too close to the eye for safety. The double does not lend itself particularly well to the mounting of telescope sights, and I am skeptical as to whether the average double is accurate enough for a telescopic sight.

Some British authorities have recommended double rifles for use on mountain game in the Himalayas. I cannot think of a type of rifle less adapted for mountain hunting. Doubles have been made in all calibers from the .22 Savage High Power to the .600 Nitro Express, but in the smaller calibers for plains and mountain use, and for precision shooting, the disadvantages of the double far overcome its advantages.

The double rifle is a European (and largely a British) institution. Back in the muzzle-loading days a few double rifles, usually over and unders, were made in the United States; but in recent years the only American doubles that I have heard of being manufactured were two or three in .405 Winchester made experimentally at the Winchester plant on Model 21 Winchester shotgun actions. Those rifles were so expensive to put together and to regulate that with American wage standards, the Winchester people decided that the manufacture of double rifles in this country was not economically feasible.

Now and then, in sporting magazines, one reads that there would be a field for a medium-caliber, medium-powdered double rifle in this country for woods hunting where shots had to be taken very fast. I am very doubtful about this and I can think of no better way for a manufacturing concern to go broke than to put out such a rifle. Furthermore, I do not think that a double would do anything that a light, properly stocked lever-action would not do.

A type of action which is purely an American institution and which has achieved considerable popularity in this country is the pump- or slide-action as exemplified by the now obsolete Remington Model 14 and Model 141. Like the lever-action, the pump is exceedingly complicated. It is also a very fast action, faster even than the lever, and it is a natural to operate from the shoulder. Those Remington rifles ejected the cases to the side and had solid tops. They were, therefore, ideally suited for the mounting of low-power, wide-angle scopes for woods use. The cartridges for which they were chambered, particularly the .30 and .35 Remington rimless cartridges, were entirely ample for woods hunting of deer.

Slide-action rifles are a good bet for the once-a-year deer hunter who does his scatter-gunning with the common pump-action shotgun. Even though he may practice very little, he is used to the action and he is used to the feel of it. He can usually do better at jump shooting of deer in the woods with such a rifle than he could with one of another type. The Remington people have discontinued the Model 141 because of the expense of manufacture, but the firm followed it up with the Model 760 early in 1951, a pump-action rifle made in .300 Savage and .30/06, as well as in the old, but popular, .35 Remington.

The semi-automatic or self-loading rifle is primarily a weapon of war. The United States uses such a rifle in the caliber .30, M-1 or "Garand," which has enormously increased the firepower of the American infantryman. The action is gas operated and of the turn-bolt type like the Mauser. Consequently, it is very strong. The Germans used semi-automatic rifles, also gas operated, to some extent—the Gewehr Model 41 and Model 43—and so do the Russians. The British, I understand, are tooling up for a new semi-automatic rifle for a small 7 mm. cartridge. In time, all of the world's armies will have to follow suit.

It is seldom, though, that the hunter needs the rapidity of fire afforded by the semi-automatic rifle. If he is much of a shot he ought to make his first bullet count. In these days of small bag

THE BIG-GAME RIFLE

limits a hunter does not have a multiplicity of targets like the combat infantryman and it is seldom that his life would depend on rapidity of fire.

The semi-automatic is usually not as accurate as the bolt-action, and it is generally a heavy, clumsy-looking rifle. There is a tendency today to legislate against semi-automatic rifles for sports hunting. Winchester developed a handsome gas operated semi-automatic rifle which they entered in competition against the M-1. As a sporting weapon it had real possibilities, but Winchester never put it into production, probably because they felt it belonged to a class of weapons that would be legislated against. The Johnson semi-automatic rifle which was produced by Johnson Automatic, Inc., of Providence, Rhode Island, for a couple of Allied governments during the war, also had possibilities as a sporter because it could be chambered for excellent sporting cartridges like the .30/06 and .270, but only experimental sporting models were made.

The various semi-automatic sporting rifles which Winchester turned out were rather heavy and clumsy and were made for cartridges of low and medium power which were pretty well behind the parade of cartridge development. They were never popular and, for the most part, have been discontinued. In fact Winchester advertises the semi-automatic in .351 caliber as largely for law enforcement officer use.

The Remington Models 8 and 81 rifles are now obsolete. They were recoil-operated—heavy, clumsy, and slow to point. Few of them were ever found in the hands of real riflemen, but they were chambered for more efficient cartridges than were rifles of the same class made by Winchester.

Most good shots and good hunters would be just about as well off with single-shot rifles as with anything else, but the day of the single-shot is over. There is so little demand for single-shot rifles that I do not know of any single-shot action suitable for high powered cartridges being manufactured at the present time. At one time, however, the single-shot action was quite popular in the United States for long, heavy, powerful black-powder cartridges which would not operate well through the early repeating actions. Many heavy single-shot rifles chambered for very powerful cartridges for the largest game were made in England in the 80's, 90's, and early 1900's on the fine Farquharson actions. Rifles for big black-powder cartridges were also made in the United States on Sharps, Sharps-Borchard, Remington-Hepburn and Winchester Model 79 single-shot actions.

There is still a fairly brisk demand in the United States for those old single-shot actions to be used in building up varmint rifles for rimmed cartridges. Favorites are the Winchester Model 79 and the Sharps-Borchard. When an American rifle nut can get hold of a British Farquharson action he is exceedingly pleased. As one of the nuttier gun nuts, I have long had sort of a yen to get hold of a British Farquharson. I would have it made into a single-shot .30/40 and I would equip it with a good scope sight. Whether I would actually take it hunting and leave my .30/06's and .270's at home I can't say but at least it would be fun to play with.

Factory Made Big-Game Rifles

Winchester Repeating Arms Company of New Haven, Connecticut, is the greatest sporting arms factory in the world, an institution with an enormous plant in which are manufactured double-barreled shotguns, repeating shotguns, .22 bolt-action and slide-action rifles, bolt-action and lever-action big-game rifles, single-barrel shotguns, shotgun ammunition, center-fire metallic cartridges and rim-fire metallic cartridges. Winchester is unique. No other firm that I know of in the history of arms manufacture has turned out as many different kinds of sporting weapons in as great a quantity.

Winchester manufactures the world's finest factory produced bolt-action big game rifle, the Model 70 Winchester. It also manufactures the world's finest double-barrel shotgun, the Model 21. It manufactures the pump-action shotgun by which all other pump-actions are judged, the Model 12. It produces the world's best big bore target rifles, the Model 70 Winchester bolt-action target rifle and the Model 70 Bull Gun. It also manufactures, in the Winchester Model 52 .22 target rifle, one of the world's great small bore target arms, its only rival being the Remington Model 37. It manufactures the world's finest .22 sporting rifle, the Winchester Model 52 sporter.

Although an old firm and a conservative one, it has yet been a pioneer. It was the American factory that developed the .22 Hornet, the .220 Swift, and the .270 W.C.F. Over the years it has been instrumental in developing the majority of American center-fire cartridges. It pioneered in adapting its rifles to the excellent .300 and .375 H. & H. belted Magnum cartridges, and in the use of chrome molybdenum and high chrome barrel steels.

The Model 70 Winchester is a bolt-action sporting rifle of the turn-bolt type. It is descended from the Model 98 Mauser through the 1903 Springfield, which greatly influenced the design of the Model 54, the predecessor of the Model 70. Model 54 bolts and receivers were made of nickel steel, I understand, and so were the original Model 70 actions. Present day Model 70 actions are made of heat-treated chrome-molly steel which is exceedingly strong, hard, and tough. The Model 70 has one of the finest trigger and sear mechanisms in the world—one that gives a clean, crisp, sharp pull. It is of original Winchester design. Bolt handle is correct for low scope mounting and the Model 70 rifles now have a most excellent side safety. Floorplate is hinged and there is a release plunger in front of the trigger guard. Trigger guard itself is milled. Winchester barrels are among the world's most carefully drilled, reamed, rifled, and gauged. Bolt stop is neat and well designed and independent of the sear and trigger. The Model 70 is equipped with a speed lock.

The Model 70 first appeared in January, 1937. At various times it has been made in .22 Hornet, .220 Swift, .250/3000 Savage,

.257 Roberts, .270 Winchester, .30/06, .300 H. & H. Magnum, .375 H. & H. Magnum, 7 mm. Mauser, .35 Remington, and .300 Savage. A few were also chambered for the 7.65 mm. Mauser cartridge and the 9 mm. Mauser cartridge.

Within recent years the following calibers have been dropped: .250/3000, 7 mm., 7.65 mm., 9 mm., .35 Remington, and .300 Savage. At one time the Model 70 was made with a 20-inch barrel but that Model has been discontinued. I understand that there are plans to put on the market a Model 70 Featherweight rifle in .30/06 and .270 calibers which will weigh about 7 pounds with 22-inch barrel and factory open rear sight. The standard Model 70 sporter with 24-inch barrel in .30/06 caliber weighs 7¾–8 pounds. Because of the smaller holes in the barrel, the .22 Hornet and .220 Swift are heavier and, of course, with its barrel of larger diameter, the .375 Magnum is also heavier.

In standard grade, the Model 70 has a stock which is a bit on the bulky side but nevertheless well shaped, ideal for iron sights and not at all bad for scopes. As this is written, Winchester is planning to put out a special standard grade high comb stock for use exclusively with scope sights.

The Super Grade Model 70 stock has detachable sling swivels instead of the fixed swivels of the standard grade, more and somewhat better checking, better wood, a composition forend tip, and a cheek piece.

The Model 70 is also made in the National Match model with a special uncheckered Marksman stock. Swivels are for 1¼ inch military-type slings. Barrel is standard sporter weight.

The Model 70 target rifle has the same Marksman stock but the barrel is heavier, and the Bull Gun has a still heavier barrel and is chambered only for the .300 Magnum and the .30/06.

Prior to World War II, Model 70 Winchester rifles were built by skilled, experienced workmen. They were assembled like watches and Model 70 bolts worked as smooth as glass. They were very carefully bedded in their stocks and I never saw one that would not shoot excellently. In fact it was not uncommon, particularly in the .220 Swift, .22 Hornet, and .270 calibers, to pick up standard Model 70 Winchesters from over the counter, fit them with scope sights and then get groups that ran right around one minute of angle.

Since the war there has been tremendous pressure on any rifle builder to get into fast production and Winchester Model 70 rifles that have come through in the past years have not been as carefully adjusted and bedded as pre-war Model 70's. Often the stock needs a bit of rebedding and the breech mechanism some smoothing up. However, they are fine rifles and any little extra care put on them pays off.

The only criticism of the standard Model 70 rifles that could be made is that they are a bit too heavy and, by the time a scope is put on them, they will weigh around 10 pounds, and some will weigh even a bit more. The comb of the standard stock is a bit too low to be ideal with scope sights and the stock can be greatly improved by reshaping and taking some of the wood off. In the design of the Model 70 stock probably too much consideration is given to target rather than to sporting needs.

The Custom Gun Department of Winchester can furnish Model 70's specially tuned up, with stocks of fine wood, and with engraving that ranges from simple to ornate.

The Winchester Model 94 Carbine

For a deer rifle for short and medium ranges, and for a rifle for general saddle use, the old Winchester Model 94 carbine is still around and has been around for fifty years.

The carbine has the famous Model 94 Winchester action. It is chambered for the .25/35, .30/30, and .32 Special Winchester cartridges. With a 20-inch light barrel and full magazine, the carbine weighs only around 6 pounds. Because of its flatness and lightness and short over-all length it still remains a favorite for saddle use with Western cattlemen and, since the .30/30 cartridge is distributed all over the world, it is a favorite weapon for trappers and frontiersmen.

How many Model 94 rifles and carbines were manufactured I cannot guess but back in 1927 the one millionth Model 94 was presented to Calvin Coolidge, who was then the President of the United States.

THE WINCHESTER MODEL 64

The Model 64 is simply the old Model 94 with a new modern pistol grip stock with fuller forend. The sporting or "Deer Rifle" model with the 24-inch round barrel weighs about 7¾ pounds. With a good receiver peep sight as made for the Model 94 by Redfield, Lyman, Williams, the Model 64 Deer Rifle is excellent for fast shooting at moderate ranges in the woods. It is equipped with detachable sling swivels.

THE WINCHESTER MODEL 71

The Model 71 Winchester lever-action, side-gate loading repeating rifle is a modernization of the old Model 1886 with parts somewhat simplified and strengthened to handle the powerful .348 Winchester cartridge, the only cartridge for which the rifle is chambered.

It has a most excellent stock for use with iron sights with a full round forend and a nicely shaped pistol butt stock. It weighs about 8 pounds with a 24-inch barrel. It is not suitable for scope mounting because the big .348 cases eject straight up and the scope has to offset too far to one side.

The Model 71 is one of the two lever-action rifles which can be considered powerful enough for use on any North American big game including moose and grizzly bear, and in the hands of a good shot it should also be ample for Alaska brown bear. No

THE BIG-GAME RIFLE

finer woods rifle is made anywhere and its choice is a particularly wise one when hunting elk and moose in heavy timber.

Model 721 and 722 Remington Rifles

The Remington Arms Company with their arms manufacturing plant located at Ilion, New York, is one of the great arms factories of the world, a firm which is over 100 years old and which has manufactured rim-fire rifles, center-fire rifles, double and repeating shotguns, and, formerly, automatic pistols and revolvers. Remington also manufactures, at its Bridgeport plant, all types of rim-fire and center-fire metallics and shotgun shells.

The firm got into the manufacture of Mauser-type bolt-action sporting rifles in undertaking to make the Pattern 14 rifle for the .303 British cartridge during World War I. The rifle became the U. S. Model 1917 for the .30/06 cartridge when the United States got into the war. The same tools were utilized to bring out a bolt-action sporting rifle after the war. The result was the Model 30 Express on the "Enfield" action chambered for the Remington rimless line of center-fire cartridges—.25, .32, .30, .35, and for the .30/06. The rifle was never particularly popular in its original form. It was later modified with a better trigger, to cock on the uplift of the bolt, and it was equipped with a better stock. Just prior to the last war it came out in the form of a Model 720 with still another stock and further minor changes in the mechanism but very few of these (only a few thousand, I understand) were manufactured.

The various revisions of the U. S. Model 1917 had always been expensive to manufacture so Remington engineers designed a completely new bolt-action big-game rifle, the Model 721. Like any Mauser-type bolt-action rifle it locks with two big strong lugs at the head of the bolt turning into recesses in the receiver ring, but otherwise it is radically different. The bolt has a recessed head to enclose the head of the cartridge case and it does not have the Mauser-type extractor, but instead it employs a circular spring extractor fitted within the bolthead. There are no extractor cuts in the barrel. The result should be an exceedingly strong bolt-action, perhaps the strongest of all bolt-actions.

The Model 721 is a production job. Unlike other Mauser-type actions the receiver is not a forging. Instead, it is apparently milled out of bar stock. The bolt handle is welded on instead of being forged with the body of the bolt. Trigger guard and foreplate are formed by a single stamping and the floorplate cannot be removed except with a screwdriver. The excellent trigger mechanism with its crisp single-stage pull is made from stampings; likewise the safety. The Model 721 is a production rifle, much easier to tool up for and much easier and cheaper to manufacture than the Model 70. It is not a gun nut's rifle, but for the man who simply wants utility out of a rifle it is a very good one. The Model 721 is made in .270, .30/06, and .300 Magnum. The Model 722 with its shorter action is made for the .222 Remington varmint cartridge, the .257, and the .300 Savage.

Various gunsmiths have done what they could to improve the looks of the Models 721 and 722. A firm in California makes a milled trigger guard with hinged detachable foreplate for the rifles. Other gunsmiths have fitted Arisaka trigger guards and floorplates to the actions and have hinged them. The Model 721 and Model 722 are a bit rough looking but the actions can be stoned to smooth them up very nicely. The rifles run a good deal lighter than the standard grade Model 70 Winchester rifles as the .30/06 in Model 721 will weigh 7¼–7½ pounds and in .300 Savage the Model 722 weighs around 7 pounds. Like practically any factory rifle obtainable today the bedding of the Model 721 and Model 722 often leave a bit to be desired, but it is usually no great trick to do a little rebedding. When that is done the rifles will deliver excellent accuracy. I put a shim under the forend of a sample Model 721 in .30/06 to give a little upward pressure on the barrel and, when I had fitted a telescopic sight, I had no trouble getting groups which would run about 1½ minute of angle—fine accuracy for a light sporter.

Besides the standard grade stock, the Model 721 is available with high combed checkered stocks for scope use and on special order the rifles can be obtained with fancy wood, engraving, etc.

The Model 99 Savage

Another time-tried and proved lever-action big-game rifle manufactured in the United States is the Model 99 Savage which is manufactured by the Savage Arms Corp., of Chicopee Falls, Massachusetts. Particularly in the .300 Savage caliber, the Model 99 is one of the most popular of all American big-game rifles.

At various times the Model 99 has been made in many different calibers with different barrel lengths and barrel weights, both round and octagon. It has also been made with many different styles of stocks in both solid frame and take-down.

At the present time, however, the Model 99 is made only in .250/3000 and .300 Savage calibers and only in the Model 99 EG and the Model 99-R and RS, all solid frame models.

The Model 99 action employs a rotary magazine with recesses for each cartridge, one which is very similar to that used in the famous Austrian Mannlicher-Schoenauer. The action has an indicator which shows how many cartridges are in the magazine. The Model 99 action has a very strong breech block or bolt which abuts against the rear of the receiver. As it is made today of strong heat-treated alloy steel, the Model 99 action should, I believe, take 50,000 pounds pressure. I know of some which have been used by handloaders with high pressures. Some have even been rebarreled to take the .22/250 varmint cartridge which is a very hot number. The Model 99 is ordinarily the most accurate of the lever-action rifles, probably because butt stock is attached to the receiver with a long, strong screw running the full length

FACTORY BIG-GAME RIFLES

of the stock. The Model 99 is ideally adapted to scope use because the cases are ejected at the side.

In .300 Savage caliber, with a 150-grain bullet at approximately 2,700, and a 180-grain bullet at close to 2,400, the .300 Savage is adequate for any North American big game in the hands of a good shot. Almost all solid-frame Model 99 Savages in .250/3000 shoot with excellent accuracy, and because of the rigid action the fired cases can be reloaded. For a man who wants a good flat saddle rifle, equipped with a scope sight, to be carried on horseback a great deal, I do not know of a better bet than the Model 99 in .250/3000 because the fast-stepping little 100-grain bullet will reach out across canyons at relatively long ranges and yet tag a deer with plenty of authority.

If world conditions do not change radically, the Model 99 should, one of these days, be out with a new center-fire big-game cartridge with a heavier bullet than is available in the .250/3000 and higher velocity than is available in the .300.

The Savage-Stevens Company also makes a little .30/30 bolt-action carbine which is the cheapest of all American big-game rifles. It is a production job, but for the man who wants a rifle at minimum cost to hunt deer with, it is satisfactory.

Savage makes rim-fire rifles, pump and double shotguns and has made handguns. It is one of the largest manufacturers of inexpensive .22 rifles in the world. The Model 99 Savage is its principal prestige item and an arm in which the company takes great pride.

The Marlin Lever-Action Rifles

The only big-game rifle made by the Marlin Arms Company of New Haven, Connecticut, is the Model 336, which is available in rifle and carbine models chambered for the .30/30, .32 Winchester Special, and .35 Remington calibers. Like the Winchester, the Marlin is a lever-action side-gate loading rifle with a visible hammer. Unlike the Winchester, the Marlin ejects the cases to the side and is consequently suitable for scope mounting. Marlin stocks are very good in design with hand-filling semi-beavertail forends and good butt stocks. Carbines weigh 6½ pounds, or thereabouts, and the rifles about 7 pounds. The Marlin Model 336-A-DL is fitted with detachable sling swivels and the stock is checkered.

Original Mauser Sporting Rifles

As this is written, the great Mauser Werke at Oberndorf, Germany, is not in production and if genuine Mauser rifles are ever again manufactured it will probably be elsewhere in Germany, but no book on big-game rifles would be complete without something about the Mauser factory and Mauser sporting rifles. The Mauser Werke was once, and may be again, one of the world's greatest sporting rifle manufacturers and Mauser actions in the "white," or unblued, were sold by the Mauser Company to large and small gunsmiths all over the world.

The Mauser firm was primarily a manufacturer of military rifles. It sold hundreds of thousands of Model 98-type rifles in various calibers all over the world—to China, Turkey, Yugoslavia, Mexico, to name but a few. It was also one of the principal suppliers of Model 98-type rifles to the German government before and during the last war and, of course, during the first World War. German military rifles made during World War I were marked Waffenfabrik Mauser and those made for use in World War II were given the code marks "byf" and "S/42." Besides rifles, the Mauser Werke also manufactured the big Mauser military pistol for the 7.63 mm. Mauser cartridge and occasionally for the 9 mm. Luger cartridge, and the Mauser pocket pistol for the 7.65 mm. Browning short or, as it is known in the United States, the .32 Automatic Colt Pistol cartridge. Most British magazine rifles were built on Mauser actions imported from Ger-

FACTORY BIG-GAME RIFLES

many, and custom gunmakers in the United States, such as Griffin & Howe, Hoffman, and Neidner, largely built rifles on Mauser actions.

The actions on which the Mauser sporting rifles were built and which were used by custom gunmakers in Germany and in other countries were all of the Model 98 pattern with two locking lugs at the front of the bolt and an auxiliary safety lug at the root of the bolt. Genuine Mauser actions came in four lengths. The standard Model 98 military and sporting action has an over-all length from the front of the receiver ring to the rear of the tang of 8¾ inches. It was used for such cartridges as the 8 x 57, 8 x 60 and .30/06. It came in various modifications with double set and ordinary military single trigger, with square bridge, and with two types of hinged floorplates. It was also modified with a special side safety upon occasion. Another action, sometimes known as the Model 1912, is ¼ inch shorter and usually, but not always, has a small receiver ring. This is the action used particularly for the 7 x 57 cartridge and it is similar to the Czechoslovakian VZ-33 action or G-.33/40 as it was known after it was taken over by the Germans. Actions of this type were used to some extent by Yugoslavia and also by Mexico. Many Mexican military actions were sold in this country after World War II and advertised as "short" actions, whereas they were very definitely not genuine Waffenfabrik Mauser short actions.

The genuine short action has an over-all length of 8 inches or ½ inch shorter than the 7 mm. action and ¾ inch shorter than the standard action. It was strictly a sporter action manufactured by the Mauser Werke for the 6.5 mm. Short (or 6.5 x 54) the 8 mm. Short (or 8 x 51) and the American .250/3000 Savage cartridge. Rifles using these actions were made with both sporting half-stocks and full-length Mannlicher-type stocks with barrels 20 inches long. All the actions I have seen have had hinged floorplates with lever-type release on the floorplate. Some have had double-set triggers, some the standard single military trigger. Prior to the last war the firm of Griffin & Howe in New York

THE BIG-GAME RIFLE

used to import these little "K" actions and build beautiful little featherweight .250/3000 Savage and .35 Remington rifles around them. Often the completed rifles with iron sights weighed only around 6¼ pounds.

The Magnum Mauser actions had an over-all length of 9 inches or ¼ inch longer than the standard Model 98 action. Diameter of the receiver ring was exactly the same and except for the longer receiver, bolt, floorplate, etc., the actions were identical to the regular Model 98. So far as I know, the Magnum Mauser actions were always made with a square bridge and they were always made with hinged floorplate with the release button in the forward part of the trigger guard. Griffin & Howe and Hoffman imported those actions for their .300 and .375 H. & H. Magnum rifles. They were used in considerable numbers by the famous British rifle making firms like Holland & Holland for a great variety of Magnum cartridges, and these big Magnum Mauser actions were the basis of the famous Halger rifles which are mentioned in a preceding chapter.

Completed Mauser sporting rifles were sold all over the world. Stoeger Arms Corporation of New York was the American agent for Mauser. Considerable numbers were sold unaltered in England and in Canada, and in Africa they were great favorites because they were strong, simple, and reliable and considerably cheaper than British built magazine rifles.

The Mauser factory furnished, as we have seen, short action rifles for 6.5 x 54, 8 x 51, and .250/3000 Savage. The Model 1912 actions were made into 7 x 57's and sometimes into 8 x 57's. Factory made Mausers on the Magnum action were available in .280 Ross and .404 Magnum. Other calibers for which Mauser rifles were regularly furnished were 9 x 57, 9.3 x 62, .75 x 68, .30/06, and .318 Wesley Richards.

The Mauser rifles were furnished in a great variety of styles of stock, engraving, barrel length, types of magazine release, sights, etc. Some were fitted at the factory with German telescopic sights on Mauser factory mounts.

FACTORY BIG-GAME RIFLES

For the most part, the genuine Mauser rifles are not particularly fancy rifles. Wood for the stocks is good, sound, plain wood but not fancy. Checking is neither very fine nor very precise. Stock design is European and conservative. Finish of the rifles built on Mauser actions by such firms as Sempert and Kreighoff is usually a good deal better. Details of finish and fitting on the original Mausers cannot compare to that of the rifles turned out by Griffin & Howe.

MANNLICHER-SCHOENAUER RIFLES

One of the largest manufacturers of sporting rifles in Europe is the great Steyr Werke at Steyr near Vienna, and the Mannlicher-Schoenauer sporting rifle the concern turns out has been one of the standard sporting rifles of the world for almost a half century. The Mannlicher-Schoenauer action is not as strong as the Mauser but it is apparently strong enough for high intensity cartridges like the .270 W.C.F. Like the old Model 88 Mannlicher, the Mannlicher-Schoenauer has a removable bolthead and the locking lugs are borne on a thin shell. The Mannlicher-Schoenauer magazine is a rotary or "spool" magazine like that used on a Model 99 Savage. There is a recess for each individual cartridge and, of course, the size of the recesses is different for the various cartridges. One could not, for instance, use 6.5 cartridges in an 8 x 56 magazine or vice versa. A serious fault with the Mannlicher-Schoenauer design is that the bolt handle passes through a split receiver bridge and scopes cannot be mounted low. Another fault is that the bolt handle is about halfway up on the bolt and, as a consequence, operating the bolt from the shoulder is difficult and awkward.

The Mannlicher-Schoenauer was first put out in 1903 for the 6.5 mm. Mannlicher-Schoenauer cartridge and early Mannlicher-Schoenauers were designated as to calibers by model numbers. As we have seen, the Model 1903 is the 6.5, the Model of

THE BIG-GAME RIFLE

1905 is chambered for the 9 mm. Mannlicher-Schoenauer cartridge, the 8 mm. is the Model 1908 and the 9.5 the Model of 1910.

After World War I a great many Mannlicher-Schoenauer rifles for the 7 x 57 and .30/06 cartridges were imported into the United States by the Sequoia Importing Company of San Francisco, and those I have seen are marked Model 1924.

Almost without exception Mannlicher-Schoenauer rifles were made, until recently, with double-set triggers. Stocks were of the typical German type—too long of butt stock, with low, thin combs. They were made with forends that ran the full length of the barrel and also with half stocks of the sporting type. However, the rifle which one thinks of when Mannlicher-Schoenauer is mentioned is the little 6.5 mm., Model 1903, with the 18-inch barrel and the full-length stock.

After World War II the Mannlicher-Schoenauer rifles were turned out in 7 x 64, .270 W.C.F., .30/06, and 9.3 x 62 as well as in the old-line "standard" Mannlicher calibers. Rifles were available with the traditional Mannlicher-Schoenauer full-length carbine stocks and also with 24-inch barrels and rifle-type half stocks. In 1951, however, the Stoeger Arms Corporation of New York, the American agents, imported new models with stocks designed to American ideas with higher, fuller combs, fuller forends, etc. Workmanship, particularly in metal, has always been excellent with the Mannlicher-Schoenauer rifles and particularly with old type stocks they have an interestingly foreign and exotic look.

FABRIQUE NATIONALE RIFLES

Another great European manufacturer of rifles is the Fabrique Nationale de Armes De Guerre of Herstal, Belgium. The company has been second only to the Mauser Werke as a supplier of military small arms to the world's governments.

FACTORY BIG-GAME RIFLES

For many years F. N. has not only built military rifles but has sold Model 98-type Mauser actions to gunsmiths. Since the war many thousands of those F. N. actions have been imported by Firearms International of Washington, D. C., and it is the principal action on which custom rifles have been built since World War II in this country. It has been revised with a bolt handle adapted to low scope mounting and a low safety which does not interfere with scope mounting. It is made in two standard magazine lengths—one for short cartridges like the .250/3000, .300 Savage and the other for longer cartridges like the .30/06 and .270.

Firearms International has also imported into this country many completed F. N. Mauser sporting rifles in .250/3000, .257, 7 mm., .270, and .30/06 with well-shaped and well-designed stocks of good grade European walnut, well-checkered and finished, with and without receiver sights. Those I have tested have been very accurate.

Besides Mauser-type rifles and actions, Fabrique Nationale manufactures Belgian Browning automatic shotguns, over and under Browning shotguns, automatic pistols, etc.

Swedish Husqvarna Rifles

Since the end of World War II a fair number of Swedish Husqvarna rifles built in Sweden around F. N. Mauser actions have been imported into the U. S. and Canada in .30/06, .270, and .220 Swift calibers. They are sound, but by no means fancy, rifles with light barrels. Those I have seen have had beechwood stocks. Finish, stock, and metalwork have not been on a par with that of the F. N. Mauser in those that I have seen. There is nothing much that can be said against the Husqvarna rifles and nothing much that can be said for them. They are just mass-produced and undistinguished factory rifles.

THE BIG-GAME RIFLE

Czechoslovakian Brno Rifles

Another foreign bolt-action big-game rifle which has sold fairly well in the United States is the Czechoslovakian Brno rifle. So far as I know the weapons have come here only in 7 mm. and 8 mm. calibers, although they are also manufactured in Czechoslovakia in 8 x 60 and 7 x 64. They are very fine little rifles built on a sporting modification of the Czechoslovakian VZ-33 small ring Mauser action. Bolt is of the butter-knife variety which turns down close to the stock. Safety is of the side variety and the action is of the small ring, small thread type. Stocks are available in sporting half stock and full-length Mannlicher type. Barrels are light and 20 inches in length. Triggers are of the double-set variety.

The rifles are light, short, and handy. Because of the butter-knife bolt handle turned down close to the stock they are thin and light and excellent for saddle scabbard use. Almost always the wood of the stock is absolutely first class European walnut showing a good deal of contrast. Checking is fine, precise, and well done. The comb is a bit too low for American tastes and for scope mounting, but the stocks are handsome and have an exotic foreign air. For the man who does not mind the butter-knife bolt handle and the double-set trigger and who wants a featherweight rifle this looks like a most excellent bet.

British Imports

The Birmingham Small Arms Company of England, has exported into Canada a great many .30/06 and .270 rifles built around American-made Model 1917 Enfield actions obtained by purchase and by lend-lease. They are sound enough rifles but about all one can say for them is that they are just rifles and if you point them right they will kill a deer.

FACTORY BIG-GAME RIFLES

The Remington Model 760

The long awaited Remington pump-action big-game rifle for the .30/06 cartridge was announced to the trade in January, 1952. For those who want a powerful, fast-operating, quick-pointing big-game rifle and who shoot a pump-action shotgun at feathered game and clay targets, the new rifle is the business. Besides being made in the .30/06, it is also available in .300 Savage and in .35 Remington calibers.

The Model 760 is a *hunting* rifle for short and moderate ranges. It is not a target rifle, not a remodeled military rifle, not a gun nut's rifle. In .30/06 it weighs 7½ pounds.

For iron sights the rifle is well stocked, fast to come up. The pistol grip is good, the slide forend hand-filling. The thing points like a good shotgun. Action operates as slick as grease and the man used to the slide-action shotgun can put two shots into a moose with it as fast as he can break the doubles at skeet.

The rifle uses a rotary bolthead with multiple lugs turning into recesses in the receiver. Bolthead is enclosed as in the Remington Model 721 bolt-action rifle, and it uses a plunger-type ejector and a spring extractor, also like the Model 721.

Because of the design, the barrel is free-floating, a doubtful virtue if top accuracy is desired with a sporting weight barrel. Magazine is of detachable box type, and the hunter can carry his ammunition in a couple of extra ones and reload in a flash.

The Model 760 is a real hunting rifle and one to appeal to the woods hunter and the shotgun man. It is not a mountain rifle as it is not as accurate as the best bolt-actions. But it is fast to operate, faster than the fastest lever-actions. It should sell very well!

CHAPTER V

Custom Rifle Making

THE TERM "custom-made rifle" covers a multitude of sins. One custom-made rifle may be a beautifully finished work of art. The stock may actually fit the purchaser. The metalwork may be fine and precise, the action as slick as grease, the trigger pull exactly what the owner wants, the barrel lapped like a mirror, the rifle fitted with special sights. Trigger guard and floorplate may be beautifully engraved and the owner's initials may be on a gold plate inletted into the stock. The wood may be specially selected European walnut, the checkering incredibly fine and precise, and the shape a thing of grace and beauty. Another "custom-made rifle" may be a cobbled up monstrosity turned out by someone with neither taste nor skill. It may simply be a rough Model 98 Mauser action fitted with an unlapped, crooked, poorly contoured barrel with an outsize chamber. The stock may be a machine-shaped blank so poorly inletted that there are gaps between metal and wood that you could stick a dime in, the trigger pull rough and hard, the bolt lift hard, the sights cock-eyed. Alas and alack, there are more custom rifles like the second than like the first, just as there are more homely gals than beauties and more tough, poorly cooked steaks than good ones. The really fine custom rifle is a work of art and in a class by itself. The poor custom rifle is, in every sense, inferior to the standard factory product. Often, strangely enough, there isn't much difference in the price between the two. Particularly after the last World

CUSTOM RIFLE MAKING

War, when the demand for big-game rifles greatly exceeded the supply, some fearful atrocities were put together and sold at prices which should buy genuinely fine weapons. In many cases dream rifles turned out to be nightmares.

Custom rifle making has always flourished in Great Britain and on the Continent. In the British Isles the game all belongs to the land owner and the man of moderate means, particularly if he is a city dweller, has about as much use for a big-game rifle as he has for an atomic bomb or a dinosaur in his backyard. Patrons of the rifle makers are wealthy men and there are not many of them. As a consequence, rifles for use in the British Isles are pretty largely handmade to the specifications of the individual customer. The sporting rifle industry in Great Britian is relatively so small that no manufacturer there ever tooled up to produce a Mauser-type action which was the basis for most of the British magazine sporting rifles. Instead, actions were imported from Germany and sometimes from Belgium. Famous British custom gun-making firms like Rigby and Holland & Holland imported German actions, fitted their own barrels to them and stocked them. Larger firms like the Birmingham Small Arms Company exported rifles to the colonies which were, for the most part, slightly remodeled British short model Lee Enfield military rifles in .303 British caliber. Since cost is of no great importance to a wealthy man, a great many of the British sporting rifles manufactured by the fine old craftsmen of London and Birmingham were double-barrel rifles built on what really amount to shotgun actions and quite a few were single-shots built on the excellent Farquharson falling block action manufactured by various concerns in England. Actually, from what I have seen, I believe that a good many of the so-called custom-made British magazine rifles (which to an Englishman almost always means a rifle built on the Mauser action) made prior to the last war had a minimum of British work on them. Instead I believe they were often simply restocked German or Belgian Mausers or Austrian Mannlicher-Schoenauers. Custom-made British big-game rifles are seen at their best in the beautiful double-barrel rifles, which are handsomely stocked, adjusted like fine watches, and sold with exquisitely made and finished sole leather cases.

French custom gun makers turned out many excellent double-barrel shotguns, but I believe in most cases they imported the tubes and possibly the frames from Belgium. French gun makers also restocked German Mauser barreled actions usually purchased from the Mauser Werke. Like the British, the French made no repeating sporting actions and no French military action was suitable for sporting purposes. Apparently the city-dwelling Frenchman of ordinary means did no hunting and the small French landowner did his gunning with a beaten up old shotgun of some sort or other, very often an ancient pin-fire job.

Germany, on the other hand, was full of custom gunsmiths, and there are whole communities in Germany where almost every male citizen is a gunsmith. Suhl, in Thuringia, is such a city. To turn out a custom rifle most of these gunsmiths purchased their Mauser actions from the Mauser Werke or possibly from Sempert and Krieghoff, or from Simson, who also turned out Model 98-type Mauser actions. Often they purchased their barrels from the same sources, but in some instances they made their own. In addition, these German gunsmiths got hold of thousands of Model 98 Mauser military actions after World War I was over. Sometimes they simply lapped the barrels to get rid of the rust and then stocked the rifles and sold them as 8 mm. sporters. Sometimes they fitted new barrels. During the German inflation in the early 1920's thousands of these remodeled military rifles were imported into the United States and sold for as little as $25., often with German telescopic sights thrown in free.

The firm of Sempert and Krieghoff, of Suhl, exported to the United States many really excellent sporting rifles usually in 7 x 57 and .30/06 with stocks more to American taste than is the case with most German creations.

Actually, the German custom gun makers and factories had

pretty much of a monopoly on the world's rifle trade prior to the last war. They sold tens of thousands of Mauser-type magazine rifles to South Africa, to Mexico, and all the big-game sections of the world. Even in Canada, right next door to the United States, the Germans sold a surprising number of bolt-action magazine rifles.

Training for the trade of gunsmithing in Germany is rigorous and a long apprenticeship is involved. When a man becomes a genuine gunsmith he is a pretty good all-around man. The best of the German smiths can take a piece of bar stock and a file and turn out an action for a double-barrel shotgun or a three-barrel gun, filing out, fitting, polishing, and hardening all the parts. Or a German gunsmith, if he has to, can also do a good job of engraving. He can make and fit a stock. In other words, he is an all-around man.

Labor is not highly paid in Germany. It is much less expensive than in the United States and less expensive than it is in Great Britain. As a consequence, the clever German gunsmiths made all kinds of interesting gadgets, the cost of which would be prohibitive in the United States. It is common, for instance, to find a scope-sighted rifle in Germany with an adjustable comb that will pop up to scope height when a button is pressed. The ordinary German three-barrel gun or "drilling" is so complicated to manufacture and adjust that with American costs one could hardly be produced to sell for less than $1,000. Since labor was cheap, German custom guns ordinarily had, what to American eyes, is an amazing amount of engraving. A job could be put on in Germany for $25. that would cost at pre-World War II in the U. S. at least $100.

German custom rifles were interestingly and carefully made, but in such essentials as barrel and chamber dimensions they seldom came up to American standards. Their chambers were not uniform and often they had excess headspace when they left the maker. Barrels ran over-size and under-size as each German barrel maker either had his own notions as to the proper bore and groove diameter and the type of rifling, or else paid no great amount of attention to such things.

Not only did the German custom gun makers sell weapons to the colonies, but they also sold them to rifle enthusiasts all over Europe who lived in countries without a gun-making industry. Well-to-do Swedes, Norwegians, Finns, Poles, and Hungarians ordinarily went to Germany for their doubles, their combination guns, their single-shot rifles, their fancy Mauser magazine rifles, because the double rifle bought in Germany, let us say, could ordinarily be purchased for about half the price that the same thing would cost in England. Whether the quality of this rifle would be equal to that of a British made double or not is rather doubtful.

The Germans themselves afforded an enormous market for rifles and the Germans were a nation of rifle nuts and big-game hunters. When American soldiers went into Germany toward the end of World War II they found rifles in practically every home. They shipped back tens of thousands of them, many of them excellent weapons. Apparently the man of moderate means in Germany had a much better chance to do some hunting than in England or in most countries on the Continent. Particularly in Bavaria, shooting at rifle matches, usually offhand at 300 meters, was almost as much of a national pastime as playing golf or watching baseball games is in the United States.

Besides the great Steyr Werke, which factory-produced the famous Mannlicher-Schoenauer rifles, Austria had many custom gun makers who built all types of the guns and rifles made in Germany and who also restocked and "customized" Mannlicher-Schoenauer rifles and Mauser rifles imported from Germany. Like the Germans, the Austrians, particularly the mountaineers, did a good deal of hunting. The villages owned communal grazing land in rough mountains and high upland pastures where they hunted chamois, roe deer, and the *hirsch*, or red deer. In Austrian inns in the Tyrol it is common to see, mounted on little plaques, the tiny chamois horns and roe deer antlers. The same thing that is said of the Austrian mountaineers can also be said of the hardy and ingenious Swiss.

The fine old flintlock and caplock muzzle-loading big-game rifles made in the United States were all custom jobs, mostly made in Pennsylvania. The early gunsmiths were German. In the pioneer farmers, frontiersmen, and explorers they found a ready market for their wares. Usually these custom gunsmiths purchased their locks from specialists and, hence, did not make the whole rifle "lock, stock, and barrel"; but they made the individual rifle for the individual customer.

When the breech-loader, and later the repeater, came in, most rifles were made by factories with new machinery and with interchangeable parts. Actually the machine production of rifles is an American institution, and the rest of the world learned how to do it from the early American gun makers. Factory produced Sharps and Remington big-bore buffalo rifles replaced the handmade muzzle loaders, and the custom gunsmith had little chance to compete in the production of repeating rifles with such firms as Winchester. Consequently custom rifle making just about died in the United States, and about the only patrons of custom makers during the 90's and early 1900's were the Scheutzen riflemen who competed with special target rifles in offhand shooting.

Revival of custom rifle making in the United States came about after the development of the Model 1903 Springfield for the .30/06 cartridge. Some of the more erudite riflemen were not happy with the ballistics of the common factory-produced repeating rifle of those days. For the most part these riflemen were target shots as well as big-game hunters. They were used to shooting the Model 1903 Springfield on rifle ranges and admired the accuracy and flatness of trajectory of the cartridge. They wanted sporting rifles on the same action for the same cartridge. In those days an officer of the U. S. army or National Guard, or a member of the National Rifle Association, could purchase a 1903 Springfield service rifle from the United States government for around $15. Many bought these rifles, hunted up gunsmiths who could make stocks, and had them restocked and adjusted for sporting use. Sporting sights were fitted, barrels and metalwork were polished and blued, barrels were sometimes shortened and turned down for lighter weight. Up until about the time of the first World War this was just about all the real custom gunsmithing that was done in the United States. Many double-barrel shotguns were made to order with special dimensions in the factories and rifles were obtainable with finer wood, better checking, and engraving, but the private gunsmith had, for the most part, degenerated into a repairman who reblued guns, made small parts, etc.

Custom gunsmithing in the United States really got under way after the first World War. For a good many years no factory bolt-action rifle was furnished with a genuinely good stock, as the early stocks on the Model 30 Remingtons and Model 54 Winchesters were pretty sad specimens. Both of these rifles were purchased by gun enthusiasts who had them restocked by custom stock-makers. In addition tens of thousands of military rifles—Model 1903 Springfields, Model 1917 Enfields, .30/40 Krags, 7.62 mm. Russians, etc.—were turned loose at very moderate prices by the American government. They were restocked and altered by small gunsmiths, reblued, fitted with sporting sights. Some of these early tinkerers developed into very fine gunsmiths and stock-makers.

R. G. "Bob" Owen, then of Saquoit, New York, is an Englishman who had learned stock making in the Birmingham gun trade. He came to the United States and since he found a demand for custom gun stocks he went into the business. Possibly more than anyone else, he is responsible for stock design of fine custom gun stocks made today. Owen stocked dozens of Springfields, sent the metal parts to Germany for engraving and turned out some very beautiful rifles. He also imported barreled Mauser actions in various calibers from Germany and stocked them. Owen is still making stocks at Port Clinton, Ohio. Another pioneer stock-maker who developed during the 1920's was the late

CUSTOM RIFLE MAKING

Alvin Linden of Bryant, Wisconsin. Like Owen, Linden was foreign born. He was a Swede who had a very thorough training in woodwork in the old country and who came to this country and found employment in the Pullman shops near Chicago in the days when fine Pullman cars were finished with intricate cabinet work. He later went to Wisconsin and worked in the woods. An accident crippled him. He had to find an indoor job so he turned to stock making. Linden, or "Ole Scratch," as he called himself, excelled at beautiful lines on his gun stocks and in turning out incredibly fine and precise checkering. He was an intelligent, salty, and highly articulate man and he wrote a series of booklets on stock making which have profoundly influenced custom gun stocking in the United States. Checking designs as employed by many custom gun stockers today derive directly from Linden. Ole Scratch was an artist as well as a fine hand craftsman. At one time I had seven rifles stocked by Linden and no two of the stocks were shaped or checkered to the same pattern, yet anyone who knew his work could instantly tell that any of them was a Linden stock.

The late R. D. Tate of Dunsmuir, California was also an excellent pioneer custom stock-maker in this country. So was a remarkable man named Adolph Minar who lived in the little village of Fountain, Colorado, and turned out some of the most beautifully checkered and shaped stocks ever made in this country. He died in the middle 1930's but I still have an old Springfield stocked by him and I shall always keep it.

August Pachmayr, of Los Angeles, the father of Frank Pachmayr, the custom gun maker and manufacturer, carried on the custom gun tradition in Southern California where he restocked and altered many Springfields and built rifles on Mauser actions, and even turned out completely handmade shotguns. Old August is still alive. He was Bavarian trained and his fine painstaking work is in the best tradition of German craftsmanship.

The Neidner Arms Corporation of Dowagiac, Michigan was one of the early concerns where a custom rifle could be built

THE BIG-GAME RIFLE

complete except for the action. Neidner, himself, was German and a fine and precise workman who made all sorts of rifles for both varmint and big-game hunting and for target shooting. Neidner was, I believe, the first custom barrel maker in the United States and the name Neidner on the barrel stood for quality just as "Sterling" does on silver. Neidner's stock-maker, Tom Shelhamer, was a pioneer gun stock designer and maker who is still practicing his art, and he has turned out some of the finest gun stocks ever made anywhere.

In the early 1920's two large firms specializing in custom gunsmithing were founded, Griffin & Howe, now at 202 East 44th Street, New York, and Hoffman Arms Company, first of Cleveland, Ohio, and later of Ardmore, Oklahoma. Griffin & Howe was founded by Seymour Griffin and James Howe. Seymour Griffin is still with the firm, which is now controlled by Abercrombie & Fitch, the famous New York sporting goods store. Howe left the concern early. Frank Hoffman was the founder of the Hoffman Arms Company, which built many fine rifles and employed many famous workmen such as John Dubiel, John Wright, and Eric Johnson. Griffin & Howe is still doing business and a lot of business, but the Hoffman Arms Company had a pretty rocky time for one reason or another. Both firms advertised and made the average man conscious of the fact that their rifle could be handsomer than the average factory product. The firms restocked and altered many 1903 Springfields and also imported short, standard, and Magnum Mauser actions from the Mauser Werke in Germany, to build custom rifles around. They were instrumental in introducing such excellent foreign cartridges into the United States as the .300 and .375 H. & H. Magnum and also the .275 Magnum. They developed wildcat cartridges of a good deal of merit such as the .35 Whelen, the .400 Whelen, and the .350 Griffin & Howe Magnum.

After World War II custom rifle making got a tremendous shot in the arm. No sporting rifles had been made for about five years and hundreds of thousands of young men returned from

CUSTOM RIFLE MAKING

military service and wanted sporting rifles to hunt with. Many of these men had learned to camp out in the army and had learned to shoot rifles and had become interested in them. Many of them who had served in the European theater brought back Model 98-type German Mauser rifles which were suitable for rebarreling and restocking. Many of them had picked up some knowledge of gunsmithing in the Ordnance Department of the U. S. Army.

This putting together of guns in small shops became an industry of no small importance. Prior to the war there was only a handful of barrel makers. Neidner Arms Corporation made barrels and so did W. A. Sukalle, of Phoenix, Arizona, and J. R. Buhmiller, of Eureka, Montana. All of these shops were small ones and could not begin to supply the demand. At the same time there was a lot of barrel making machinery available as surplus. Many concerns went into the business of making and furnishing barrel blanks to gunsmiths. John Buhmiller greatly expanded his production. P. O. Ackley, rifle maker of Trinidad, Colorado, tooled up to furnish barrels in just about any length, twist, and caliber. Today there are probably dozens of custom barrel makers. Some of them furnish only the barrel blanks for gunsmiths to thread, chamber, and contour, but some not only furnish blanks but fit finished barrels to customers' actions.

There are now all kinds, sizes, and conditions of custom gun makers in the United States. Some are like Griffin & Howe, of New York, which occupies an entire floor in an office building, a large concern which employs many workmen—specialists in stock making, barrel fitting and chambering, file work, and engraving. Other concerns are strictly one-man businesses and the same man does the metalwork on the action, alters the bolt, fits a new safety, adjusts the trigger pull, laps, threads, contours, and chambers the barrel, then blues all metal parts, makes the stock from the rough blank, shapes it, checkers it, polishes it, and finishes it. Such a workman is Alvin Biesen, West 1620 Nora, Spokane, Washington. Except for the action he will turn out a com-

THE BIG-GAME RIFLE

plete rifle, and the rifles that he produces are among the finest obtainable anywhere. He is one of the best stock-makers who has ever practiced the art and his stocks are as fine as those turned out by the late Alvin Linden.

Other gunsmiths do only fine metalwork and turn over the stocking to specialists. Others like Leonard Mews, 932 West Summer Street, Appleton, Wisconsin, do only fine stock work.

A new and large rifle making concern which has come to the front since the war is Weatherby's, Inc., 2793 Firestone Blvd., South Gate, California. The concern imports Mauser actions from Belgium, barrels them with their own barrels, stocks them, fits sights, etc. The firm is well known for the Weatherby Magnum cartridges designed by Roy Weatherby, the founder of the company. They are cartridges of very advanced ballistics and have been used on big game all over the world.

Frank Pachmayr, the manufacturer of the Pachmayr Recoil Pads, the POWER-PAC choke device, Lo-Swing scope mounts, etc., also has a custom gun department which fits, chambers, and contours barrels, fits sights, completes fine custom stocks, etc.

As this is written in 1951, custom gun making in the United States is in a very healthy condition. The poor workman and the gyp artists have been pretty well shaken out of the trade because they cannot compete with factory rifles. The best workmen have survived and, I believe, the finest bolt-action magazine rifles in the world are being made right in the United States. If a man wants a big-game rifle handsomer than the ordinary, to fit him, to incorporate his ideas as to weight, stock, etc., the world is his oyster.

CHAPTER VI

Planning the Custom Rifle

Getting a custom rifle made up is beset with many pitfalls which the beginner can avoid if he exercises care and takes advice, but most of us learn the hard way. The custom rifle maker who is to turn out the hunter's dream weapon should be chosen with care. There are some very excellent gunsmithing firms and some very poor ones. Many custom rifles are things of beauty and accuracy to be cherished for a lifetime and some of them, alas, are pieces of junk—crude, homely, and inaccurate. Let it be said that as a rule the so-called custom rifle which can be sold at a price comparable to that of a factory made rifle is usually no great bargain. A *good* custom rifle will necessarily be more expensive than the factory rifle because of the greater amount of handwork which must go into it. It is very difficult to produce custom rifles at a profit. No one has ever got rich doing it, and because of the great expense of handwork, most custom gunmaking firms have had their financial troubles.

A man thinking of having a custom rifle made up is first confronted with the problem of whether he should turn the entire job over to one concern or whether he will have the metal work done in one shop and the stock made in another. Some concerns can do the whole job, even to the engraving. Others specialize in one type of work. The pioneer gunsmithing firm of Griffin & Howe of New York, will remodel the action, fit, chamber, and contour the barrel, fit sights, make and checker the stock and engrave the metal parts. On the other hand, W. A. Sukalle, the famous barrel maker, will make and fit the barrel and do all of the metal work, but he does no stock work. Keith Stegall, Box 696, Gunnison, Colorado, an able stock-maker, does no metal work. Alvin Linden, the famous stock-maker, did only minor metal work and blueing and most of the metal work and barrel fitting on Linden's rifles was done by Emil Koshollek, 517 South Michigan Ave., Stevens Point, Wisconsin. West Coast gun concerns who can undertake an entire job, including engraving, are Weatherby's, Inc., 2793 Firestone Blvd., South Gate, California; Kerr Sporting Goods, of Beverly Hills, California; and Pachmayr Gun Works, 1220 S. Grand Ave., Los Angeles 15, California.

It is easier, when deciding to get a rifle built up, to turn the whole set of specifications over to one firm and have them carry it through. Nevertheless, most rifle enthusiasts get a great creative satisfaction out of drawing up the specifications for a rifle and do not object to dealing, let us say, with a metal man and barrel fitter, a stock-maker, and an engraver—if engraving is wanted. One word of warning: before anyone undertakes to have a custom rifle built he should see examples of work turned out by the concern. Individual stock-makers have their own styles. A man who admires the type of stocks turned out by Griffin & Howe isn't going to be happy with one turned out by Weatherby, and the man who fancies the Weatherby stocks will not care for the Griffin & Howe or Shelhamer styles.

Let us assume that the man wanting a custom rifle has decided on the caliber. His next step should be to decide on his choice of action. If he is content with a standard caliber available in the Winchester Model 70 and with the standard Winchester Model 70 twist and type of rifling, and if he does not want a barrel heavier or longer than Winchester factory standards, a standard grade Model 70 Winchester rifle is a good basis to begin on in having a custom bolt-action rifle built up. The action can be smoothed out, the trigger pull adjusted, the whole barrel and

PLANNING THE CUSTOM RIFLE

action polished and blued and a custom stock fitted to the customer's specification. The Model 70 rifle, a fine job in itself, can easily be the basis for an exceedingly fine and fancy sporter.

The Model 70 Winchester actions are not available alone, nor are barreled actions. Winchester sells only completed rifles. Consequently, if a man wants a rifle of a caliber not available in the Model 70 or a barrel longer or heavier than standard, it would not pay him to purchase a complete Model 70 rifle just for the action. Instead he should consider some other type of action. Most custom gunsmiths use the F.N. Mauser action variously remodeled, smoothed up, and in some cases specially heat-treated. Weatherby's, Inc., for example, opens up the F.N. Mauser magazine and remodels bolt face and extractor for even the big blown-out .300 Weatherby Magnum cartridge. Many Model 98 Mauser military actions of German, Czech, Belgian, or Polish manufacture are floating around the country. Some are excellent and in almost every way equal in quality to the commercial F.N. actions. Many, however, are rough and soft and, of course, the late Model 98's with stamped trigger guards and floorplates are not suitable for custom rifles. As a rule, Czech and Belgian actions are better than the German, but any action made prior to 1942 is usually good. The better ones can have bolt and safety altered for low scope mounting, the magazine hinged with a release button put in the trigger guard, and it is even possible to cut in two and shorten a Model 98 Mauser for short cartridges like the .250/3000.

Many Springfield Model 1903 actions are also available and can be remodeled to be suitable for fine custom sporters; likewise the British Pattern 14 or the U. S. Model 1917. Since they are longer than the Model 98 and Springfield actions they are somewhat more suitable for remodeling to take the long cartridges like the .300 and .375 H. & H. Magnum cartridges. I, for one, have never particularly admired the looks of the 1917 action. It is entirely possible to remodel the Remington Model 721 and Model 722 actions to improve their looks. They can be fitted

THE BIG-GAME RIFLE

with milled trigger guards and floorplates either by adapting them from a Jap Arisaka or purchasing them from a firm which specializes in their manufacture.

Let us assume now that our customer has decided on the action he is to use, whether he will furnish it himself or whether he will obtain it from the gunsmith. He has also decided on the caliber. He should next decide on the weight of the finished rifle. Actions can be lightened slightly and a real saving in weight can come from using an aluminum trigger and magazine box made by Holland and Holland of England. A major factor in the weight of the completed rifle is the length and contour of the barrel. When a customer is drawing his complete specifications he should specify that the rifle should weigh no more, let us say, than 8½ or 9 pounds, or whatever figure strikes his fancy and fits his needs. From then on it is up to the gunsmith, who can weigh the action, the sight equipment, a stock of about the same specifications, and who can then contour the barrel accordingly. In drawing up specifications for a custom rifle this weight business is of utmost importance. Many a customer has written rather vaguely that he wanted a "light" rifle and then has been disappointed when the finished weapon turned out to weigh 10½ or 11 pounds, complete.

METAL WORK ON ACTIONS

A good metal man can do many things to a rifle action to improve the looks and utility and to lighten it. Let's take a look at some of them. The trigger guard of a fine custom rifle should always be narrowed from front to rear. This lightens the action somewhat by taking off a bit of metal. It also adds to the appearance. Furthermore it improves the utility of the action because it makes it easier for the trigger finger to reach the trigger without bumping into the rear part of the trigger guard. Another thing that can be done which improves both the looks and the utility of the rifle is to have the floorplate hinged and a quick release button put in the forward part of the trigger guard, something which was done on the high-grade Mauser actions turned out in Germany. In the United States the job has been done by W. A. Sukalle, 1120 E. Washington, Phoenix, Arizona; Tom Burgess, E. 823 Sinto Ave., Spokane, Washington; Roy Dunlap, 2319 Fort Lowell Road, Tucson, Arizona; Alvin Biesen, West 1620 Nora, Spokane, Washington; and George Schielke, Rural Route #2, Trenton, New Jersey. Perhaps others have also done it but if they have I have not seen the work. The bolt handle, if a scope is to be used, should be altered for low scope mounting by either cutting off the bolt and welding on at a lower angle or by forging the bolt. The bolt handle can be filed down to smaller diameter and more graceful shape without losing necessary strength, and it can be bent back for easy grasping. The bolt knob itself can be knurled or it can be checkered in the style made famous by Griffin & Howe. If the customer wishes, the bolt handle can be flattened and checkered on the underside. Particularly if the rifle is to be used in a saddle scabbard the bolt handle should be turned down close to the stock but not so close that it makes grasping it difficult.

On a fine custom rifle the trigger should always be checkered, because a checkered trigger on which the finger will not slip is conducive to good, clean let-off of the shot. Some triggers can be bent to give a more graceful curve and the whole trigger narrowed down. Trigger pull should be adjusted to give a clean, crisp let-off of about 3½–4 pounds or, possibly better still, a special trigger can be fitted. A very excellent, crisp one-stage trigger is made my the Dayton-Traister Company, 34 S.E. 66th Ave., Portland 16, Oregon. It is the best single-stage trigger that I have ever seen. I have Dayton-Traister triggers on several rifles. Another most excellent trigger is the single-set trigger made by the Miller Single Trigger Company, of Millersburg, Pennsylvania. When unset this Miller trigger has a beautiful, crisp one-stage pull which lets go like a glass rod breaking. The trigger is

THE BIG-GAME RIFLE

set by pushing forward and then the merest touch will let it off. Springfield actions can be greatly improved in appearance by streamlining the magazine cutoff housing to a cigar shape and by reshaping the tang to the Mauser pattern. Where Springfield actions and unaltered Model 98 military Mauser actions are used with low mounted telescopic sights another safety should be substituted.

Various safeties are on the market and available to gunsmiths but one of the most suitable for fine custom rifles is the one turned out by W. A. Sukalle, 1120 E. Washington, Phoenix, Arizona. It is available to gunsmiths but must be individually fitted. The other is the slide-button type made by the Anderson Gun Shop, 1203 Broadway, Yakima, Washington. One version is located on top of the tang exactly like the safety of a double-barrel shotgun and the other version is located on the side.

The bolt can either be blued or it can be engine turned. The conscientious gunsmith will always carefully go over any action to see that the locking lugs at the head of the bolt bear evenly in the locking lug recesses and to correct the condition if they do not.

The man getting a custom rifle will have considerable leeway in choice of barrel length, twist, contour, etc. Standard length for sporting barrels in most calibers is 24 inches. However, this is a mere custom which probably derived from the original length of the Model 1903 Springfield barrel. For sporting use I much prefer the 22-inch barrel in calibers like the 7 mm., .270, and .30/06. Such a barrel is handier to carry in rugged mountains where the rifle often has to be strapped over the back. It is also handier in a saddle scabbard, and the shorter barrel results in a handsomer, more compact, and slightly lighter rifle. Velocity loss with the chopped-off barrel is so slight as to be ignored.

I do not believe that the barrels of rifles in .30/06 or .270 caliber should ordinarily be shorter than 22 inches because if they are the muzzle blast is increased to the point where it becomes

PLANNING THE CUSTOM RIFLE

unpleasant. However, if a man wants a short, light saddle rifle for a cartridge consuming less powder, such as the 7 mm., .257, or, .250/3000, he might well go to a 21- or even a 20-inch barrel. With the Magnum calibers like the .300 or .375, I do not think the barrel should be shorter than 24 inches and I prefer 25 or 26, as a short-barreled Magnum has a muzzle blast that would knock the ears off a brass monkey. Let us say then that for the average big-game rifle for all-around use the 22-inch barrel is difficult to improve upon.

The custom barrel makers usually make their barrels with six grooves and with six narrow lands. This type of rifling is presumably more accurate and also shorter lived than the 4-groove type with wider lands which is generally found in factory rifles for most big-game calibers. Actually I do not believe the number of grooves makes much difference, as there are many other factors which contribute to accuracy besides the type of rifling in the barrel. Factory rifles in .30/06, .270, and .300 Magnum have a twist of one turn in 10 inches. For ordinary hunting I prefer a 1–12 twist in both the .270 and .30/06. With that twist, excellent accuracy is obtained even with the 220-grain bullet in the .30/06 over game ranges, and with the 150-grain bullet in the .270. If the man ordering a custom rifle would plan to use the 150-grain bullet in the .30/06, let us say, or the special 160 or 170-grain bullets in the .270, he would be wise to select the standard 1–10 twist. A 7 mm. to be used with light bullets like the 130, 145, and 150-grain should have the 1–12 twist, but for all-around use with bullets weighing up to 175 grains, I would prefer the 1–10 or even 1–8½. Probably the best twist for .300 Magnum for use with all bullet weights is the 1–12, although excellent accuracy with 180-grain bullets is obtained with a twist of 1–14.

Ordinarily it is necessary only for the customer to specify to the barrel fitter the finished weight of his rifle complete with sights, and then the barrel fitter will contour the barrel to bring

THE BIG-GAME RIFLE

the weight within limits. However, if the customer wants to specify the barrel contour, here are some suggestions.

For a light .25 caliber rifle the barrel can have about the following contour: a cylinder 1.25 inches in length forward of the receiver ring and one inch in diameter; then the straight taper 1.75 inches long to .75; then another straight taper to .50 at the muzzle. Such a barrel contour with a Mauser action and a stock of medium weight will result in a rifle which will weigh 7–7¼ pounds with iron sights, or around 8 pounds with a scope.

A lightweight .30 caliber rifle could have the cylindrical portion 1.05 inches in diameter and extending 1.25 inches forward of the receiver ring; then the taper 1.75 inches in length to .850; then the straight taper to the muzzle which will measure .550. A 7 mm. or .270 barrel could come down to .50 at the muzzle. With a light stock and a barrel 22 inches in length so contoured a .30/06 will come out without sights to weigh around 7 pounds, and a .270 to around 7¼.

The standard Springfield .30 caliber service barrel has a cylindrical portion 1.14 inches in diameter which tapers to .956 and then has a straight taper to the muzzle of .647. A standard 1903 Springfield barrel with a Springfield action and a fairly light stock without sights will weigh from 7½–8 pounds, or from 8½–9 pounds with a scope.

While we are at it, some weight figures for various actions might not be amiss. The Springfield 1903 action weighs about 2 pounds, 12 ounces; the 1917 Enfield action 3 pounds, 5½ ounces; the Model 98 Mauser 2 pounds, 10 ounces; and the Winchester Model 70 action about 3 pounds. The moral of that one apparently is that the man ordering a light custom rifle will save a little weight by using the Mauser action.

Different barrel makers contour a barrel somewhat differently than I have outlined here. Some, for instance, use a longer cylindrical portion and then instead of using a straight taper they use a convex taper to the point where the straight taper begins to the muzzle. Again it is wise for the customer to see the barrel fitter's favorite contours before he jumps.

The Custom Rifle Stock

The standard gun-stock material of the world is walnut, and almost without exception the best gun-stock material available for the deluxe custom rifle is a really fine piece of European walnut. It is light, strong, and tough. It weighs 35–40 pounds per cubic foot, and it will take and hold fine checking. European walnut comes from trees growing the thin-shelled or "English" variety of nuts. It is variously known as Circassian, English, Italian, and French walnut, depending on where it is grown and what it looks like. A great majority of the European walnut blanks that reach this country are grown and cut in the Rhone Valley in France. However, it is a custom, if the particular stock blank shows a lot of color contrast (particularly if it contains yellow streaks as well as light and dark brown), to call it Circassian. If the blanks are light in color, they are often called English or Italian. Chances are that, whatever they are called, they actually came from France.

The European walnut most desirable for gun-stock material is straight grained and streaked with vivid contrast between the lighter body wood and streaks that are so dark brown as to be almost black. The best walnut is grown in a mild, dry climate where the trees grow slowly because of lack of moisture and are not subject to severe winter temperatures. Wood is now coming on the market from thin-shelled walnut trees grown in California. Some of it is as fine as the best walnut grown in Europe, but much is light in color and rather soft because it was grown in irrigated walnut groves.

Before the last war it was quite easy to obtain French walnut blanks of the highest grade at from $10. to $25. a blank. Now, very ordinary French walnut blanks with no contrast whatsoever sell from $10. up and a really fine piece of walnut will cost from $35. up. The best supply of good French walnut blanks that I have seen since the war was over was at the shop of Griffin & Howe in New York.

The commonest gun-stock material in the United States is American black walnut. Probably 95 percent of all gunstocks are made of this material. Walnut trees grow all over the United States from the Atlantic to the Pacific. There are many thousands of walnut trees in the Ozark region of Arkansas and Missouri where E. C. Bishop and Sons, of Warsaw, Missouri, cut and cure black walnut trees for their rough shaped and inletted stocks. The firm also furnishes walnut blanks to many of the rifle and shotgun manufacturers.

Some of the better American walnut is very good indeed, almost as good as European. It is somewhat softer and heavier than European walnut and it does not take as fine checking nor hold it as well. Nevertheless, many beautiful stocks are obtained from American walnut trees, particularly at points where the roots and branches branch out from the main trunk. Shotgun butt stocks particularly are made from fine burl American walnut with very fancy figure and often a good deal of color contrast.

The poorest walnut grows in swamps and along river bottoms. Then it is soft, spongy and open-grained. If linseed oil alone is tried on such wood, it will practically never get through soaking it up and eventually it will turn almost black. Many black walnut trees grow in the semi-arid canyons of the Southwestern mountains, usually at altitudes of from 4,000 to 5,000 feet. I have never seen one of those native Arizona black walnut trees cut, cured, and converted into gun-stocks. It seems to me, though, that the conditions for growth are ideal and should result in excellent rifle stock material.

Another type of wood which is fairly often used for gun-stocks is rock maple in either the birdseye or the "tiger flame" variety. Maple has about the same density as walnut, weighing around 37 pounds per cubic foot. The wood is very hard and a bit on the brittle side but not too brittle to be used in gun-stocks. It holds checking well but is more difficult to check and work than good European walnut. It was a favorite with the old custom gunsmiths who built the flintlock and cap and ball Kentucky rifles.

As it finishes up, maple is practically white and for the best appearance should be colored. The late Alvin Linden, the famous stock-maker who did much to popularize the use of maple for stocks, used the Japanese "Suigi" fiinish which consists of scorching the wood lightly with a blow torch. The treatment brings out the contrast in the grain that results in some very beautiful and spectacular stocks though they are a bit on the gaudy side. Another system is to oil-finish a maple stock with linseed oil in which some burnt umber has been added. To some of the more conservative stock-makers and rifle enthusiasts, maple is too gaudy, and they would not be caught dead with a maple stock. However, good maple is gaining in popularity as gun-stock material and anyone having a custom stock made should consider it.

Another interesting wood for gun-stocks is Oregon myrtle, which grows along the coast in the mountains of southwestern Oregon and northwestern California. The myrtle tree is a cone-shaped evergreen varying in height from 20 to, I believe, about 40 feet. The wood itself is curious stuff. If it can be obtained with good figure, and properly cured and dried, it is excellent gun-stock material. Weight is about like that of walnut. It takes and holds fine checking as well as the best European walnut and is very strong. It is, I have been told, very difficult to dry. It should be cut into planks, then the planks sunk under water for at least two years. Then the wood should be thoroughly air-dried and then kiln-dried. Myrtle has more variety of color, figure, and contrast than any wood I have ever seen. I have seen myrtle which could be taken for birdseye maple, myrtle that looked like the finest Circassian walnut, myrtle with no more contrast than a pine plank, and myrtle that was all contrast. Typical myrtle, though, is a light-colored wood which when oil-finished will turn sort of a tan, and much of it has no great figure. The very best is light but strongly marked with brown to black streaks which often form ornate figures. Sometimes one runs into a myrtle blank with dark, rich green streaks as well as brown. I have a fine .270 stocked with a myrtle blank which I picked up myself at Marshfield, Oregon, after sorting over perhaps 150 or 200 blanks, some good, some bad, some indifferent. This one was correctly cut, thoroughly dry, beautifully figured and the result is one of the finest gun-stocks I have ever seen.

Another wood which has seen some use, particularly in California, in recent years is the screwbean mesquite. Roy Weatherby has turned out a good many stocks of that wood. It is a very heavy wood and a very strong wood weighing about 50 pounds per cubic foot. When finished up, it is dark reddish-brown with black streaks. Mesquite can be made into very handsome stocks, but the excessive weight bars its use for anything except rifles which are intended to be heavy.

These woods I have mentioned are the favorites. Others are occasionally used. The late Alvin Linden made many stocks of beech which he stained or gave the Suigi finish. Cherry and apple are sometimes used, and so are mahogany and rosewood. For the most part, however, the man wanting a fine custom gun-stock cannot go wrong on good European walnut and his second choice should be American black walnut.

Modern American stocks for sporting rifles derive from the old muzzle-loading Kentucky rifles, which in turn were stocked in a style imported from Germany by the original emigrant rifle makers. Butt stocks were very short with great drop at comb and heel. Buttplate was small and crescent-shaped—the so-called "rifle" buttplate. The forearm was narrow with little to hold on to. Many profess to love the lines of these old Kentuckys but I have always found them miserable things to shoot, clumsy, muzzle-heavy, and even painful. The stock does fairly well for the

PLANNING THE CUSTOM RIFLE

offhand position but for no other, and if used with a heavy load it is murder! The crooked stock causes the comb to rise up and smack the cheekbone and the sharp points of the crescent buttplate will dig into the shoulder.

Until fairly recently as time goes, most American sporting rifle stocks showed strongly the influence of the old Kentucky. The older Winchester, Savage, and lever-action Marlin rifles had relatively short buttstocks with rifle buttplates and skinny little forends. I remember a Model 95 Winchester for the powerful .405 Winchester cartridge I shot once. When I say once, I mean *once!* That miserable stock almost killed me.

Until about the time the 1903 Springfield came out, few riflemen paid much attention to the stocks on their weapons. They simply did their best to shoot what they could get. Since they didn't know any better they were happy. Apparently stock designers gave the matter no thought either. They just put out stocks in the conventional manner and let it go at that. The stock on the Model 1903 Springfield service rifle was very bad as compared to the excellence of the rifle itself and the cartridge designed for it, and a few bold and original riflemen began to experiment in any attempt to get more suitable sporting stocks. The immediate inspiration for these on the Springfield sporters was the typical stock for the European bolt-action sporter as made in Germany. The foreign jobs, although an improvement on American stocks, were still far from perfect. Combs were too low and too thin and there was too much drop at heel. Forends were too skimpy. The first of the new stocks for the Springfield were made in Los Angeles by a German gunsmith named Hans Wundhammer, who was persuaded to give his sporter stocks fuller forends, higher, thicker combs, less drop at heel, broad, flat buttplates instead of the small curved rifle buttplates. I have seen one of those first sporter stocks, which was built for and owned at the time by the late Captain E. C. Crossman. It isn't a bad looking stock at all.

The fact that the new gospel on stock design was still not

widely disseminated is shown by the appearance of the first Model 30 Remington and Model 54 Winchester stocks which came out just after the first World War. The stock on the Remington had a rifle buttplate that would half kill you with the recoil of a .30/06. The Winchester Model 54 stock had excessive drop at comb and heel and the buttplate was too small and set on at an angle which gave so little pitch down that the butt was apt to slip down under the shoulder. Along in the 1920's, the Springfield Arsenal, through the efforts of the National Rifle Association, brought out a Model 1903.30/06 rifle known as the N.R.A. Sporter. Although it had far too much wood on it and was surely no thing of beauty, the basic dimensions were a great improvement over those of any factory made sporting stock heretofore available. The N.R.A. Sporter, by the way, once sold complete to the members of the National Rifle Association with good stock, smooth-working, well-adjusted action, with a good trigger pull, fully polished and blued barrel, and Lyman 48 receiver sight for $40. It was the first genuinely well-stocked sporting rifle that many shooters got their hands on. One can imagine how happy this competition made Remington, Savage, and Winchester, as those firms did not have the American taxpayer as an angel and in setting the retail prices for their own wares, they had to cut the wholesaler and the dealer in on some of the gravy. The N.R.A. Sporter made the officials of those companies squawk no end, but the sale of that good rifle had the result of improving the factory products. For use with iron sights, later stocks on the Remington Model 30 rifles and Winchester Model 54's were a vast improvement.

Considerable thought was being put into the design of rifle stocks by intelligent stock-makers along in the 1930's. Although the telescopic sight had not come into wide use at the time, the stocks were well designed for iron sights and those turned out by Griffin & Howe, Tom Shelhamer of Neidner's, Hoffman Arms Company, Bob Owen, and Alvin Linden had good dimensions and good lines.

PLANNING THE CUSTOM RIFLE

When the telescopic hunting sight came into wider use, stocks began to be designed for use with scope sights only. A great many stock-makers were target shots only and were pretty much unaware of the problems of the big-game hunter. Consequently, the target stock has had a good deal of influence on sporting stocks. Much of it is not too happy as the target stock has too much wood on it, too full a forend, too curved a pistol grip.

A good sporting stock should enable the shooter to get a shot off quickly and accurately and it should also be a thing of beauty. Many fine sporting stocks are handsome but are of little aid in accurate shooting. Many others which hold and shoot well are homely and clumsy. The very best sporter stock design results in a stock with handsome, graceful lines and one which also enables the man behind it to do his best work.

Today most sporting stocks are designed for use with telescopic sights to be used on a bolt-action rifle. This is responsible for special problems since the comb can be no higher than the withdrawal of the bolt will permit. Unless some thought goes into comb design this often results in too little support for the face, because the use of the telescopic sight raises the line of sight considerably over that of iron sights. A development in sporter stock design which has come to the fore in the past ten years or so is the use of the Monte Carlo comb. Just how successful this has been, we shall see.

First let us look at the component parts of the stock and see what the function of each is. Because the work of holding the rifle firmly against the shoulder is largely accomplished by the right hand, the pistol grip is of great importance. The rifle is held more firmly against the shoulder than is the shotgun and consequently the pistol grip has to have more of a curve. The best design is a sharp, full curve *slightly* flared at the grip cap for better holding. The straight grip, such as is found on many double-barrel shotguns and on the old Model 1903 Springfield military stock, has no place on a rifle at all because the straight grip cramps the wrist and hand and makes a firm hold awkward.

THE BIG-GAME RIFLE

Actually I suspect that the straight grip has no place on a shotgun either if it is equipped with single trigger. In late years such a grip has been put on certain high grade double guns because it is the conventional thing to do. The closeness and fullness of the pistol grip and also the parabolic curve or flare toward the grip cap is often exaggerated by certain stock-makers and the result is not only a homely pistol grip but a clumsy one. Very often pistol grips are made with a swell on the right side for the hollow part of the palm. This was worked out well before the first World War by one of the original stockers of Springfield rifles, Hans Wundhammer, of Los Angeles, whom we have mentioned. For my part I think the importance of the famous Wundhammer swell is greatly exaggerated. It is not at all bad and may even be helpful if the man who has ordered the stock is present when the grip is being shaped so that the stock-maker can fit the swell into his hand. But if the swell does not fit exactly, it is worse than useless. Most pistol grips are too large for any hand except that of a giant. My hands are not large for my size. Although I am tall I would say that my hands are about average. A pistol grip running from $4\frac{1}{2}$–$4\frac{3}{4}$ inches in circumference is just about right for me. Larger pistol grips are clumsy. Many come as large as $5\frac{1}{4}$ inches. It is often said that the small pistol grip is weak and will break. This is not true if the grain was cut correctly when the original stock blank was sawed out. Grain should always run parallel to the grip. Good stock woods are strong. Actually the rifle stock does not take nearly the shock and abuse that a baseball bat does, and a baseball bat is small in diameter at the grip.

The comb of the rifle stock should be rounded up from the grip and should give protection so that the nose will not bump on the thumb around the grip. Many otherwise fine stocks have combs that do not project high enough above the grip proper to protect the nose. Since the comb cannot be higher than the withdrawal of the bolt will permit, it should, if telescopic sights are to be used exclusively, be thick and well rounded. In comb design, thickness can be substituted for height and the same support obtained from a relatively low, thick, round comb that could be obtained with a much higher and thinner comb. Stocks for most European bolt-action sporting rifles are particularly bad in respect to the comb because they are thin as well as lower than necessary.

For a bolt-action rifle used with telescopic sights the comb should usually be just as high as withdrawal of the bolt will allow and drop at that point is, therefore, controlled by the bolt. Drop at heel, in the best design, should be very little greater than drop at comb. If I plan a rifle stock to be used with both iron sights and scope I order drop at heel to be ½ inch greater than

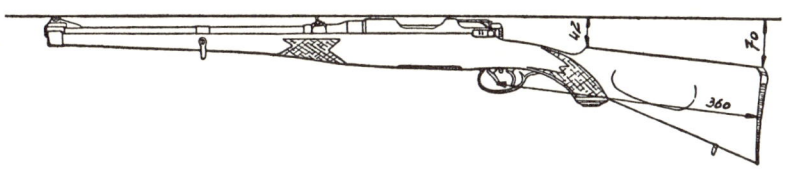

The Mannlicher-Schonauer carbine illustrated represents the classical European stock. Comb is much thinner than the best American design and there is more heel drop. Americans have always liked the exotic looks of these little carbines, and any sporter stocked full-length of the barrel is in this country said to have a "Mannlicher" stock.

drop at comb. If I order the rifle to be used with scope sights only, I specify drop at heel exactly the same as drop at comb. The straight-stocked rifle mounts faster and points more accurately. A straight-stocked rifle also gives much less apparent recoil because drop at heel tends to accentuate the jump of the muzzle when the powerful rifle is fired—something which bangs the comb up against the cheek and makes a man think he is being killed.

Many sporting stocks are made today with Monte Carlo combs in an attempt to get a buttstock with the point of contact for the cheek higher than the point of the comb can be. This design is not bad, if the man shoots with his head relatively high. It is not a bad deal either for a man with sloping shoulders because one can have considerable drop at heel and yet a fairly high point of contact for the cheek midway up the stock. For the stock crawler—the man who runs his neck out and his head forward—the Monte Carlo comb is absolutely worthless—just extra wood to be carried around, since his cheek makes contact with the comb only at one point. If this place where his cheek comes against the comb is at the point of the comb, it does absolutely no good to raise the comb toward the rear with a Monte Carlo. This stock crawler, then, cannot use the Monte Carlo and derive any benefit from it. Furthermore, I, for one, have never particularly cared for the looks of the Monte Carlo. In extreme examples some of them look about as aesthetic as canoe paddles.

The forend of the stock should be of such a shape that it can be grasped firmly and the rifle swung with it by the left hand for running shooting. It has the further function of keeping the hand away from a hot barrel. However, the game shot faces an entirely different problem in that respect than does the target shot. Actually it is seldom that the hunter fires more than two or three shots in succession. Consequently the barrel never becomes very hot. He does not need wide so-called "beavertail" forends favored by target shots. The best type of forend for the sporting rifle is, I believe, modified pear-shaped which is flattened on the under side yet gives a beaver-tail effect for quick, sure grasping. Actually a forend that is round in cross section is not at all bad. Some of the early Griffin & Howe stocks had forends so made and they were not only efficient but handsome.

A detail of good shaping on the fine sporter stock is the cutting away of the wood above the trigger guard so that the hand can get to the trigger without any cramping of the index or trigger finger.

Early cheek pieces on American sporting rifles were of the British design called "Whelen" or "Baker" in this country. (I am illustrating such a cheek piece.) They were not too successful except for the man who shoots with his head pretty much straight up since the forward edge will cut into and bruise the cheek with recoil if the shooter has any tendency to crawl his stock. The best type of cheek piece is the modified Scheutzen stock type

PLANNING THE CUSTOM RIFLE

which flows into the comb. Then the man who shoots the rifle can crowd right up on the comb without getting his cheek bruised. Many cheek pieces are made with the surface which goes against the cheek rounded. I do not care for this type of shaping because such a cheek piece comes in contact with the cheek only at one point. The best type of cheek piece is almost flat, so as to allow full contact between cheek piece and face from top to bottom. A man with a full face can even use a concave cheek piece.

The comb should be cut away—undercut or "fluted"—on the right side to give a space for the fleshy part of the hand at the base of the thumb.

Some rifle stocks are things of beauty because of their lines. Many are ugly for the same reason. The finest engraving in the world and the best checking and carving will not make a rifle stock with poor lines anything but homely. To say why one stock is handsome and another is not is almost as difficult as to say why one girl is a beauty and another girl with similar features is quite ordinary in appearance. All girls have the same quota of eyes, noses, and mouths, just as stocks have pistol grips, cheek pieces, and forends. A few rules can be laid down, however. One is that lines should either be straight or they should be segments of a circle and that lines should flow into one another and seem to belong. For example, on the best stocks the line from the bottom of the buttstock from the tow of the stock up toward the pistol grip should, if it were continued, run into the base of the trigger as it disappears into the action. Shad-belly curves from the bottom of the buttstock have no place and result in ugly lines. The line of the underside of the forend should also be straight.

Another rule for creating a handsome stock is that large slab-sided spaces should be broken up. The space on the left side of the stock of a bolt-action rifle between the trigger and the receiver ring is large and blank. Its appearance is greatly improved if the wood under the boltstop is fluted to break up the flat sur-

THE BIG-GAME RIFLE

face. Of course the different actions give the artistic stock-maker different problems.

The best way for one to get a stock of handsome and pleasing design is to pick the stock-maker who turns out the type of stock the man ordering admires. There are some stock-makers who can do fine inletting, good checking, but who have no artistic eye. Many stock-makers are equally good in their inletting, checking, and finishing, yet they also have an eye for line and turn out graceful and handsome-appearing stocks. Stock-makers simply cannot change their style—or at least very few of them can. The late Alvin Linden was one of the most versatile of all stock-makers and although all of his stocks looked like Linden

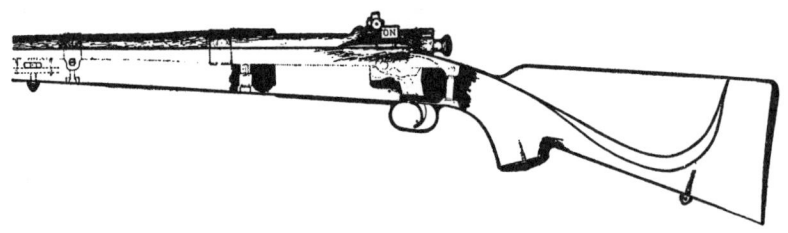

Cut away view of modern bolt-action rifle stock the way the late Al Linden built one. Notice the full, close pistol grip, the cheek-piece merging into the comb. Notice also the attachment of the front swivel base forward of the band which ties barrel and forend together.

stocks, no two of them were exactly alike. He was constantly experimenting and improving and adapting his style to various actions and conditions. More than any other stock-maker I have had any experience with, Linden could really make a stock to specifications and could vary his style to suit his customer's needs and ideas. Some stock-makers simply cannot do this and although they may turn out fine-looking stocks all of them are as alike as two peas in a pod. The prospective purchaser of a custom stock, then, should, if he possibly can, look at some of the products of his stock-maker. If he doesn't like their appearance he should forget about that particular stock-maker because the chances are that he will be unhappy with the result. One of Roy Weatherby's stock-makers probably would not do much of a job of

PLANNING THE CUSTOM RIFLE

turning out a stock in the style of Griffin & Howe, and one of the Griffin & Howe stock-makers would drop dead if he were asked to turn out a Weatherby stock.

My own tastes in stocks are relatively conservative and I like very much the lines of the stocks turned out by Alvin Biesen, Tom Shelhamer, Griffin & Howe, Bob Owen, and Morgan Holmes.

A school of stock-making known as the California school has grown up on the West Coast in the past ten or fifteen years. Some apparently like the California-style stocks immensely. They are marked by very thick cheek pieces usually made necessary because the stocks have excessive cast-off and these thick cheek pieces simply bring the line of support back where it ought to be. They are also marked by very long and excessively flared pistol grips, by Monte Carlo combs which run clear back to within a couple of inches of the heel of the stock. In many cases the stocks have excessive drop at heel. This style of stocking is an extreme one and in many cases it substitutes cure in one dimension for a fault in another. Excessively thick cheek pieces, as we have seen, are made necessary by excessive cast-off and the marked Monte Carlo by excessive drop at heel. There is no use for those long pistol grips unless a man has an unusually large hand. Most of these stocks have excessive wood in the forend and too much wood all around. Actually one of the greatest faults of most custom stock-makers is leaving too much wood in the stock. There are few custom sporter stocks that cannot be benefitted by the removal of some wood.

If a man is of more or less average height and build he can be quite well fitted with a stock of more or less standard dimensions. A man around 5 feet 8 inches tall should take a length of pull of about 13¼ inches. I am a six-footer and 13½ inches is about right for me, and 13¾ inches is definitely a bit awkward because it is too long. A man under 5 feet 8 inches can use a length of pull of about 13 inches and a very short man or a small woman can use a length of pull of about 12¾. The man with a very large hand needs a larger pistol grip but I very seriously doubt that he ever needs one larger than 5 inches in circumference. The average hand is best fitted with one about 4¾ inches in circumference, and the small hand can take one around 4½ inches. It is better for the pistol grip to be slightly on the small side than slightly on the large side. The man with a thin or even a medium face needs all the comb height he can get on a bolt-action rifle and a fairly thick cheek piece about ⅝ inches thick on the lower edge. The man with a very wide face and high, wide cheek-bones will be murdered with a comb of that sort, however, and a man so built should make his physical characteristics plain to his stock-maker. Likewise the man with a large hand will do better with a somewhat fuller forend because the large hand finds it difficult to grasp a small forend. Never should anyone try to transfer dimensions of a shotgun stock to a rifle. The shotgun stock should be longer, as rifle and shotgun are shot in an entirely different manner. As a rule, the shotgun stock should be about ¾ inch longer than a rifle stock. I, as an example, am correctly fitted with a length of pull on a rifle stock of 13½ inches whereas 14¼ inches about catches me with a shotgun stock.

Unless the rifle stock is on a weapon of great power and heavy recoil, the best looking and longest wearing buttplate material is knurled steel. It can be plain or it can have a trap which covers a hollowed out portion in the butt stock to carry emergency cleaning rod, perhaps an extra round or two of ammunition, etc. The steel buttplate should be fairly wide and flat to distribute recoil evenly. It will stand up under much hard use and it protects the wood of the stock. A rifle equipped with a steel buttplate can also be fired somewhat more accurately because there is less give and jump to a steel buttplate than to a rubber one.

If a rifle has considerable recoil, or if the man shooting it is sensitive to recoil, it should be equipped with a rubber recoil pad. Many excellent ones are made, notably those turned out by the Pachmayr Gun Works. A rubber recoil pad will not bruise the shoulder and for many it takes the sting out of shooting heavy rifles. I have never considered the rubber recoil pad, however, as handsome as the steel buttplate, and I agree with Tom Shelhamer when he said that seeing a fine rifle stock with a rubber recoil pad is like seeing a man in evening clothes wearing rubber boots.

For my own rather conservative tastes the best type of pistol grip cap is one of plain or lightly engraved blued steel. About the best grip caps and buttplates manufactured in America are those made on special order by Emil Koshollek, 517 S. Michigan Ave., Stevens Point, Wisconsin. They are beautifully knurled and very handsome. I do not care for fancy pistol grip caps with inlaid diamonds, and I do not care for white spacers between the grip cap and the wood nor between the recoil pad and the buttstock. Some grip caps are made of ivory, some of red, yellow, and green plastic. Some love them. I do not! It is the convention these day to have a forend tip on a sporting rifle. Originally these tips were made of black horn which was obtained from East Indian water buffalo. In many cases horn is very handsome but it has a tendency when very dry to crack and split like the hoof of a dead horse or the horn of an expired range cow. Possibly better are tips of some type of plastic, although some good stockers use ebony or some other dark wood that finishes up black.

Many types of finishes can be used on sporter stocks and all of them have their admirers. Some like shiny finishes put on with shellac and lacquer. Some like coats of spar varnish. I have had the best luck with linseed oil finish put on over some good filler. Actually, if a man takes his time and has a high-grade close-grained stock blank to work on, he needs to have no other finish than linseed oil. Professional stock-makers don't like to monkey with a straight linseed oil finish because to put on a good one actually takes several months. In the old days, when people had more leisure, fine stocks were almost entirely finished with linseed oil. Coats were applied until the stock was filled and the surplus oil gummed on the outside. Then, by one means or other, this surplus oil was cut off clear down to the bare wood. Then the finish was put on by rubbing in a little bit of oil each day and wiping off any surplus until coat after coat, each microscopically thin, was put on the stock. Such a finish is very handsome and very durable and if it is scratched a little bit the scratch can be rubbed out with another application of linseed oil.

Particularly on some factory stocks the lacquer finish is very unsatisfactory and a little contact with rocks in ordinary use will make the finish fall off in big flakes.

Fine, precise checking is one of the marks of a fine rifle and the best shaped and finished and inletted stock will be ruined by coarse, clumsy checking. In many eyes the same stock can also lose beauty and value by checking and ornamentation that is too fancy and too ornate. In recent years many stocks have been ornamented with fancy inlays and woods of different color or with ivory and plastic. It is my conservative opinion that such fancy work detracts from a fine stock, just as gaudy jewelry detracts from the appearance of a pretty girl. However, anyone who likes it can name his own poison. Other stock-makers specialize in carving stocks, particularly in Germany. I have seen stocks with hunting scenes carved on them—dogs chasing mountain lions, javelinas destroying rattlesnakes, etc. My own feeling is that if I want to look at pictures I will look somewhere else rather than on gun-stocks.

The finest type of ornamentation for the gun-stock, and also very useful ornamentation, is fine, precise checking of pleasing design with fine, sharp diamonds running from 22–26 lines to an inch. There are many pleasing checking designs; some of the older types are derived from the English and are a variation of diamonds. Some are based on Fleur-de-lis patterns. The late Alvin Linden is, I believe, pretty much responsible for getting away from the diamond design in stock checking. Good, sharp diamonds make the stock easier to hold and to grasp. In some of the best examples of fine checking, wood is cut away before it is checked so that the wood around the checking pattern stands out in bas-relief. Some fine sporters have engraving on the metal

PLANNING THE CUSTOM RIFLE

parts. If engraving is genuinely well executed and artistically designed it adds much to the beauty of the rifle. A man can spend as little as $25 to get some scroll engraving on the floorplate and trigger guard or as much as $1,000 if he wishes to have floorplate and trigger guard elaborately engraved in relief, and engraving put on the receiver ring and on the barrel. Engraving is usually quite good or very bad and there are only a handful of competent steel engravers in the United States. There are many poor ones and their work should by all means be avoided.

A few of the custom gunsmiths such as Griffin & Howe have enough engraving to do to warrant their employing an engraver who works on the premises. Most custom gunsmiths, however, have so little demand for engraving that they send their engraving out.

The finest rifle is by no means the fanciest rifle and usually a man gets more for his money in a custom rifle if he invests it in fine wood with good figure and contrast, excellent stock work, and fine, sharp checking of pleasing pattern. If he wishes he can ornament the stock with a gold or silver nameplate either forward of the toe of the buttstock or inlaid into the forend. Such a name or initial plate individualizes a rifle and does not add greatly to the cost.

The best custom rifles fit the owners, shoot beautifully and are a joy to own. They will not shoot any better than a well tuned-up factory rifle, but the man who loves guns can get a creative thrill in planning his rifle and the custom job gives him leeway in weight and special barrel dimensions and twist specifications, choice of wood and shape of stock. The owner of a custom rifle can take a good deal of pleasure, if he is that kind of a guy, out of having a rifle that is exactly like no other in the world.

CHAPTER VII

Rifles and Cartridges for Forest Game

THE WHITETAIL deer is in numbers, and in area of distribution, and possibly in intelligence, the No. 1 North American game animal. Because he is prolific and because he is smart enough to adapt himself to civilization, he is able to exist in great numbers close to large centers of population. Those who live in great urban centers like Philadelphia, Pittsburgh, Detroit, New York, Chicago, and Boston have a chance to hunt whitetails on a week-end trip. To them the whitetail is "big game." Because so many can hunt him, he is one of the best friends that the arms and ammunition industry has ever had, since probably nine out of ten center-fire cartridges, above .22 caliber, are sold to people who are plotting his destruction. Whitetails of one variety or another are found from Maine to Florida, from northern Idaho to Arizona.

This most popular of all North American big-game animals is almost always a dweller in brush and forest. He is not a large animal and he is not particularly difficult to kill. Because of his habitat, shots at him are usually fairly short and, over most of his range, far more whitetail deer are killed within 100 yards than beyond. Black bear are found just about wherever whitetail deer are found and, like the deer, the black bear gets along well with civilization. The possibility of running into a bear lends spice to a week-end whitetail hunt all over the wooded East, and the er-

RIFLES AND CARTRIDGES FOR FOREST GAME

roneous notion that the black bear is a dangerous animal lends still more spice.

Probably at least 50 percent of all North American hunters who go after big game are primarily whitetail deer hunters who secondarily have hopes of obtaining a black bear. The average whitetail buck probably weighs around 135–140 pounds clean dressed. The average black bear does not weigh too much more. In some sections of the United States, bears run larger than in others, but a black bear weighing, when clean, 300 pounds is an exceedingly large one and probably the average adult black bear will weigh between 150 and 200 pounds.

The American pioneers killed the Eastern whitetail deer and black bear with muzzle-loading Kentucky rifles which were about as powerful as the modern .32/20. This does not mean, though, that a .32/20 would be a wise choice for a modern American hunter. The American pioneer was a woodsman used to seeing game in its native habitat. He had the skill to track down and finish off a wounded animal. Game was plentiful and relatively tame and he almost always held his fire until he could get a good standing shot at a vital portion of the animal.

Today things are different. The average forest hunter for whitetail deer is a city man. He seldom has much skill in tracking, and he is not nearly as good a shot as the pioneer. Deer hunting with him is the climax of the sporting year and not a work-a-day matter as it was with the pioneer. He is apt to blaze away the moment he sees a deer. He does not wait for a standing shot with vital areas exposed, and probably he couldn't hit the vital area every time even under the most favorable circumstances. He shoots at his deer on the run and instead of driving his bullet into the heart-lung area or coolly breaking the neck, he often hits the animal in the hams, in the abdominal cavity and in other non-vital areas. Furthermore, over much of the whitetail country there is an enormous density of hunters, and if a man does not kill his deer in his tracks and get to it immediately, he is apt to find another hunter standing over it and another

THE BIG-GAME RIFLE

hunter's tag on its antlers. In the course of every year, in my capacity as a gun editor, I get dozens of letters from hunters who have hit bucks hard and then followed the blood trails only to find that other hunters have claimed their bucks. Conditions under which deer are hunted today differ vastly, then, from conditions of the pioneer days, and a rifle and projectile which were entirely adequate then are not so now.

Since shots at whitetail deer average short, it is not necessary for the whitetail hunter to have a rifle using a cartridge which gives a very flat trajectory, as almost any center-fire smokeless cartridge shoots flat enough for 100–125 yard ranges. The antelope hunter on the Western plains may have to take his trophy buck at 400 yards or more. He needs not only very flat trajectory but the finest of accuracy. The whitetail hunter doesn't have much use for either. Whitetail shooting is almost always offhand shooting, and given the most accurate rifle in the world, the average whitetail hunter would do well to keep his shots in a one-foot circle at 100 yards offhand. The whitetail hunter, then, has no particular use for super-duper accuracy. Shots at whitetail are very often taken when the game is partially obscured by brush, and the bullet has to drive through brush on a relatively straight line in order to kill the game. Under those conditions, an ultra high velocity bullet is actually a handicap because it is much more apt to be deflected than a heavier, slower moving bullet.

Some years ago I did some extensive experimenting by shooting various bullets through brush at a life-size, life-color deer target on a big sheet of wallboard. My findings were that the average amount of deflection upon striking the brush were directly in proportion to the velocity of the bullet, the weight of the bullet, and the profile of the bullet. The faster a bullet traveled, the more it was deflected. The lighter the bullet, the more it was deflected. The sharper the point, the more it was deflected. Bullets from the .220 Swift almost always blew up on the twigs and reached the target only in fragments. Spitzer-pointed

[112]

RIFLES AND CARTRIDGES FOR FOREST GAME

100-grain bullets fired from a .257, and similar 130-grain bullets fired from a .270 reached the target about once or twice in five shots. The 180-grain bullet from the .30/06, if it was spitzer-shaped, hit the deer about half the time, but if of round nose shape hit the target about two-thirds of the time. Even the big 300-grain bullet in the .375 Magnum showed considerable deflection. The best performer that I tried was the 200 grain round nose soft-point bullet at 2200 f.p.s. in the .35 Remington. It was my conclusion, however, that any time a man takes a shot at deer behind brush and misses the deer he has a ready-made alibi because even the comparatively slow-moving round-nosed .35 Remington bullet can be deflected enough by a twig to miss a deer ten or fifteen feet behind the twig, and about one-third of the .35 Remington bullets I fired at the deer target showed that they had turned sidewise or "keyholed" when they hit.

For brush and forest use, then, our bullets, whatever the caliber, should best travel at a moderate velocity, have considerable weight, and a round or even a flat nose, if such a bullet be obtainable. Spitzer shape, light weight, and ultra high velocity are all disadvantages. The best missile I found for driving through brush reliably on a straight line was the heavy, slow-moving, slow-spinning shotgun slug.

Because most of my hunting has been done in mountainous country which is relatively open and where shots tend to be long, most of my big-game rifles are bolt-action jobs. Most of them are for cartridges of high velocity and flat trajectory. Many of the gun writers hunt under similar conditions so they tend to write about bolt-action rifles and cartridges designed for them. This has resulted in many whitetail hunters going after deer with antelope rifles. The bolt-action is not a virtue in itself for big-game hunting but a necessity forced upon the hunter because the bolt-action is the only one which will stand the pressures of high intensity big-game cartridges designed for mountain and plains use.

Because the whitetail is often shot under very poor conditions

Griffin & Howe, Inc. 202 East 44th St., New York

WORK ORDER

WORK ORDER NO. _____

Date _____

Name _____

Address _____

Shipping or Delivery Instructions _____

NATURE OF WORK

Caliber _____ Type _____ Weight _____ lbs.

Parts or materials furnished by customer _____

ACTION

Type _____
Bolt (turned down or standard; plain or checkered) _____

STOCK

Grade and Color of wood _____
Type of grip _____
Length from front of trigger to center of butt plate _____
Drop of comb from 100 yard line of sight (open sights) _____
Drop at heel from 100 yard line of sight (open sights) _____
Cast off (not advised except for a very thick face) _____

BARREL

Type (light, standard or heavy; ribbed or plain) _____
Length (24 in. is standard) _____
Front sight base (G&H ramp is standard) _____
Barrel band (type and location, if desired) _____
Remarks _____

SLING SWIVELS

Type desired (Whelen or loop) _____
Location of forward swivel (through forearm or on barrel) _____

Pitch (slope of butt plate)_____	**SIGHTS**
Type of butt plate_____	Type of front sight (ivory or gold; large, small or medium)_____
Type of forearm (light, medium or heavy; standard or beaver tail)_____	Type of rear sight_____
	Type of telescope and mount (if desired)_____
Forearm tip (Buffalo horn or plain; knobbed or round)_____	**ENGRAVING**
Length of forearm from receiver (standard 10 in.)_____	Type of engraving desired_____
Type of checkering_____	_____
Remarks_____	_____

Ammunition to be used_____

Miscellaneous instructions_____
_____
_____
_____
_____
_____
_____

Accessories and equipment ordered_____
_____
_____
_____
_____

Delivery by_____ Time_____ hours

Shipped_____

for good aim—on the move, through the brush, in poor light—the whitetail hunter ideally should have a rifle with an action which can be operated easily from the shoulder so that a second shot can be driven in rapidly in case the first shot is not effective. A bolt-action is simply not that action because the average once-a-year deer hunter is not going to take the time to practice so that he can operate the bolt from the shoulder in rapid fire. What he needs is some other type of action—a lever-action, a slide-action, or even a semi-automatic.

The Winchester Model 94 carbine, if equipped with proper sights, is a pretty good deer rifle. Because of the better designed stock, the Winchester Model 64 Deer Rifle is still better, particularly if equipped with a barrel shorter than 24 inches. The Model 99 Savage rifles are excellent and so is the now obsolete Remington Model 141 slide-action. All of these rifles can be operated from the shoulder while the hunter is keeping his eye on the sights and on the target.

Of all the factory produced deer rifles that I have ever seen I believe that the best was the Savage Model 99-T, which was discontinued at the time the United States got into the second World War and which has never again been manufactured. It was a light rifle, weighing only about 7 pounds. Although accuracy of the hair-splitting variety is not necessary for a brush rifle, the Model 99-T in .250/3000 caliber that I had was as accurate as most heavy-barreled varmint rifles and it was routine to shoot groups with it, after I put a telescopic sight on it, that ran right around one inch per 100 yards. The Model 99-T had a good hand-filling forend which was easy to grasp and it enabled the man behind it to point it very speedily for running shooting. It had a fairly high-combed buttstock which was exactly right for iron sights. It was equipped with an open "U" rear sight with a white line and with a red bead front sight—the best combination of open iron sights that I have ever seen for woods shooting. I have always regretted that the little Model 99-T was discontinued since it was the best stocked rifle that Savage ever produced for saddle use and for woods hunting. Perhaps some day it will be put back into production.

The woods rifle should be as light as possible. Light weight and fast handling generally go together. Light weight usually doesn't go with the best accuracy but, as we have seen, shots in the deer woods are not long and hair-splitting accuracy is not necessary. Our once-a-year whitetail hunter is usually pretty soft, and the lighter the rifle he has the less it burdens him down, the more spring he has in his arms and legs at the end of the day, and the faster he can get into action. The nearer the deer hunter can come to getting a rifle which weighs complete with sights around 7 pounds, or better still 6½ pounds, the better off he is. The deer rifle should be so stocked that the man behind it can shoot it almost as quickly and as naturally as he does his favorite shotgun. That is one of the reasons why the men who do a lot of shooting with a pump shotgun are very well off with a slide-action Remington, as those rifles handle, feel, and operate about like the common American type of pump shotgun.

In spite of the fact that I have recommended lever-action rifles, the best rifle I, myself, ever had, I believe, for brush shooting of deer was a bolt-action. It was a very light custom made 7 mm. Mauser with a 21-inch barrel, and a Lyman 1-A cocking piece rear sight. The aperture was large and close to the eye. The stock was very straight—about like that of a fine quail gun. The forend was exactly right. I never had a rifle that I could get onto a target quicker with than I could with that one. There was never any hesitation about finding the target through the large aperture of that cocking piece sight, as it seemed I could almost see the whole world through it. All I had to do was to put the front sight on what I wanted to hit and press the trigger.

The first time I took that rifle on a hunt I made a "double" on buck mule deer in a thick patch of *cholla*. Working the bolt between shots from the shoulder I believe I killed those two deer in not much over a second and I rather doubt if I could have killed two quail with a pump-action shotgun any faster. On an-

THE BIG-GAME RIFLE

other occasion, I killed three running javelinas at about 65 yards, and my distinct impression (probably incorrect) was that the first javelina was still rolling when the third one fell. It gives you the idea, anyway. That little rifle was not a particularly accurate one and since I am an accuracy nut I was annoyed by this fact. I have always regretted that I sold it.

In spite of the fact that a considerable number of states outlaw the use of semi-automatic rifles, I am convinced that for most hunters the ideal action for short-range woods shooting at medium-sized game is the semi-automatic. The ideal semi-automatic, though, is not with us. The Remington Model 8 and Model 81, both now obsolete, were heavy and clumsy. They were hard to get on with and they did not point naturally. The ideal whitetail rifle would be one on the order of the M-1 carbine but shooting a more powerful cartridge. As this is written, there is considerable talk of producing a new United States military rifle to take the place of both the heavy M-1 rifle in .30/06 and the M-1 carbine for the little carbine cartridge. This new cartridge would be very much on the order of the .300 Savage giving the 150-grain bullet a muzzle velocity of about 2700 f.p.s. The rifle is supposed to weigh only about 7 pounds. When and if such a rifle is produced and when and if it can be available to the American deer hunter, it should be about what the doctor ordered, *but* with a little heavier bullet at a somewhat lower velocity.

SIGHTS FOR THE WOODS RIFLE

Probably more than half of all whitetail deer killed annually are killed with rifles equipped with open sights. The average man who knows little about rifles and shooting first becomes familiar with the open sight and because he is used to it he demands it. Most factory rifles are equipped with open sights because they are very cheap to manufacture, and factories have to put some

RIFLES AND CARTRIDGES FOR FOREST GAME

sort of sights on the weapons they sell so that the casual hunter can take a rifle from the rack in the sporting goods store and go out and shoot at something with it. To equip rifles with the more expensive type of peep sight would boost the retail price from $8 to $12 and make them more difficult to sell.

The open sight, particularly the kind usually preferred by people who know little about sights, is about the worst sight that anyone could ever use for forest game. Preferred open sights are of the buckhorn and semi-buckhorn variety. Both have big, useless ears sticking up which do nothing but blot out the game and the scenery. The very best in open sights will blot out half the game. The worst types of open sights blot out from ¾ to ⅞ of the game. Deer hunting is done under the stress of excitement. Shots at deer are more often than not taken in rather poor light. In any forest much light is cut out, and in the fall in northern latitudes, the light is none too good at best. Our hunter will sight in his rifle so he hits the point of aim, let us say, with a "fine" bead at 50 yards. Then when the big buck comes tearing across the opening, our excited hunter doesn't pull the front bead down fine into the notch and, consequently, he overshoots. Exactly the same tendency is present in poor light. Our hunter wants to see the bead. The farther down into the notch he pulls the bead the darker it becomes because more light is cut out. In order to see the bead he doesn't draw it down fine, and again he shoots over.

On many occasions I have tried shooting the little running deer in shooting galleries with the .22 rifles with the miserable open sights usually found on shooting galleries' .22's. When I take extra care I can knock over those running deer. Let me get a little careless, though, and fail to bring down the front bead into notch and right over the deer's back the bullet will go. Actually the open sight is obsolete even in its best form—the side, shallow U or V. In its worst form, the buckhorn or semi-buckhorn, it is not only obsolete but it is actually a handicap to the hunter which increases the deer's chances of survival by at least 50 percent.

THE BIG-GAME RIFLE

By far the best type of iron sight for the deer rifle is the peep. The old adage "Always hold low on a deer" does not apply to the peep. The peep with a large aperture and fairly close to the eye is an exceedingly fast sight. With it one does not have to bother to draw the front bead down into the notch. All one has to do is look *through* the peep, put the front bead on what one wants to hit, and press the trigger. It is that simple! The eye naturally centers the bead in the middle of the aperture and the man shooting a peep sight does not have to worry or even think about centering his front peep. His eye does it naturally and automatically. Most hunters are not aware of this optical principle and when they get their first peep sight they are worried because they can see so much through it. They think that if they can see through a sight without difficulty and it appears to be so easy to use, it cannot possibly be any good. My own first experience with peep sights came with the old Model 1903 Springfield which had a miserable little hole on the slide much too far from the eye. When I got my first good peep sight, a Lyman 48, I put in it the smallest target disc that I could find. When I tried to use it on game I had a shot late in the evening at a buck standing in the shadow of heavy timber. I could not even see the buck through that tiny hole and it finally walked away unscathed. I might have denounced all peep sights then but I did not. Instead I did some experimenting. I shot groups with the disc in place and then I shot groups without the disc. I found that I could shoot just about as small a group and I could shoot it far faster and with less strain by using the large aperture.

The best place to mount a peep sight is as close to the eye as it can be put. In the case of a rifle of relatively light recoil and with a stock long enough, an excellent place to mount the peep is on the tang. The Lyman 1-A tang peep is usually so mounted. Another good location is on the cocking piece of a bolt-action rifle. The closer the peep is to the eye the more one can see through, just as one can see more through a keyhole with his eye right on it than he can by standing back some distance from it. There is only one grave danger, however, in having a peep sight close and that is that under certain conditions the peep sight can be driven into the eye. This is particularly dangerous with a rifle using a tang peep if the recoil is fairly heavy and the stock is a bit too short. On an uphill shot there is a very real danger of injury. Some years ago a gun writer took a new wife up into the Alberta Rockies for a hunting trip. She took a shot at a goat sharply above her on a hillside and she was using a short-stocked Model 99 Savage in .300 caliber, which has fairly heavy recoil. When she fired, the peep sight was driven back into her eye. She was taken to a physician, after a long and painful pack trip, and the eye had to be removed.

Today the most widely used peep sights are those mounted on the receiver. Excellent ones are made for practically any type of rifle. They are more accurate than open sights, particularly when one has to shoot swiftly. They are also far easier to adjust than open sights. Actually so difficult to adjust are most open sights that anyone who really wants to sight his rifle will save money by getting a receiver sight put on immediately. Most receiver sights come from the factory with a little target disc included. It is my advice that anyone who has no target ambitions, but plans only to hunt big game, take the disc out and throw it as far as possible. Some receiver sights have little built-in turned-down discs. They also should be unscrewed and likewise thrown away because they have been known to get turned up in the way at the wrong time.

The deer rifle should be light and short-barreled. It should be stocked like a shotgun for quick pointing. It should also, I believe, be equipped with sling swivels for a light carrying sling. It is not once in seven blue moons that the whitetail hunter will use his gun sling for shooting in the conventional way, as a mountain hunter will, but when the whitetail hunter has to walk long distances the sling is a great aid in carrying. At best a rifle is a clumsy and awkward burden if it has to be carried over the shoulder the way a parading soldier carries his, or carried in the arms as one would carry an infant.

Cartridges for Light Forest Game

Several deer cartridges survive in low pressure smokeless loadings from the black-powder era and are still used to some extent on deer. The .38/40 W.C.F. and the .44/40 as used in the Winchester Model 1892 rifles and carbines killed many thousands of deer in their day. Both use bullets of good weight and large diameter. Both get through brush quite well. For ranges to around 50 yards they are satisfactory but the muzzle energy of a .38/40 is only 685 foot-pounds, as now loaded and that of the .44/40 is only 750 foot-pounds. Both cartridges are shy on power and in the hands of anyone but the coolest, most experienced, and most expert shot they allow too high a percentage of deer to get away wounded, to go off and die, or to be claimed by some other hunter.

The .38/55 with its 255-grain bullet at a muzzle velocity of 1310 f.p.s. and a muzzle energy of 985 foot-pounds is a more satisfactory cartridge but it is certainly no powerhouse, and since it is growing rapidly obsolete there is no particular reason for anyone to buy a .38/55 at this late date. Occasionally someone turns up with an old Model 1886 Winchester in .45/70, a cartridge which uses the 405-grain bullet at a muzzle velocity of 1310 f.p.s. with a muzzle energy of 1545 foot-pounds. That old charcoal burning cartridge is a very good deer cartridge up to about 125 yards, and, as a matter of fact, because of its big, heavy bullet of large diameter, it is a good forest cartridge for practically any game. However, the recoil is quite heavy and few hunters can do their best shooting with it. Furthermore, good old cartridge though it is, the .45/70 is about on its last legs. No rifle

RIFLES AND CARTRIDGES FOR FOREST GAME

has been manufactured for it for many years, and only a hobbyist would now be justified in purchasing a .45/70.

Under no circumstances can the .25/20, .32/20, or .22 Hornet cartridges be considered deer cartridges. A typical .25/20 load is an 86-grain bullet with a muzzle velocity of 1400 f.p.s. with 400 foot-pounds of muzzle energy and a typical .32/20 cartridge gives the 100-grain bullet a muzzle velocity of 1280 f.p.s. with a muzzle energy of 365 foot-pounds. Deer, of course, have been killed by the .22 Hornet and a man who gets a good shot at a standing deer so he can hit it in the head or break the neck or even shoot it right through the heart will get himself a deer. The Hornet bullet is much too light, though, and gives too little penetration ever to be used on deer except in the direst emergency.

For many years it has been said that the two lightest cartridges that should be used on whitetail in the woods are the .25 Remington rimless and the .25/35 Winchester. In ballistics the two cartridges are practically identical as both use the 117-grain bullet driven at 2300 f.p.s. in the .25 Remington and at 2280 in the .25/35. Muzzle energy runs around 1375 foot-pounds in the case of the .25 Remington and 1350 in the case of the .25/35. Many states have written these ballistics into law by making it illegal to hunt deer with a cartridge giving less than 1,000 foot-pounds of energy at 100 yards.

I wouldn't call either of those cartridges particularly good deer cartridges. They will do, but neither gives as high percentage of instant kills as the heavier cartridge of the .30/30 class. Neither bullet gets through brush particularly well. Actually both cartridges are obsolescent. They can still be used, of course, but they are by no means ideal. In spite of all this I would not hesitate myself to hunt deer with either of them but if I did so I would not take rear-end shots. I would hesitate to shoot at running deer, and even under the best circumstances I would expect now and then to have to chase a deer a considerable distance.

THE BIG-GAME RIFLE

The standard deer cartridge in the United States is the .30/30. More deer are probably still killed with .30/30 rifles than with any others. I would consider the .30/30 a very poor cartridge for mountain and plains use, but in the hands of a good shot it is still an excellent whitetail and black bear cartridge for wooded country. Standard ballistics of the .30/30 are taken with the 170-grain bullet at a velocity of 2200 for a muzzle energy of 1830 foot-pounds. At 100 yards the energy is 1405 foot-pounds, and at 200 yards, 1065. The .30/30, then, delivers at 200 yards about the same energy as the .25/35 or .25 Remington delivers at 100 yards.

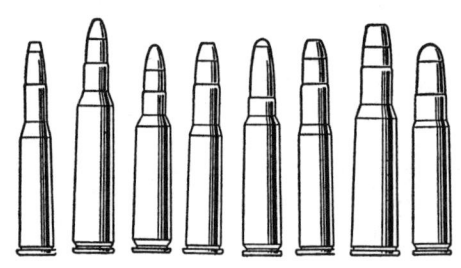

American loaded cartridge suitable for deer. Left to right: .25/35, .257, .250/3000, .30/30, .300 Savage, .32 Special, .348, .35 Remington.

A well placed shot with a .30/30 bullet of suitable weight and construction will almost always kill a deer within a few jumps to at least 150 yards. The best bullet for the .30/30 is the old fashioned soft-point with considerable soft lead exposed at the tip. In recent years luck with the .30/30 has not been so good with the new bullets like the Remington Core-Lokt and the Winchester Western-Silvertip for the simple reason that the bullets do not expand quickly enough to give one-shot kills on light game. Deer and black bear are both relatively small, fragile, thin-shelled animals. Their flesh is soft. The problem in bullet construction for such light game is not depth of penetration but expansion. There is no heavy hide to penetrate, no big massive bones to break, no heavily muscled meat to drive through in order to get into the vital area. Cartridges of the .30/30 class do not have the velocity to expand heavily constructed bullets. What is needed is a bullet with a soft lead core, a thin jacket and either a large, soft nose of lead, or a deep hollow point. With the old-fashioned bullets with their large exposure of soft lead at the nose, a very high proportion of the whitetail shot did not move out of their tracks because the bullets opened up rapidly. If they did move they didn't go far with a lung shot. In the last few years, though, with the adoption of the controlled expanding bullets, many a whitetail properly hit has run a quarter of a mile or more. A decade ago, or more, when I was hunting antelope in northern Arizona a fellow hunter brought me the carcass of an antelope he had killed with the .30/30 with a 170-grain Remington Coke-Lokt bullet. He had shot the antelope as it ran away. The bullet had entered between the hams and, believe it or not, had come out of the forehead. Of course he killed his antelope. Let us suppose he had hit that antelope sidewise. He probably would never have known that he hit it at all.

Other cartridges of the .30/30 class with almost identical ballistics are the Winchester .32 Special with the 165-grain bullet at 2260 with a muzzle energy of 1870 foot-pounds, the .30 Remington rimless with the 170-grain bullet at 2200 foot-pounds, and the .32 Remington rimless with the 170-grain bullet at a muzzle velocity of 2200. I have heard hunters argue that the .32 Special killed better than the .30/30. As the figures show, such an argument is simply ridiculous. However, there are enough hunters who believe that so that it still pays Winchester to make the Model 64 Deer Rifle in .32 Special.

In spite of the fact that most shots at whitetail in wooded country are taken within 100 yards, it would still be foolish to sight in a deer rifle of the .30/30 class to put the bullet at point of aim at 100 yards. Instead, I believe, the iron sighted rifle of the .30/30 class should be sighted in to put the bullet 2 inches high at 100 yards. Then the bullet is on the nose at 150 yards, and about 5 inches low at 200. In that way the occasional fairly long shot across a ravine is much easier to make. Let us suppose that our deer was 200 yards away. Our hunter held right in the middle of the deer's chest. The bullet would drop 5 inches and he would be apt to get his deer, although the shot, of course, would be on the low side. Suppose, on the other hand, that he had sighted his rifle in for 100 yards and forgot to hold high. Then at 200 yards the bullet would drop 9 inches and our hunter would miss the deer. No man can shoot offhand well enough to tell whether or not his rifle is shooting 2 inches high at 100 yards. When not one deer hunter in a thousand is enough of an offhand shot to keep all of his shots in a 12-inch circle at 100 yards, it is useless to worry about a 2-inch trajectory rise at that distance.

A very good cartridge, almost an ideal woods cartridge for deer, is the .35 Remington. It uses the 200-grain bullet at a muzzle velocity of 2180 f.p.s. with a muzzle energy of 2110 foot-pounds. Trajectory is about like that of the .30/30 and the .35 Remington should likewise be sighted in to put the bullet 2 inches high at 100 yards. Because of the somewhat heavier bullet at somewhat larger diameter the .35 Remington has a reputation for giving a higher percentage of one-shot kills than the rifles of the .30/30 class. As this is written, the Remington Model 81 automatic and the Remington Model 141 slide-action rifles for the .35 Remington have been made obsolete. However, the cartridge is too good a deer cartridge to let die and Remington has chambered the new Model 760 for it. Marlin makes a lever-action deer rifle in .35 Remington caliber. The Winchester Model 70 has been made in .35 but the combination was never popular because the boys who wanted .35 Remingtons did not want bolt-action rifles and those who wanted bolt-action rifles did not want them for the .35 Remington. The Model 30 Remington Express bolt-action for the .35 was also manufactured at one time. Prior to World War II various custom gunsmiths, notably Griffin & Howe of New York, made very fine light bolt-action woods rifles on genuine Waffenfabrik short Mauser actions in .35 Remington.

RIFLES AND CARTRIDGES FOR FOREST GAME

Rifles and Cartridges for the Heavier Woods Game

Moose are, more often than not, dwellers in heavy woods and they are much larger and much harder to kill than the whitetail deer. Whereas, as we have seen, a whitetail will dress out at 150 pounds or less, a moose will dress out from 1,000–1,200 pounds, and in some cases even 1,400 pounds. Since moose have larger bones, heavier muscles, and more meat to shoot through, they should be hunted with a much more powerful rifle than one which is adequate for deer. I have shot a half dozen or so moose myself and I number among my friends northern guides and trappers who have lived on moose for thirty and forty years. Many of them use .30/30 rifles, but it is seldom that they kill a moose in its tracks. Routine, when a trapper uses a .30/30 on a moose, is for him to take one good, carefully aimed shot high through the lungs. The moose goes off. The trapper sits down, smokes a cigarette, or even brews himself a pot of tea. He is an expert tracker and after he has waited for half an hour or so he picks up the moose's track and follows it. Then he finds the moose lying down. Apparently moose are quite sensitive to pain and when wounded they hurt all over. If they are not badly frightened by quick pursuit, they ordinarily lie down fairly quickly. Our trapper then sneaks up on the moose as it lies there, plants a bullet in the head and has himself a moose. Unless one of the big deer is struck in the spine or in the head, or unless the neck is broken it is seldom that a moose is killed with one shot with any cartridge. Nevertheless the sportsman hunter who is looking for a trophy wants a much more powerful rifle than the .30/30 in spite of the fact that the .30/30 is North America's No. 1 moose killer. Our sportsman, for example, will often take a hindend shot at a moose, something which the native Indian would never do if he could get out of it.

My own first moose was killed in heavy fir and spruce timber beside a little creek known as Compton Creek high in the Alberta Rockies north of Jasper Park and not far from the British Columbia border. Since it was killed under rather typical moose-hunting circumstances, I shall describe the hunt. I had an Indian guide named Isaac, and for several days we had been attempting to stalk moose. We would climb 1,000 or 1,500 feet upon the side of the mountain and then with powerful binoculars we would try to find bull moose below us along the creek in the heavy timber. We would locate the moose by some conspicuous landmark such as a dead tree and then attempt to stalk quietly upwind or crosswind to find the moose and shoot him before he was aware of our presence. The moose is a difficult animal to stalk. He has a marvelous nose and wonderful ears and he hasn't the slightest bit of curiosity. He will move off like a great black shadow at the first whiff of tainted air or the sound of a breaking twig. I had never killed a moose and was raring to shoot a moose because most people think of the moose as the typical Canadian game animal. For a week we hunted with no luck whatsoever. Every time we arrived at the place were the moose was supposed to await us he would be gone. Finally one day I grew weary of this game of hide-and-seek. I spent the morning in camp resting and doing some washing and then I told Isaac that instead of climbing mountains and spying out moose I was going to try to still-hunt them, just as I had still-hunted whitetail deer. I put on a pair of hunting shoes with leather uppers and rubber bottoms. The wind was blowing gently toward the head of the creek so as quietly as I could possibly go I hunted downstream taking pains to avoid brushing my clothes on dry branches and being careful not to break any twigs. There were a lot of moose along that creek. I could see their big droppings, big deer-like tracks, places where the bulls had horned the brush to clear the velvet from their massive antlers. I had been hunting about an hour when right on the other side of some stunted Alpine fir I saw a big bull rise out of his bed and take off on legs that looked ten feet long. I was carrying a .270 Model 70 Winchester rifle with a 2½-x scope and I was using the 130-grain Silvertip bullet. There was a lot of brush and limbs between me and the moose, but I got off a good shot at the shoulder. The moose kept on going, but there was a tremendous rain of twigs and brush cut off by the bullet. The second shot, fortunately, was in the clear between two big trees as the moose was quartering away from me. I worked the bolt rapidly from the shoulder and I put the crosshairs against the curve in the paunch in the hope that the bullet would drive up into the lung cavity. I pressed the trigger with the crosshairs looking just right and the moose probably no more than 40 or 50 yards away from me at the most. Nothing happened. The moose disappeared before I could work the bolt again.

I got a belated attack of moose fever and stood there trembling, wondering how in the world I could miss an animal bigger than a horse at that distance. The more I thought about it, though, the more convinced I was that I couldn't possibly have missed him. I took up his track and after following it about 50 yards I found evidence that he had fallen to his knees because the imprints of both knees were there in the soft, mucky soil. I tracked him a few yards farther to a little opening filled with Arctic willow and suddenly that moose rose up before me looking, to my startled eyes, as tall as a giraffe. He took off on a tremendous trot, but this time I had a beautiful shot and squeezed it off with the crosshairs swinging along just behind his shoulder. The moose took off, again showing absolutely no signs of being hit. I had yet to see a single drop of blood. Once more I took up the track and this time I followed him perhaps 150 or 200 yards, and there this great, massive creature, the largest deer living or extinct, lay as dead as a mackerel. The first shot had been exactly where I had called it. It had driven through the paunch and had stopped in the lobe of the right lung. He had lain down because he was a very sick moose, indeed, and if I had followed the practice of the Indian and the trapper of sitting down and smoking a cigarette or brewing myself a pot of tea, I am sure that the moose would have been dead when I tracked it down the first time. The second hit was also where I had called it and as the moose ran off he was drowning in his own blood.

I killed my first moose with a .270 using the 130-grain bullet, but the .270 is a long way from being the ideal moose cartridge. There was no sign whatsoever of that first shot. Not even a bullet fragment had reached the moose and apparently the bullet had entirely disintegrated on the limbs through which it was fired.

When I killed that moose I was a hunter of considerable experience and one with some confidence in his ability to shoot. A greener hunter might never have attempted to track the moose, convinced that he had missed because the moose gave no sign of being hit.

Since that time I have shot several moose with the .270, but it is only a so-so moose rifle. It is made with no other type of action than the bolt and is thus handicapped for forest use. It uses relatively light bullets at high velocity, and they do not get through twigs, leaves, and brush very well. As still another consideration, the diameter of the .270 bullet is so small that it will almost never leave a blood trail from the entrance hole. If a man must choose the .270 for moose he is better off with the 150-grain factory load like the Remington soft-point Core-Lokt and still better off with the special custom made bullets like the 160-grain Barnes or M.G.S. bullets. With the .30/06 the best bet for moose is the 220-grain bullet at about 2400 f.p.s. velocity, not because it is any better killer on moose than the 180-grain bullet but because, with its lower velocity and greater weight, it gets through more brush.

The finest woods cartridge for heavy game that we have, and also a very excellent one-shot killer on deer, is the .348 Winchester cartridge made for the fine Model 71 Winchester rifle. Actually, if a man does not mind the recoil, the light, excellently stocked Model 71 with its fast operating lever-action is a spectacularly successful choice for any type of woods hunting from deer on up to moose and grizzlies. The best known bullet for the

RIFLES AND CARTRIDGES FOR FOREST GAME

.348 is the 200-grain bullet at a muzzle velocity of 2530 f.p.s. and with a muzzle energy of 2840 foot-pounds. This is an excellent deer cartridge which will lay a deer low with practically any solid hit which gets inside the body cavity. The .348 is also loaded with the 150-grain bullet at a muzzle velocity of 2890 and a muzzle energy of 2780 foot-pounds. Within 150 yards, there is no more sudden deer killer, and this load will give as high a percentage of one-shot kills as will the 150-grain bullet in the .30/06 and the 130-grain bullet in the .270.

For moose and grizzly in heavy woods alone, though, for the .348 I would prefer the 250-grain Silvertip bullet with a muzzle velocity of 2380 with 2980 foot-pounds of muzzle energy. That cartridge is a powerhouse. Because of its moderate velocity it gets through brush very well. The great weight and the rigid construction of the bullet enable it to drive on through with a broadside shot on a moose or an elk. I have never killed a grizzly with that bullet, but those who have claim that even on the big bear it gives a high percentage of one-shot kills. For the man who hunts in forest and who wants to hunt all game from deer on up, I can think of no better bet than the .348. Furthermore, the Model 71 Winchester rifle is one of the finest stocked rifles ever turned out by any factory anywhere. It handles like a flash and points like the finest shotgun.

A couple of other good cartridges for heavy forest game in North America are the now obsolete .35 Winchester and the .405 Winchester. The .35 Winchester is no longer loaded, but if a man has a .35 Winchester rifle it is not difficult to neck down .405 Winchester cases to .35 and load them. As formerly loaded, the .35 W.C.F. used the 250-grain bullet at a muzzle velocity of 2200 f.p.s. The .405 Winchester cartridge is still manufactured, although the Model 95 Winchester rifle for it was discontinued back in the middle 30's. The present load gives the 300-grain bullet a muzzle velocity of 2220 f.p.s. with 3285 foot-pounds of muzzle energy. In the Model 95, particularly with the rifle buttplate often seen, the .405 kicked like the dickens. The old Model

THE BIG-GAME RIFLE

95 was rather a clumsy rifle and an awkward one to carry because the box magazine protruded right where one would grasp it for balance. However, the .405, because of its big heavy bullet, was an excellent killer to use even on dangerous game such as lion and tiger and Alaska brown bear.

Very often the man hunting in Canada for moose will want to use the same bolt-action rifle that he would use for mountain game. If he does he can use the 220-grain bullet in the .30/06, the 150-grain bullet in the .270, the 220-grain bullet in the .30/40 Krag or the 175-grain bullet in the 7 mm.

In some areas elk are found in heavy timber, although the elk, more than the moose, tends to be an animal of semi-open mountain and canyon country. An elk is not as large as a moose but it is a big animal weighing possibly on occasion and in the case of an exceedingly large and fat bull 1,000 pounds on the hoof. Any big animal is hard to kill and this applies to the elk. In the Jackson Hole country of Wyoming and in Arizona where I have hunted elk, shots tend to be fairly long—from 150 to 350 yards, let us say—and any good mountain rifle like the 7 mm., .270, or .30/06 is also a good elk rifle. In the famous Selway and Lochsa country of central Idaho, elk are found in brush and timber, but in many instances the country is so noisy that it is exceedingly difficult to get close to elk, and then shots have to be made at long range across great canyons. For a stalker who can get close in heavy timber a good moose rifle is also a good elk rifle, but the man who takes the long shots across the canyons needs a fairly powerful flat-shooting rifle—nothing less than the standard 7 mm. The .270 with the 130-grain bullet is a fine little cartridge for broadside shots such as one usually gets in rough canyon country. One of the best elk hunters I know, John George of Lewiston, Idaho, has used a .270 on elk for years. I have killed relatively few elk, but for most of them I used the .270. For thick, heavy country, however, I would prefer a heavier bullet.

Just as the man who hunts moose and grizzly in heavy timber may want to do it with his mountain rifle, the man who hunts deer in brush and timber may want to do so with an all-around rifle which he can use in a pinch on varmints as well as on big game. The .250/3000 Savage is a good combination for whitetail deer and varmints in spite of the fact that the 100-grain bullet is rather easily deflected by brush. The same thing is true of the bolt-action .257.

Besides the .348 Winchester, another all-around lever-action rifle which can be used in a pinch on any North American big game is the .300 Savage—one of the most popular of all American calibers. With the 150-grain bullet at 2610, the .300 Savage is a pretty good mountain or plains rifle although not in the class, let us say, with the .270 or .30/06. With the 180-grain bullet at 2380, the .300 Savage cartridge becomes a fine one for forest use. With proper bullets that give proper expansion, it is usually a one-shot killer on deer and the relatively heavy bullet at fairly low speed gets through brush well. In the hands of a good shot, the .300 Savage with the 180-grain bullet will do for moose and it is much superior in killing power to the cartridges of the .30/30 class.

This chapter has been written with the needs of the North American hunter largely in mind. What has been said, however, about the small whitetail deer of North America will apply equally well to the little Rae deer of the Central European forests, and to the many deer of Asia.

The great .375 Magnum cartridge, although really a cartridge for heavy and dangerous game, which will be discussed more fully in another chapter, can be used on both moose and elk in heavy timber. In fact, some experienced hunters advise its use. For my part, I have been somewhat skeptical as to its desirability because not many hunters exist who can handle the .375 because of its very considerable weight and heavy recoil. However, if a man likes the .375 and wants to hunt moose and elk with it in the timber he is certainly free to make the choice, and he will get a higher percentage of one-shot kills and quick kills than he will with a lighter cartridge. The same thing applies to the heavy

Ballistics Of U. S. Loaded Cartridges Suitable for Forest Game

CARTRIDGE	BULLET Wgt. Grs.	BULLET Type	VELOCITY Muzzle	VELOCITY 100 Yds.	VELOCITY 200 Yds.	VELOCITY 300 Yds.	ENERGY Muzzle	ENERGY 100 Yds.	ENERGY 200 Yds.	ENERGY 300 Yds.	MID-RANGE TRAJECTORY 100 Yds.	MID-RANGE TRAJECTORY 200 Yds.	MID-RANGE TRAJECTORY 300 Yds.
25 Remington	117	Soft Point	2,300	2,020	1,760	1,530	1,375	1,060	805	610	0.9	4.5	11.0
25–35 Winchester	117	Full Patch	2,280	1,970	1,690	1,440	1,350	1,010	740	540	1.0	4.5	12.0
25–35 Winchester	117	Soft Point	2,280	1,970	1,690	1,440	1,350	1,010	740	540	1.0	4.5	12.0
30–30 Winchester	150	Op. Pt. Exp.	2,380	2,060	1,770	1,510	1,890	1,415	1,045	760	0.9	4.0	11.0
30 Remington	170	Soft Point	2,220	1,930	1,680	1,460	1,830	1,405	1,065	805	1.0	4.5	12.0
30–30 Winchester	170	Soft Point	2,220	1,930	1,680	1,460	1,830	1,405	1,065	805	1.0	4.5	12.0
303 Savage	190	Soft Point	1,960	1,740	1,530	1,350	1,620	1,280	990	770	1.3	6.0	14.5
303 British	215	Soft Point	2,160	1,940	1,740	1,550	2,230	1,795	1,445	1,145	1.0	4.5	11.5
32 Winchester Special	170	Soft Point	2,260	1,960	1,690	1,450	1,930	1,450	1,080	795	1.0	4.5	12.0
32 Winchester Special	165	Op. Pt. Exp.	2,260	1,950	1,670	1,430	1,870	1,395	1,020	750	1.0	4.5	12.0
32 Winchester Self-Loading	165	Soft Point	1,390	1,190	1,060	980	710	520	410	350	2.6	12.5	31.0
32 Remington	170	Soft Point	2,200	1,910	1,640	1,400	1,830	1,380	1,015	740	1.0	5.0	13.0
33 Winchester	200	Soft Point	2,180	1,870	1,600	1,360	2,110	1,555	1,135	820	1.1	5.0	13.5
8 × 56 m/m Mannlicher-Schoenauer	200	Soft Point	2,150	1,940	1,750	1,570	2,055	1,670	1,360	1,095	1.1	4.5	11.5
8 × 57 m/m Mauser	170	Soft Point	2,530	2,210	...	...	2,415	1,845	...	...	0.8	3.5	9.0
348 Winchester	150	Soft Point	2,880	2,380	1,930	1,550	2,765	1,890	1,240	800	0.6	3.0	8.5
348 Winchester	200	Soft Point	2,520	2,160	1,840	1,560	2,820	2,075	1,505	1,080	0.8	4.0	10.0
35 Winchester Self-Loading	180	Soft Point	1,390	1,170	1,040	960	775	545	430	370	2.5	13.0	31.0
35 Remington	200	Soft Point	2,180	1,870	1,590	1,360	2,110	1,555	1,125	820	1.0	5.0	13.0
35 Remington	200	Op. Pt. Exp.	2,180	1,870	1,590	1,360	2,110	1,555	1,125	820	1.0	5.0	13.0
351 Winchester Self-Loading	180	Metal Case	1,850	1,560	1,310	1,140	1,370	975	685	520	1.5	7.5	19.0
351 Winchester Self-Loading	180	Soft Point	1,850	1,560	1,310	1,140	1,370	975	685	520	1.5	7.5	19.0
375 H. & H. Magnum	270	Soft Point	2,720	2,460	2,220	1,990	4,440	3,630	2,960	2,375	0.7	3.0	7.0
375 H. & H. Magnum	300	Full Patch	2,580	2,300	2,040	1,790	4,435	3,525	2,770	2,135	0.7	3.5	8.5
38–40 Winchester	180	Soft Point	1,310	1,090	960	870	685	475	370	305	3.2	15.5	37.5
38–55 Winchester	255	Soft Point	1,320	1,150	1,050	980	985	750	625	545	3.0	13.5	32.5
401 Winchester Self-Loading	200	Soft Point	2,140	1,750	1,420	1,170	2,035	1,360	895	610	1.1	5.5	16.5
405 Winchester	300	Soft Point	2,220	1,940	1,690	1,460	3,285	2,510	1,905	1,420	1.0	4.5	12.0
44–40 Winchester	200	Soft Point	1,300	1,070	940	860	750	510	390	330	3.3	17.5	38.0
45–70 Government	405	Soft Point	1,310	1,160	1,060	990	1,545	1,210	1,010	880	2.8	14.0	32.5

RIFLES AND CARTRIDGES FOR FOREST GAME

wildcat cartridges like the .333 O.K.H. which uses a 250-grain bullet at about 2700 or the .35 Whelen which uses a 250-grain bullet at about 2750.

For any forest game, then, the cartridge should drive a round-nosed, relatively heavy bullet at moderate velocity so that it can penetrate brush well. For the lighter types of forest game like the whitetail deer and black bear the bullets should be easily expanded at this moderate velocity because animals of that sort are light and thin-shelled and do not offer much bullet resistance. For heavier game, of course, one needs a much more powerful cartridge. In any case, the rifle should be relatively short-barreled, light, handy, and fast operating.

The best sight for forest use is the aperture or peep, and in recent years telescopic sights for deer hunting are becoming much more popular. Indeed, the low mounted wide angle hunting scope with a conspicuous reticule like the flat, wide, flat-topped post is a most excellent sight for forest use. In the chapter on telescopic sights and mounts more material on the selection of a scope for woods hunting is presented.

CHAPTER VIII

Rifles and Cartridges for Mountain Game

IN EUROPE there are two schools of thought on what rifles and cartridges should be like for mountain game. Best known among the mountain hunters on the Continent itself are the Austrian and Swiss chamois hunters and, from all I can read, one of their most favored combinations is the little Model 1903 Mannlicher-Schoenauer carbine chambered for the 6.5 x 54 Mannlicher-Schoenauer cartridge and weighing with iron sights only around 6½ pounds. Both the rifle and the cartridge are interesting examples of a combination which evolved because of a certain set of circumstances. Swiss and Austrian mountain hunters carry their rifles themselves. They hunt small, thin-shelled animals in very rough, steep country. They often have to do what amounts to real Alpine work to get shots at chamois. They have to sling their rifles across their backs by the sling strap and then climb up a cliff or very steep hillside using both hands. Consequently, the rifle they have chosen is a light one with a short barrel. Excess weight in the mountains greatly handicaps a hunter, particularly the one who is middle-aged and soft from too much sitting at a desk. A long-barreled rifle is downright dangerous to carry if the hunter has to do any real rock work. On many occasions I found myself, when hunting desert sheep in the rough and rocky mountains of northern Sonora, in positions where if I had carried a long-barreled rifle I might have been thrown off a cliff. Our little Mannlicher-Schoenauer carbine is light, then, and short of barrel. It takes a cartridge of moderate power because the chamois and roe deer which were hunted in the Swiss Alps, in the Tyrol, and in the Bavarian Alps are little animals and easy to kill. Although the Mannlicher-Schoenauer 6.5 x 54 cartridge is loaded with bullets of various weights, a typical loading is the 160-grain bullet at a muzzle velocity of around 2200 f.p.s. and a trajectory about like the American .30/30. Undoubtedly this little carbine was satisfactory or else it would not have been so popular. Most of the time such a rifle would be entirely adequate for the work because short and mid-range shots are far more common in mountain hunting than many people believe. Nevertheless, under most North American conditions the little Mannlicher-Schoenauer would not be so good. The cartridge does not have enough shock power for long-range shots or poorly placed shots. Nor is it a very accurate cartridge, particularly when fired in that little carbine. Its genuine virtues are that the Mannlicher is light, short, and handy, and the cartridge has a mild recoil.

British sportsmen did much hunting in the high mountains of Asia. Trips to the Indian frontier, all during the time of the British occupation of India, were taken for sheep and goats by hundreds of British officers and civil servants. They habitually used much heavier and much more powerful rifles. Unlike the Swiss, Austrian, and German chamois hunters, the British did not carry their own weapons. Instead, they transported themselves over those incredibly rough, high, and rugged Asian mountains and let their shakaris carry their rifles. They did not touch them until it was time to shoot. Under those circumstances the weight of the rifle and the length of the barrel made little difference, and it is indeed true that the long-barreled, fairly heavy rifle will settle down quicker and is easier to hold comparatively steady when the man who is shooting it is winded. The British used much more powerful cartridges because their shots probably averaged a good deal longer than did shots at chamois in the

THE BIG-GAME RIFLE

Alps, and the animals they shot at were larger. Chamois and roe deer are both small animals, smaller than the smallest American whitetail deer, but some of the Asiatic sheep and goats are fairly large and rugged animals and the goats, particularly, seem to take a good deal of killing. British hunters, therefore, used more powerful cartridges. A favorite for British officers was the remodeled .303 British Lee Enfield because, for the serviceman, both rifles and ammunition were cheap. Other Britishers used, for the mountains, such cartridges as the .280 Ross and some even recommend cartridges like the .375 H. & H. Magnum and the .300 Magnum in the belted form for Mauser magazine rifles and in the rimmer or flanged, as the British call it, for falling-block single-shot rifles and doubles.

In his book "Notes On Sporting Rifles" Major Gerald Burrard says that he prefers, for mountain hunting, a rifle weighing over 9 pounds, and of all the available weapons he prefers a double-barreled hammerless ejector. The great advantage of the double, he says, is that the hunter can get off his second shot with no movement to work the bolt and no noise of reloading and hence does not frighten the game.

If the hunter considers the hammerless double-barrel too expensive, Burrard recommends a double with hammers and if that is unavailable he prefers a single-shot on a falling block action. He writes:

> "Personally I detest magazine sporting rifles. They make a vile noise in reloading, never balance as well as a double or falling block, and add extra length to the weapon. . . . Magazines are also complicated in mechanism and there is the ever present liability of a jam."

I must confess that I cannot follow the Major·all the way. I cannot imagine a more unsuitable rifle for mountain hunting than a double. Because of the extra barrel, a double is heavy for its caliber. A double is difficult to put good sights on. It is very rare indeed that the two barrels will shoot together at a long range. The Major may have a point when he lists as an advantage the fact that one can get off a second shot with a double without movement. The advantage is very slight and ordinarily a game animal realizes that something is amiss when a bullet cracks over his back, smacks into the rocks beyond, and he hears the bellow of a high-powered cartridge going off. It is true, as the Major says, that sometimes an animal will locate the hunter by the sound and movement of his reloading, but most of the time he will already have done so.

The more I read of British sporting literature, the more convinced I am that accuracy standards among British sportsmen is not particularly high. If they were they would not be satisfied to use double-barrel rifles for mountain shooting with their doubtful ability to group both barrels together. Nor would they be satisfied with miserable open sights which are adjusted by the rifle maker and which are practically impossible for the hunter to do anything about.

Like the Austrian, the American who hunts in the mountains usually carries his own rifle. In much mountain hunting there is no particular reason to do so except that it is an old American custom. Since he has no caddie to lug his musket around, he needs a lighter rifle than the Britisher who has a gun bearer. Like the Britisher, though, the American often hunts in mountain country where he is apt to encounter game which requires a fair amount of killing power. A cartridge like the 6.5 mm. Mannlicher-Schoenauer or any other cartridge with ballistics of the .30/30 class is a very poor cartridge for mountain use and anyone trying to hunt in the mountains with such a cartridge is greatly handicapping himself. It is true that in certain areas shots at mountain game are often surprisingly short. As this is written, I have shot eighteen rams of all North American species—desert, bighorn, Stone, and Dall. The majority of them have been shot at under 200 yards within .30/30 or 6.5 Mannlicher-Schoenauer range. I stalked the last desert bighorn I killed to within 35 yards and the last Dall sheep I shot, which incidentally was one of the

THE BIG-GAME RIFLE

finest Dall rams ever taken, to within 65 yards, and he went down 85 yards from the muzzle of the rifle. However, I once saved my bacon on a sheep hunt by killing two fine rams, because I could get no closer, at about 350 and 400 yards. Usually the sheep hunter will get a shot at moderate range but he should always be prepared to reach out and tag one at long range if conditions demand.

In some areas the topography and vegetation make long shots the rule rather than the exception and make running shots more common than standing shots. In the high, rugged mountains of the Southwest, the little Arizona whitetail deer is more often than not shot across wide canyons and on the run. The reason it is seldom that one gets a good shot at a buck on his side of the canyon is that the rocks and the brush make going so noisy that the deer can hear the hunter and slip off in front of him. A favorite way to hunt those beautiful little deer is for one hunter to go up one side of a canyon and a companion to go up the other. Then each hunter shoots at animals the other hunter moves. I have no notion of how many whitetail deer I have shot under those circumstances, but it is quite a few because I grew up in the Southwest and hunted the deer for years in Arizona and Sonora. Because of the country, the deer have to be jumped rather than stalked and shots at them average much farther than the shots I have had at sheep. Whereas my average shot at sheep has averaged about 175 yards, shots at the little whitetails have averaged, I believe, close to 250 yards. The same type of shooting is also had in many areas at the fine Western mule deer. In some sections elk are found in comparatively level country where the hunter can travel quietly, but in others, most shots are taken across big, deep canyons at ranges which to an Eastern hunter seem absolutely fantastic. The Rocky Mountain goat is hunted under conditions similar to those under which sheep are hunted. Sometimes the hunter can get right on top of his goat, but again he may have to knock him off at 300 yards or more. When I was hunting in the Selkirks for goats in 1947 I killed a goat at less

RIFLES AND CARTRIDGES FOR MOUNTAIN GAME

than 300 yards, but my companion had to reach out and tag his at what I believed was over 500. This same companion, Ken Niles, the radio announcer, was hot as a pistol on that trip and shot a couple of nice buck mule deer across canyons at not far from 500 yards.

The mountain rifle should be fairly light and it should be fairly short of barrel. The best type of action is the bolt because only the bolt-action, with very few exceptions, has the strength and rigidity to hold the high intensity cartridges suitable for mountain hunting. Because long shots do pop up now and then the mountain rifle should use a cartridge with high velocity, flat trajectory, and great accuracy.

My favorite factory made mountain rifle is the Model 70 Winchester in such excellent calibers as .30/06 and .270. The Model 70 has an excellent action and is available for suitable cartridges. There is just one thing wrong with it. For most people it is too heavy by the time a scope is fitted, as with scope and mount it will weigh 10–10½ pounds. If a man is young enough, strong enough, and tough enough to lug a Model 70 weighing 10½ pounds with scope, sling, and loaded magazine over the hills, he should be fixed up. For my part, as I grow old and lazy, I like a lighter rifle. Most people will not find a 9½ pound rifle too burdensome, but it is better if it weighs less, just as long as it is accurate and flat-shooting. Anyone who has ever done real mountain hunting knows a couple of pounds difference in the weight of a rifle become very important at the end of the day. The mountain rifle should be scope-equipped and, under most conditions, the scope should be mounted with a low, strong bridge mount and there need be no other sight on the rifle. The ideal mountain rifle, then, will weigh complete with scope and sling from 8–9½ pounds, with one weighing less than 9 pounds to be preferred. It should have a barrel no longer than 22 inches. It should be equipped with a scope of about 4-x like the Stith 4-x Bear Cub, Lyman Challenger, or the Weaver K-4. The rifle should fire a cartridge with a bullet weighing at least 125 grains at a velocity of at least 2900 foot-seconds. In spite of its light weight, the mountain rifle should be capable of grouping into 1½ minute of angle or into 3 inches at 200 yards, 4½ inches at 300 yards. It isn't often that accuracy that precise is needed but occasionally it will save a hunter's bacon. I remember once when gilt-edged accuracy got me a very fine buck. I had to break his neck at about 225 yards or not get him at all, since he had seen me and was standing behind a tree with only his head, and part of his neck, exposed. If my rifle had not been capable of grouping into 3 or 4 inches at that distance under hunting conditions I would not have brought home the buck.

As this is written, Winchester is toying with the idea of bringing out a lightweight Model 70 which in .270 and .30/06 will weigh about 7 pounds with open iron sights and about 8 pounds with a scope. With such rifles available, the problem of a light, accurate mountain rifle can be solved without going to a custom gun maker. The Remington Model 721 in .30/06 or .270 weighs ordinarily around 7¼ pounds. With the 24-inch barrel cut to 22 and a scope mounted, the Model 721 will come in permissible limits.

A very satisfactory way to get an ideal mountain rifle is to go to a good custom gun maker. The customer should absolutely specify in this case that his finished rifle in 7 mm., .270, .30/06, or whatever caliber he chooses, should not weigh more than 8 pounds.

As I write this I have just finished sighting and tuning up a beautiful little mountain rifle which was custom made to my specifications. Tom Burgess, East 823 Sinto Avenue, Spokane 13, Washington, did the metal work, fitting a light 22-inch 7 mm. barrel to Czech VZ-24 action. He altered the bolt handle for low scope mounting, thinned it down to neat and graceful lines and saving a little weight. He streamlined the trigger guard, hinged the floorplate and put a quick release button on the forward part of the guard. He fitted a Dayton-Traister trigger and a Sukalle safety, mounted a Weaver K-4 on the Buehler top bridge mount. Russ Leonard, also of Spokane, made a trim and handsome stock for it, beautifully shaped and bedded. The little rifle will group into 1½ minute of angle all day long. So straight is the barrel, so correct the chamber, and so excellent the bedding that it will put any bullet from 130–160 grains with full-power loads at comparable pressures into a 4-inch group at 200 yards. The little rifle will be a joy to hunt sheep with, and with it there would be no need to run from the biggest grizzly that ever walked, just so long as one had him in the open.

I have done much mountain hunting with a 2½-x scope. Such a scope is much preferable to iron sights of any sort, but it isn't as good a scope for mountain use as the 4-x which I think is the best all-around compromise, because even with a mountain rifle someone will sometimes hunt in timber where he needs a fairly wide field. However, many mountain hunters are trying the fine 6-x scopes such as the Stith 6-x Bear Cub, Unertl 6-x Condor, the Weaver K-6, and the big Zeiss and Hensoldt scopes of the same power. For the longest ranges, the 6-x scopes are excellent. They give fine definition and one can see to hold precisely with them. I still think, however, that the 4-x is the best all-around bet.

Cartridges Suitable for Mountain Hunting

The .250/3000. About the lightest cartridge which I would consider at all suitable for mountain hunting is the good little .250/3000. It is an exceedingly accurate little cartridge and one which is most pleasant to shoot because of the mild report and recoil. Furthermore, it is available in the Model 99 Savage for the man who prefers the lever-action. The best load for the .250/3000 is the 100-grain bullet at a muzzle velocity of 2810 and a muzzle energy of 1755. The little .250/3000 is entirely adequate for mule and whitetail deer and also for sheep to 250 yards. Beyond that distance the falling off in the velocity will result in wounded animals unless the shots are right on the but-

THE BIG-GAME RIFLE

ton. The handloader can step up the velocity of the 100-grain bullet with permissible pressures to a bit better than 2900 f.p.s. At the present time, the .250/3000 is available in an American factory rifle only in the Model 99 Savage. However, one can get Belgian-made barreled F. N. actions imported into this country by Firearms International Company, 6521 Kerby Hill Road, Washington 20, D. C., and can also get complete F. N. Mauser rifles which shoot beautifully but which are a bit heavy, and which weigh about what the Model 70 Winchester will.

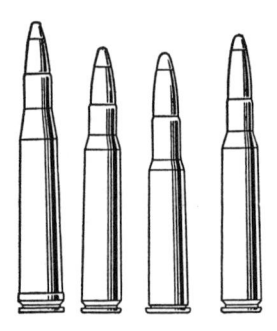

American cartridges suitable for mountain game. (Left to right: .300 H. & H. Magnum, .3006, .30/40, .270 W.C.F.

Anyone wanting the lightest possible rifle and willing to spend the money can have a skilled gunsmith shorten and lighten the Springfield or Mauser action by cutting it in two and welding it, or he can, if he is lucky, secure a genuine Waffenfabrik short Mauser action. Then he can have a featherweight .250/3000 built which can come out as light as 7½ pounds with scope. Such a little rifle, light, short, and handy, would do beautifully for most mountain work, particularly for a woman, a boy, or a light man, and it would be a thing of beauty which would warm the cockles of a gun nut's heart forever. Before the last war, Stoeger Arms Corp., used to import from Germany little K-Mausers in .250/3000 like that, and I do not believe they weighed, with iron sights, more than about 6¼ pounds. Griffin

& Howe used to import the actions and build such rifles on them. They were little beauties.

The .257 Roberts. Another very excellent cartridge for a short, light mountain rifle for the lighter varieties of game and one which can be used in a pinch on the larger animals—even on grizzlies in the open—is the .257. The cartridge came out in the early 1930's. It is a 7 mm. case necked to .25 caliber with the same shoulder slope retained. It is an accurate cartridge and one with very mild report and recoil. Developed as a long-range woodchuck cartridge, it has since been widely used on the smaller varieties of big game. Actually, although I have owned various .257 rifles, both factory and custom made, since the cartridge came out, I have done very little hunting with it for big game and have used it mostly as a varmint cartridge. My wife, though, has been hunting since 1934 with a .257, a light job with barrel and metal work by Sukalle and stock by Griffin & Howe. Not only has she done a lot of shooting with it, but hers is the rifle on which my two sons cut their teeth as big-game hunters. The three of them have killed between thirty and forty mule and whitetail deer, antelope, and javelinas with the rifle. They have used, for the most part, the 100-grain bullet handloaded to about 2950 f.p.s. I do not believe they have ever lost a wounded animal. Even with large mule deer the 100-grain bullet at that velocity seems to be a one-shot killer up to 250 yards, if the bullet is placed in the chest cavity.

The man wanting to use the .257 on larger game and at longer ranges can load the 120-grain Speer or Arizona Bullet Company bullet to right around 3000 f.p.s., or the 125-grain Barnes bullet to around 2900 f.p.s. Then he has a rifle which compares quite favorably to the .270, as either of those loads give a trajectory practically as flat over 300 yards as does the .270 with the 130-grain bullet at 3140. It is not difficult to remodel a Model 70 Winchester in .257 by shortening and turning down the barrel and by fitting a new stock into a light, handy mountain rifle. The

THE BIG-GAME RIFLE

Remington Model 722 on the short Remington action weighs only about 7 pounds with iron sights, and can be had to weigh around 8 pounds with a scope. It makes a most excellent combination.

The 7 x 57 Mauser. One of the finest cartridges for all-around use is the famous 7 mm. Mauser, a cartridge which was one of the original center-fire small bore high velocity cartridges brought out for the Spanish government around 1893. It is a cartridge which has had a long and checkered career in the United States, one which is handicapped by a foreign name, one which has had its periods of prosperity and adversity but which has so many virtues that it has always refused to die. Right now 7 mm. Mauser ammunition is available from the factory only with a 175-grain bullet at a muzzle velocity of 2460 in a 29-inch barrel and with muzzle energy of 2350. That is the original 7 mm. Mauser loading. It is not a bad load and it has been used on big game all over the world, even on elephants, with full-metal cased bullets. In the hands of a cool, careful, crack shot who places his bullets exactly, this cartridge, with that long relatively heavy bullet, is deadly even on the largest game. As loaded today with the 175-grain bullet, the 7 mm. Mauser cartridge is an excellent one for woods and forest use even on large animals like elk and moose. It is not, however, a particularly good mountain cartridge because the moderate velocity gives a trajectory that is too curved to make sure hits a certainty at the longer distances.

If the owner of a 7 mm. wants to make a mountain rifle out of it he must use hand-loaded ammunition. Then he has something. An excellent sheep and mule deer load which I am using in my present 7 mm. Mauser is the 130-grain Speer bullet with 44 grains of Government No. 4895 powder, Lot No. 27277. From the trajectory the velocity appears to be between 2800 and 2900, or not far behind the .270. Pressures are apparently in the .270 class or between 50,000 and 55,000 pounds per square inch. Such a load, of course, should never be used in an old Model 93 or Model 95

RIFLES AND CARTRIDGES FOR MOUNTAIN GAME

Mauser action or in one of the ancient Remington single-shots for that cartridge; but such pressures are perfectly all right with modern brass cases and in good Model 70 Winchester, Model 30 Remington, or Model 98 Mauser actions. Another good load is the 145-grain Speer bullet with 44 grains of DuPont No. 4064 for a muzzle velocity of about 2800 f.p.s., or 42 grains of No. 3031 for a velocity of 2830. Either of those loads approximates the old Western load of the 139-grain open-point bullet at a velocity of about 2850. I have never seen a hunter who used the 7 mm. with that load who did not like it. The combination of velocity, bullet weight and sectional density, thickness of jacket, hardness of core, and diameter of open point made it a perfectly balanced and deadly cartridge. Back in the early 1930's I killed ten head of big game with that cartridge with twelve shots. It was too bad that Western ever discontinued the load, but there simply was not enough demand for it to make it profitable.

For the man who is hunting in country where, in addition to animals the size of sheep and goats, he will encounter larger game like moose and grizzly bear, he might well use the 160-grain Speer or Barnes bullet with 49 grains of No. 4350 for a velocity of around 2700 f.p.s. That load, by the way, shoots with beautiful accuracy in a 1–10 twist. To show how versatile the 7 mm. is for the handloader one can use the 175-grain factory bullet with 47 grains of No. 4350 for a muzzle velocity of about 2500 f.p.s. and pressures under 50,000 pounds per square inch.

Even with the heaviest loads a light 7 mm. does not have objectionable recoil and report. Report is a sharp, but not unpleasant, crack instead of a heavy, hollow boom as it is with a .30/06. The 7 mm. is a grand little cartridge and one which pays big dividends to the rifle nut and handloader.

The .270 Winchester. There isn't a better mountain cartridge of moderate recoil in existence than the .270 Winchester. I have owned various .270 rifles and have shot them ever since the cartridge first came out in the Model 54 Winchester in the fall of 1925. For a long time the .270 languished in the doghouse and was far less popular than the .30/06. However, it has caught on tremendously since the war and now, if custom rifles as well as factory rifles are considered, it probably outsells the older cartridge. Since I have been using the cartridge for over twenty-five years and since I have carried .270 rifles from the mountains of northern Mexico to the Alaska border I have had about as much experience with the .270 as has anyone. With the 130-grain factory load at 3140, the .270 has a little edge on the .30/06 with the 150-grain bullet and the 7 mm. with the 140-grain bullet. It has a point-blank range of about 25 yards more than either of the others. In arriving at that conclusion I am applying the following criterion: let us suppose that we do not want our bullet to deviate from the line of aim more than 4 inches—and such deviation is not too much for big game. The .270 has about a 25-yard greater point-blank range than the .30/06. The .270 makes up in speed what it lacks in bullet weight. It kills just as well as the 150-grain bullet in the .30/06 and from considerable use with both cartridges I would say that on light and medium weight game the .270 will give a somewhat higher proportion of instantaneous kills. That is a statement which cannot be scientifically proved and which hinges on the question of which is more important, velocity or bullet weight, inflicting severe wounds and great shock. I'll string along with velocity. I base this on having shot probably seventy-five or eighty head of big game with the .270 and also having killed at least one hundred coyotes with it. When I first started using the .270 I noticed that any time I got one of those vicious 130-grain bullets in the chest cavity of an animal the size of a deer the kill was almost always instantaneous. I have killed many deer with that bullet and with similar ones, including the 120-grain Barnes bullet, so quickly that I did not know what happened to them. It is difficult for most hunters to realize that even with low-power, wide-angle scopes they lose sight of the game for an instant. In that brief, almost unapparent, interval after I have pressed the trigger, I have had game disappear absolutely, blotted out like a chalk figure erased from a blackboard, I have had that happen many times. I have shot some black bear and one grizzly with the 130-grain bullet in the .270 and I have been surprised at how quickly it has killed them. The one grizzly I shot with the .270 was killed instantly in its tracks and so were all of the black bear except one. With one exception, all the caribou I have shot with the .270 have been killed in their tracks. Of the several moose I have shot with the .270, however, I have yet to kill one in his tracks. There is simply too much meat on a moose to expect an instantaneous kill.

In spite of the fact that I have done almost all of my hunting with the 130-grain bullet in the .270, it wouldn't surprise me greatly if the best all-around load for that cartridge was a good 150-grain sharp-pointed bullet hand loaded with 55 grains of No. 4350 to give a muzzle velocity of 2960. By the time it has reached 300 yards, that bullet has caught up and passed the 130-grain bullet, and beyond that it will shoot flatter with greater retained velocity and energy. The 150-grain sharp-point bullet so loaded is a great favorite with the more thoughtful and skillful north Idaho elk hunters who kill elk across wide canyons at fantastically long ranges.

The two longest shots I have ever made on big game were both made with the .270. One was at a big bull elk in the Jackson Hole country of Wyoming. My guide and I got our glasses on him as he lay surrounded by his harem of cows. We finally worked within about 600 yards and stopped above him on the rim of a timberline basin. We could stalk no closer because we had run out of cover. For a moment we planned to crop back and work up a tongue of timber in the basin and get closer, but the plan played out when we discovered that the timber was full of lesser bulls hanging around to chisel in on the big bull's harem. There was nothing to do but shoot from where we were, since if we had attempted to get closer one of those keen-eyed cows would have spotted us and then we would have had to let that beautiful bull get away or to gamble on a long-range running shot.

THE BIG-GAME RIFLE

I shot the bull from what amounted to a bench rest. I found one stone which would do for a seat and another which would do for the rest. I took off my down jacket, put it on the larger rock, and used it to rest the forend on. By marking off in our minds the distance to the bull in 100-yard units we arrived at an estimate of about 600 yards. I also compared the size of the 4-minute Lee dot in my 2½-X scope with the width of the bull's body and arrived at the same figure. I then held accordingly. The bull lay facing us. The first shot entered his mouth, broke the lower jaw, and came out. This was a piece of bum luck because estimation of range and hold were both exactly right and I should have killed that bull with one shot if the bullet had landed a little higher or a little lower. Startled and hurt, but unable to locate the source of the danger, the bull jumped to his feet and stood broadside. Holding as before, I squeezed another shot off and the guide said he saw the dust fly right behind the bull's shoulder. I put down the rifle and picked up my own glass. I could see the bull was dying on his feet, weaving back and forth on rubber legs. In a moment he collapsed.

Another very long shot with the .270 which I will never forget took place in northeastern Wyoming not too far from Gillette where I was hunting with some companions in September, 1950. A big buck antelope stopped on a hillside across a wide, shallow basin spotted with sagebrush and dry grass. I estimated the range to be 500 yards, got into a good solid position, and held accordingly. An instant after I had touched the trigger the antelope went down. Three men paced the distance and got 485 long paces.

There is no American factory made cartridge which has a longer sure hitting range than the .270. Furthermore it is a cartridge that gives a mild enough report and recoil so that most people can shoot it accurately. Ammunition is widely distributed and if a rifleman can shoot even fairly well the .270 will give him enough power to use on any North American big game in open country.

RIFLES AND CARTRIDGES FOR MOUNTAIN GAME

I wouldn't call the .270 an Alaskan brown bear rifle by any means. Those who have used it in Africa say that the 130-grain bullet is too light for most of the larger African antelope and that the 150-grain bullet is better. Actually, from what I hear of African hunting, the .270 is not a particularly good cartridge to choose. There is always the possibility that the comparatively light bullets might go to pieces on the heavy chest muscles of a charging lion, and of course the .270 would be next to worthless for the heavy, thick-skinned, dangerous game such as a cape buffalo or rhino. Just as the .270 is by no means a one-shot killer on moose, neither would it be much good for the enormous African antelope-like eland.

Nevertheless, with its fine accuracy, its high velocity, its flat trajectory, its great shock power on game of medium weight, the .270 is a most excellent mountain cartridge for anything from Arizona whitetail deer to elk, caribou, and goats, and also for Asiatic sheep and goats. It is a fine cartridge for Rocky Mountain hunting in the far North where in addition one is apt to run into grizzly bear. The .270 is one of the most popular of all American cartridges and it deserves to be. Factory rifles for it are available in the famous Model 70 Winchester, the Model 721 Remington, the Belgian FN, and the Swedish Husqvarna Mausers, and in the Austrian Mannlicher-Schoenauer both in rifle and carbine form. Even the British custom gun makers build .270 rifles on Mauser and Pattern 1914 actions. The cartridge is not only loaded in the United States and Canada but also in England and, I believe, also in Sweden, Belgium, and Austria. It is one of the world's great mountain cartridges.

The .30/06. For about twenty years, from about 1915 until about 1935, the gun writers of this country did a pretty good job of overselling the .30/06. It was, they wrote, the only choice as an all-around big-game cartridge and the only choice for a long-range target cartridge. It was also, they said, the most accurate and highly developed high-power center-fire cartridge and it was a good varmint cartridge. Anyone who did practically anything

THE BIG-GAME RIFLE

with a cartridge other than the .30/06 was, it seemed, a chump.

But gradually a lot of territory once claimed for the .30/06 has been shot out from under it. When the .270 came along in the middle 1920's, the .30/06 had a real rival as an all-around cartridge, and when this country broke out with a rash of hot centerfire .22's, beginning with the Hornet, in the early 1930's, the .30/06 rapidly went into the discard as a varmint cartridge. Even in the field of long-range target shooting, the .30/06 has taken the back seat for a good many years to the .300 Magnum.

There isn't any doubt but that for 1,000-yard target shooting, the .300 Magnum, with its higher velocity, has the edge on the .30/06. Nor is there any doubt that there are many cartridges much more suitable for varmint shooting. With its fairly heavy recoil, loud report, and heavy bullet, the .30/06 is a very poor choice as a varmint cartridge. At the present time, there is a tendency to shoot at the .30/06 in a field where it genuinely shines —as an all-around big game cartridge. It isn't, I have read, much of a cartridge for elk, caribou, moose, and grizzly, and a man hunting Alaska brown bear with a .30/06 would practically be playing fast and loose with his life. Not long ago I saw a list of cartridges for elk hunting. The .30/06 was not among them! I may be a dull fellow indeed, but when I saw that the 8 mm. Mannlicher-Schoenauer and the 8 mm. Mauser with 236-grain bullets were listed for elk and the .30/06 was not I did a double take. What possible superiority either cartridge could have over the .30/06 I cannot fathom since, with the 220-grain, the .30/06 has a bullet of better sectional density, almost as great a weight, and a higher velocity.

Actually the .30/06 is not only a good mountain cartridge but a very satisfactory all-around cartridge. With the 150-grain bullet at a velocity of 2960 it is not far behind the .270 for mountain shooting at medium game. With the 180-grain bullet at around 2700 f.p.s., the .30/06 has sufficiently flat trajectory for most mountain shooting and also gives great shock power and ample penetration for heavy game like bear, moose, and African antelope. With the 220-grain bullet at about 2450 f.p.s., the .30/06 has been used with the greatest success on Alaska brown bear, on charging African lions, and on all heavy African antelope. The .30/06 is one of the world's most versatile cartridges.

It is probably the most widely used all-around big game cartridge in the world and it deserves to be. Ammunition in that caliber has been loaded in Canada, Germany, England, Sweden, Belgium, Mexico, Austria, and probably even in Russia and China. Wherever big game is shot the .30/06 is a top cartridge. It is one of the favorite cartridges used by the Canadian and a favorite cartridge used by the hunters in the great game fields of Africa. Most of the arms making countries of the world have brought out .30/06 rifles of one sort or another. Let us look at them: in the United States .30/06 rifles have been made in the 1903 Springfield at the Springfield and Rock Island arsenals, and by Remington. Winchester has produced the Model 1895, the only lever-action .30/06 ever manufactured, as well as the bolt-action Model 54 and the Model 70. Rifles in .30/06 were produced by Charles Newton. Model 1917 Enfields in .30/06 were made by Winchester and Remington and the Eddystone arsenal during World War I. Savage has produced .30/06 rifles in the Model 40 and Model 45. Remington made the various Model 30 rifles, the Model 720 and the present Model 721. Johnson Automatics Trust, of Providence, Rhode Island, produced the Johnson semi-automatic military and sporting rifle in .30/06. Winchester and Springfield arsenal produced the M-1 Garand, the present military rifle used by American services in .30/06.

Most English custom makers built .30/06 rifles on Mauser or Model 1917 Enfield actions.

In Germany, .30/06 sporters were manufactured at the famous Mauser Werke and variously marked 7.62 x 63 or 7.6 U. S., and by many German custom makers such as Kreighoff, J. P. Sauer, etc.

In Austria, the famous Mannlicher-Schoenauer of the Model 1924 and the Model 1950 were chambered for the .30/06 and marked 7.62 x 63. Belgium has produced .30/06 rifles at the great Fabrique Nationale plant and they are regularly imported into the United States. Sweden makes the Husqvarna Mauser rifles in .30/06 and exports them to this country and Canada. Even Mexico makes .30/06 rifles on the Mexican "Mauser" action which is actually a strange cross-breed between the Mauser and the Model 1903 Springfield.

The .30/06, then, is truly an international cartridge, even more so at this time probably than the 7 mm. and 8 mm. Mausers. It has been used for war and hunting all over the world.

Because the .30/06 is a powerful, well balanced, and accurate cartridge, and because .30/06 ammunition is available all over the world in various bullet weights and types, I do not think anyone ever makes a mistake in getting a .30/06 for his all-around rifle.

Because the .30/06 has a bit more recoil than the .270 and definitely more recoil than the 7 mm., it is not wise to attempt to make up the .30/06 to weigh 8 pounds with scope. The limit on the underside for the mountain rifle should be about 8½ pounds, with the extra half pound of weight going into the barrel. My own favorite .30/06 sporter weighs 9¼ pounds, and I do not think I would care to have it much lighter.

For mountain hunting I do not think there is much doubt that the best .30/06 load is with the 150-grain bullet at 2960 f.p.s. Bullets of this weight should be of spitzer-shape to hold velocity well. For most mountain game the bullet should be fairly easily expandable. Long-time favorites of mine have been the Western open point 150-grain and the Remington bronze point. I have never tried the 150-grain Winchester-Western Silvertip but there is no reason why it shouldn't be excellent. With a good scope-sighted .30/06 sighted in to put the bullet 3 inches above point of aim at 100 yards, one has a point-blank range of about 275 yards, since the bullet is on the nose at 250. Being an excellent mountain cartridge is only one of the attributes of the .30/06. The 180-grain load in the .30/06 is the best for all-around use where one is apt to encounter both light and fairly heavy game. It does quite well for light game, but don't let anyone tell you that it will give as high a percentage of instantaneous kills as will the 150-grain bullet or the 130-grain .270 bullet. Most of the 180-grain bullets are constructed to hold together, and on a light animal a very high percentage of the energy has been expended blasting down trees and cracking rocks on the far side of the game. Heavy bullet construction and moderate impact velocity in the 180-grain simply do not allow the blasting effect of the fragmentation one sees in the lighter and faster bullets. The 180-grain bullets will average quicker kills on larger animals like elk and big bull caribou than they will on lighter game, because the larger animals offer more resistance and absorb a higher proportion of the energy.

I once shot a large Dall ram high through the lungs at over 300 yards and he was on his feet giving no signs of being hit for about 5 or 6 seconds before he toppled over. I shot a desert sheep through the lungs with the same 180-grain .30/06 bullet and he gave no signs of being hit. I hunted him up and found him lying in the rocks about 75 feet from where I had last seen him. The shot was a very easy one and I could not see how I could possibly have missed. A 150-grain bullet would have killed him in his tracks.

The 150-grain bullet in the .30/06 is very deadly on animals of elk class as well as on animals of the sheep-mule deer class if the hunter has a good broadside shot, but if the shoulder has to be broken or a good deal of tissue penetrated before the vital area is struck, the 180-grain is better. Once I tried deliberately to break a big bull caribou's shoulder at about 170 yards with the 150-grain bullet in the .30/06. The bullet went to pieces in the shoulder with a crack that sounded like a pistol shot. It didn't even knock the bull off his feet. Most 180-grain .30/06 bullets would have gone clear through, breaking both shoulders.

Particularly with the Remington 180-grain pointed Core-Lokt .30/06 bullet, it seems to me that there is no need, on any of the stuff I have ever shot, for a bullet giving more penetration. Once in the Yukon I put four of these bullets rapid fire right behind the shoulder of a big rangy grizzly that measured 7 feet, 7 inches from nose to tip of tail as it lay dead. The bear was on a sandbar and every bullet fired went clear through the bear and cracked against rocks on the other side. The same sort of bullet broke the shoulders of another grizzly and sailed on through both shoulders of a big bull caribou. For years the favorite brown bear medicine of Hosea Sarber, famous Alaska game warden and guide, was the 172-grain Western Tool and Copper Works bullet loaded to about 2750 f.p.s.; since he felt the load adequate, and since he has killed more brownies than I have ever seen I can see no way except to take his word for it.

For African hunting the .30/06 with the 220-grain bullet compares very favorably with cartridges designed by the British for magazine rifles; and on African plains game, cartridges such as the .318 Wesley Richards and the .333. Stewart Edward White used the .30/06 with the old Remington 220-grain delayed mushroom and the Western 220-grain boat-tail, with only a pinpoint of lead exposed, and he killed dozens of lions with them. He felt that for charging lions the .30/06 so loaded was superior to the .405 Winchester.

Long ago, though, for the lighter mountain game, I settled on the 150-grain factory load or on handloads with 55 grains of No. 4320 and the 150-grain bullet, which have always given me good accuracy, long case life, and good killing power. Velocity is probably about 2925—2950 f.p.s., and pressure probably below 50,000 pounds. With the 180-grain bullet, 49.5 grains of the same powder is a good bet, likewise 56 grains of No. 4350.

The .30/06, then, is not only one of the world's great mountain cartridges but one of the world's great all-around cartridges. It has a bit more recoil than the 7 mm. and it doesn't shoot quite as flat as the .270. It doesn't have the power of the .375. For versatility, though, it is a tough one to beat, and for the man who can take a little more recoil and a little more weight the .30/06 is a good bet for practically anything except the heaviest African and Asiatic game.

The Brenneke 7 x 64 mm. A very popular European cartridge, which is the European equivalent of the .270 W.C.F., is the Brenneke 7 x 64. It was developed by Wilhelm Brenneke, the famous bullet designer and manufacturer of Leipzig, Germany. In 1946 the late William Krippner had an article in the "American Rifleman" on the 7 x 64 which praised this fine cartridge. I remember the occasion very well because I remember the article and I also remember the flood of mail from lads who discovered that, willy-nilly, they had picked up 7 x 64 rifles in Germany. Exactly when the 7 x 64 was developed I do not know. I recently had a letter from a German-born gunsmith who is now practicing his trade in Philadelphia, saying that he had used the 7 x 64 in Germany and in Africa prior to the first World War. The 7 x 64 is one millimeter longer than the .30/06 case and it takes a standard size 7 mm. bullet like that used in the 7 x 57. It is, then, very much like the .270 W.C.F. and almost identical to the various 7 mm./06 wildcats which have been developed from time to time in this country. The 7 x 64 case is smaller toward the head than the .270 or .30/06 and the powder capacity is a bit less. The shoulder is sharper. Right after the war I made a swap for a 7 x 64 and, I believe, had the first set of 7 x 64 dies ever made by Pacific Gunsight Co., of San Francisco. I found that cases used less powder than the .270 with bullets of the same weight. There are many 7 x 64 owners in this country because apparently tens of thousands of those rifles were manufactured in Germany, not only by Brenneke, but by all kinds of German manufacturers and small gunsmiths. My first 7 x 64 rifle was a Brenneke, my second was made by Germania Waffenfabrik, at Suhl. Since all foreign 7 x 64 cases have Berdan primers and cannot be used with the Boxer-type American primer I formed 7 x 64 cases by running .30/06 brass through 7 x 64 dies in an arbor press and then blowing them out. Best stunt, of course, would be to size unnecked .30/06 blanks. From what I saw of the 7 x 64 I could

THE BIG-GAME RIFLE

not go hog wild over it. It did not use as much powder as the .270 and with the 145-grain Speer bullet I found 52 grains of No. 4350 about tops. I seriously doubt if that load gave over 3000 f.p.s.

However, German figures for the 177-grain 9 degrees boat-tail bullet give a muzzle velocity of 2940, which for the weight and sectional density is really something. I pulled some bullets on German ammunition and found the stuff loaded with 57½ grains of Rottweill flake powder. That much of a charge of the slowest burning American powder, No. 4350, would be a terrific over-charge, so apparently we can only assume that Rottweill flake burns more slowly than any American powder. If these figures are indeed the McCoy the claims that a 7 x 64 is a much better long-range killer than the 180-grain bullet in the .30/06 at 2700 f.p.s. would indeed be justified.

German figures give retained velocity at 100 yards of 2780 f.p.s.; at 200 yards, 2620 f.p.s.; at 300 yards, 2470 f.p.s.; at 400 yards, 2325 f.p.s.; and at 500 yards, 2190 f.p.s. Figures also claim that trajectory over 300 yards of 5.36 inches, which is slightly flatter than the mid-range trajectory at that distance of the .270 with the 130-grain bullet. If these figures are correct, the 7 x 64 in German loadings is a considerably more powerful cartridge than the .270.

I do know, though, that 7 x 64 ballistics cannot be reached with it or any other similar cartridge in the United States with American powders. If their figures are correct we have no powder that can compare with this German flake powder.

Waffenfabrik Mauser rifles were never manufactured in 7 x 64 caliber. Many other manufacturers in Germany turned them out, however. The Steyr Werke in Austria made Mannlicher-Schoenauer in that caliber. Brno Mauser rifles in 7 x 64 made in Czechoslovakia are coming into the United States and into Canada. Apparently pressures of the 7 x 64 German factory loads are not too rough, in spite of the heavy powder charge, because the Germans put 7 x 64 barrels on all kinds of actions, in-

RIFLES AND CARTRIDGES FOR MOUNTAIN GAME

cluding those with the receiver ring cut clear through to form a dovetail for scope mount base.

There isn't any doubt but that the 7 x 64 is a good cartridge. Considering the fact, though, that one cannot use European cases and that one cannot reach advertised German ballistics with any American powder, there is no use in anyone's knocking himself out with longing for a 7 x 64. It is a great cartridge as it was loaded in Germany, but with American powders it is no better than the .270, and probably is not as good. It is, however, an entirely adequate mountain cartridge and one of the best. Anyone who has a 7 x 64 rifle, therefore, and who is content to get custom handloads in that caliber or to import his ammunition from Czechoslovakia or Sweden can do very well on any North American big game with this exceedingly interesting cartridge.

The nearest .270 load to the 7 x 64 is a 160-grain bullet like the M.G.S. or Barnes loaded with 52 grains of No. 4350 powder for a velocity of around 2800 f.p.s. It would not have quite the power of the 7 x 64 Brenneke, but it wouldn't be so far behind.

The 8 x 57 Mauser. In the United States the 8 mm. Mauser cartridge is pretty much looked down on and it is difficult for most of us to realize that it is one of the most popular and widely used cartridges in the world. One of the original center-fire smokeless powder cartridges, it was developed for the Model 1888 German service rifle which is called by the Model 88 Mannlicher and the Model 88 Mauser, as well as the "Schilling Mauser" and "Haenel Mannlicher." It was originally loaded with a 236-grain bullet at a velocity of around 2100 f.p.s. and at moderate pressures. Then in 1905 the heavy bullet was dropped for military use and a slightly larger 154-grain bullet at the then very high velocity of about 2900 f.p.s. in the stronger Model 98 rifle became the German standard. In Germany, the original cartridge with the smaller bullet is known as the 8 x 57-J and the Model 1905 cartridge the 8 x 57-JS. The older ammunition can be used in rifles with the later type of rifling, but using the Model 1905 ammunition in a rifle with the Model 1888 rifling results

THE BIG-GAME RIFLE

in very high pressures. In addition, the Germans made a rimmed version of the 8 x 57-JS cartridge known as the 8 x 57-JR. It is exactly the same, except that it is rimmed. The 8 x 57-R, an older rimmed cartridge, also for doubles, falling-block single-shots, and combination guns is a straight-taper job like the American .32/40.

A great variety of rifles for the 8 x 57 came into the United States—Model 88 military rifles, sporting rifles on the same actions and with the same barrel dimensions, later Model 98 military rifles, Genuine Mauser sporters, and all manner of strange and sloppy rifles built on surplus World War I actions. Loading for all these has presented quite a problem.

To be on the safe side, American 8 mm. Mauser ammunition has used bullets which are undersize for a rifle with Model 1905 rifling and pressures have been held down. Standard American factory 8 mm. Mauser cartridge is loaded with the 170-grain bullet at a muzzle velocity of 2530 f.p.s. with pressures well under 40,000 pounds.

Because the 8 mm. Mauser cartridge was one of the earliest high velocity, smokeless powder, center-fire cartridges and because rifles for it were cheap, it was widely used in hunting, particularly with the original 226-grain bullet for a muzzle velocity of around 2300 f.p.s. The cartridge was an adequate but not spectacular killer and in killing power it was about on a par with the original 220-grain load in the .30/40 Krag and the 215-grain bullet in the .303 British.

The American factory load with the 170-grain bullet is a passable deer cartridge for woods use and every year thousands of American hunters go afield with 8 mm. Mauser rifles which are converted German military rifles.

It is seldom that the American sportsman would spend much money remodeling an 8 mm. Mauser with the original barrel, but anyone owning one and wanting to handload can step up performance considerably over factory ballistics. The Speer 170-grain bullet with 52 grains of No. 4320 to give a muzzle velocity

[160]

RIFLES AND CARTRIDGES FOR MOUNTAIN GAME

of about 2700 f.p.s. puts the cartridge not very far behind the standard 180-grain load in the .30/06 in power. Trajectory would be comparable and so would killing power. One can also load the various 150-grain 8 mm. bullets with as much as 54 grains of No. 4320 for a muzzle velocity of about 2850. Then the 8 mm. becomes a very satisfactory flat-shooting mountain cartridge, one not far behind the .30/06 in performance.

The Germans made various other 8 mm. cartridges including the 8 x 60 "Magnum." After the Versailles Treaty the Germans were forbidden to manufacture rifles for the 8 x 57 cartridge and the 8 x 60 was a substitute made at the Mauser Werke. As the name implies, the case was 3 mm. longer than the 8 x 57 and, of course, 8 x 57 ammunition could not be used in 8 x 60 rifles. Velocity was somewhat higher but not spectacularly so. The presence of both 8 x 57 and 8 x 60 rifles in the United States has resulted in the creation of a rather interesting wildcat, so unshortened .30/06 brass could be used in the rifles. Both rifles have been rechambered to a wildcat cartridge variously known as the 8 mm./06 or the 8 x 63. The cartridge is simply a .30/06 case necked up to 8 mm. or about .32 caliber. With equivalent bullet weights, slightly more powder can be used than in the .30/06 with comparable pressures since with the same ogive a 150-grain 8 mm. bullet, let us say, has less bearing surface than a .30 caliber bullet. The cartridge is really an excellent one and particularly with the long, heavy bullet it will give good performance on the heavier types of big game.

.270 and 7 mm. Magnums. Because of the wide popularity of the .270 W.C.F. cartridge and because of the many good .270 caliber bullets available, there has been a good deal of experimenting with various wildcat .270 Magnum cartridges. One of the best known is the .270 Weatherby Magnum, which is based on the .300 H. & H. case shortened to the same length as that of the .270, necked to .270, and "blown out" or "fire formed" by shooting in a rifle chambered for the .270 Weatherby Magnum. A couple of years ago, I borrowed a rifle in that caliber from

THE BIG-GAME RIFLE

Weatherby and kept it around a couple of months loading for it and shooting it. With the 130-grain bullet it would take about 10 grains more No. 4350 than would the standard .270—67 as against 57 grains—and produce about 200 f.p.s. higher velocity. In the rifle I toyed with, pressures were not tough with that much powder. I had no extraction difficulty and the primer pockets remained tight. With the 150-grain bullet, 65 grains of No. 4350 produced 3140 f.p.s., again about 200 f.p.s. higher than is possible to obtain with the standard .270 and also with about 10 grains more powder.

Various other experimenters have brought out .270 Magnum cartridges, but the only other I have had much experience with is the .270 Ackley Magnum, which is, like the Weatherby, based on the shortened and blown out .300 H. & H. case. It uses a little less powder (about 3 grains as a rule) than the Weatherby and gets somewhat less velocity. The Ackley rifle I played with was heavy but very accurate. Once when making a drop test by shooting from the back window of a station wagon I discovered I had made a 6-inch group at 500 yards.

Various experimenters have worked on 7 mm. "Magnum" rifles to push fairly heavy 7 mm. bullets fast with a lot of powder. Jim Wilkinson, formerly of Illinois, and now of Prescott, Arizona, has for years used a 7 mm. based on the .30 Newton case necked down. He swears by it. P. O. Ackley, the custom rifle manufacturer, can furnish barrels in both .270 and 7 mm. for wildcats based on the .30 Newton case.

Ackley furnishes a 7 mm. Magnum based on the shortened H. & H. Magnum case. So does the Mashburn Arms Co., of Oklahoma City. A 7 mm. on the .30/06 case was developed many years ago by the late Major Charles Askins, and the .285 O.K.H. is also a 7 mm. on a .30/06 case. I have never seen any velocity figures on this last one, though.

The Mashburn 7 mm. Short Magnum looks like a very high-class cartridge. It is similar to the 7 mm. Ackley Magnum. The Mashburn 7 mm. Long Magnum is the .300 Magnum case necked

RIFLES AND CARTRIDGES FOR MOUNTAIN GAME

down, kept at its original length and blown out—a sort of a super .280 Dubiel. I have seen no chronograph data on either cartridge. The designer of the two cartridges told me, though, that he feels that the Long Magnum would need a 28- or 30-inch barrel in order to develop full velocity. My own hunch is that the shorter cartridge is probably better and that the long job would probably be over bore capacity with any existing sporting powder.

Latest Weatherby Magnum cartridge is also a 7 mm., and in the present state of technical development in this sinful world I think it is about as good a long-range mountain cartridge as one can get. I have always had a hunch that with the shortened Magnum case, the 7 mm. caliber would be better than .270 because the greater area of the base gives more for the powder gas to push on, and a bullet of equal weight would have less bearing surface.

Weatherby's first version of his Magnum came about because G.I.'s returning from the European theater brought in dozens of 7 x 64 rifles for which no American ammunition was available. Others brought in standard 7 x 57's and wanted some goat glands put in them. Weatherby made up reamers to rechamber these rifles for the shortened Magnum case with a conventional 30-degree shoulder and did some loading and chronographing so he could furnish some dope.

Results were encouraging, so the next step was to make up a set of reamers using the radius shoulder which is a trademark of the Weatherby cases. For the man who wants great power and long-range accuracy, yet with recoil and muzzle blast that won't knock a man out from under his hat, this looks like our baby.

Best bullets are the 145-grain and 160-grain, which in the 7 mm. Magnum out-class the standard .270 W.C.F. as much as the modern jet fighter is ahead of a World War II P-51. With 70 grains of No. 4350 the 145-grain bullet can be driven at a muzzle velocity of 3,475 f.p.s., which would mean that the bullet would turn out not far from 3,900 foot-pounds of muzzle

THE BIG-GAME RIFLE

energy. The 160-grain bullet in front of 68 grains of No. 4350 has a velocity at the muzzle of 3360 and about 4,000 foot-pounds of muzzle energy. With that loading for the 145-grain bullet, retained velocity at 100 yards is 3,123 or about what the standard .270 produces at the muzzle with a bullet weighing 15 grains less. At 200 yards, retained velocity is 2,825.

At 100 yards, the 160-grain bullet is still traveling along at 3,011 f.p.s. faster than the lighter 150-grain .30/06 bullet is traveling at the muzzle, and at 200 yards, that long, relatively heavy bullet is still zipping along at 2,757, which is about as fast as a bullet of the same weight can be driven in the standard 7 mm. at the muzzle.

By way of comparison, factory dope gives the standard .300 H. & H. cartridge with the 180-grain bullet at 2,900 f.p.s., 3,365 foot-pounds of muzzle energy, and retained velocity of 2,700 and 2,500 f.p.s. at 100 and 200 yards respectively. With the 160-grain bullet, which is probably the best bet for long-range big-game shooting, the 7 mm. Magnum should be poison on elk, moose, and grizzly, and probably very bad medicine on the Alaska brownies, which I have never hunted.

I have played around with two 7 mm. Weatherby Magnum rifles. Both have had 1–12 twists. First had a 26-inch barrel, the second a fairly light 24-inch barrel. What the answer is I do not know, but the rifle with the shorter and lighter barrel produced better groups than did the first—about 1½ minutes of angle, which is remarkable for a standard weight rifle of that power.

With the 145-grain Speer bullet I sighted in to print the group 4 inches high at 200, and the group is at point of aim at approximately 350 yards. All of this means that on an animal like an elk we have a rifle with a practical point-blank range of around 400 yards. Such a stretched-string trajectory, coupled with good bullet weight and efficiently retained velocity, would take a good many headaches out of shooting at long and uncertain ranges.

The 7 mm. Weatherby Magnum cartridge is still not so completely developed but that the curious experimenter could add to the knowledge about it. For example, so far as I know, chronograph tests have not been made with cases with the new shoulder and 175-grain and 180-grain bullets. I'd also like to see what can be done with the Speer 130-grain bullet. With the 175-grain bullet, 65 grains of No. 4350 gave 2,900 f.p.s. I have seen no dope on any bullet weighing 100–110 grains. With those light bullets it should be possible to crowd 4,000 f.p.s.; but such a load has no particular place in the scheme of things as the bullet would be too light for most big game and too noisy and unnecessarily destructive for varmints. The 140-grain M.G.S. bullet gives the astounding muzzle velocity of 3,550 f.p.s.

For big-game shooting the 160-grain bullet looks like the best bet. High velocity is well retained because of the good sectional density, and killing power out where the game is should be spectacular. Here is a cartridge with more power and a flatter trajectory than the .300 Magnum, yet with a light enough recoil so that it can be shot accurately. No one will think he is touching off a .22 rim-fire when he lets one go with the 7 mm. Magnum, but the recoil is not too bad. To me, it seemed more than that of the .30/06 in a standard-weight rifle, less than that of the .300 Magnum. Offhand, I'd say the *apparent* recoil is about like that of the .348.

Weatherby builds rifles for the 7 mm. Magnum on Belgian F.N. Mauser actions, which have been specially heat-treated in this country. He uses his own chromed barrels which, he claims, have double the life of barrels not plated. I have shot one of the rifles about 500 times now with full-power loads and still see no sign of throat erosion, whereas some would probably be apparent with a non-chromed barrel. Pressures are not bad. I have run into no extraction difficulty and no stretching of primer pockets. Cases should last a long time.

Cartridge of the 7 mm. Weatherby Magnum, like that for the Ackley and Mashburn Magnums, is about the same overall length as the .270 or .30/06 and as a consequence any "standard" action can be used—Model 54 or 70 Winchester, 98 Mauser,

THE BIG-GAME RIFLE

Ballistics of Cartridges Suitable for Mountain Game

CONTINENTAL CARTRIDGES	BULLET WEIGHT	MUZZLE VELOCITY	MUZZLE ENERGY	
6.5 Mannlicher-Schoenaeur	160	2160	1660	(Canadian figures)
7 x 57 Mauser	140	2900	2787	(British data)
7 x 57 Mauser	175	2460	2350	(American data)
7 x 57 Mauser	130	2950		(Hand load)
7 x 57 Mauser	160	2800		(Hand load)
7 x 64 Brenneke	154	2735	2559	(German data)
7 x 64	162	2883	2978	" "
7 x 64	173	2686	2769	" "
8 x 57 Mauser	154	2906	2884	" "
8 x 57 Mauser	185	2624	2826	" "
8 x 60 Magnum	185	2932	3499	" "
6.5 x 68 Vom Hofe *	123	3444	3253	(Vom Hofe figures)
7 x 73 Vom Hofe	170	3293	4085	" " "
8 x 68 Vom Hofe	187	3280	4460	" " "

* The figures of the Vom Hofe cartridges are included simply to show that the evolution of high-intensity cartridges was going on on the Continent as well as in the U. S. The Vom Hofe company was apparently similar in size to the Weatherby company in this country. The 7 x 73 Vom Hofe is comparable to the 7 mm. Weatherby Magnum and the 8 x 68 Vom Hofe to the .300 Weatherby Magnum.

1917 Enfield, or high number Springfield. A simple way to get one would be to have a Model 70 Winchester in 7 mm. Mauser rechambered, bolt face and extractor altered. The same job can be done on a Model 98 Mauser in 7 x 57 or 7 x 64 or on a Model 30 Remington in 7 mm.

Czech sporting Mausers made at Brno have good strong actions, but not enough metal around the chamber to permit rechambering, and 7 mm.'s on Model 93 and 95 actions are not strong enough.

This 7 mm. wildcat is one of the most interesting big game cartridges I have played with in many years, and it, and the similar high performance 7 mm.'s, fill a small but important niche.

AMERICAN FACTORY LOADED CARTRIDGES

CARTRIDGE	BULLET Wgt. Grs.	VELOCITY Muzzle	VELOCITY 100 Yds.	VELOCITY 200 Yds.	VELOCITY 300 Yds.	ENERGY Muzzle	ENERGY 100 Yds.	ENERGY 200 Yds.	ENERGY 300 Yds.	MID-RANGE TRAJECTORY 100 Yds.	MID-RANGE TRAJECTORY 200 Yds.	MID-RANGE TRAJECTORY 300 Yds.
250 Savage	100	2,810	2,490	2,180	1,900	1,755	1,375	1,055	800	0.6	3.0	7.0
257 Roberts	100	2,900	2,530	2,190	1,870	1,870	1,420	1,065	775	0.6	2.5	7.0
257 Roberts	117	2,630	2,330	2,050	1,790	1,800	1,410	1,095	835	0.7	3.0	8.0
270 Winchester	100	3,540	3,210	2,890	2,600	2,785	2,290	1,855	1,500	0.4	1.5	4.5
270 Winchester	130	3,140	2,820	2,530	2,260	2,850	2,295	1,850	1,470	0.5	2.0	5.5
270 Winchester	150	2,770	2,490	2,220	1,970	2,560	2,065	1,645	1,295	0.6	3.0	7.0
7 x 57 m/m Mauser	175	2,460	2,220	1,990	1,780	2,350	1,915	1,540	1,230	0.8	3.5	9.0
7.62 m/m Russian	145	2,810	2,570	....	....	2,545	2,130	....	....	0.6	2.5	6.5
30–06 Springfield	150	2,960	2,720	2,480	2,260	2,920	2,465	2,050	1,700	0.5	2.5	6.0
30–06 Springfield	150	2,980	2,650	2,350	2,070	2,960	2,340	1,840	1,430	0.6	2.5	6.5
30–06 Springfield	180	2,720	2,520	2,335	2,157	2,960	2,540	2,190	1,870	0.6	2.8	6.8
30–06 Springfield	180	2,710	2,420	2,150	1,900	2,940	2,340	1,850	1,445	0.7	3.0	7.5
30–06 Springfield	180	2,710	2,420	2,150	1,900	2,940	2,340	1,850	1,445	0.7	3.0	7.5
30–06 Springfield	220	2,410	2,190	1,970	1,780	2,840	2,345	1,900	1,550	0.8	3.5	9.0
30–40 Krag	180	2,480	2,210	1,950	1,710	2,460	1,955	1,520	1,170	0.7	3.5	9.0
30–40 Krag	220	2,190	1,980	1,780	1,600	2,345	1,915	1,550	1,250	1.0	4.5	11.0
300 H. & H. Magnum	180	2,930	2,630	2,340	2,080	3,435	2,765	2,190	1,730	0.5	2.5	6.5
300 H. & H. Magnum	220	2,610	2,380	2,160	1,950	3,330	2,770	2,280	1,860	0.7	3.0	7.5
300 Savage	180	2,380	2,140	1,910	1,700	2,265	1,830	1,460	1,155	0.8	4.0	10.0

THE BIG-GAME RIFLE

British Factory Loaded Cartridges

	BULLET WEIGHT	MUZZLE VELOCITY	MUZZLE ENERGY	
.240 Belted H & H	100	2900	1869	
.246 Purdey	100	2950	1934	
.26 Belted B.S.A.	110	3100	2350	
.275 Flanged Nitro Express (H. & H.)	160	2575	2357	(Rimmed version of 7 x 57)
.280 Ross	140	2900	2617	
.280 Ross	160	2700	2592	
.300 H. & H. Magnum or .30 Super	150	3000	3000	
	180	2700	2915	
	220	2350	2700	

They deliver a lot of energy at long range with a flat trajectory, yet their recoil is moderate and rifle weight can be kept down to a total weight of 9–9½ pounds, or the point where a man does not have to be a Samson to lug one around.

Particularly should they shine in country where fairly large animals have to be taken at the longer ranges—caribou in the winter when they are very wild and where they can hear the crunch and squeak of the hunter's snowshoes, wary bull moose above timberline before the rut, elk across the canyons of Idaho's Selway. Because of the very flat trajectory these super 7 mm.'s would also be what the doctor ordered for shots at antelope when they are found on flat plains where stalking close is often impossible. Anyone who would want a terrific long-range coyote rifle would only have to get one of these Super 7's and put a 10 or 12-x target scope on it. Then he could really have himself some fun in an open plains country!

The .300 Magnums. Since the middle 1920's an increasing number of mountain hunters have carried rifles chambered for the cartridge which in this country has always been known as the .300 Holland & Holland Magnum, but which in England is

Loading and Chronograph Data for the Weatherby Magnum Line of Mountain Cartridges

.257 WEATHERBY MAGNUM

Powder Weight	Powder	Bullet	Pressures	Muzzle Velocity	Foot Pounds of Energy
60	4064	100 W	OK	3540	2778
62	4064	100 W	Caution	3650	2958
64	4350	100 W	OK	3480	2685
65	4350	100 W	OK	3550	2794
60	4350	117 r	OK	3220	2687
58	4350	125 W	OK	3070	2616
60	4350	125 W	OK	3230	2890

.270 WEATHERBY MAGNUM

Powder Weight	Powder	Bullet	Pressures	Muzzle Velocity	Foot Pounds of Energy
65	4350	130	OK	3160	2876
67	4350	130	Near Max.	3335	3195
69	4350	130	Caution	3430	3390
70	4350	130	Max.	3460	3450
65	4350	150	OK	3140	3277
67	4350	150	Max.	3245	3489

7 MM. WEATHERBY MAGNUM

Powder Weight	Powder	Bullet	Pressures	Muzzle Velocity	Foot Pounds of Energy
65	4350	139	OK	2980	2742
67	4350	139	OK	3060	2890
70	4350	139	OK	3320	3396
72	4350	139	Watch	3400	3562
74	4350	139	Max.	3475	3710
65	4350	154	OK	3010	3099
68	4350	154	OK	3125	3344
70	4350	154	OK	3200	3546
60	4350	175	OK	2715	2855
63	4350	175	OK	2830	3112
65	4350	175	OK	2900	3268

THE BIG-GAME RIFLE

Loading and Chronograph Data for the Weatherby Magnum Line of Mountain Cartridges (*Continued*)
.300 WEATHERBY MAGNUM

		FORMED CASES			
Powder Weight	Powder	Bullet	Pressures	Muzzle Velocity	Foot Pounds of Energy

The following ballistical data was compiled using Super Speed cases.

Powder Weight	Powder	Bullet	Pressures	Muzzle Velocity	Foot Pounds of Energy
75	4350	150 FP	Mild	3065	3118
77	4350	150 FP	Mild	3180	3361
79	4350	150 FP	Mild	3265	3532
80	4350	150 FP	OK	3350	3730
82	4350	150 FP	50,000 a	3455	3957
84	4350	150 FP	Caution	3540	4167
85	4350	150 FP	Caution	3625	4365
86	4350	150 FP	Max.	3660	4462
75	4350	180 S.T.	Mild	3085	3792
77	4350	180 S.T.	50,000	3205	4084
79	4350	180 S.T.	OK	3290	4300
80	4350	180 S.T.	Caution	3330	4422
82	4350	180 S.T.	Max.	3400	4611
73	4350	220 S.T.	Mild	2810	3856
75	4350	220 S.T.	OK	2935	4193
77	4350	220 S.T.	Caution	3000	4400

Note: The Weatherby Magnum line of cartridges is highly developed in that they have been in use for several years by hundreds of hunters from Alaska to Africa. For many reasons, the above data should serve as a guide only. For one thing Remington, Winchester-Western, and Speer cases made for the line of cartridges differ greatly in powder capacity, and a lot that is moderate in a Remington case, let us say, is poison in a Speer case. Chambers vary, bores vary. Some rifles are freebored, others are not. I load 78 grains of No. 4350 in my own .300 Magnum rifle with the 180-grain bullet, 70 grains of No. 4350 with the 140-grain bullet in the 7 mm. Magnum. This last is with Speer cases.

known as the Super .30. It was developed before the first World War by the famous London rifle making firm of Holland & Holland, which has made many rifles for it on Magnum Mauser actions. In England the cartridge is loaded to almost exactly the same velocities as are given bullets of various weights by the .30/06 in this country—a 150-grain bullet at 3,000 f.p.s., a 180-

RIFLES AND CARTRIDGES FOR MOUNTAIN GAME

grain bullet at 2,700 f.p.s., and a 220-grain bullet at 2340 f.p.s. Remember, then, that anything you read about the performance of the .300 that is written by an Englishman can be duplicated by our common or garden variety of .30/06.

With better American powders, performance is stepped up considerably. The 180-grain bullet is given 2,900 and the 220-grain is driven at 2,610. Pressures are pretty high, close to 55,000 pounds per square inch, and the .300 is, like the .220 Swift, so rough on barrels that Winchester Model 70's are now made with barrels with a high chrome content to resist the rapid erosion.

The Hoffman Arms Co., first of Cleveland, Ohio, and then of Ardmore, Oklahoma, and Griffin & Howe, of New York, pioneered the .300 Magnum cartridge in this country, and during the 1920's they built many rifles in that caliber for the better-heeled sportsmen on the same Magnum Mauser actions that were used by the English. The rifles were pretty heavy. They usually had 26-inch barrels and with iron sights they weighed from 9½–10½ pounds. About 1937, Winchester brought out the Model 70 rifle in .300 (and also in .375) and anyone who had about $65 in his pocket in those days could have a .300, a luxury which before that time could be afforded only by the well-heeled. At this writing, the Model 70 has almost exactly doubled its 1937 price.

For the size of the case the performance of the .300 H. & H. has always been a disappointment. It has a slight shoulder and great body taper, since it was designed for British Cordite powder, and American powder pressures have run high, velocity low, and barrel life short. Various experimenters have tried blowing out the long tapered case to give a sharp shoulder and more powder capacity. The result is a great improvement with stepped up velocity and apparently no more pressure.

Blown out .300 Magnum cartridges have been designed by Ackley, Powell, Pfeifer, and others, but the best known is the .300 Weatherby Magnum. Ballistically it is an enormous improvement over the standard .300 H. & H. It will drive a 180-

THE BIG-GAME RIFLE

grain bullet at between 3,100 and 3,300 f.p.s. depending on how hot one wants to load it. It is the flattest shooting cartridge I have ever played with, and in a good rifle it is very accurate.

The only thing wrong with it is that the recoil is heavy, too heavy for anyone who doesn't do a lot of shooting. It is also unnecessarily powerful for mountain game like mule deer and sheep. I have shot only two head of big game with the .300 Weatherby, a Rocky Mountain goat and a grizzly, and both were killed instantly in their tracks, just as a woodchuck would be killed with a Swift.

My own feeling about the cartridge is that it is seen at its best on Alaskan brown bear and on the larger African plains game. For mountain use, I'd prefer the 7 mm. Weatherby Magnum if I wanted to carry something more powerful than the .270 or .30/06.

CHAPTER IX

Problems of the Saddle Rifle

ONE of the most delightful ways to shoot big game is to hunt from horseback. It is particularly to be recommended for the office worker who is soft or for the middle-aged man who has lost much of the spring of his legs and whose wind is short. In thick woods and heavy brush it is useless to attempt to hunt from horseback because a horse makes too much noise and it takes too long for the hunter to jump off, grab his rifle, and take a pop at a running deer.

Certain areas in North America, however, are made to order for horseback hunting. In much of the Southwest, elk, mule deer, and turkeys are found in relatively open forest of Gambel's oak and yellow pine with very little underbrush. Here one can see from 200 to 400 yards and the mounted hunter usually has time to get off his horse, pull out his rifle, and take a shot. In southern Arizona and the upper Sonora zone of northern Mexico, little whitetail deer are found in rolling grassy hills with live oaks growing in the heads of the canyons and on the north side of the slopes. I have hunted in country in northern Sonora so smooth, with hunting so good, that I could ride anywhere at a trot, country that was so open that I could keep a deer in sight for a half mile.

In other sections of the country which are not so favored, a horse will take much of the wear and tear off a hunter's legs by getting him up into country from which he can hunt. Even in southern Arizona I used to ride to the top of a ridge, then tie my horse, take out my rifle and hunt the heads of the draws and canyons on foot.

Over the northern Rockies, clear into Alaska, a hunter who goes out with a pack outfit will ordinarily leave camp on horseback. Often he will still be on horseback when he spies moose above timberline early in the season, grizzlies eating berries or digging varmints, and caribou wandering aimlessly on the great upland caribou barrens. Then he can get off, tie his horse, and make his stalk. Even when sheep hunting the northern hunter will go out on horseback, climb with his horse as far as he can, then tie and finish his climb on foot. I have often actually spotted sheep when mounted. Once Frank Golata and I were leading a pack string down Nevis Creek where it ran into the Bessa River in the northern British Columbia Rockies. We saw a bunch of seven mature rams lying on a ledge far above us on the canyon wall. I stepped off of the horse, took a .270 out of the saddle scabbard and laid it across my knees as I sat down. Then I glassed the rams and saw one I wanted. I shot him off the ledge and he fell over with a terrific splash a good 300 or 400 feet straight down into the swift, cold water.

The choice of a saddle rifle is a fairly complicated one and it depends on what is to be hunted, how much the rifle is to be carried, and what sort of shots must be taken. Many Western cattlemen seldom go out on the range without a rifle in the scabbard. Primarily they are not hunting big game. They take the rifle along because they may get an opportunity to take a shot at a coyote or even at a bobcat or mountain lion. Now and then, of course, they get a favorable opportunity at a deer and pick themselves up a piece of meat. It can hardly be said that those Western stockmen carry their rifles. They actually "wear" them. They want rifles which can be carried in a saddle scabbard day in and day out, rifles that are so short, so light, and so unobtrusive, that they hardly know that they have them. They

PROBLEMS OF THE SADDLE RIFLE

want a rifle so carried that they can ride their horse on a dead run without having it bounce and jounce around.

The long time favorites of such cattlemen are the lever-action Winchester Model 94 carbines in .25/35, .30/30, or .32 Special. They are reasonably powerful, fairly flat-shooting, but best of all they are light, short, and above all they are flat. The standard Model 94 carbine has a 20-inch barrel, but before it was necessary to register rifles with barrels less than 18 inches, Winchester turned out a special short-barreled Model 94 for just that use. The barrel was only 15 inches long. It was an overgrown horse pistol with a muzzle blast that would make your ears ring for a week. With the short barrel and the very short sight radius, those little rifles, particularly with open sights, were very difficult to shoot accurately but they would do for 100–125-yard shooting and many ranchers liked them. Few Western cattlemen are gun nuts. Many are very fast shots on running game at short range but few attempt to do much long-range shooting. They would be better off, as a rule, with their saddle rifles using cartridges of higher velocity and flatter trajectory because since the horse is a noisy beast, a high percentage of the shots they get are at running animals. I have always felt that probably the best choice for the saddle rifle which is to be carried a lot and used a lot by a good shot would be a light Model 99 Savage like the Model 99-T in .250/3000 caliber. With the 100-grain bullet stepping along at over 2800 f.p.s., trajectory is flat and not so much lead is necessary on running game. The .250/3000 within 200 yards is a most excellent deer cartridge, killing, as a rule, better than the cartridges of the .30/30 class. For those ranchers who are not hopelessly prejudiced against the bolt-action, the little 6.5 Mannlicher-Schoenauer carbine is excellent. It has about the same ballistics as the .30/30 but the small diameter, very long bullet gives deeper penetration and in a pinch does pretty well on animals even as large as elk. The Marlin Company makes a good carbine in .30/30, .32 Special, and .35 Remington. It has a

20-inch barrel and anything that can be said about the Winchester saddle carbines can also be said about the Marlins.

The deer hunter who plans to do his hunting from horseback is faced with a somewhat different set of circumstances. He is primarily hunting and can, therefore, use a somewhat heavier rifle than the rancher, as his horse will seldom go faster than a walk. Because he has gone out particularly to hunt deer and the whole success or failure of his trip hinges on his getting a deer he should have better sights. His rifle should be reasonably light and fairly flat, because riding with such a rifle under the leg is much more comfortable than to do so with a heavy, bulky, thick weapon. Since any shots obtained by the horseback hunter are apt to be running shots and fairly long ones, the horseback hunter should have a fairly powerful, flat-shooting rifle.

Horseback hunting is right up my alley. I have hunted on horseback off and on for more years than I like to remember. I have stepped off horses and shot mule deer, whitetail deer, wild turkey, elk, black bear, and sheep. The more I have hunted on horseback, the more convinced I am that the good saddle rifle for the man who plans to do much of his deer hunting from horseback is very similar to the ideal mountain rifle which we described in a previous chapter. It should be fairly short of barrel, fairly light, and it should be chambered for a high velocity, flat-shooting cartridge. It should be accurate. Because a higher proportion of the shots the mounted hunter will get will be in open country and at fairly long range, the bullets should be light, fast-moving and sharp-pointed. A telescopic sight is a tremendous boon to the mountain hunter because he can see better with it and shoot better with it, particularly at moving game.

The best mountain cartridges I have ever used have been the 7 mm. with the 139-grain bullet at about 2,850, the .270 with the 130-grain bullet at 3,140, and the .30/06 with the 150-grain bullet at 2,960. For deer only the .257 is also an excellent mountain cartridge and the one with which my wife has done much of her hunting. In that caliber the 100-grain bullet at a velocity between 2,900 and 3,000 f.p.s. is to be preferred and it appears to be adequate, certainly up to 250 yards, even with large mule deer.

One of the last heads of big game that I killed with the 7 mm. Mauser was a big Rocky Mountain mule deer in the Kiabab forest north of the Grand Canyon in northern Arizona. The previous day my wife had killed a buck but I was looking for an exceptional head and although I had seen several I had not popped a cap. We were hunting at about 7,500–8,000 feet, up in the yellow pines where a few spruce and fir also grew on the north slopes of the ridges. We had passed up a couple of small bucks but I had not even got off the horse. It was still early in the morning, still cold, and the heavy frost of the night before lay on the ground.

Then my wife said quietly, "Do you want that big buck over there in the sun?"

I glanced to my left where she indicated and there in a patch of sunlight which shone on him as bright and clear as a spotlight on a stage stood a big buck with a beautiful, massive, five-point head. I stepped off the horse, put the crosshair of the 4-x scope right behind the buck's shoulder and pressed the trigger to send the vicious little 139-grain open point bullet on its way. That buck was killed instantly dead in his tracks—and I mean in his tracks.

In the Western mountains shots average pretty long and the hunter travels on horseback. I have killed many Arizona white-tail deer by stepping off a horse and taking a shot, many in southern Arizona and many in northern Sonora. One time, some years ago, I sat down and tried to recapitulate how far my average shot had been and under what conditions it had been taken. About three-fourths of the deer were killed at well over 200 yards. The average range was, I believe, right around 250 yards, with some killed running as far as 325 yards.

Under such conditions, where the hunter does not have time to stop and think, but has to get off a horse, sit down instantly,

THE BIG-GAME RIFLE

and shoot almost as soon as his hind end touches the ground, he needs a fast bullet that gets there right now, strikes a hard blow, and does not make it necessary for him to do any figuring on trajectory.

Of the various cartridges I have used for this type of shooting, I think the 130-grain .270 load definitely has the edge on any of the others. The 150-grain .30/06 load, which I have also used a lot, is a good one but the 130-grain .270 bullet has a somewhat greater point-blank range and gives a somewhat higher percentage of instantaneous kills. This is very important in horseback hunting because the deer are frightened and moving and unless they are hit hard they can often run a considerable distance. It is very necessary that the animals show that they are hit.

When I have used the .270 it has been very seldom that a deer I have hit solidly anywhere has ever traveled more than 10 feet after I hit him before going down at least temporarily.

I remember one occasion when I was hunting in Mexico with a .30/06 with the 150-grain Remington bronze-point bullet. For several days I had hunted high on the shoulders of a great towering mountain called Sierra Azul. Live oaks grew in the draws and were scattered over open grassy meadows. I had seen many whitetail does and fawns and a couple of small bucks, but I had not fired a shot. Then a friendly Mexican suggested that I ride up the canyon and hunt a series of low ridges, barren, unhospitable, and over-grazed by cattle. He said he had been in there the week before and had seen several large bucks. I had hardly got into the country and was riding along watching on every side, when I saw what I thought to be a doe and a fawn climbing up the head of a canyon up an almost straight up-and-down slope about 250 yards away. I had no scope but decided to shoot anyway, since before I had left camp my companion and I had agreed to bring home meat of some kind, because we were completely out of anything with protein in it to eat. I stepped from

PROBLEMS OF THE SADDLE RIFLE

the horse, took a couple of shots at the larger animal and apparently missed. By this time it was over the ridge but the smaller one, which I took to be a fawn, stopped right on top of the ridge for an instant and the gold bead came to rest right behind the shoulder. I pressed the trigger and it went down. When I got around there the "fawn" was a big four-point buck. I walked over to the place where the other deer had crossed and found a tremendous blood trail. Another buck with a fine head was lying just across the ridge in some brush. If I had had a 4-x scope for those shots I would never have thought I was shooting at a doe and a fawn. Actually many Southwestern hunters are now using 6-x scopes like the Weaver K-6 and the Stith 6-x Bear Cub. The horns of those little whitetail deer are not conspicuous and often they are difficult to see on perfectly legal bucks at over 100 yards. When a deer jumps, our hunter piles off his horse, grabs his binocular, and takes a look at the deer to see if it is a legal buck. Then he drops his binocular, picks up his rifle. By that time the deer is often out of sight. With a good 6-x hunting scope, our hunter can see instantly whether the deer is legal or not and fire the moment he sees antlers. I have used 2½-x scopes considerably for that type of hunting but I do not care for them. Out at 300 yards or over, it is often, under poor conditions of visibility, impossible, with a 2½-x scope, to see antlers even on a pretty large whitetail. I have passed up such shots at good bucks because I could not check with glasses and shoot quick enough. At other times with a 2½-x scope I have only been able to see a sort of a fuzz over the ears because the definition of the scope is not sufficient. I learned that this indistinct fuzz I could see showed that the deer had antlers and knowing no more than that I have killed deer, but in every way a 4-x scope is preferable, and for that long shooting, even a 6-x with sufficient width of field and the definition is superb.

The horseback hunter can use the standard factory bolt-action rifles with their 24-inch barrels, but particularly the Model 70 is somewhat too heavy. On a round-backed horse it has a tendency to pull the saddle over to the side on which the rifle is hung. An ideal saddle rifle is the Mannlicher-Schoenauer carbine in .270 and with 20-inch barrel imported from Austria by the Stoeger Arms Corp., of New York. Another very good one is the little Czech 7 mm. carbine imported from Czechoslovakia by the Thalson Company of San Francisco. The Czech rifle has a flat or "butter-knife" bolt handle, which cannot be recommended for rapid fire but which makes the rifle flatter and easier to carry in a saddle scabbard and easier to jerk out.

The man who does his hunting on horseback and who plans to jump off and take a pop at a deer or an elk should carry his rifle in a scabbard with the butt to the rear and the scabbard passing under the stirrup leather. So the rifle will not fall out of the scabbard when the horse is climbing up hill, the butt should be higher than the muzzle and at an angle of about 30–45 degrees. Then the hunter, when he sees game, can step off his horse on the left side, reach back, grab the rifle by the butt, and jerk it out of the scabbard. If the rifle is carried with the butt forward along the horse's neck, the sudden grab that the excited hunter makes for the butt will often frighten the horse. He will jump and perhaps the hunter will miss the butt of the gun. Then if he has to chase the horse around to get his rifle, the deer will be out of sight before he can shoot. With the rifle carried in the position that I have described, the horse can run off without making much difference, since all the hunter has to do is hang onto the butt of his rifle. He can find his horse later.

Some Western hunters, particularly with very short-barreled carbines, will carry the weapon on the right side, butt high and to the rear, and grab the butt as they get off. However, this is not practical for a heavier rifle with a long barrel.

In the years when I was doing a lot of horseback hunting in the Southwest and often taking three or four annual trips into Mexico, as well as hunting in Arizona, I believe I could get off the horse, grab my rifle, sit down and start shooting in a matter

Herb Klein of Dallas, Texas, with Paddy Jim, Indian guide, with one of the great Dall sheep heads of all time. One of the horns of this great ram had an outside curve of 47½ inches when the ram was killed, but it is undoubtedly smaller now, for all sheep heads shrink. Klein shot this ram on 52 Mountain, in the Yukon, about twenty-five miles off the old Whitehorse–Dawson City winter road, in 1950. He used a .300 Weatherby Magnum rifle with the 180-grain bullet driven at about 3,300 foot-seconds.

A Barren Ground caribou with a good head killed by O'Connor in the White River country of the Yukon in 1945. Bull was one-shot kill with 180-grain .30/06 bullet at 425 paces.

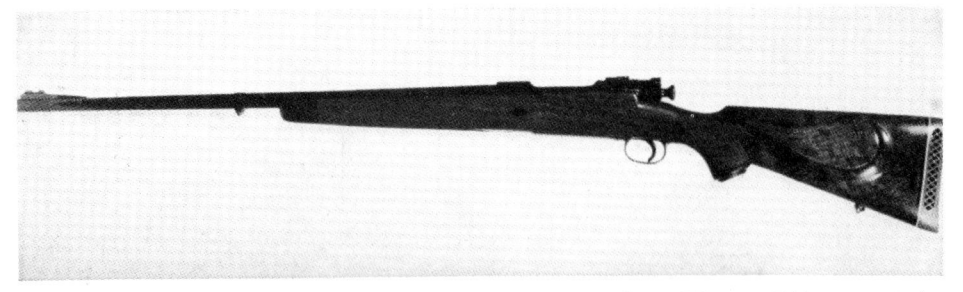

A fine .30/06 Springfield stocked by R. G. "Bob" Owen, Port Clinton, Ohio, one of the older stock-makers who is responsible for the lines of the present "classic" sporting stock for bolt-action rifles. Note that the swivel base for the front sling swivel is attached directly to the barrel—something which is often seen in British magazine rifles and older American bolt-action rifles.

A deluxe .270 owned by the author. It was built on an F. N. Mauser action by Alvin Biesen of Spokane, Washington. Scope is a Stith 4-x Bear Cub with double adjustments and on a Griffin & Howe mount. After this picture was taken the scope blocks were removed and a Lyman 48 receiver sight fitted.

The wood is a spectacularly marked piece of Oregon myrtle, yellow-brown in color with sweeping dark lines. Bolt handle has been altered. Floor plate is hinged, with release button in the trigger guard. A Miller single-set trigger has been fitted.

This is a typical deluxe Continental rifle built by Richard Marholdt of Innsbruck, Austria. The action is Mauser. It is fitted with the double-set trigger so dearly loved by Continental sportsmen. The flat or butterknife bolt handle is also a Continental touch. The entire action is elaborately engraved.

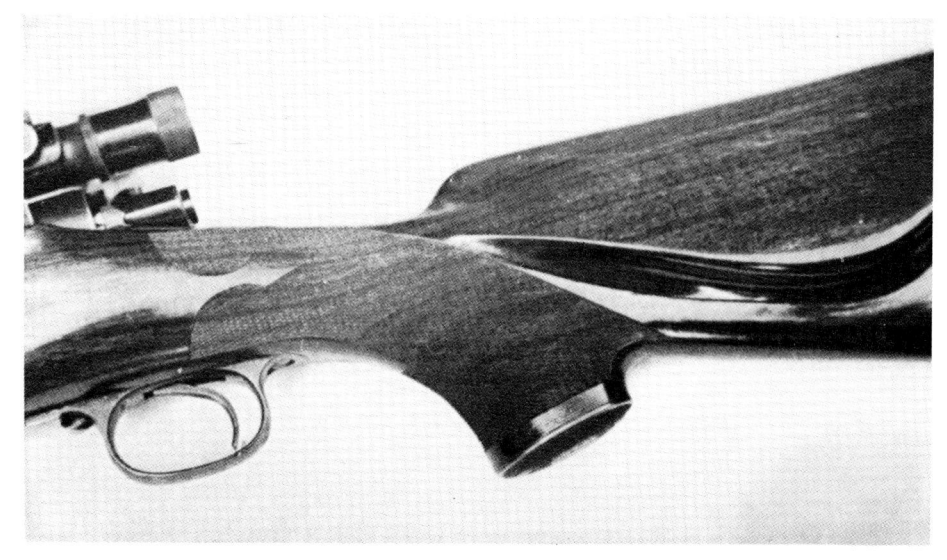

Detail of modified Scheutzen cheek piece on a Winchester Model 70 .270 stocked by the late Alvin Linden. Such a cheek piece enables the hunter to crawl right up to point of comb without having his cheekbone knocked off when the gun is fired.

The photo above shows a standard Weatherby Magnum rifle built on an F. N. Mauser action and fitted with a Stith 2½-x Bear Cub scope on a Buehler top mount. The lower photo shows the little Brno Mauser made in Czechoslovakia and imported into this country in fair numbers—note the Continental touches: the sling swivel on the barrel, the double-set triggers, and the butterknife bolt handle.

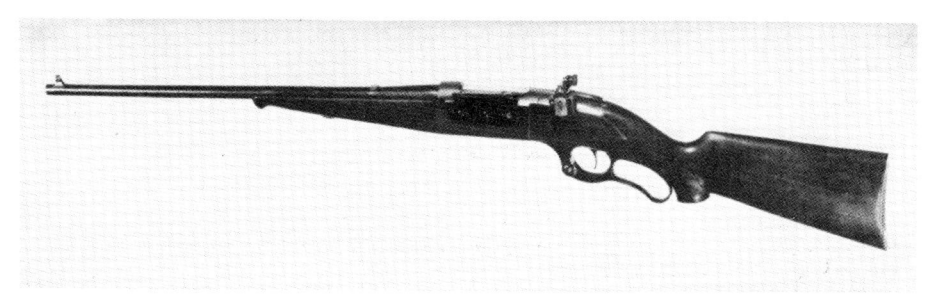

A good deer-rifle, a Model 99 Savage fitted with a Lyman 57-SA receiver sight, which is fast, close to the eye, and generally preferable to the open sight.

Two views of a highly engraved and handsome sporter on a Mauser action built by Bob Owen. Scope is a Stith 4-x Bear Cub with double adjustments and on a Griffin & Howe mount. The stock is fitted with a silver nameplate which Owen makes out of 25-cent pieces.

This is the little Savage Model 99-T in .250/3000 caliber, one of the finest stocked lever-action rifles ever built, and one of the most accurate. The man shooting the rifle is Carroll Lemon, Tucson, Arizona, a rifle enthusiast and big game hunter.

A fine .30/06 sporter built by Alvin Biesen on a Mauser action. It is fitted with a Lyman 48 receiver sight, the slide of which has been shortened. Floor plate has been hinged and release button is in the trigger guard.

A high grade Remington Model 721 in .30/06 caliber, which has been fitted with the Williams Foolproof receiver sight.

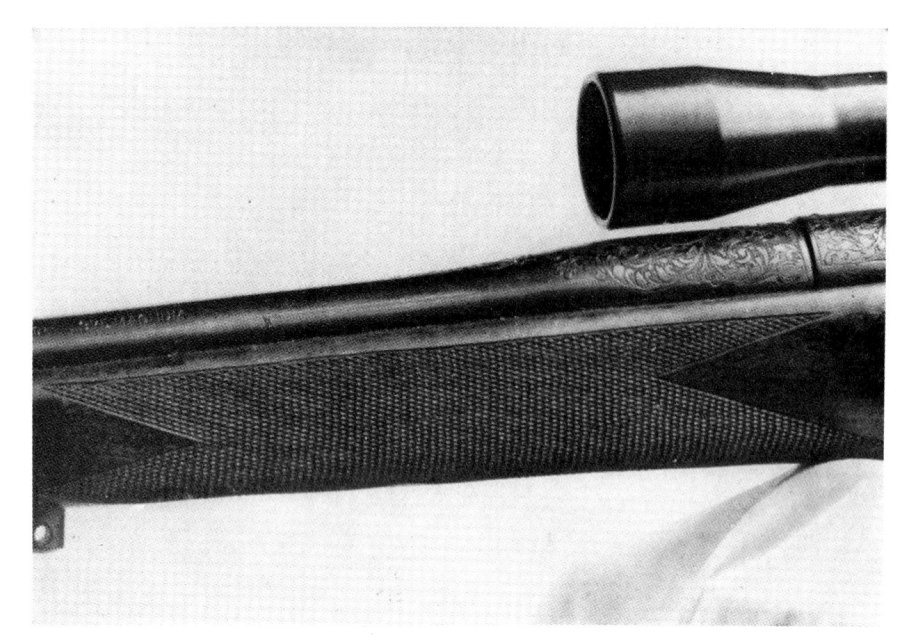

Details of the checking of the forend and engraved receiver and barrel on a fine custom sporter turned out by Keith Stegall of Colorado.

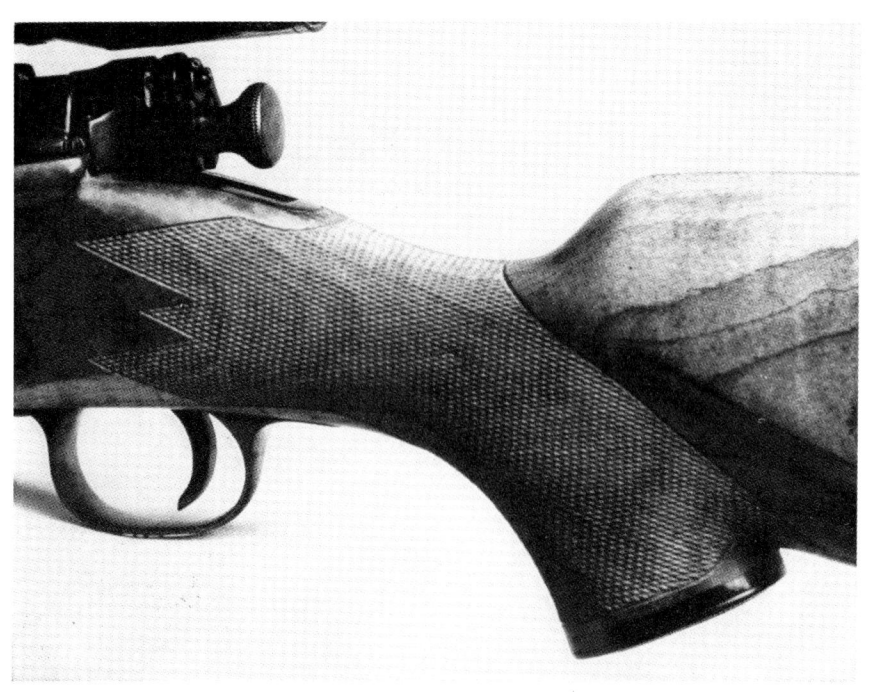

Showing details of comb, pistol grip, and checking on a Springfield rifle stocked by Keith Stegall.

A standard grade Winchester Model 70, which probably is basically the finest of the world's factory-produced sporting rifles.

A deluxe Biesen .270 owned by the author. Photo shows details of checking and of the hinged floor plate.

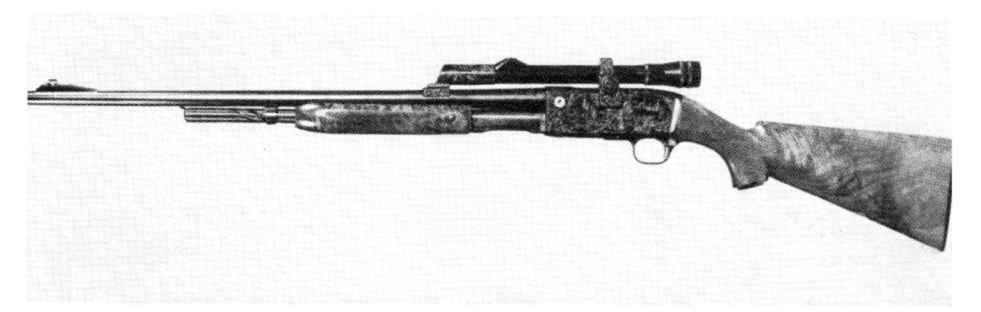

A deluxe and highly engraved Remington Model 141 slide-action rifle fitted with a Stith Streamline mount and a Stith 2½-x Bear Cub scope. In .35 caliber this is a very effective woods rifle.

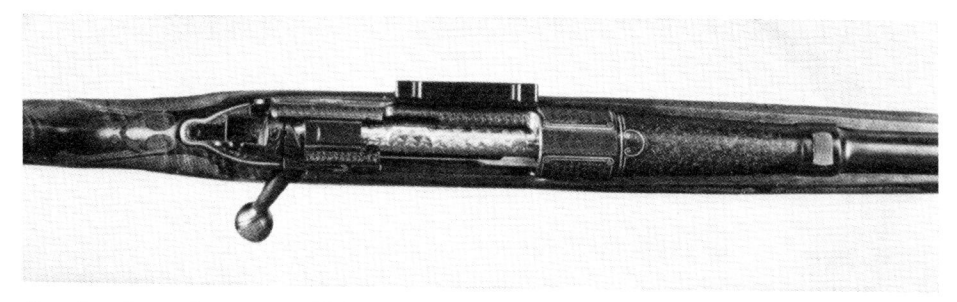

Details of an ultra fancy, highly engraved, Winchester Model 70, turned out at the Winchester factory and owned by Dr. Russell Smith of Petersburg, Alaska. Base for the Griffin & Howe side mount remains on the rifle.

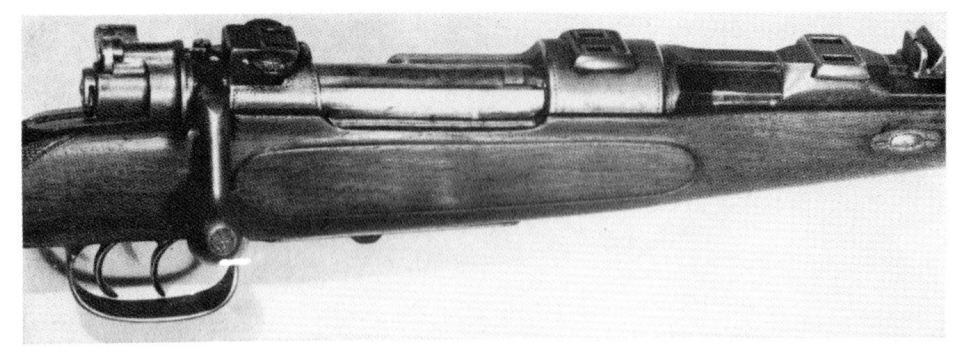

A typical German sporting rifle on a Mauser action. Note the panel over the magazine and the base for scope mount dovetailed into the receiver ring.

Williams "Foolproof" receiver peep sight on a Winchester Model 70 rifle.

Three views of a custom-made Weatherby sporting rifle with a stock of birdseye maple. This is an exceedingly elaborate rifle with engraved floor plate and trigger guard which had been gold plated. Stock design is of the California school—and so are the fancy stock inlays. Tastes in rifles are like tastes in women—what is one man's dream is another man's poison. Many do not care for stocks this fancy, but others love them.

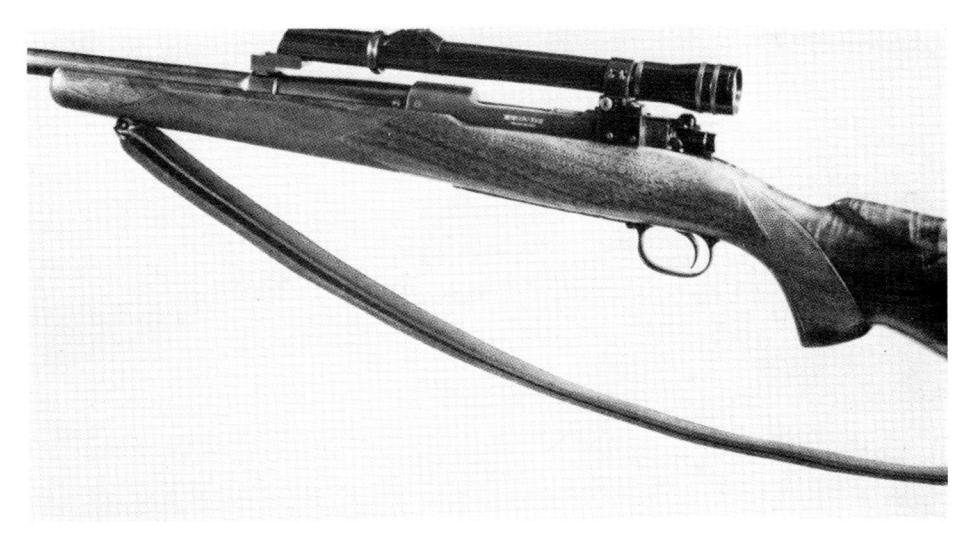

Winchester Model 70 standard grade rifle fitted with a Stith Streamline mount with Stith 2½-x Bear Cub scope. Mount incorporates windage, as scope does not. This is a very strong and satisfactory mount for saddle scabbard use.

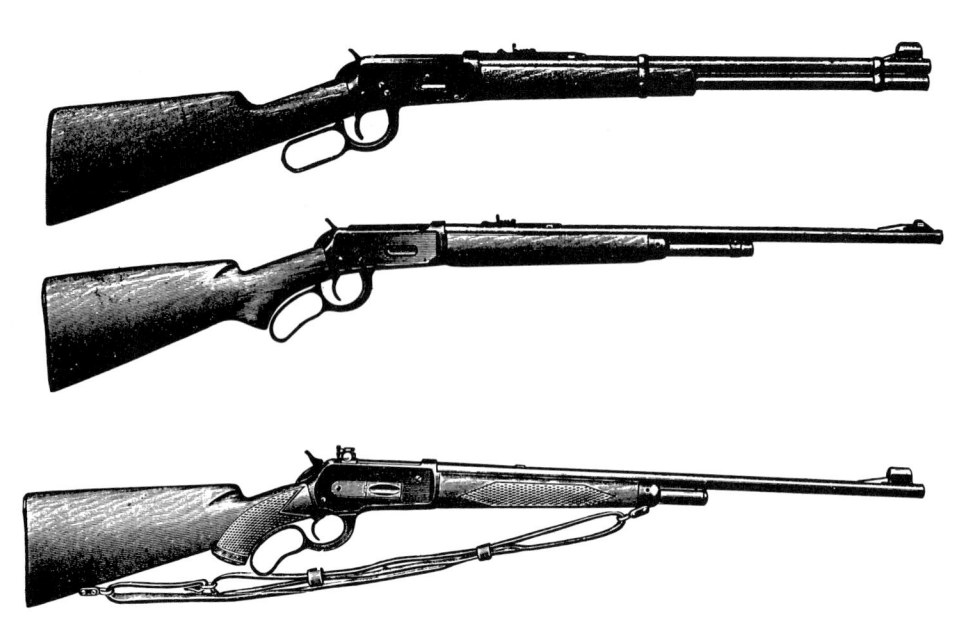

Three Winchester lever action rifles for forest use. Top: The old Model 94 carbine, which has been made with but little change for well over a half century and which in .30/30 and .32 Special is the classic deer rifle. Middle: The Model 64, which is a Model 94 with a modernized stock. Bottom: The Model 71, a modernized Model 86. It is the most powerful of the lever action rifles and is made only for the big .348 Winchester cartridge.

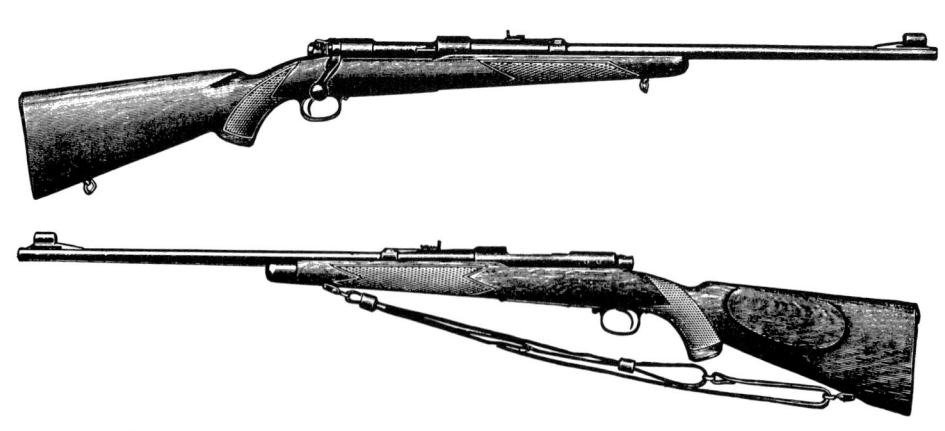

The Winchester Model 70 bolt-action big-game rifle made in .22 Hornet, .220x Swift, .257, .270, .30/06, .300 and .375 Magnum isn't the fanciest of the world's big-game rifles but probably the soundest. The Model 70 is shown here in Standard Grade (above) and Super Grade (below).

Another Austrian sporter fitted with a 4-x scope on the typical high German mounts. Apparently this rifle is built on a Mannlicher-Schoenauer action and the stock, of course, is of the Mannlicher or full-length type. The stock carving is typically Austrian and so is the stock design.

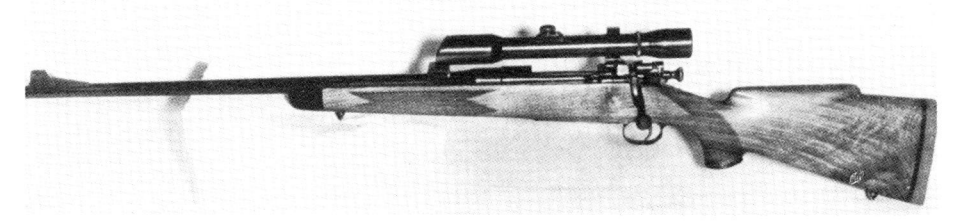

A Springfield with a left-hand bolt action and a Weaver K-4 scope on Stith Streamline mount. The stock was made by that old master stock-maker Tom Shelhamer of Dowagiac, Michigan, who was for many years with the old Neidner Arms Corp.

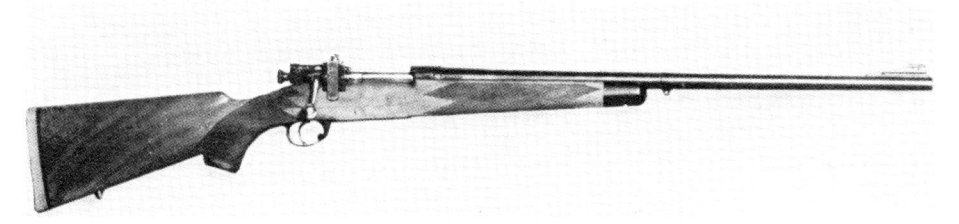

Here is a fine rifle for heavy, soft-skinned big game. It is a .35 Whelen once owned by the author. Remodeling of the action, hinging of floor plate and fitting release button and trigger guard as well as barrel work was done by W. A. Sukalle, 1120 East Washington, Phoenix, Arizona. Stock was built by the late Alvin Linden. Springfield action was used and stock is built along classic lines.

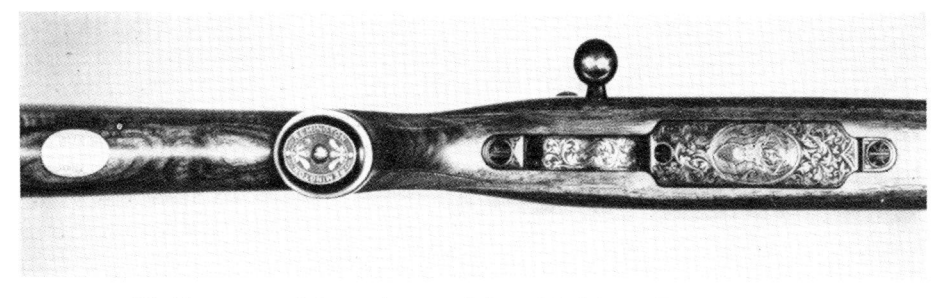

Highly engraved floor plate on deluxe Model 721 Remington rifle.

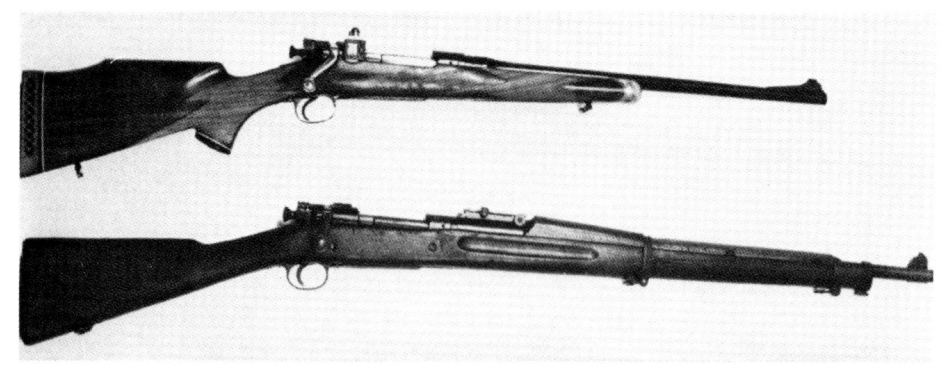

Ronnie King, one-time gunsmith at Lewiston, Idaho, specialized in building featherweight sporters. Here is a remodeled .30/06 Springfield which is shown in contrast to the standard Model 1903 Springfield unaltered.

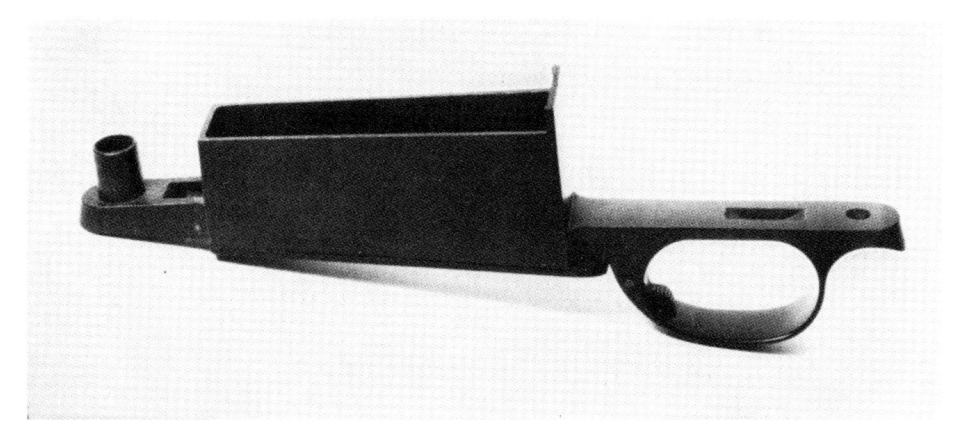

The lightweight magazine stocks and trigger guard assembly made for Model 98 Mauser and 1917 Enfield rifles by Holland & Holland of England. Assembly is similar to that used on the fine Magnum Mauser actions turned out by the Mauser Werke of Germany prior to the war.

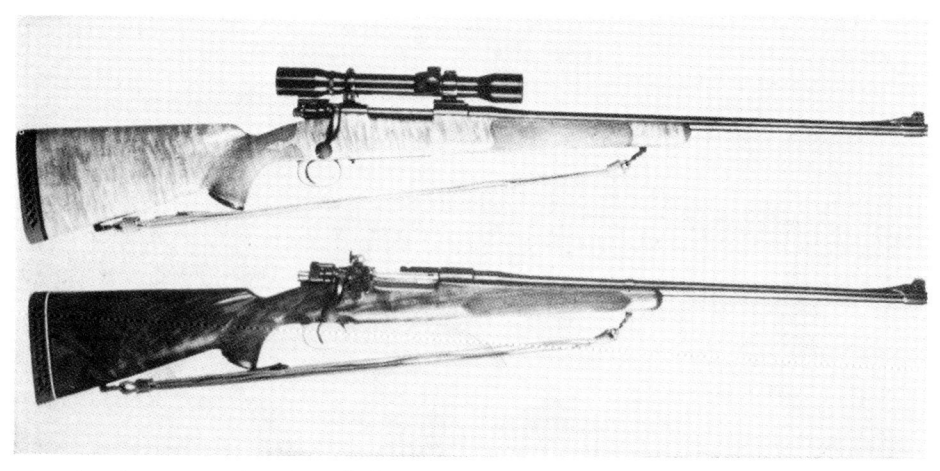

Two handsome sporting rifles built on Mauser actions by George Schielke, Trenton, New Jersey. Schielke not only stocked the rifles but did all metal work.

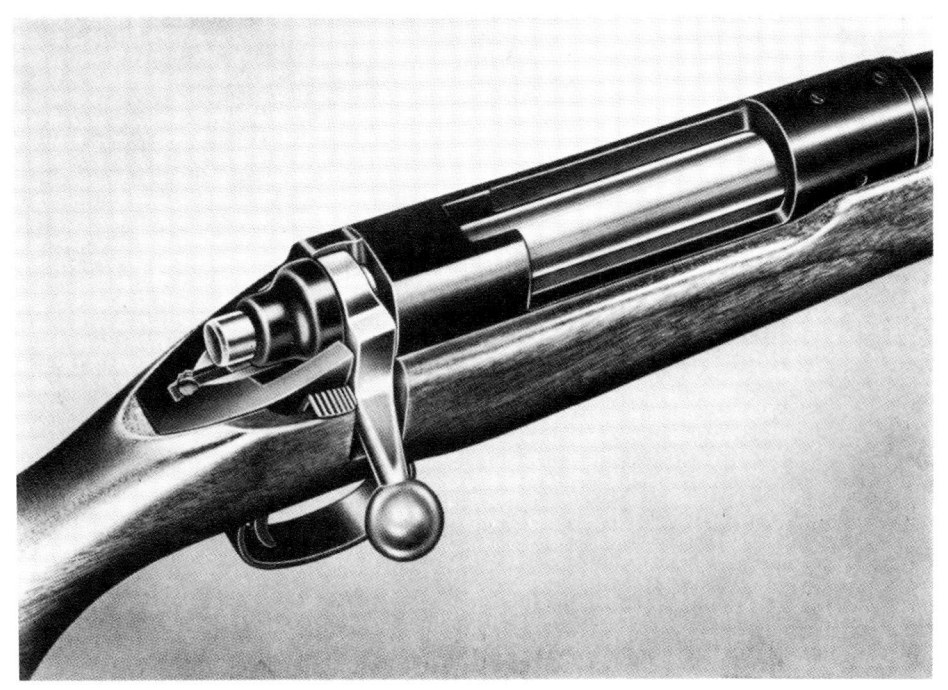

Action of a Remington Model 721 rifle which is currently made for the .270, .30/06, and .300 Magnum cartridges. The action is a modification of the Mauser but of new and novel design in many respects and very strong.

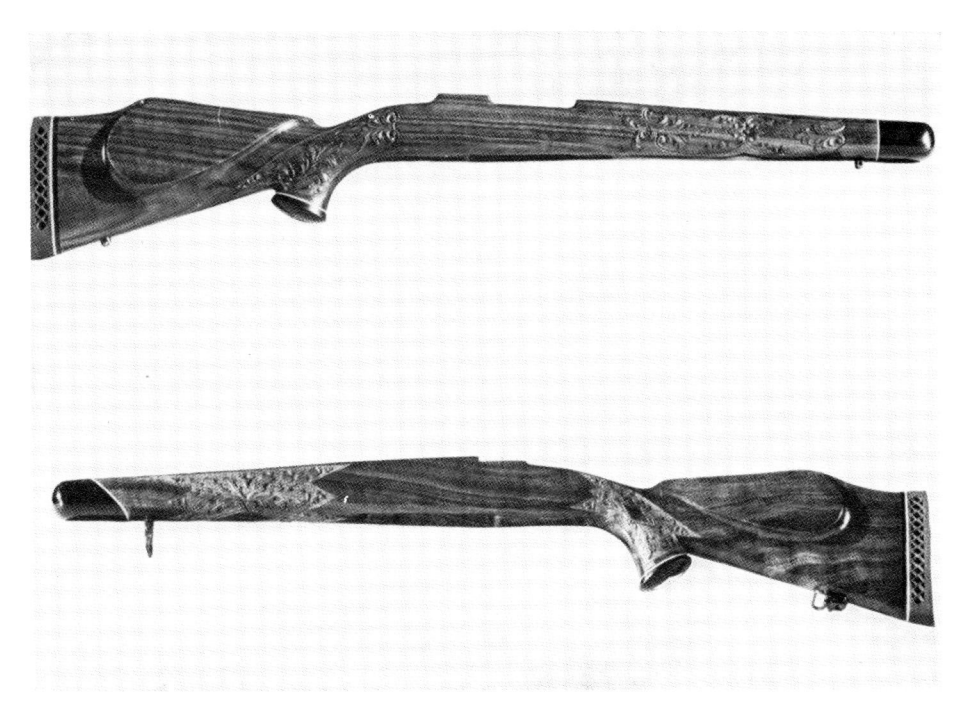

Carving on stock turned out by Weatherby's, Inc. With the Monte Carlo comb and long, flared pistol grip, this is a typical California stock.

Highly engraved and specially stocked Winchester Model 70 rifle turned out by the Custom Department of Winchester Repeating Arms Company of New Haven, Connecticut, and owned by Dr. Russell Smith, the rifle collector and big-game hunter of Petersburg, Alaska.

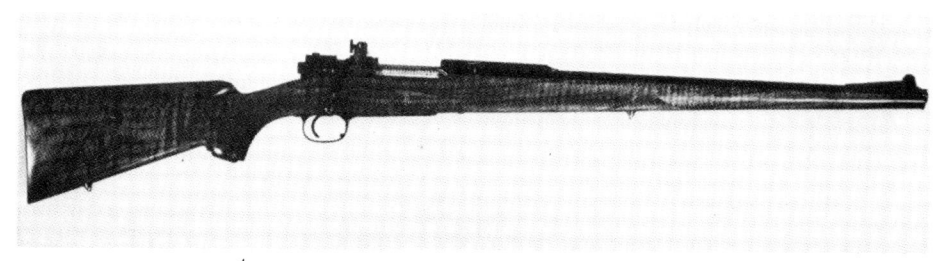

Mannlicher-type stock made by Al Biesen of Spokane, Washington. Rifle is a .30/06 on a Mauser action fitted with Lyman 48 and three-leaf open sights on a short rib.

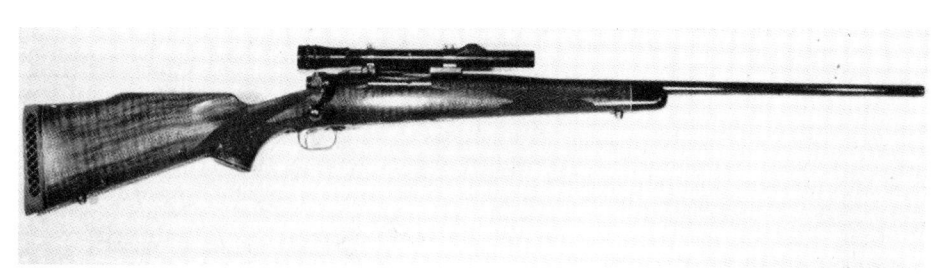

The author's .300 Weatherby Magnum, remodeled Model 70 Winchester stocked by Leonard Mews of Wisconsin, one of this country's best stock makers. Scope is Stith Bear Cub 2½-x on Redfield Jr. mount.

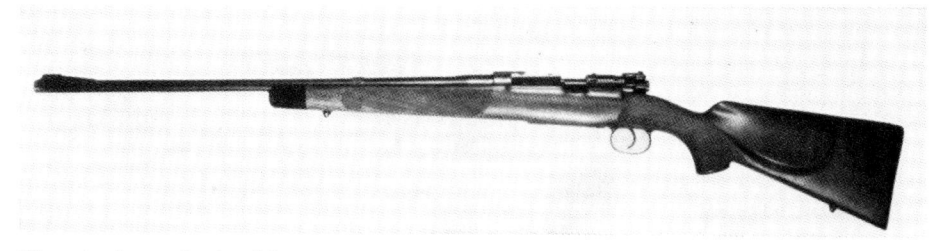

Here is the author's old .270. It was stocked by Alvin Linden. Action is a Model 98 Mauser and all action work and barrel fitting was done by W. A. Sukalle of Phoenix, Arizona. Linden used a plain but very hard and dense piece of Circassian walnut for the stock. Checking runs 26 lines to the inch. The old rifle is now on its third barrel and, counting everything from coyotes to moose, it has probably knocked over around a hundred head of game.

The Model 1950 Mannlicher-Schoenauer in .270, .30/06, and .257 calibers, as imported into this country by the Stoeger Arms Corp., of New York; it is an excellent lightweight mountain-rifle.

A very fine rifle once owned by the author. It is a remodeled 1903 Springfield with a stock by Alvin Linden. A black-and-white photo cannot do justice to the wood which is suigi finished maple. Stock was checked after the suigi finish was put on and checking is much lighter than the rest of the wood.

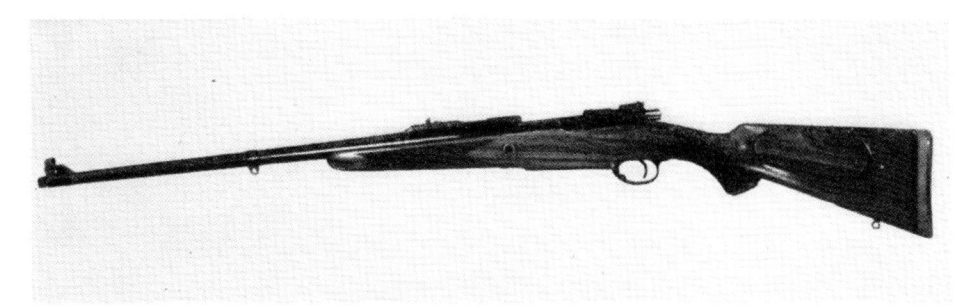

A beautiful .375 Magnum built by the originators of the cartridge, Holland & Holland, 98 New Bond Street, London, W. 1. Prior to the war the firm used the Magnum Mauser action for the .300 and .375 Magnum cartridges but since the war they have had to use Model 1917 Enfields and remodeled standard Model 98 and Belgian F.N. actions. This rifle is fitted with the light metal trigger guard and magazine box assembly with hinged floor plate turned out by Holland & Holland not only for their own rifles but for rifles turned by other custom gunsmiths both in England and in the United States.

Bradford O'Connor shooting a fine, lightweight, mountain rifle owned by the author. It is a 7 x 57 built on a Czech VZ 24 action. Floor plate has been hinged with release button in the trigger guard, bolt handle altered, Sukalle safety installed. Scope is Weaver K-4 on Buehler mount. Barrel and metal work was done by Tom Burgess, Spokane. Russ Leonard of Spokane built the light, handsome stock. Complete rifle weighs 8 lbs. on the nose and is a joy to carry and to shoot.

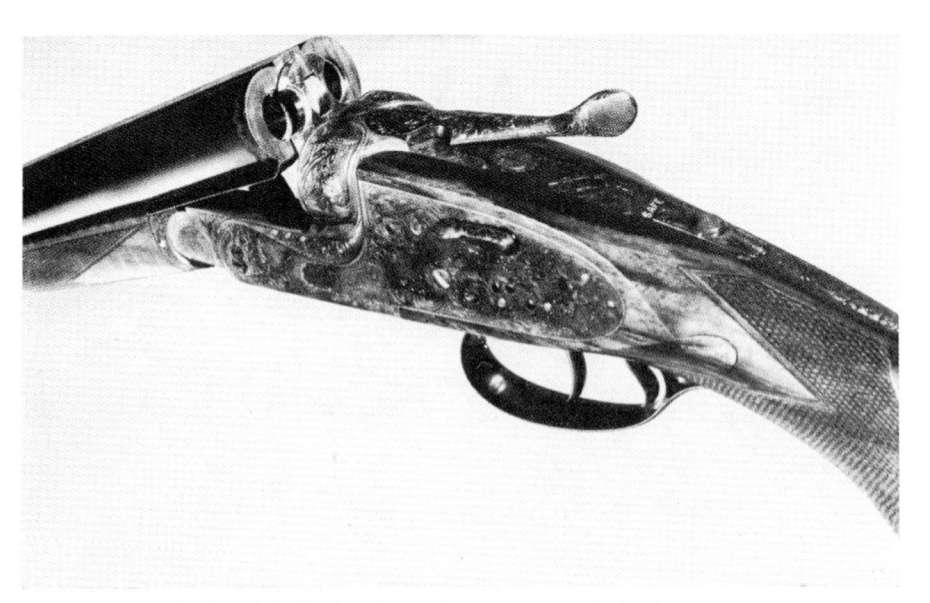

Holland & Holland double built on a side-lock action.

A fine double built by Holland & Holland of London. This one is for the .375 flanged Magnum cartridge, but a rifle for the .465 Nitro Express would be similar in appearance.

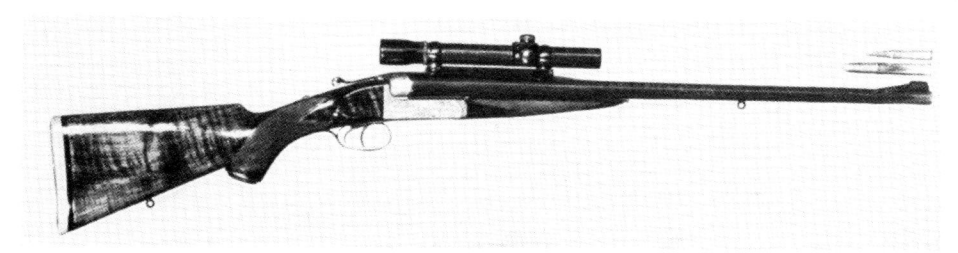

Maynard P. Buehler, the manufacturer of the Buehler scope mounts, as a hobby buys powerful double rifles and fits them with telescopic sights on the Buehler mount. This one is a .475 No. 2 Nitro Express. It was built by Halliday of London. Buehler handloads the cartridge with 100 grains of Hi-Vel No. 2 and a 570 grain bullet.

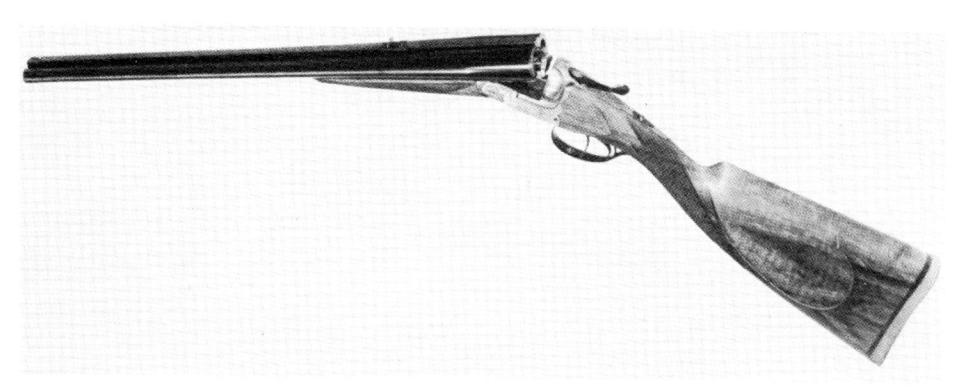

A Belgian-made double rifle for the .475 No. 2 Nitro Express cartridge built in Belgium and imported into the United States by Continental Arms Corp., 697 Fifth Avenue, New York. Belgian double rifles run about half the price of the better British doubles.

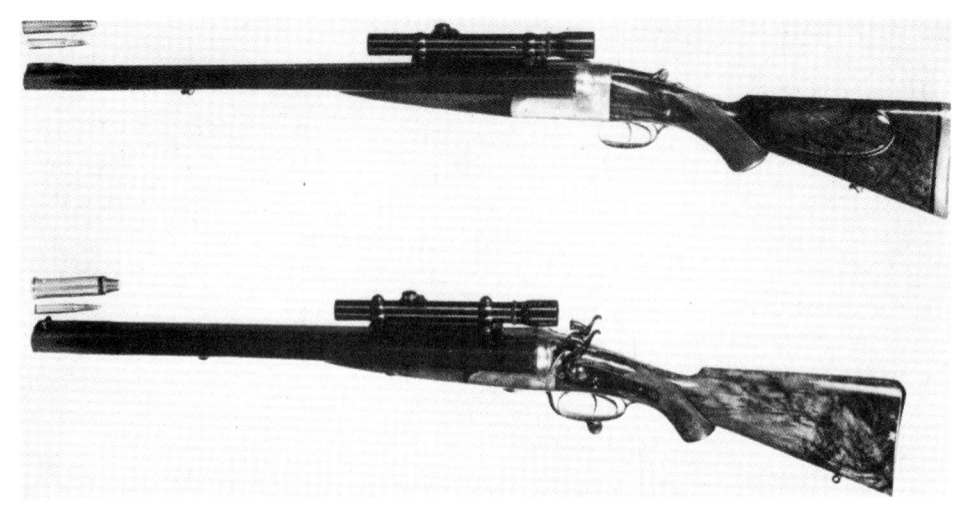

Two more heavy double rifles from the collection of Maynard Buehler. The top rifle is a .577 Nitro Express—one of the most powerful cartridges ever built and one that turns up around 7,000 pounds of muzzle energy. This rifle weighs a full 17 pounds. The cartridge is compared to that of a .30/06 in the illustration. The rifle below is a terrific 8-bore black powder rifle which is loaded with 10 drams of FG black powder and a lead bullet weighing 1,250 grains. Muzzle velocity is 1500 f.p.s. and muzzle energy 6,290 foot-pounds. The rifle gives 162 foot-pounds of free recoil, whereas the recoil of the average .30/06 sporter, which is considered quite a rifle in the United States, runs from between 16½ to 19 foot-pounds. Buehler claims he enjoys shooting it.

British sportsmen, particularly army officers who were not very well heeled, often used single-shot big-game rifles rather than doubles because they were less expensive. Here are two from the Buehler. Both are built on the Martini action. The top rifle is a .500 x .450 x 3¼ inch built by Westley Richards. It uses 140 grains of black powder with the 325 grain lead bullet for 1,950 foot-seconds of muzzle velocity and 2,745 foot-pounds of muzzle energy. The bottom rifle is a .577 x .450.

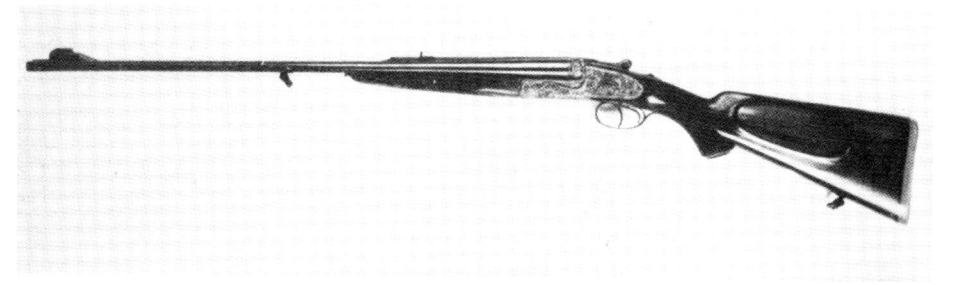

A beautiful Holland & Holland double for the British rimmed version of the .300 Magnum cartridge. This is the royal model, hammerless ejector.

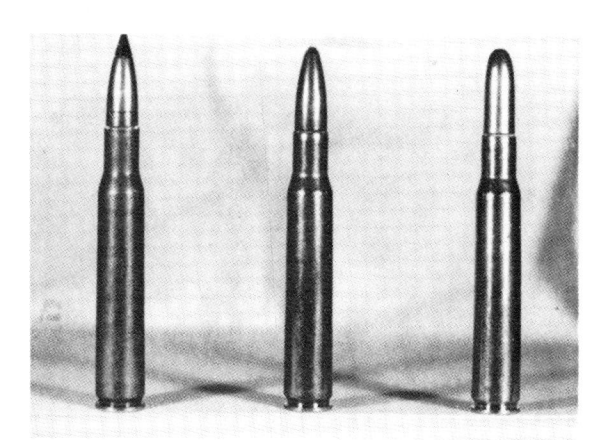

Three most popular loadings of the famous .30/06 cartridge. Left to right, they are: the 150-gr. Remington bronze point; 180-gr. Remington pointed softpoint Core-Lokt; and 220-gr. softpoint Core-Lokt.

Some good mountain-cartridges. Left to right: 7 x 57, 7 x 64, .30/06, .30/06, 7 mm. rimmed Magnum for single-shot and double rifles, .275 H. & H. Magnum, 7 mm. Weatherby Magnum, 7 mm. Mashburn long Magnum.

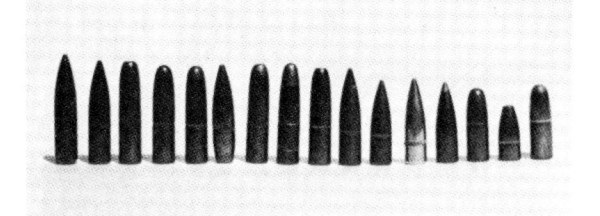

An enormous variety of bullets in .30 caliber are available for .300 Magnum rifles. These bullets are of various weights and types, ranging from 110 to 225 grains.

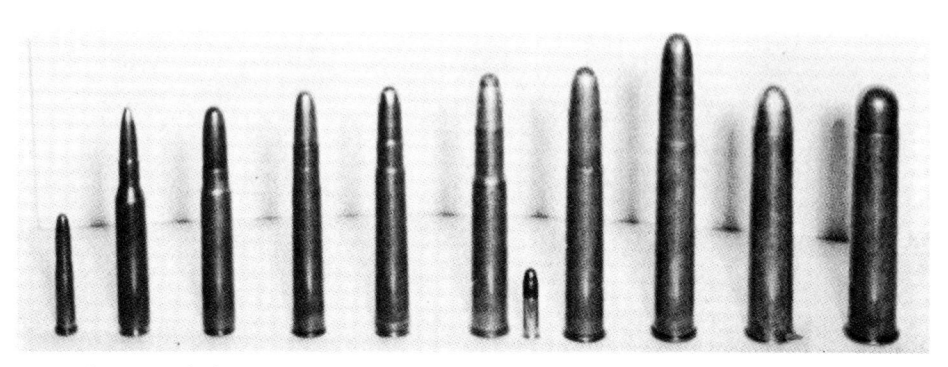

Cartridges for African use contrasted to some smaller ones. Left to right: .22 Hornet, .270 Winchester, 9.3 x 62 mm., .360 Nitro Express, .375 H. & H. Magnum, .400 Jeffrey, .22 Long Rifle, .470 Nitro Express, .475 No. 2 Nitro Express, .577 Nitro Express, and .600 Nitro Express.

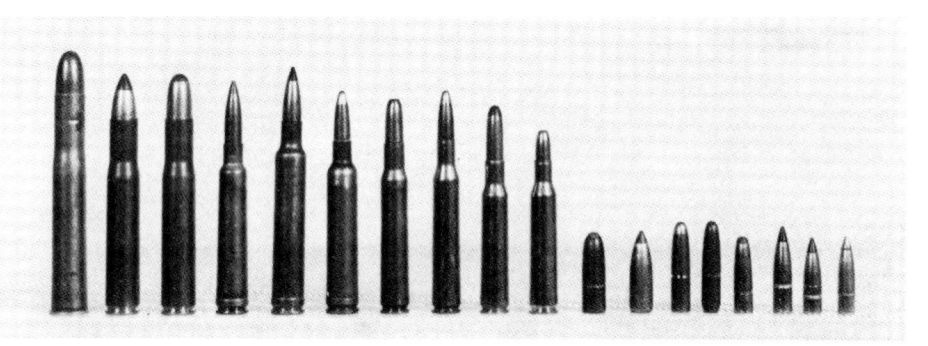

Big-game cartridges: Left to right—.470 Nitro Express, .404 Magnum for magazine rifles with spitzer softpoint bullet, .404 with round-nosed softpoint, .275 H. & H. Magnum, .300 Weatherby Magnum, .270 Weatherby Magnum, .30/06 with 220-grain bullet, .270 with 130-grain Silvertip bullet, 7 x 57, and .257. Game bullets shown are the 300-grain softpoint .375 Magnum bullet, 250-grain .375 Magnum bullet made by Fred N. Barnes of Colorado, 220-grain Winchester Silvertip in .30 caliber, and Western pinpoint bo~tail .30 caliber, 150-grain .270 softpoint, 180-grain .30 caliber Remington bronze point, 150-grain .30 caliber Remington bronze point, and 130-grain .270 Winchester pointed softpoint.

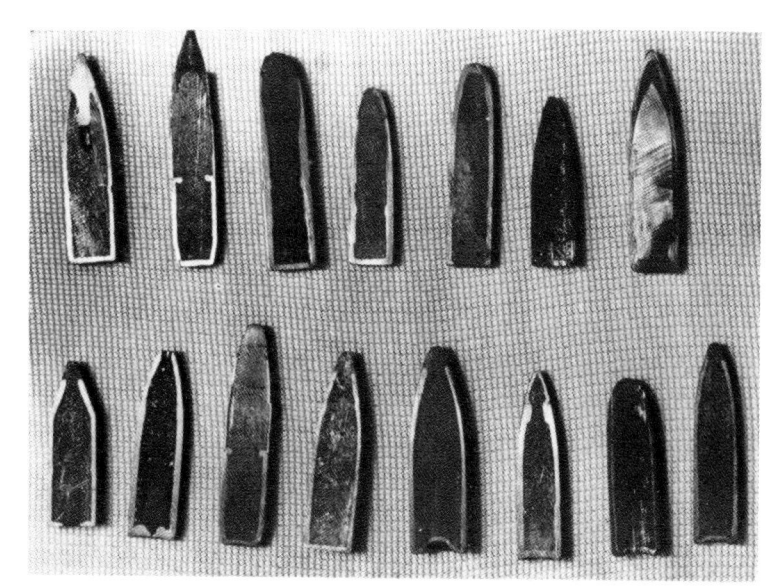

Sectioned bullets showing different types of construction. Top row, left to right: 180-grain .30 caliber Remington bronze point, German 177-grain H-jacket boattail for the 7 x 64 Mauser. Bullet has hollow copper cap, lead in forward portion is soft, rear portion alloyed very hard. 220-grain .30 caliber Remington softpoint Core-Lokt, 130-grain .270 Winchester Silvertip, 175-grain full-metal cased 7 mm., 130-grain .270 Speer softpoint, .30 caliber military armor-piercer bullet. Bottom row, left to right: 150-grain spire point Hornaday .30 caliber bullet, 172-grain openpoint .30 caliber bullet made by Western Tool & Copper Works of Oakland, California, German H-jacket boattail bullet in 8 mm. caliber, Speer spitzer softpoint 180-grain .30 caliber, Speer spitzer softpoint 250-grain .30 caliber, 130-grain .270 Winchester pointed expanding, 150-grain round-nosed full-metal cased bullet, 150-grain Speer spitzer bullet for the .270.

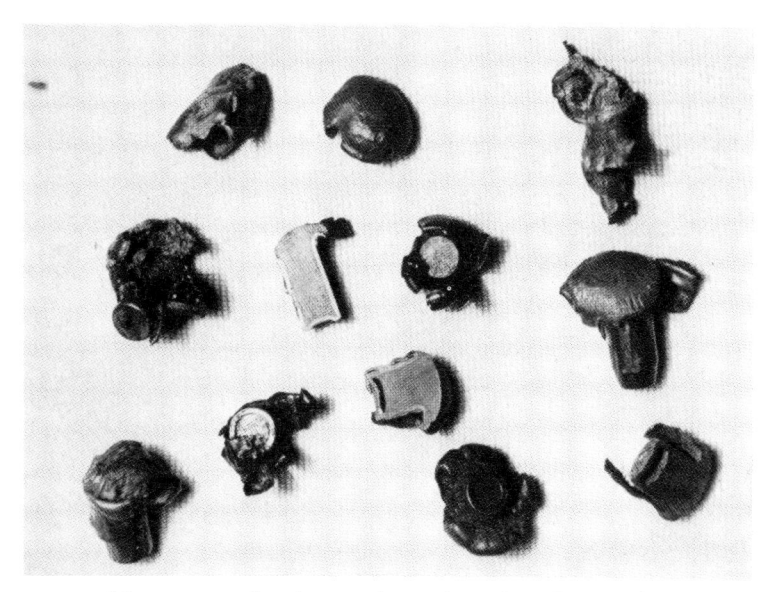

Bullets recovered from game, showing mushrooming effect. Notice that some of the bullets have shed but little of their weight and would give deep penetration. Some have pretty much gone to pieces. Such bullets will give quicker kills with chest shots on light and medium game. The boattailed bullet at the right flattened itself on the far shoulder blade of a moose after penetrating through ribs and lung cavity.

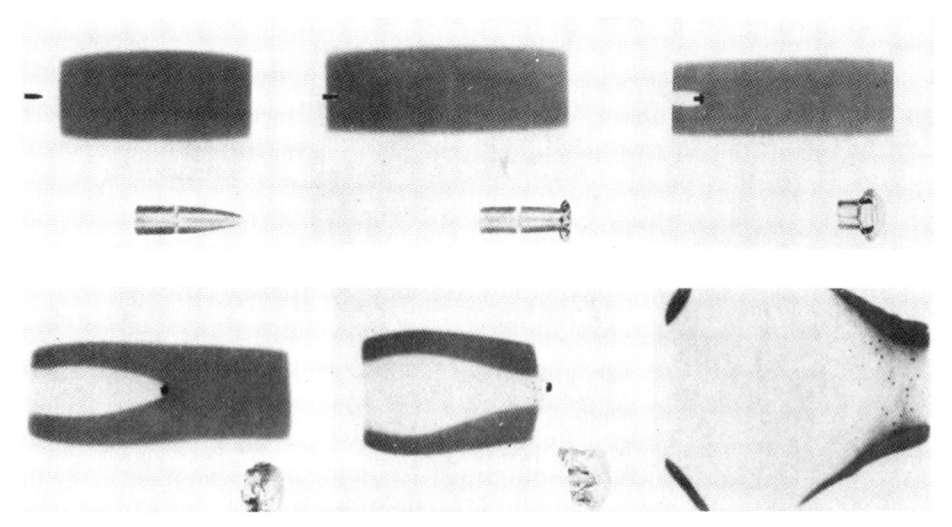

A series of photos showing the action of the Remington pointed softpoint Core-Lokt in gelatin blocks that approximate animal flesh. That bullet, which I have used, gives very deep and reliable penetration.

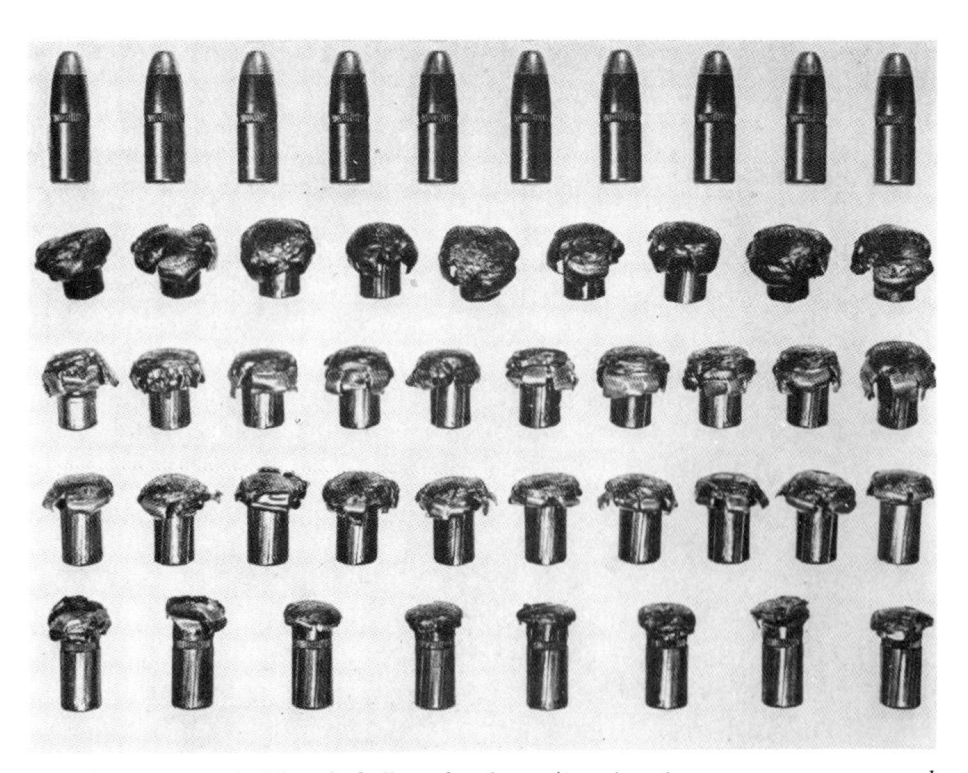

Winchester 150-grain Silvertip bullets, showing uniformity of upset at 50, 100, 200, and 300 yards.

The late Alvin Linden, shown with a pattern sheet drawn for one of his fine booklets on restocking rifles. Rifle nuts suffered a severe loss when Linden died, because he was one of the most original and versatile stock makers ever to practice the trade in the United States.

The author (center) kibitzing while a Winchester Model 70 is assembled at the Winchester factory.

Alvin Biesen, crack gunsmith and stock maker, at work in his basement shop at his home in Spokane, Washington.

Bluing department of Weatherby's, Incorporated.

Checking a Weatherby stock, apparently of mesquite wood. Photo shows guide lines for checking pattern.

Stocker at Weatherby's fitting trigger guard and floor plate assembly into stock.

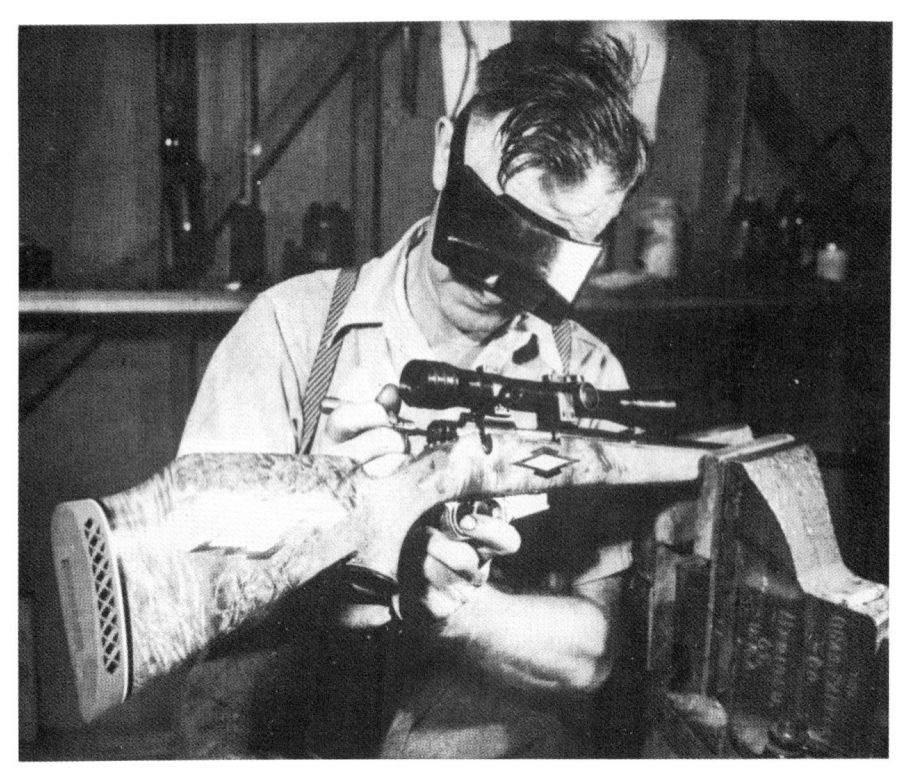

Workman making final adjustments on custom-made Weatherby sporter.

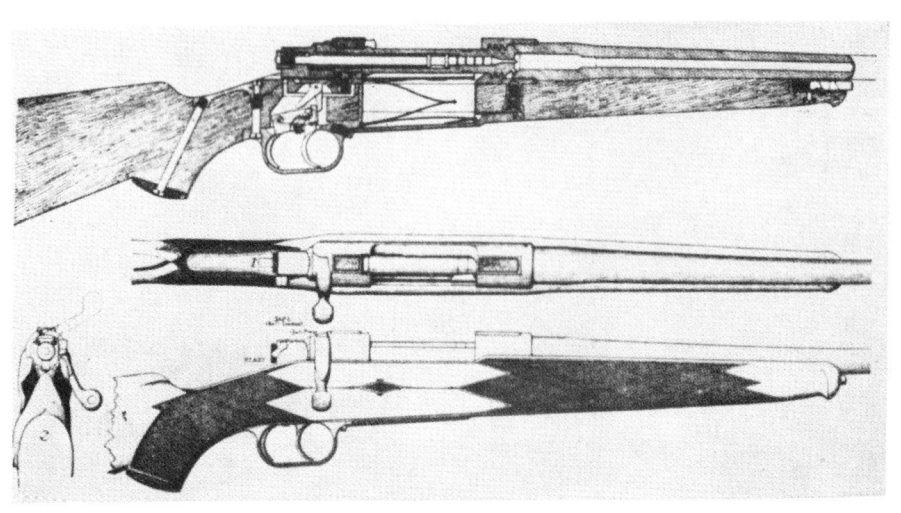

The Newton rifle had many original and excellent features of design, although because of production and financial difficulties the Newton Company was never able to manufacture any great number.

Stocks for Weatherby sporters are first shaped and inletted by expensive and complicated machinery. Afterwards they are finally fitted and shaped up by handwork, but the machine inletting and shaping saves many hours of expensive hand labor.

Roy Burch, top barrel-man at Weatherby's, straightening barrel with overhead clamp.

The late Alvin Linden inletting a walnut plank for barrel and action of a sporting rifle. Linden used no machine-shaped and inletted blanks, but did all his work by hand.

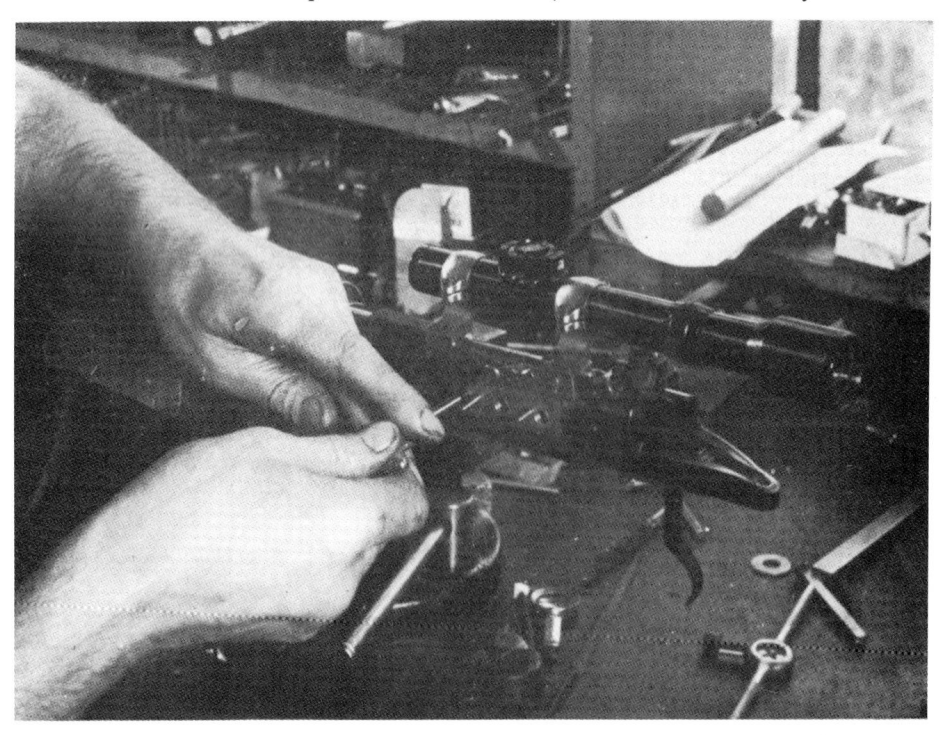

Fitting the base of a Griffin & Howe side telescope mount to rifle in the shop of **Griffin & Howe** *of New York.*

Engraving an action in the shop of Griffin & Howe of New York.

Adjusting for elevation a Stith 4-x Bear Cub. Both windage and elevation are within the tube of the scope. It is mounted by a Griffin & Howe mount.

Adjusting elevation with a Lyman 48 receiver sight. With its quickly removable slide a Lyman 48 is an excellent bet for a rifle on which scope and iron sights are to be interchanged quickly.

A Weaver K-4 scope on a fine Winchester Model 70 restocked by Pachmayr Gun Works of Los Angeles, and fitted with the Pachmayr Lo-Swing mount.

The base portion of a Stith Master Mount on a Remington Model 721. This mount enables the same scope to be used on as many rifles as bases are available for, since all windage and elevation adjustments are in the mount.

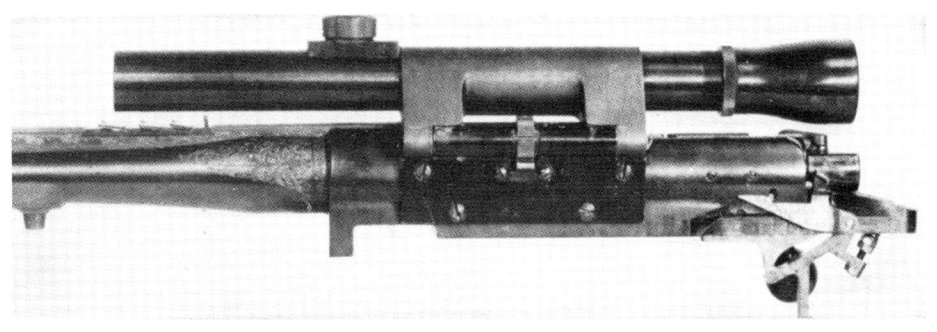

The Pachmayr Lo-Swing mount fitted to the side of the receiver of a Winchester Model 70 rifle, showing the rigid attachment of the form-fitting base, and the knurled finger-wheel to remove upper portion of mount. This mount is a great favorite in Alaska, where it is often necessary to get a fogged or waterlogged scope quickly out of the way.

When the hunter is actually doing his hunting on horseback, the best place to carry the saddle scabbard is on the left side, with the butt to the rear and at an angle of about 45 degrees. Since the hunter gets off the horse on the left side, he has only to reach back with his right hand, grab the rifle by the small of the grip and yank it out. Carried this way, the butt pointed up, the rifle will not fall out of the saddle scabbard and the scabbard itself will not fill up with brush and twigs as happens if the open part of the scabbard is pointed forward. Furthermore, the hunter does not have to make a grab for the butt of his rifle by the horse's head, something which often spooks a jittery horse. In much of the West, where timber is not too thick and the country not too rough, deer are commonly hunted from horseback.

Here is an excellent scabbard made by the Schoellkopf Company of Dallas, Texas. The stiff leather boot protects the butt of the rifle from scratches by brush and twigs and keeps the scabbard itself from filling up with twigs and debris. In the northern Rockies the horse is usually ridden out to the point where the stalk is begun, and the hunter almost never hunts from horseback. The scabbard is ordinarily carried on the right side with the butt forward because then the weight is right on the cinch and does not pull the saddle over to the right. A rifle carried in this position is worthless where game is actually jumped from horseback; it takes too long to get the rifle out of the scabbard.

Here is another excellent saddle scabbard with an attached flexible boot which zips up to enclose the butt or which can be folded back and tied down by strings on the scabbard. The picture was taken in northern British Columbia.

Showing the adjustment of a one-piece Whelen-type sling. Here is the loop through which the upper left arm is thrust. The two keepers will keep the sling snugly in position. Swivels are of the quick-detachable Winchester type.

Robert Chadfield-Taylor of New York and San Francisco, taking it easy on his horse in southern Arizona and hopefully looking over a canyon below him for deer. Notice how the rifle is carried.

Bradford O'Connor taking a shot at a caribou in the Atlin district of northwest British Columbia. For greater steadiness he is resting his rifle on a rolled-up Eddie Bauer down jacket. Note the leather cartridge box, which holds a full box of cartridges, at his belt.

The sitting position is the queen of hunting positions, and with a tight sling it is almost as steady as prone. Notice here that the flat of the left arm is well over the knee against the flat part of the shin. The sling is high on the upper arm and the left hand jammed hard against the swivels. The rifle is a custom-made .270 on an F. N. Mauser action built by Alvin Biesen and equipped with Lyman 48 receiver sight with a Stith Bear Cub scope on Griffin & Howe mount.

Sitting position without sling. Body is bent well forward and left elbow is well forward of the left knee. Forend of rifle rests against the heel of the left hand.

A good offhand position, particularly for a long shot. For running game the left hand should be farther forward on the forend.

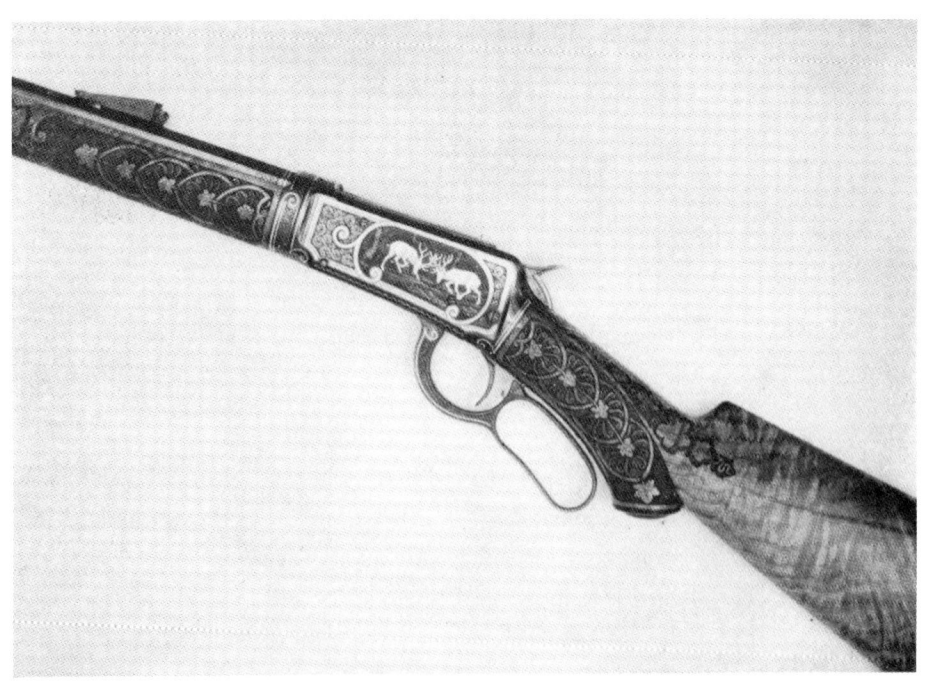

A beautiful and highly decorated Winchester Model 1886.

A running deer target at the Lewiston Gun Club, Lewiston, Idaho. This running target is only 60 yards away, yet the man who gets in the black usually wins a turkey. Most shots are behind.

The Montana mount shown here with a Unertl 4-x Hawk scope on a Model 70 Winchester is a quickly detachable yet very strong and rigid mount.

Bradford O'Connor sighting in a rifle from a bench rest, shooting over a sandbag.

Montana mount on that old favorite deer hunter's rifle, the Model 94 Winchester. Because of the top ejection the scope is, of course, offset to the left.

A Weaver K-4 scope on a beautiful Model 70 Winchester in .257 restocked by the Pachmayr Gun Works of Los Angeles. Mount is the Pachmayr Lo-Swing mount.

Two-piece Buehler top mount with a Lyman 4-x Challenger scope on a Winchester Model 70. The Buehler mount is an excellent one when the rifle is to be permanently equipped with a scope.

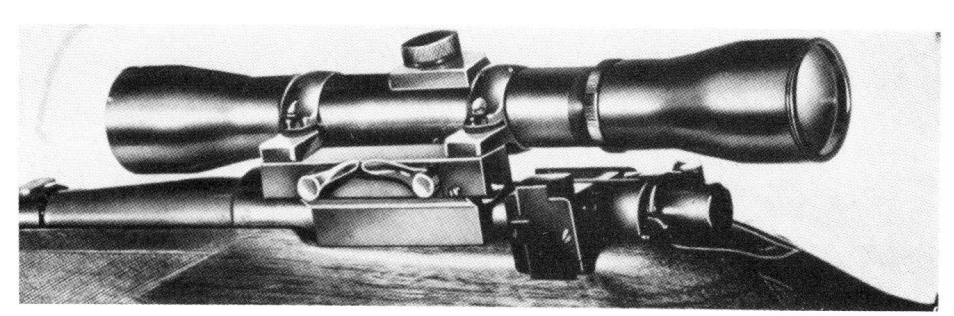

Model 70 Winchester rifle fitted with a Lyman 4-x Challenger scope with a Griffin & Howe double-lever, quick-detachable side mount—one of the earliest successful American mounts, and one that has been used all over the world for almost a generation.

This picture is typical of the African plains country in British East Africa. The safari wagon is shown and hunters are hanging a topi in a tree for lion bait.

This American hunter killed this black-maned African lion with a .300 Weatherby Magnum which is rapidly winning a reputation as an African plains rifle for dangerous, soft-skinned game.

The zebra of British East Africa is as large as a small horse and takes plenty of killing.

Roy E. Weatherby, rifle manufacturer, with an African water buck shot with the .300 Weatherby Magnum rifle which the gunbearer is carrying.

A shot of the open "bush" in British East Africa where much game is found. Notice that the tall grass would make a prone shot impossible and a sitting shot very difficult. In country of this sort most shots must be taken offhand.

Ralph Hammer of Redlands, California, with a rare Hunter's antelope shot at 350 yards with the .300 Weatherby Magnum, using a 180-grain bullet.

A big bull eland is as large as a Jersey bull. This one was shot with a .300 Weatherby Magnum by Mr. Hammer.

Ethel Hammer with an African wart hog that was shot at 150 yards with a .300 Weatherby Magnum.

This fine rhino, a thick-skinned and truculent beast, was killed by Ralph Hammer with a .450 Watts Magnum using the 500-grain full-metal cased Barnes bullets with 75 grs. of 4895 powder. The .450 Watts Magnum is an American wildcat as far as ballistics goes, on the order of the big British double elephant rifles.

This hunter is taking a rest on a tree for a long shot in the East African bush.

This small African antelope could easily be taken with a .25/35 or even a .25/20.

The Hammers with a record-class topi shot in Africa. This animal has 20½-inch horns. The world-record horns are 22 inches.

Mrs. Ethel Hammer's tremendous bull elephant, with tusks weighing 103 and 105 pounds.

This is a terrific African trophy—an enormous bull elephant with tusks weighing 126 and 136 pounds. It was shot by the Hammers on their African expedition.

Mr. and Mrs. Ralph Hammer of Redlands, California, with a male lion shot with a .375.

A fine Urial or Shapo ram (Ovis vignei) shot in Iran by Colonel Afgani of the Iranian army. He used an 8 x 57 Mauser. The Urial is one of the smaller Asiatic sheep, much smaller than the big Argalis. It is a magnificent trophy. (RIGHT) Colonel Afgani and guides with two Urial rams.

The author's best desert mule deer. This big buck was taken about 200 miles south of the American border in Sonora and only about 20 miles from the sea. It was shot at about 70 yards with a .270 Winchester with a 130-grain Silvertip bullet.

Bradford O'Connor, right, and guide Harry Johnson of Atlin, British Columbia, measuring the head of a tremendous caribou shot by Bradford in 1951. It is No. 4 in the world's records.

Jerry and Bradford O'Connor warming their hands over an ironwood fire in late December on the Sonora desert while Ivon Nelson of Tucson, Arizona, looks on. Both desert mule deer and desert whitetail deer were taken on this trip.

Iranian hunters really pile them up when they get the chance. When they got into this herd of ibex they shot nannies as well as billies.

Frank Golata, the famous Stone sheep guide of Dawson Creek, British Columbia, with a black bear shot by Dr. Wilson DuComb, of Carlisle, Illinois.

A good Rocky Mountain mule deer shot with a .257 by Eleanor O'Connor in northern Arizona.

Guide with a fine Rocky Mountain mule deer killed in the north Kaibab of Arizona in 1934 by the author. Rifle used was a .30/06 Springfield using the 150-grain Remington bronze point factory load.

This fine Arizona whitetail buck was shot with the 130-grain Winchester pointed expanding bullet from the author's old .270. The Arizona whitetail is one of the smartest and most beautiful of all North American deer, and this fellow has an exceptional head.

A scene from Arizona's annual buffalo "hunt." Notice the rounded-up herd standing in the background. In spite of its size the buffalo does not seem to carry much lead.

A very old picture from Alaska taken back in the days when the limit in Alaska on Dall sheep was three rams per hunter. The hunter at left is apparently armed with a Mannlicher-Schoenauer, the tough-looking character at the right has a Model 95 Winchester lever-action. Four out of the five rams should have been passed up. Only the one at the extreme left is a trophy ram—and he is nothing to write home about.

Jack O'Connor with a Wyoming bighorn shot at about 200 yards from across the canyon with a .270 using the 130-grain bullet.

Red Early of Hunt, Texas, with a fine desert bighorn ram killed in northern Sonora, Mexico, with a .300 Magnum.

Jack O'Connor with a good Stone ram shot off the Prophet River in the northern British Columbia Rockies in 1946. The head measured 15¼ by 41½ when it was thoroughly dried out, and is No. 10 in world records. Rifle used was a .270 stocked by Bob Owen. Load was the 130-grain Winchester expanding bullet with 49.5 grains of No. 4064 powder.

O'Connor lining up on a couple of bull caribou in northern British Columbia.

O'Connor with an Osborn Caribou shot on the Caribou Range out of Richards Creek in northern British Columbia in 1946.

Roy Hargreaves, guide and outfitter, of Mt. Robson, British Columbia, with a big grizzly shot in Alberta by Jack O'Connor in 1943.

A pack outfit coming down the hillside into a creek bottom in northern British Columbia.

An antelope, shot in New Mexico, with a record head.

Eleanor O'Connor with a fine buck antelope head that measured almost 17 inches around the curl. It was shot in northern Arizona with a scope-sighted .257 and the 100-grain bullet.

Roy Hargreaves skinning out a caribou head in the Copton Creek country of Alberta.

Roy Hargreaves is holding the head of an Alberta bighorn shot with the .270 and the 130-grain bullet by Jack O'Connor in 1943. Head measured 15½ by 39½.

A very fine Stone sheep shot by Major James Workman, Belfast, Ireland, in British Columbia's Cassiar country in 1931. The head measured 13¼ x 44¼.

Bradford O'Connor with his first ram, a handsome little Fannin killed in the Eva Lake country of northwest British Columbia.

Herb Klein of Dallas, Texas (left) and Jack O'Connor shown with two very fine Dall sheep heads taken in the Yukon in 1950. Klein's head measured 47½ inches on the right horn.

These big mountain caribou are almost as large as bull elk and make beautiful trophies. These two were "shot" with a Super Ikonta B.

It is on little jack camps like this that the game is usually got. The photo shows Bradford O'Connor alongside two Fannin sheep heads while Harry Johnson and Watson Smarch, guides, finish their supper.

The present world record Stone sheep, shot by L. S. Chadwick of Cleveland, Ohio, on Lapp Creek, which flows into the Prophet River in northern British Columbia.

A Canadian bighorn with a fine, rugged, and massive head shot in Alberta. The photo is by F. H. Riggall.

The Whitehorse Inn in Whitehorse, Yukon Territory, the jumping-off place for many big game expeditions. The picture shows Alex Davis of Whitehorse, famous Yukon outfitter, with his truck. Odin Hogan, the cook, is sitting in the truck and Red Early of Hunt, Texas, one of the author's hunting companions, is beside him.

Jack O'Connor (left) with a fine Dall ram shot in the Yukon in 1950 with the .30/06 and the 150-grain bullet. The head measures 15 x 43⅝. It is extraordinarily heavy and massive for a Dall sheep head and is one of the great Dall sheep trophies of all time. This ram was hit first at 65 yards and went down at about 85 yards.

A herd of bighorn rams in the southern Alberta Rockies. The photo is by F. H. Riggall.

Vernon Speer, bullet manufacturer, with bull moose shot with the .35 Whelen and 250-grain bullet of his own manufacture.

Eleanor O'Connor shot this young buck mule deer in northern Arizona. It was a one-shot kill with a .257 at 250 yards.

Bradford O'Connor leveling down on a caribou bull in northwest British Columbia in 1951.

A typical prewar British magazine rifle. This is by Jeffery. It is built on a square-bridge Magnum Mauser action imported from Germany and has a whole parade of open sight leaves on a short rib. Ramp front sight is also typically British.

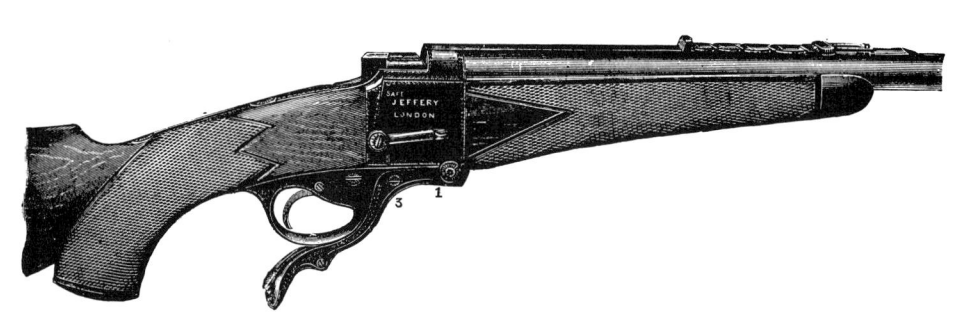

A Jeffery single shot built on the strong British Farquharson falling block action. These single shots were made for all rimmed cartridges for the .22 Savage Hi-Power to the .600 Nitro Express.

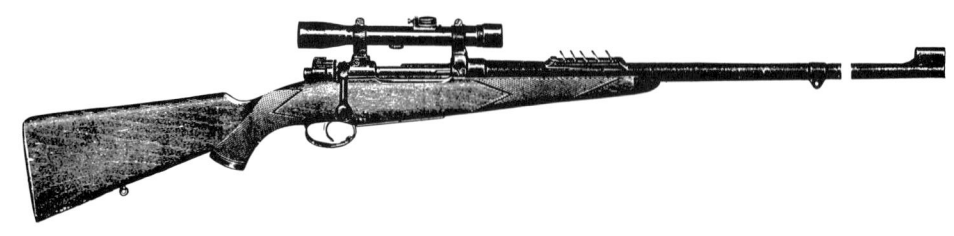

A Jeffery magazine rifle showing the typical British and Continental way of mounting a scope, high to clear the unaltered bolt-handle and with a tunnel to peer through at the open sights.

Breaking camp in the Yukon. Hunter's bedrolls and duffle bags are laid out in front of the cook tent and rifles of the three hunters are piled up in the foreground of the picture.

A man doesn't necessarily have to be young to hunt sheep. This nice Fannin ram was killed by Dr. E. G. Braddock (left) of Lewiston, Idaho, in 1951 when Doc was 70 years old. A horse could be ridden clear to the top of this particular mountain.

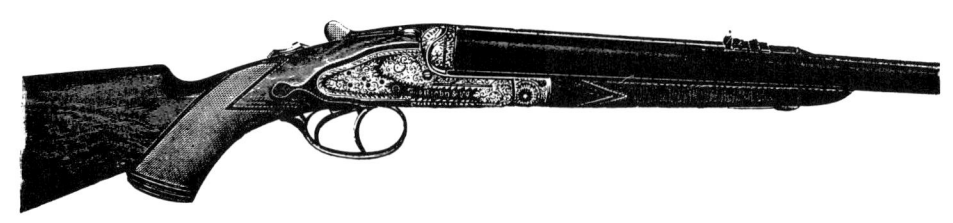

A Rigby best quality double rifle.

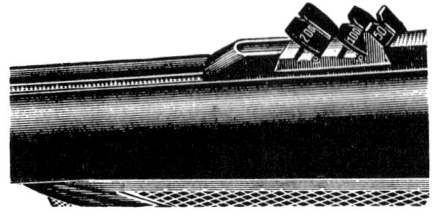

Close up of sight leaves on double rifle, for 50, 100, and 200 yards.

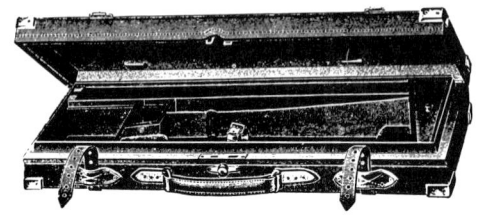

A British oak-and-sole leather case for a double rifle.

It is the British and Continental practice to bring out rimmed versions of rimless cartridges designed for magazine rifles. They are used in doubles, in falling block single shots, and in that German specialty, the three-barrel gun or "Drilling." The first three cartridges illustrated (left to right) are the 7 x 57-R, 8 x 57-R, and 9 x 57-R, rimmed counterparts of the Mauser 7 x 57, 8 x 57, and 9 x 57 cartridges. The next cartridge is the 9.3 x 74-R, a powerful cartridge for use on soft-skinned dangerous game and a favorite for double rifles. The last is the 9.3 x 72-R, much used for the rifle barrel in three-barrel guns. It is a black-powder and low-pressure smokeless job.

The old black-powder cartridges were displaced by those designed for smokeless powder. Here are some old-time favorites (left to right): .38/72, .45/90, .45/70, .38/55, .40/65. The .405 W.C.F. cartridge was a smokeless-powder job for the Model 95 lever action Winchester, but it plainly shows the effect of black-powder case design. Until the advent of the .375 H. & H. Magnum, it was, with its 300-gr. bullet at 2200 f.p.s., the most powerful of American factory-loaded cartridges.

Original Mauser Magazine Sporting Rifle, Type K, pattern No. 176

Original Mauser Magazine Sporting Rifle, Type B, pattern No. 40

Original Mauser Magazine Sporting Rifle, Type A, pattern No. 1
with standard and four leaves' sight

Mauser catalog illustrations showing genuine Mauser rifles made at the Mauser Werke with three lengths of actions and in different styles. The rifle at the top has the short or K action. It is suitable for such cartridges as the .250/3000, .35 Remington, .300 Savage, and in Germany was made in .250/3000, and in 6.5 and 8 mm. Short. The middle rifle has the standard length Model 98 action used in 7 x 57, 8 x 57, 9 x 57, etc., and adaptable to the .270 and .30/06. Stock is typically German. The bottom rifle is on the long square-bridge Magnum Mauser action. The Mauser people used it for such cartridges as the .280 Ross and .404 Magnum. The British imported it for their Magnum magazine rifles, as did Hoffman, Griffin & Howe, and Neidner in the United States. The stock shown here is designed to please the British market.

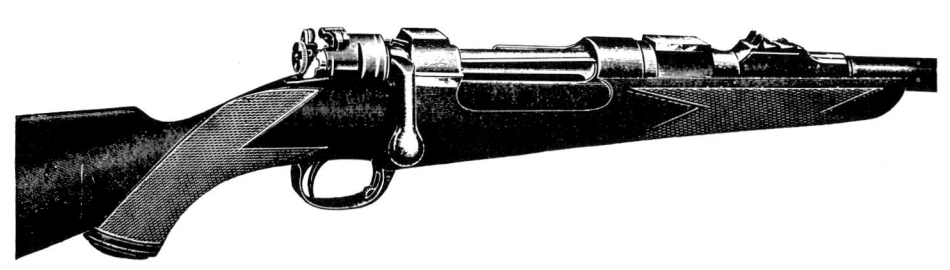

British magazine rifle built on Magnum Mauser action, showing details of action, with release button for hinged floor plate in forward part of trigger guard.

Herb Klein of Dallas, Texas, and a big 58-inch Alaska moose shot in the Yukon in 1950.

Here Watson Smarch congratulates Bradford O'Connor on a fine billy shot in the Cassiar district of northern British Columbia. The North American Rocky Mountain white goat is a fine and interesting trophy and one that in spite of his moderate size carries a lot of lead. Bradford used a .270 with the 130-grain Dominion semi-spitzer softpoint bullet.

An Indian hill tiger shot by Dr. Curt von Wedel, of Oklahoma City.

A little southwestern javelina weighs only about 40 to 55 pounds on the hoof but it is an interesting and fairly rare trophy.

Arthur Popham, Kansas City attorney, with a big grizzly shot with a blown-out .300 Magnum and the 180-grain bullet.

PROBLEMS OF THE SADDLE RIFLE

of three or four seconds. Often such speed in getting into action is all that will get a man his game.

In the northern Rockies it is very seldom that a man actually hunts from horseback. Instead he simply rides out to where he is going to hunt, ties his horse and hunts on foot. It is seldom that he will have to get off and shoot immediately as Northern game seldom lies tight and jumps suddenly as a deer will do. Our Nothern hunter, then, does not need to be able to get off his horse and go into action immediately. He is simply using his horse as a means of transportation for himself and his rifle. Since most Northern horses are of work stock, heavy, round-backed, and ill-adapted to carrying a saddle, it is not advisable to carry the rifle on the left side, butt to the rear, as I have described. If the heavy rifle is so carried it will pull the saddle over to the left. It will make riding uncomfortable and it will be hard on the horse's back. The best place to carry a rifle under those circumstances is on the right side, butt to the front, with the muzzle angling sharply down. In this way most of the weight is on the cinch. The rifle has a tendency to pull the saddle to the right, but the hunter, every time he gets off or on, has a tendency, because of his weight on the saddle, to pull the saddle to the left and the two things more or less balance each other and make the saddle tend to ride on an even keel. Furthermore, even if a fairly quick shot is offered, those phlegmatic Northern plugs are not easily buggered and they don't seem to mind if a man runs around their head and grabs a rifle—something which would drive a hot-blooded Southwestern horse crazy.

It is very seldom that one runs into a genuinely good saddle scabbard in a sporting goods store, one suitable for a scope-sighted bolt-action rifle, and the best way of acquiring a suitable scabbard is to take up the matter with a good saddle maker. The average factory produced scabbard is too short and too skimpy to carry the average rifle with a telescopic sight. It should be made of good stout saddle skirting leather and it should be long enough so that it covers the rifle about halfway along the stock.

Particulars of Original Mauser Magazine Sporting Rifles and Ammunition

English Measurements

Designation of Rifle and Cartridge		Mauser .354 5	Mauser .366 6	Mauser .423 7	Savage .250/3000 * 8	Ross * Rimless .280 9	U.S.A. 1906 .300 * 10	W.R. Express .318 * 11	Eley .404 * 12
Length of barrel of rifle	inch.	23.60	23.60	23.60	21.60	23.60	23.60	23.60	23.60
" " carbine	inch.	19.70	—	—	—	—	19.70	—	—
Total length of rifle	inch.	44.80	44.80	44.80	40.30	45.30	45	45	45
" " carbine	inch.	40.80	—	—	—	—	41	—	—
Weight of rifle	lb.	7.15	7.3	7.5	5.95	7.7	7.4	7.7	8.2
" " carbine	lb.	6.85	—	—	—	—	6.85	—	—
Weight of bullet	grains	247	285	347	87	150	150	250	400
" " powder	grains	46.3	54	64.8	—	—	53.5	—	82
" " cartridge	grains	455	502	602	278	467	383	475	748
Length of cartridge	inch.	3.03	3.29	3.23	2.52	3.449	3.331	3.523	3.504
" " bullet	inch.	1.102	1.181	1.044	.85	1.228	1.095	1.495	1.165
Muzzle velocity (V_0)	f. s.	2296	2346	2313	3080	2870	3000	2230	2160
" energy (E_0)	f. lb.	2885	3486	4123	1840	2710	2980	2700	4173
Height of trajectory 100 m.	inch.	1.025	.922	.922	.60	.70	.60	.98	.86
at a range of 200 m.	inch.	4.60	4.40	4.55	2.4	2.59	2.4	4.13	3.9
300 m.	inch.	11.70	10.67	11.40	6.3	7.0	6.3	8.74	10.0

* To comply with the demand emanating from countries where Mauser cartridges are sometimes not easy to obtain, we are making our rifles also for the following cartridges: .250/3000 Savage, .280 Ross rimless, .300 U. S. 1906, .318 W. R. and .404 Eley. Rifles cal. .280, .318 and .404 are made in type A only.

Page from Mauser catalog giving ballistic data on cartridges for which Mauser rifles were made for export.

Ballistics of Holland & Holland Rifles

MAGAZINE RIFLES

Description of Cartridge	Types of Bullets Available	Muzzle Velocity ft. per sec.	Muzzle Energy ft. lb.	100 Yards Velocity in ft. per sec.	100 Yards Energy in ft.-lb.
.240 Belted Rimless............100 gr.	Semi-pointed soft-nosed	2900	1870	2652	1560
.275 Magnum Belted Rimless....160 gr.	Semi-pointed soft-nosed	2675	2550	2439	2120
.30 Super Rimless............150 gr.	Semi-pointed soft-nosed	3000	3000	2698	2425
" " ....180 gr.	Soft-nosed	2700	2915	2426	2355
" " ....220 gr.	Soft-nosed	2350	2700	2141	2242
.375 Magnum Belted Rimless....235 gr.	Copper-pointed	2800	4090	2535	3360
" " ....270 gr.	Semi-pointed soft-nosed Solid	2650	4210	2415	3496
" " ....300 gr.	Soft-nosed, or W.R. Capped Soft-nosed	2500	4070	2253	3390
.375 * Flanged Nitro-Express 2½-inch case ..270 gr.	Solid Soft-nosed	1975	2340	1760	1860
.400/.375 * Rimless H. & H. Schonauer....270 gr.	Solid	2175	2840	1930	2235

* For old pattern rifles.

Page from catalog of Holland & Holland, London, showing ballistics of cartridges for which the company makes magazine rifles. Notice that in England, the .300 Magnum (or .300 Super as Holland & Holland has always called it) is loaded to exactly the same ballistics as the .30/06 is in the United States.

Such a scabbard protects the butt from bad scratches from twigs and brush, and it protects the telescopic sight from rain and snow. It is necessary, usually, to get a scabbard custom made to fit the individual rifle. The scabbard must fit the rifle. Particularly if there is much over-hang to the scope and the scope is wedged into the scabbard with the weight of the rifle on it, the mount may bend and change point of impact. This is particularly true of side mounts.

The Northern hunter who uses his horse simply as transportation, and often uses the side mount, can well remove the scope and carry it in his saddle bags when he is on horseback. It is almost never that he will get a quick shot that does not give him time enough to put the scope back on. If he should, he can use his iron sights. The Southwestern or Western horseback hunter, though, needs the lowest, strongest top mount for his scope that he can get. Perfectly satisfactory ones are the Stith Streamline, Redfield, Tilden, or Buehler. They are strong and rigid, they protect the scope well and are in every way satisfactory. I have used all of them on horseback. The strongest and most rigid of the side mounts and one which is entirely suitable for horseback hunting is the Noske side mount made by R. Noske of San Carlos, California. I have a Noske mount on an ancient .270 that I have carried thousands of miles on horseback. It has never given me the slightest trouble.

For the average horseback hunter, then, the recipe is a fairly light rifle with a fairly short 21- or 22-inch barrel fitted with a good solidly mounted scope of 4 or 6-x and chambered for a high velocity flat-shooting cartridge like the .30/06, .270, or 7 mm. or even one of the fast stepping .270 or 7 mm. wildcats. Great weight should be avoided in the saddle rifle. So should bolt handles that stick out too far, such as those on the Model 1917 Enfield, the Remington Model 30, and the FN Mauser.

As another tip, the rifle should not be carried in a scabbard with a sling on, and as a consequence the saddle rifle should be fitted with quickly detachable swivels so the sling can be removed and carried in the saddle bags. If the sling is left on it will, in spite of hell and high water, work out of the scabbard and the loop will eventually catch on a limb and jerk the rifle out. I have violated the rule myself, and I have had rifles go clattering to the ground as a consequence.

CHAPTER X

Rifles and Cartridges for Heavy, Soft-Skinned Game

THERE is very little heavy game in North America (or at least heavy game in the Old World sense) and as a consequence most of this chapter will be devoted to rifles and cartridges for use on the plains and in the open scrub of Africa.

Large North American animals (large only in the North American sense) are the moose, Alaska brown bear, grizzly, and polar bear. The big Alaska moose found from northern British Columbia to the limit of trees in Alaska will often weigh 1,400 or 1,500 pounds. Brown bear from Kodiak Island and the Alaska peninsula may occasionally weigh as much as 1,500, and now and then a polar bear, which is larger than usually believed, will be almost as heavy. The grizzly hardly belongs in this classification from the standpoint of size, since it is a rare grizzly that will weigh over 600 pounds. Old *Ursus horriblis* is a tough customer, though, and he has probably chewed up more people than the brown bear, so we'll include him here for his disposition, if for no other reason.

Some writers have made an attempt to put elk in this classification, but although the elk, like any other animal, will carry a lot of poorly-placed lead, he is not difficult to kill with rifles of the .270–.30/06 class. I have shot several elk with a .270, and in every case where I placed the first shot in the heart-lung area, I had a one-shot kill. A friend and hunting companion of mine,

Dr. E. G. Braddock, of Lewiston, Idaho, is a passionate varmint shot who shoots almost every week of the year when chucks, hawks, crows, and magpies are out. He is able to place his shots well and has killed several elk with a .257 Roberts and the 100-grain bullet.

Actually there might be some argument about placing moose in this class also, because although the moose is a large and substantial animal he seems to be easily hurt and will ordinarily go off and lie down even with a fairly superficial wound and he can then be followed up and finished off. Particularly for the American who hunts in the Canadian north, in northern British Columbia and the Yukon, there isn't much reason to carry an especially heavy rifle for moose, because at the time the big bulls are hunted in late August and early September they are ordinarily above timberline, sometimes miles from timber, and even if they cannot be knocked down with the first shot they will be in sight long enough to absorb two or three other bullets. I have shot only about a half-dozen moose. I have seen about the same number killed. I have never seen a moose killed in his tracks with one shot. From my own experience, then, it would seem that a rifle of the .30/06 or .270 class will almost never knock a moose down in his tracks with a shot in the heart-lung area the way the same rifle would smack over a deer, sheep or even an elk. I have had many good moose hunters tell me that my experience is exceptional and that they have killed many moose instantly with one shot with rifles of both calibers. I can only accept their testimony, in spite of the fact that this seems strange to me, as I have never put a poorly-placed bullet into a moose.

Back in 1945, Myles Brown and I were riding along with a couple of Indians and a jackcamp outfit on our way from our main camp where Harris Creek runs into the Generc River in the Yukon to where we were going to set up a jackcamp to hunt sheep on Moose Horn Creek near the foot of Mt. Nazahat. As our little pack outfit wound around through the buck brush and willow above timberline on a caribou barren, I saw something

THE BIG-GAME RIFLE

brown and furry-looking sticking up out of the willows about a quarter of a mile ahead. I signaled for Myles to stop, got off the horse and took out my binoculars. I had wondered if this brown fuzzy object were a grizzly bear, but the glass showed me that what I had seen was the top of the antlers of a big bull moose still in velvet. A closer look showed he had a companion with him.

Myles and I stopped the pack train and held a council of war. I wanted an Alaska moose and at this time the antlers were hard enough so that the velvet could be stripped off of them. Myles was somewhat less enthusiastic because he had killed many large moose. We agreed, though, to sneak up and look them over and if they were exceptional to pop them off. We got into position about 100–125 yards from them, then I shouted to get them to their feet. Both were exceptionally fine bulls when they got up and took off on their long legs. I shot rapidly and put three 130-grain .270 bullets right through the lungs of my moose before he staggered and went down. One of the guides yelled: "That last shot got him!" as he fell. Actually it was nothing of the sort. All three shots were in the lungs and what got the moose was the cumulative effect of the three shots and not the one shot.

Myles's moose was hit only once, through the paunch with a 220-grain .30/06 bullet. It had given no indication of being hit and the guides were inclined to believe that he had escaped the fusillade unscathed. We were able to watch him run for about a mile since we were on a ridge and the whole country was spread out before us. Finally he went to a little lake surrounded by a thick and narrow band of willows and lay down right by the water's edge. The Indians then decided that he had been hit, so Myles and one of the guides took off after him while I watched with the glass. Presently they kicked him out of his sanctuary. Myles shot again and the moose staggered into the water and went down. The last shot was through the neck.

That moose of mine had a fine head with a very massive

RIFLES FOR HEAVY, SOFT-SKINNED GAME

cupped-up palm and a 57-inch spread; but Myles's moose was, for a time, the Yukon record, as after the skull had been sawed in half for packing and the antlers had had thirty days to dry and shrink, it still had a spread of 69¾ inches.

The last moose I shot was also above timberline in a willow patch off of Lapp Creek in the far northern Rockies. We had seen the moose and his companion about a mile away from the other side of the creek and we stalked him to within about 200 yards. The willows were so high that I had to shoot offhand but I squeezed off three shots with the .270 using the 130-grain bullet as carefully as if I were doing my best to get a possible on the army A target at 200 yards offhand. I could hear the first shot plunk into the moose. He was immediately a very sick moose and staggered around groggily while I shot twice more. Then he went down. All of the bullets went right through the lungs and again it was the cumulative effect that got him, although I am sure the moose would have died in a few minutes or so from the first shot.

I could go on and on this way but I believe these incidents will show that a hunter is a bit optimistic if he expects one-shot kills with rifles of the .270 or .30/06 class. I think these incidents also show that for most Northern moose hunting, rifles of that class are adequate even though they are not one-shot killers. The moose simply cannot get away in the open country and would quickly lie down if they did. In a more heavily timbered country the use of a more powerful cartridge would probably be justified.

There is no doubt whatsoever that the grizzly can be a pretty bad actor. In the Canadian Rockies from the border of the United States to that of Alaska, I believe grizzly kill or badly maul an average of about ten people a year. I know several people who have survived those maulings. Usually if a hunter gets beaten up it is his own fault. Generally it comes from following a wounded grizzly into thick brush where the visibility is poor and where the bear has every advantage.

THE BIG-GAME RIFLE

But the American sportsman hunter going after grizzly in the Canadian Rockies usually finds his bear above timberline in open country where he can put in two, three, or four shots if necessary to get the bear down.

To show what one can expect, let us kill a few bear. The first grizzly I ever shot at was up in the Alberta Rockies, north of Jasper Park. A companion and I saw the bear marching along right at timberline. We sneaked over into a good position. My companion cut loose with the 130-grain bullet in the .270 and knocked the bear down. The bear stood up on its hind feet to see what it was all about and I drove a 200-grain .30/06 bullet into its chest. It collapsed and rolled down the mountain.

Another grizzly was below me on a river bar in the Yukon about 200 yards away. I got into a good sitting position, put the top of the post reticule in the scope right behind the bear's shoulder and squeezed one off. The bear went down on its nose, got up and headed for the timber of the river bank. A second shot knocked it down again, but again it got up. The third shot knocked it down once more and it lay struggling on the sand bar. I put a fourth shot into it just because grizzlies make me nervous. When we got down to the bear it was, of course, as dead as a herring and, as chance would have it, all four shots were in the group that could just about be covered by a silver dollar. In this case I used an experimental lot of Remington 180-grain pointed soft-point Core-Lokt bullets. Every one went clear through the bear.

Another bear was stalked to about 75 yards in a basin above timberline. The bear was above me. The first shot broke one shoulder, the second the other and the bear propelled himself down the hill with his hind legs. I fired four shots before the bear stopped moving.

I have seen only three grizzlies killed with one shot. One had been wounded around the edges by a companion. The guide and I went into a willow patch and booted the bear out. When it got into the open I cracked it behind the shoulder with the 130-

grain bullet in the .270 and in that one instance the bear was killed as quickly with that one bullet as a whitetail deer would have been. It just simply collapsed and rolled down the hillside.

Another bear I saw killed with one shot was in the Yukon in 1950. My companion, Red Early, leveled down on a grizzly at about 275 yards with the 180-grain bullet in the .300 Magnum. The bullet hit right in the ear and the grizzly really collapsed.

The third one-shot grizzly was one I killed with a .300 Weatherby Magnum in the Yukon in 1949.

A rather high proportion of North American grizzly bears are shot in the open. They are not particularly large animals and in the interior, full-grown males weigh around 600 pounds. At that, though, one-shot kills are apparently not too common. If a man were hunting grizzlies alone he might possibly be justified in carrying a rifle more powerful than the .30/06 or .270 if he could handle it and shoot it well.

The only rub is that in fall grizzly hunts the grizzlies are usually shot more or less by chance when the hunter is out after other game. I, for instance, have killed most of my grizzlies on hunts where my primary objective was sheep, and I have shot them with sheep rifles. A heavier rifle will, of course, kill sheep but for mixed hunting in the far North I would not consider it particularly advisable to hunt sheep, let us say, with a .375 Magnum on the off chance that one might run into a grizzly. Few hunters can absorb enough recoil so that they can do their best work at long range with a heavy rifle. However, if a man is not recoil-sensitive and cannot be happy unless he kills his grizzly with one shot, then he would be justified in carrying, for a mixed hunt, a more powerful rifle than one of the .30/06–.270 class.

Although I may do it some time I have never as yet hunted Alaska brown bear, so all I know about such hunting is what I read and what my friends who have hunted the big animal tell me. Although many Alaska browns, particularly those found in southeast Alaska, don't average much larger than big grizzlies,

THE BIG-GAME RIFLE

some of them, particularly those on Kodiak Island and on the Alaska Peninsula, run much larger. Apparently the biggest browns weigh 1,000 pounds and more. Like any animal that has a lot of meat on his carcass, the big browns are hard to kill. They are often shot at close range and in heavy willow and alder brush where the primary requirement of the rifle is not great accuracy, high velocity, flat trajectory, but great bullet weight, momentum, and knock-down power. Many browns—perhaps the majority of them—have been shot with .30/06 rifles and bullets weighing from 172 to 220 grains. Nevertheless, I notice that most of the guides in that country, whose rifles have to be their insurance, carry .375 Magnums and use 270- and 300-grain bullets. If a man can count on a broadside shot, though, he would probably make a quicker kill with such a cartridge as the ultra high velocity .300 Weatherby Magnum which will drive the 180-grain bullet at 3,300 f.p.s. My friend, Herb Klein, of Dallas, Texas, shot his first Alaska brown in the spring of 1951 with the .300 Weatherby Magnum and the 180-grain Nosler bullet. It was a one-shot kill with a broadside shot. The heavy rifle is apparently, then, justified for the big browns, and to some extent it is justified for use on moose and grizzly.

The plains and semi-open brush country of east Africa is the area where the rifle heavier than the .30/06 really comes into its own. Apparently, pound for pound, African game is somewhat more tenacious of life than is North American game or Asiatic mountain game. Why this is I do not know. As a rule the difficulty of killing an animal is pretty much in proportion to its size. In North America there is certainly one exception and that is the Rocky Mountain goat which is, pound for pound, much harder to kill than a sheep, a mule deer, or other animals of the 250–300 pound class. Furthermore, a great deal of African game is pretty heavy by the standards of the ordinary American whitetail deer hunter who is used to thinking of 150-pound whitetail as "big game." The zebra is a pretty solid and blocky animal, as large as a small horse. The sable antelope is as big as an American elk. The Greater Kudu is a big animal and a bull eland will weigh as much as a domestic Jersey bull.

In addition, on the African plains, the hunter is apt to encounter lion, and although the lion will weigh only between 400 and 500 pounds, he can be a pretty tough cookie, and one which has mauled and killed many hunters. The African plains rifle should, therefore, have the power to knock a lion for a loop and enough bullet weight and sectional density to drive through the very heavy chest muscles with a frontal shot if the animal charges. Even where a party is hunting on the plains, the gun bearer will carry a heavy double-barreled rifle as a stopping weapon, but at that the ideal African plains rifle should have the power in an emergency to turn or smash the shoulder of a rhino or a Cape Buffalo, both of which are large, truculent, and dangerous.

Back in the 1920's the late Leslie Simpson, an American with a great amount of African hunting experience, wrote:

"What I think the average American coming to shoot in Africa should bring is a rifle taking a .350 cartridge with a heavy bullet and as high a velocity as possible compatible with pressure and weight of rifle. My idea would be a 275-grain bullet at 2,500 f.p.s., or, if this gives too much pressure, or would necessitate the rifle's being too heavy, then cut down the velocity rather than the bullet weight."

From talking to friends who have hunted in Africa and, from looking at their movies, it would seem that most African shooting, even at quite long ranges, is done from the offhand position, because in most areas, in the greater part of the year, the grass is so high that it is rare that the hunter can lie down, and much of the time he cannot even sit. This will mean, of course, that even at moderate range it is difficult to place shots exactly, and again one would need a more powerful rifle than he would in the American Rocky Mountains, where he can usually sit down and hold well enough to place his bullet exactly.

Skillful professional hunters in Africa, particularly in the early days of smokeless powder, did much of their shooting with fairly light cartridges using long, soft-nosed or full-metal cased bullets which the British call "solids." Favorites were the 160-grain bullet in the 6.5 Mannlicher-Schoenauer or 6.5 rimmed for the Model 1897 Dutch and Roumanian Mannlicher rifles. Another was the 175-grain bullet in the 7 x 57 Mauser. Some professional elephant hunters depended upon the use of those long but light solids to shoot elephants in the brain. Many hundreds of lions have been killed with them. From all I can learn, however, it would be rather unwise to carry such a rifle into Africa today except to use on the smaller antelope. There is no use in one's under-gunning himself, since the larger and heavier game animals like buffalo and elephant are not found in the open to the extent they formerly were, but instead spend more time in heavy brush. The hunter cannot pick his shots to the extent that he could on the open plains in the old days.

The thing the African plains hunter must have is absolutely reliable penetration. The bullet must never blow up near the surface and make a superficial wound. Instead, it should drive through into the vital areas even with an angle shot. I have talked to friends who have used the .270 with the 130-grain bullet in African hunting and they report that it doesn't do so well. They simply do not get the penetration with it, they claim, even on animals the size of zebra. The 150-grain factory load in the .270 is better, but still far from ideal.

Apparently about the lightest plains rifle which one should consider taking to Africa is the .30/06 with a supply of ammunition loaded with both 180- and 220-grain bullets. A 200–250 yard shot on the African plains is apparently a long one and the 180-grain load in the .30/06 certainly has flat enough trajectory for that type of shooting. With the heavy 220-grain bullets in the .30/06, sufficient penetration is apparently obtained, even on fairly heavy animals, to make the cartridge reliable if in the hands of a good shot. Stewart Edward White, the novelist, killed many lions with the .30/06, using the obsolete Remington delayed expansion mushroom—a hollow-point bullet with a full jacket over a hollow point—and with the Western 220-grain boat-tail with just a pin-point of lead exposed at the tip. I should think that the new Remington 220-grain soft-point Core-Lokt would certainly be just as good, if not better, and likewise the 220-grain Silvertip.

The .300 Magnum as it is called in the United States, or Super .30 as it is known in England, is apparently a satisfactory African plains cartridge, particularly with the 220-grain bullet.

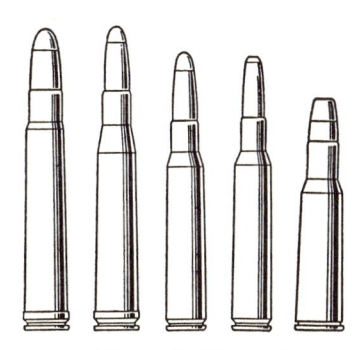

American cartridges suitable for dangerous and heavy soft skinned game. Left to right: .375 H. & H. Magnum, .300 Magnum, .30/06 with 220-gr. bullet, .270 with 150 gr. bullet, .348 with 250-gr. bullet.

As I have previously mentioned, the British figures for the .300 Magnum loadings are, for the most part, exactly the same, with identical bullet weights, as the American .30/06. The American .300 Magnum cartridge is loaded a good deal hotter because the Americans use the excellent American progressive burning nitro-cellulose powders which are much less heat-sensitive than the British cordites. The 180-grain load at 2,900 f.p.s., with a muzzle energy of 3,365 foot-pounds, should be a fine one for taking the larger African antelope at longer ranges, but the 220-grain bullet at 2,610 f.p.s., with 3,330 foot-pounds of muzzle energy should be even more useful.

The British make a rimmed or "flanged" form of the Super .30

THE BIG-GAME RIFLE

for use in double-barrel rifles. Because the actions of those doubles are not as strong as the Mauser-type bolt-action and because extraction is not as reliable, the flanged form of the Super .30 is loaded to lower velocities and less pressure than the belted form to be used in bolt-action rifles and is less powerful than the run-of-the-mine .30/06 cartridge. The 180-grain bullet is given only 2,575 foot-seconds, and the 220-grain only 2,250. It is hardly more powerful than the .30/40!

A very interesting and useful form of the .300 Magnum for African plains use or for use on any heavy, soft-skinned game is the American wildcat form of the cartridge. It is made by "fire forming" or "blowing out" the standard .300 Magnum case in an enlarged chamber. The brass expands to fit the new chamber and the result is a sharper shoulder and greater powder capacity, permitting the cartridge to be handloaded for greatly stepped-up velocity. Various forms of the cartridge are made by the Hollywood Gun Shop (PMVF), Mashburn Arms Company of Oklahoma City (.300 Mashburn Long Magnum), Pfeifer Rifle Co., 11252 Penrose Street, Sun Valley, California (.300 Pfeifer Improved Magnum); but probably the best known form is the .300 Weatherby Magnum made by Weatherby's, Inc., 2793 Firestone Blvd., South Gate, California. A blown-out form of the .300 is much more suitable for burning American powders than is the standard .300 Magnum case and, if loaded within reason, pressures are no higher, if as high as with the factory ammunition. The 180-grain bullet used in the .300 Weatherby Magnum can be driven with 75 grains of No. 4350 to about 3,150 f.p.s. This is not a top load for the cartridge at all and pressures apparently appear to be mild because cases last practically forever and there is no extraction difficulty whatsoever. Some load as much as 80–82 grains of powder for a velocity of around 3,300–3,400 f.p.s. That is quite a load! According to Weatherby's figures, 80 grains of No. 4350 will give the 180-grain bullet a muzzle velocity of 3,330 and with 4,422 foot-pounds of muzzle energy. With the 220-grain bullet one can get 2,810 f.p.s. veloc-

RIFLES FOR HEAVY, SOFT-SKINNED GAME

ity with 73 grains of No. 4350 and 3,856 foot-pounds of muzzle energy. Pressures in this load are mild. This is a boost of 200 f.p.s. of velocity over the factory load.

Recoil of the .300 Weatherby Magnum cartridge is fairly severe but not as bad as that of the standard .375. Anyone who is used to doing much shooting can learn to handle it without too much trouble, and for long shots on heavy game I know of nothing better. Trajectory is very flat. The cartridge seems to be a very well balanced one and accuracy has always been good in my experience. Once at the Burbank Rifle Range, near Los Angeles, I hit a 30-inch steel plate three times in succession from the offhand position at 430 yards. I then quit while I still had my reputation. In the United States and Canada the .300 has been used successfully on moose, grizzly, brown bear, and elk and almost always a hit anywhere in the chest cavity has meant a one-shot kill. It is the only cartridge that I have ever used that I would bet on making one-shot kills on animals the size and with the tenacity of life of moose and grizzly. I have killed both grizzly and goat instantly in their tracks with it.

Particularly with a strongly constructed 220-grain bullet one should be able to knock over instantly even an indignant lion. At least a dozen African hunters I know have used the cartridge and all are delighted with it. Ralph Hammer, of Redlands, California wrote me that the next time he goes it will be the only plains rifle that he will take. Roy Weatherby himself hunted in Africa with the cartridge and made one-shot kills even on the big, tough Cape buffalo. One of his friends killed a bull elephant with the cartridge but I would say that was taking it out of its class.

A favorite African plains rifle among British hunters is the .318 rimless Nitro-Express. Many magazine rifles on Mauser actions have been built for the cartridge, particularly by the firm of Westley Richards, and in spite of the fact that the cartridge is rimless some double rifles have been made up for it. In ballistics the cartridge is very much like the American .30/06. One load for it is the 250-grain bullet at a muzzle velocity of 2,400 in the

28-inch barrel with 3,194 foot-pounds of muzzle energy. Although no factory 250-grain bullet is loaded for the .30/06, Fred N. Barnes, of Golden, Colorado makes a 250-grain .30 caliber bullet and with 50 grains of No. 4350 one can reach approximately the same velocity, particularly since in England the velocity of the .318 is taken in the 28-inch barrel and would be somewhat lower in the 24-inch barrel, the .30/06 standard. British 250-grain bullets are furnished in various forms—solid, soft-nosed, capped, or split. The other popular loading for the .318 is a 180-grain bullet at 2,700 f.p.s. velocity, a dead ringer for the common .30/06 load. I cannot see that the .318 would do anything that the .30/06 could not do and for that reason the cartridge is, to American hunters, of academic interest only.

The .333 Jeffery, or, as it is also called, the .333 rimless Nitro-Express, is one of the most popular African plains cartridges. Magazine rifles for it were made in England by Jeffery and other concerns and there was a rimmed form for doubles known as the .333 flanged Nitro-Express and otherwise identical in case shape to the rimless cartridge. The rimmed form drives a 300-grain bullet at a muzzle velocity of 2,150 with a muzzle energy of 3,090, or a 250-grain bullet at 2,400 with a muzzle energy of 3,200. Velocities and pressures are higher in the rimless form of the cartridge, with the 300-grain bullet being given 2,200 f.p.s. and the 250-grain bullet 2,500 f.p.s. Either bullet weight has great sectional density, and particularly the 300-grain job, if bullets are at all well constructed, should drive very deep indeed.

Even with the 300-grain bullet at moderate velocity, trajectory should be flat enough, if the rifle is properly sighted in, for 200-yard shooting on plains game. The 300-grain bullet should be a lion stopper.

The case of the .333 has a larger head than the .30/06 or 8 mm. Mauser, but Springfield or Model 98 Mauser actions could have bolt face and extractors opened up to handle it. The American .333 O.K.H. wildcat cartridge was inspired by this British job. It uses a .30/06 case necked up to .33 and it is generally loaded

RIFLES FOR HEAVY, SOFT-SKINNED GAME

with the 250-grain bullet. Velocity is about 2,650 foot-seconds, and the cartridge has made a reputation for being deadlier on the heavier game than the .30/06, although it has never achieved a great deal of use or much popularity.

Another favorite for an African plains rifle is the 9.3 x 62, 9.3 Mauser, or, as the British call it, the .366. Manufacture of rifles for that cartridge was a specialty of the great Mauser Werke

German cartridges suitable for dangerous game. Left to right: 10.75 x 68, 9.3 x 62, 9 x 57, 8 x 60., .318 Wesley Richards, and .404 Magnum. The last two cartridges are British in origin but the Mauser Werke and other German factories made rifles for them.

and many hundreds were sold in Africa at about half the cost of a British magazine rifle on a Mauser action. As loaded in Germany the 9.3 bullet weighed 285 grains. It was driven at a muzzle velocity of 2346 and with 3,486 foot-pounds of muzzle energy. Loaded with that relatively heavy "H" jacket bullet, or the Stark Mantel bullet made by another concern, the cartridge seemed to be a very useful one.

The 9.3 x 62 was also quite popular among German sportsmen and many hundreds of rifles chambered for it surely must have come into the United States after the last war. I know I have had letters from many dozens of ex-G.I.'s who brought such rifles

THE BIG-GAME RIFLE

in and wanted to know how they could manage to shoot them. Ammunition is loaded in Sweden and Czechoslovakia and also probably in Belgium, and it is no great feat to get custom loaded ammunition in that caliber in the United States. Vernon D. Speer, the Lewiston, Idaho bullet maker, makes 9.3 mm. bullets, and it is simple to make 9.3 x 62 cases simply by running them through a full length 9.3 die and then trimming them, since the .30/06 case is 63 rather than 62 mm. long.

Actually the 9.3 is very similar to the American wildcat .35 Whelen, the .30/06 case necked to .35. In European terminology the .35 Whelen would be a 9 x 63 mm. It will use the same weight of bullet as the 9.3 at the same velocities. An American who wants a rifle shooting a heavier than ordinary bullet of larger diameter could well consider a .35 Whelen since barrels in that caliber are made by many custom barrel makers. Dies are obtainable from such firms as Pacific and Hollywood Gun Shop, and cases are very easy to form. Recoil is greater than that of the .30/06, but still much less than that of the .375 Magnum.

A very popular rifle for African plains shooting, or indeed for all-around shooting in Africa, is the .375 Holland & Holland Magnum. It is one of the world's great cartridges and, from the standpoint of the American, the most useful of all cartridges between the .30 calibers and the big bores of .40 and over, which have been designed for use on the very heaviest and most dangerous game. The .375 Magnum was evolved by Holland & Holland, the London rifle and gun makers, well prior to the first World War. It was widely used in both Africa and Asia and it was introduced into the United States by the Hoffman Arms Company and by Griffin & Howe, both of which concerns made up a good many .375's on Magnum-Mauser actions. Neidner Arms Corporation of Dowagiac, Michigan also built a few. The cartridge owes its popularity, however, to the fact that when Winchester, in 1937, brought out the Model 70 rifle it included the .375, and anyone with the price of a Model 70 in his pocket (or about 65 or 70 pre-war dollars) could have himself a .375.

RIFLES FOR HEAVY, SOFT-SKINNED GAME

Almost at once the .375 achieved a fair degree of popularity. It is a good cartridge. I have owned three of them. In spite of this, I have never shot a single head of big game with the .375 because I have never felt that I needed that much power. It is quite a chore to shoot a scope-sighted .375 from a bench rest, but I have done so, and one of the Model 70's will usually shoot just about as well as a good .30/06. I have shot many groups that ran between 3 and 4 inches at 200 yards with .375 rifles. I have also found it easy to stay in the 10-inch black of a 200-yard target from the sitting position for five shots with the .375. The second five shots are, however, something else again. Usually I yank a couple in the second string. Don't let anyone tell you that the .375 does not kick, because it does, and I seriously doubt if many shooters can do their best work with it, particularly with a long string of shots. Fired at game when the hunter is excited, though, I doubt if many people would be particularly flustered by the recoil.

If there is such a thing as an all-around cartridge to be used on all game, dangerous and non-dangerous, thick-skinned and thin-skinned, all over the world, it is the .375. With the lighter bullets, trajectory is flat enough to make the .375 a satisfactory sheep rifle if the man behind it can shoot it. With a full-metal cased 300-grain bullet, the .375 is not too bad for elephant, rhino, or buffalo. With the 270- or 300-grain soft-point bullet, it is a wicked stopper on soft-skinned dangerous game like lion, tiger, Alaska brown bear, and grizzly.

As loaded in England, the .375 belted rimless Magnum gives the 300-grain bullet a muzzle velocity of 2,500 f.p.s. in a 28-inch barrel with 4,070 foot-pounds of muzzle energy; 2,650 with the 270-grain bullet and 4,210 foot-pounds of muzzle energy; or 2,800 with the 235-grain bullet and a muzzle energy of 4,090 foot-pounds.

The firm of Holland & Holland pretty much specializes in that cartridge and builds double rifles for a rimmed form of it, but loads it to somewhat lower velocities—2,425 with the 300-grain bullet, 2,600 with the 270-grain bullet, and 2,750 with the 235-grain bullet. Other British concerns build doubles for the rimmed form and even for the rimless belted form.

In the United States the 235-grain bullet at something over 2,800 f.p.s. was loaded prior to the war, but now Winchester and Western load only the 270- and 300-grain bullets. The 270 semi-spitzer soft-point bullet is given a muzzle velocity of 2,720 f.p.s. with 4,440 foot-pounds of muzzle energy, and the 300-grain bullet in both full patch, or "solid," or Silvertip form is given 2,580 with 4,435 foot-pounds of muzzle energy. The reason the .375 is loaded a bit hotter in the United States is undoubtedly that the Americans use nitro-cellulose powder whereas the British still use cordite which gives a good deal higher pressure in a hot, tropical climate than in a temperate climate.

There are two schools of thought on the .375. One holds that in the hands of even a passably good shot it is sufficient for elephant and for any other dangerous game. Another school holds that the .375 has too much recoil and is unnecessarily powerful for a small bore plains rifle and that it does not have what it takes to be a stopper on dangerous game. The reaction of most of my friends who have hunted in Africa is that it is the most useful rifle an American can take to Africa. The tendency is for Americans hunting there to depend more on the .375 than on any other rifle, and not a few have killed elephants with rifles of that caliber. If I should ever hunt in Africa I shall certainly take a .375 and I shall also take a .375 if I ever go after the big Alaska brown bear. I have never felt, however, any particular desire to hunt grizzly with the .375 because a man has to lug a rifle around grizzly hunting a lot more than he has to shoot it and I have always been willing to take a couple of shots with the .30/06 to kill a grizzly and have a lighter rifle to carry around than to be burdened with the heavy .375 and kill a grizzly with one shot.

Just as he has a blown-out version of the .300 Magnum, so does Roy Weatherby have a blown-out and souped-up version of the .375 Magnum, which he calls .375 Weatherby Magnum.

RIFLES FOR HEAVY, SOFT-SKINNED GAME

With the 270-grain bullet and what he calls a moderate load, Weatherby uses 81 grains of DuPont No. 4064 to give a velocity of 2,825 f.p.s., and a muzzle energy of 5,100 foot-pounds. With the 300-grain bullet, Weatherby uses 89 grains of No. 4350 for a velocity of 2,773 and 5,112 foot-pounds of energy. Those are powerful loads, with energy, though not bullet weight, up in the elephant class. I am rather skeptical, however, as to the desirability of souping up the .375. Particularly on heavy game, the very deepest penetration is more important than high velocity and the added velocity might now and then blow a bullet to pieces at short range to give insufficient penetration and possibly dire results.

The 9 mm. Mannlicher-Schoenauer and 9 mm. Mauser cartridges were brought out to be used on the heavier African antelope and on lion. Many rifles in those calibers were sold to African settlers, again because they were cheap. The cartridges are quite similar, although not interchangeable. Neither is loaded in the U. S. but in England the 9 mm. Mannlicher-Schoenauer is loaded in the 245-grain solid or soft-nosed bullet to a muzzle velocity of 2,100 f.p.s., with 2,395 foot-pounds of muzzle energy and the 9 mm. Mauser is loaded with the same bullets at a velocity of 2,150 with 2,515 foot-pounds of muzzle energy. Neither cartridge would be particularly good. They are lacking in power and the trajectory could be a good deal flatter for plains use. The 9.5 Mannlicher-Schoenauer had a fair African following with its 270-grain bullet at a muzzle velocity of 2,200 f.p.s. and 2,905 foot-pounds of muzzle energy.

Probably the nearest rival to the .375 H. & H. Magnum for an all-around African cartridge is the .404 rimless Nitro-Express. It was a very popular cartridge prior to the war. Not only did most of the British custom rifle makers build magazine rifles for it, but so did the great Mauser Werke and other German concerns. It uses a 400-grain bullet at a muzzle velocity of 2,125 with a muzzle energy of 4,006. Its heavy bullet almost put it in the elephant rifle class. Some rifles for the .404 were also built in the

THE BIG-GAME RIFLE

United States back in the 1920's by Hoffman Arms Company and also, I believe, by Griffin & Howe.

A cartridge of more or less the same class was the German 10.75 x 68 Mauser or .443 which drives a 347-grain bullet, according to British figures, at a muzzle velocity of 2,175 and 3,641 foot-pounds of muzzle energy. The cartridge was more used by European settlers in Africa than it was by sportsmen. A few rifles in that caliber were built in the United States by the Hoffman Arms Company on standard Model 98-type Mauser actions. I shot one of them once. Recoil was pretty severe and accuracy nothing to write home about. The cartridge has been criticized for giving poor penetration on heavy game.

The .350 Rigby Magnum cartridge drives a 225-grain bullet at a muzzle velocity of 2,625. The Imperial Chemical Industries catalog lists only one bullet weight for the .350. As it is loaded it is very much the same thing as the 235-grain bullet in the .375 Magnum. It is not nearly as popular as the .375. It is handicapped by not having heavier bullets and there is no particular reason why one should choose it over the .375 or even over the .35 Whelen.

Now and then one can pick up a German 9.3 x 74-R double rather cheaply. I have seen some advertised for less than $200 that were built by good German makers. The cartridge is quite similar to the rimmed version of the .375 Magnum and if a man has a yen for a double rifle at a moderate cost this might be a bet. Ammunition in that caliber is loaded in Sweden and, I believe, in Czechoslovakia. It might be difficult to obtain in some instances and there would be no particular point in looking one up.

Another popular British cartridge designed for magazine rifles and of the all-around class is the .416 Rigby. It is very much on the order of the .404, since it drives a 400-grain solid or soft-point bullet at a muzzle velocity of 2,300 f.p.s., with 4,700 foot-pounds of muzzle energy. A few rifles of this caliber were made up in the United States by Hoffman Arms Company back in the 1920's and early 1930's and, I believe, Griffin & Howe can fur-

RIFLES FOR HEAVY, SOFT-SKINNED GAME

nish such rifles even now. It should be a very useful African cartridge.

THE BATTERY FOR AFRICAN PLAINS USE

What rifles should an American plan to take for a hunting trip on the African plains? Probably the most useful rifle would be, beyond any doubt, a .375 Magnum in the Winchester Model 70. As we have seen, there are other excellent cartridges loaded in England and on the Continent but there would be no particular point in an American going to the trouble of getting a foreign arm when he can get a strong, reliable, and inexpensive American rifle. There is little, for instance, that the .404 Eley could do that the .375 could not do. The .375 Magnum may not be an ideal elephant rifle but many elephants have been killed with it and the American hunting in Africa will go out with a white hunter who carries a heavy double barrel in something like the .465 or .470. Presumably if the American gets into trouble the white hunter is there to bail him out of it.

After the .375, probably the best bet as a second rifle for the smaller antelope and even for larger game under favorable circumstances would be the .30/06 or some other .30 caliber such as the .300 H. & H. Magnum or .300 Weatherby Magnum. If the hunter is at all recoil-sensitive he should prefer the .30/06 to the .300 Magnum because he will do better work with it.

The .30 caliber rifle should be supplied with both 180- and 220-grain bullets and the rifle should be carefully sighted in so that the hunter knows where each bullet strikes. As a usual thing with a well-bedded .30/06 sighted to put the 180-grain bullet at point of aim at 200 yards, the 220-grain bullet will strike at point of aim at about 100 yards, which is as it should be.

The British are among the world's most conservative people, and there is nothing about which they are more conservative than the matter of sights. The average British magazine rifle has a parade of open sight leaves mounted on a short rib. They are marked for 100, 200, 300, and 400 yards, and those who use them have a deep and abiding faith in them. Although the British sometimes use cocking piece and bolt sleeve sights, they have never gone in much for receiver sights. They are still open sight men. They go in even less for scopes than they do for peep sights. Some hunting-type scopes are made in England by Ross, but most scopes mounted on British rifles by the custom rifle makers were put on miserable German-type mounts.

Any magazine rifle for plains use in Africa should be mounted, I believe, with a good scope on a quick detachable side mount and it should have a good receiver sight with the largest possible aperture available. Friends of mine who have hunted there tell me that the scope mount should be of the quick detachable type always. One reason is that in the hunting cars the rifles are apt to get knocked about pretty badly and scope mounts can be bent and scopes come out of adjustment. They say that it is wise to remove the scope and carry it in a little case attached to the belt when the rifle is in the hunting car. Then when they get out of the car, they can remove the slide of the Lyman 48, put it in the pocket, and slip on the scope.

The conservative firm of Griffin & Howe tells me that they like to mount telescope sights on .375 Magnums, to be used in Africa, high enough to clear the Lyman 48. Then to use the iron sights immediately it is not necessary to remove the scope but merely to look under it. Seymour Griffin and Phil Johnstone undoubtedly know more about it than I do. For my part I would hesitate to have a scope so mounted. I have never been able to do good shooting with a high-mounted scope because I cannot get my cheek on the comb and steady the rifle. I would much prefer to have the scope mounted so low as to make it necessary to remove the slide of the receiver sight before the scope was put on.

The British are firmly convinced that the open sight with a shallow V or U, often marked in the center by a thin platinum

Ballistic Data of Cartridges Suitable for Heavy Soft-Skinned Game

CARTRIDGE	BULLET WEIGHT	MUZZLE VELOCITY	MUZZLE ENERGY	
American				
.270 W.C.F.	150	2800	2610	
.270 W.C.F.	150	2950	2850	(Hand Load)
.30/06	180	2700	2910	
.30.06	220	2410	2830	
.300 Magnum	180	2920	3400	
.300 Magnum	220	2620	3350	
.300 Weatherby	180	3290	4300	
.300 Weatherby	220	2935	4193	
.333 O.K.H.	250	2650	—	(Wildcat on '06 Case)
.35 Whelen	250	2700	—	
.35 Whelen	275	2450	—	
.348 W.C.F.	200	3530	2840	
.348	250	2350	3060	
.375 Magnum	270	2740	4500	
.375	300	2550	4330	
.405 Winchester	300	2260	3400	
.375 Weatherby	270	2825	5102	
.375 Weatherby	300	2773	5112	
British				
.318 Nitro Express	180	2700	2920	
.318 " "	250	2400	3194	
.333 Rimless	250	2400	3200	
.333 "	300	2200	3230	
.333 Rimmed for doubles	250	2400	3200	
	300	2150	3090	
.350 Rigby Magnum	225	2625	3440	
.369 Purdey	270	2525	3815	
.404 Nitro Express	400	2125	4010	
.404 " "	300	2625	4595	
.416 Rigby	400	2300	4702	
8 x 64	185	2890	3420	
8 x 75	227	2722	3788	
9 x 56 Mannlicher-Schoen.	247	2105	2429	

THE BIG-GAME RIFLE

BALLISTIC DATA OF CARTRIDGES SUITABLE FOR HEAVY SOFT-SKINNED GAME (*Continued*)

German

CARTRIDGE	BULLET WEIGHT	MUZZLE VELOCITY	MUZZLE ENERGY
9 x 57 Mauser	230	2368	2863
9 x 57 "	280	2110	2523
9.3 x 62 Mauser	231	2542	3325
9.3 x 62 "	285	2381	3600
9.5 x 57 Mannlicher-Schoen.	272	2148	2790
10.75 x 68 Mauser	347	2000	3080

line, is the fastest type of sight to use on dangerous game. About this I am exceedingly skeptical, as any open sight, no matter how good, will cut out at least half of the view of the game and will always give some tendency to over-shoot. The peep sight, on the other hand, does not have that same tendency and for my eyes, anyway, it is much faster. A great many people also feel that the hunting scope is not fast enough to use on charging game. It seems to me that a good 2½-x scope like the Lyman Alaskan with its 40-foot field at 100 yards, 20-foot field at 50 yards, 10-foot field at 25 yards, would be fast enough for practically any use, and the focus of such a scope is universal. For Africa I believe a flat top post reticule with the top of the post subtending from 4 to 6 inches would be about right, and the one to select, rather than the medium fine crosshair which is to be preferred for American use. When an American sports hunter takes off for his daily hunting jaunt in Africa he is a member of what is practically a task force. He may carry his .30/06 or other .30 caliber rifle himself. He then has a gun bearer with him with his .375 and the gun bearer is trained to put the rifle in his hand immediately. The white hunter will be tagging along with a .470 or .465 double. All in all that amounts to quite a bit of fire power.

Colonel Sandy McNab, the man who taught the army how to shoot and who has made two African trips, tells me that anyone

RIFLES FOR HEAVY, SOFT-SKINNED GAME

hunting in Africa should by all means take a varmint rifle with him because he will have a chance to shoot no end of hyenas, wild dogs, predatory hawks, etc. It is indeed, he says, the place to make a varmint hunter's mouth water. Furthermore he says that the smaller antelope can be taken nicely with a varmint cartridge. He particularly recommends the .22 Hornet cartridge because ammunition is light, easily carried, and the report is mild enough so that larger game will not be frightened off by it.

As can be seen by the accompanying German and British ballistics tables, there are many other cartridges suitable for African plains use but they are not as popular as the ones we have covered and, of course, we cannot cover them all.

CHAPTER XI

Rifles and Cartridges for Thick-Skinned, Dangerous Game

THE BIG stopping rifles, the powerful ponderous weapons throwing heavy bullets of large caliber and kicking like the devil, are arms that North American hunters know little about and have no use for if they stay in their own back yards. The rifles and the cartridges for them are a British specialty, although some rifles have been built for the big British cartridges both in Belgium and Germany.

There is no doubt that elephants can be killed very dead if a long, relatively heavy, small-caliber bullet is driven into the brain, but if the brain is missed, those light bullets will not stop one of the great animals, or even bother him greatly. The really heavy cartridges are designed to have enough power to set an elephant back on its haunches even with a head shot that misses the brain, to break the massive bones of the shoulder, to drive through on a heart shot. They are the most powerful shoulder weapons used by man, cartridges comparable in recoil and deadliness to the great American .50 caliber machine-gun cartridge.

Usually the cartridges are rimmed and of .45 caliber on up. They use a heavy charge of cordite powder at relatively low pressure. Most are used in that British specialty, the double rifle, but a good many falling-block single-shots have, in the past, been made for these Big Bertha rimmed cartridges, and some rimless cartridges in this class have been designed for use in magazine rifles built on Magnum Mauser actions.

RIFLES FOR THICK-SKINNED, DANGEROUS GAME

The British double rifle is an interesting weapon—and a very expensive one. To build one requires time, patience, and skill of the very highest order. As this is written in 1951, a Purdey hammerless ejector costs in England £325. A No. 2 grade Holland & Holland can be bought for £250 and a Model de Luxe for £350. Even with the British pound at its present price, that is a lot of potatoes. Add to that the duty and the 11 percent excise tax, and it is easy to see that one does not buy a British double rifle lightly.

Doubles are made in an amazing variety of calibers, including, strangely enough, the little American .22 Savage High Power. The famous London rifle making firm of Holland & Holland specializes in doubles for a rimmed 7 x 57 cartridge, which is either identical with or very similar to the German 7 x 57-R, a favorite caliber for three-barrel guns or "Drillings." For my part I can see no excuse for small caliber, high-velocity doubles, as there isn't anything such a rifle will do that a bolt-action will not do better and more cheaply. It may well be that it is possible to build a high-velocity double accurate enough for mountain shooting to 250–300 yards, but the job would be a tough one at best. Building real precision accuracy into a double-barreled rifle is a job that would make the labors of Hercules seem like a child's after-school chores. Doubles are all take-downs, of course, with a joint between the barrels and the frame which encourages vibration and wobble. Because of the construction there can be no stiffening of barrels and action through solid bedding into a one-piece stock. Then there is always the difficulty of getting the two barrels to shoot together under all conditions and at different temperatures.

The Rigby catalog, from which I am quoting, has some pertinent remarks on the construction of double rifles:

"Many sportsmen think that all a gunmaker has to do when he builds a double rifle is to set the barrels together so that the two axes of the bore are absolutely parallel, when the rifle will shoot. We only wish that the matter were so simple, but in actual fact the axes must seldom, if ever, be parallel. At first sight this may seem to be a very curious fact, but a little thought will soon explain the reason. When the right barrel of a double rifle is discharged the recoil very naturally throws the rifle outwards to the right, and since recoil begins to make itself felt as soon as the bullet begins its passage up the bore, this means that the axis of the right barrel will be pointing to the right of the line of original aim when the bullet actually leaves the muzzle. When the left barrel is fired an identical movement takes place in the opposite direction, i.e., out to the left, and so it is not difficult to see that the right barrel tends to throw its bullet to the right and the left to the left. In other words, the two barrels naturally tend to shoot apart. In order to counteract this tendency the barrels of all double rifles are set so that the axes are converging in the direction of the muzzle. The great difficulty in regulating a double is the determination of the correct amount of divergence. This will vary for every individual rifle, as no two barrels behave identically on firing. The vibrations and waves set up in the steel all influence the shooting to a very marked extent. The barrels are first of all set at a slightly convergent angle and then are brazed together at the breech ends. They are then held together at the muzzle with a wedge and lumps of packing are inserted at various points between the breech and the muzzle. The attainment of the best possible shooting from each barrel individually is chiefly dependent on the positions of these pieces of packing and can only be ascertained by experiment, since no two pairs of barrels require identical treatment. There is no golden rule on which to work, merely experience in the skillful cunning of a master hand. When both barrels have been made to shoot their best independently of each other they are gradually regulated to shoot together by the alternation of the position of the

RIFLES FOR THICK-SKINNED, DANGEROUS GAME

wedge at the muzzle, an extremely delicate and often tedious operation. Sometimes a pair of barrels is spoiled in the process by some unaccountable cause and then all work must be begun again with a new pair.

"But this is not all. We have already explained how the barrels naturally shoot apart on account of recoil. If the weight of the bullet is changed the recoil is also changed and a pair of barrels that may be shooting perfectly together with one weight of bullet will no longer shoot in accord. A heavier bullet naturally increases the recoil and tends to make the barrels shoot further apart while a lighter bullet lessens the recoil when the barrels will shoot somewhat across each other; i.e., the right will shoot to the left of the mark while the left will place its bullets to the right of the mark. A change in velocity has a somewhat similar effect and therefore we do not recommend firing different weights of bullets from the same rifle.

"Nitro powders are sensitive to changes of temperature and the same charge will develop a considerably higher velocity in a hot climate than in a cold. The result of this is that the barrels of a rifle which may be regulated to shoot perfectly in England will no longer shoot together in the great heat of the tropics, and inexplicable misses may very easily result, while the danger of such an eventuality can be readily seen. We are pleased to say that we have made special close study of this problem for many years and have succeeded in adapting a system of regulation of all our double rifles by which absolute accuracy, even in the intense heat of African and Indian jungles, is assured. We have been greatly assisted in our experiments by many of our customers who have most kindly shot the rifles for group under varying conditions of climate and we now regulate our doubles so that the two barrels shoot slightly apart in England. The exact distance apart depends on the temperature at the time of regulating, and in this respect we are pleased to say that our experiments have been so successful that there is no divergence of the shooting of our doubles when fired in hot climates.

"The adoption of a so-called tropical charge is an attempt in the same direction. While we recommend a slight reduction in the cordite charge simply in order to lessen breech pressure, we place no reliance on such general measures for the prevention of changes in shooting. The only certain measure is the careful regulation on their own principle of every individual rifle. We have most carefully studied the climatic conditions which prevail in all parts of the world and so regulate our rifles that our world-wide reputation for absolute accuracy is fully maintained.

"After the final regulation of the alignment of the barrels has been completed to our satisfaction, the back sight of the rifle is carefully adjusted for elevation and direction by our expert staff. We recommend, however, that the purchasers of our rifles should, if possible, shoot the weapons they select at the rifle range before the sights are finally finished."

The above is an interesting exposition of building even a fairly accurate double rifle so that the two barrels will shoot together. I, for one, will take with considerable salt the story that the Rigbys have the problem licked to the extent that their rifles shoot the two barrels together under various conditions of heat, humidity, etc. Let's say they shoot them *about* together and let it go at that. One can see how the difficulty of building such a rifle, coupled with British handicraft methods with their great use of expensive labor, would keep the price of that type of weapon very high indeed.

The advantages claimed for the double are many. It is said that they point and handle like fine shotguns if a man can look at the spot he wants to hit, throw his rifle to his shoulder, and fire in an emergency with some hope of hitting about where he wants to hit. It can be seen that this natural handling and pointing ability would be of great importance in jungle hunting for dangerous game. It is also said that the double is an absolutely reliable weapon that never jams and that even if one barrel should go bad the hunter would still have a single-shot rifle at his disposal. Another virtue claimed for the double is that the hunter always has two shots at his immediate disposal and, if he can get off the second shot with no rattle of the functioning of the bolt or lever, often game cannot locate the hunter between the two shots.

The double surely has its advantages, but it also has its disadvantages. The first, as we have seen, is the great expense. A man could outfit himself for an African trip with a whole battery of bolt-action rifles for the cost of one double. The second disadvantage is indifferent accuracy. The double surely has good enough accuracy for short-range shooting up to 100 yards, but the double is certainly no long-range rifle, as it surely must be very sensitive to slight changes in ammunition. Bullets of different weight, bullets with jackets of different hardness, the use of various lots of powder, all would, no doubt, have their effect on the point of impact obtained with this two-barreled job. At 50 yards, on an animal the size of a rhino or a target the size of an elephant's head, this probably would make little difference, but suppose one were trying to knock off a small antelope at 250 yards, then the difference would be appreciable.

The double is probably quite a reliable weapon, but not as 100 percent reliable as some would lead us to believe. Compared to the strong and simple bolt-action, the double is as intricate as a watch. Each ejector, for example, is a complicated and delicate mechanism. Furthermore, the ejectors themselves have, as compared to the ejector of a Mauser-type bolt-action, relatively little extracting power, and with a dirty or over-size case, particularly if the cartridge were fired in a dirty or pitted chamber, one could easily run into trouble. A leaf or twig can prevent the finely fitted double from closing. Advocates of doubles make a great point of two instantaneous shots being at the disposal of the hunter, but what happens when someone is up to his neck in indignant elephants and fires those two shots? Also what happens when a lion charges and the hunter misses or wounds with his first two shots? It seems to me that there would be some argument for a life-saving third or fourth shot being at the disposal of the hunter.

The double is a poor platform to put good sights on. Most are equipped with from two to four open leaf sights. They are adjusted at the factory and from then on the hunter is supposed to use them without further adjustment and be happy. Non-adjustable sights would be all right if ammunition were always precisely the same with precisely the same bullets, precisely the same lot of powder, precisely the same amount of crimp holding the bullet in the case, precisely the same hardness of bullet jacket —and if exactly the same man were always to shoot the rifle. It is no great secret though, that, particularly with open sights, no two men shoot exactly alike. It has been shown that, given the same rifle with the same adjustment of open sights, two crack marksmen will group their shots at 200 yards as much as a foot or 18 inches apart.

Then let us suppose that the man who owns a double shoots out one or both of the barrels, something which is very apt to happen if the rifle is an all-around one which is to be used on a great variety of game; then he is faced with an extremely difficult and expensive operation of fitting and regulating another set of barrels at a cost which will be at least half of that of a new rifle. With a bolt-action rifle, however, the fitting of another barrel is a simple and relatively inexpensive matter.

Undoubtedly the fact of two almost instantaneous shots at the disposal of the hunter is the great advantage of the double. The other is that doubles are built for a whole line of very powerful cartridges firing very heavy bullets. For my part, I can see but little excuse for a small- or medium-bore high-velocity double to use on the plains, but for jungle shooting at the largest and heaviest game, and for use as a life saver with great knock-down

RIFLES FOR THICK-SKINNED, DANGEROUS GAME

power, a double, along with the big cartridges for which many are chambered, has its advantages.

The first modern, high-velocity cartridges using jacketed bullets and Cordite powder were introduced for double rifles in England at the end of the nineteenth century. Typical were the

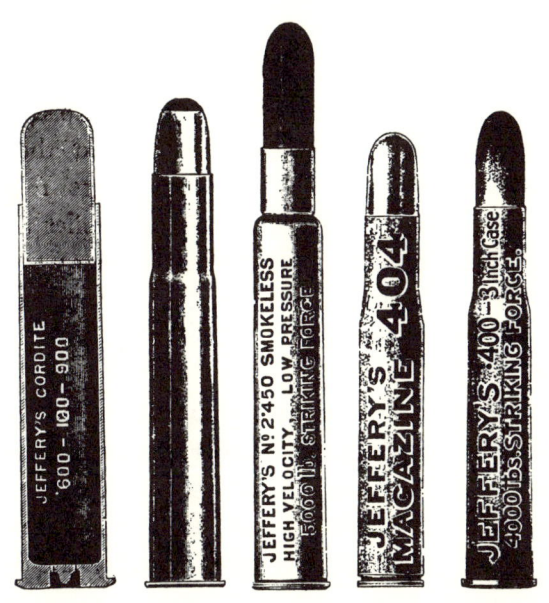

Some British cartridges for heavy thick-skinned game. Left to right: .600 Nitro Express, .465 Nitro Express, .450 No. 2, .404 Magnum, .400 Jeffery. All except the .404 Magnum are for doubles or heavy single shots and are rimmed. The .404 is rimless.

.450 caliber cartridges using 70 grains of Cordite powder and a 480-grain bullet which developed a muzzle energy of around 5,000 foot-pounds. It did not take long for those early .45 caliber cartridges to drive out of use the big 8 and 10 gauge black-powder rifles. They hit just as hard, seemed just as effective as far as knock-down power went, but kicked a lot less.

Let's take a look at these big large-bore black-powder rifles which were displaced by the Nitro-Express jobs. They must

THE BIG-GAME RIFLE

have been something. The enormous 4-bore rifle used 12 drams of black powder and a conical bullet weighing 1,882 grains which was driven at a muzzle velocity of 1,330 f.p.s., and with a muzzle energy of 7,400 foot-pounds. The rifles themselves weighed from 20 to 24 pounds! The 8-bore used a bullet weighing 1,257 grains at a velocity of 1,500 f.p.s., with a muzzle energy of 5,290 foot-pounds, and was fired in a rifle weighing from 16 to 18 pounds. The more common 10-bore used 8 drams of black powder for an 875-grain bullet at 1,550 f.p.s., with 4,660 foot-pounds of energy. The rifles that fired the cartridge weighed from 13 to 15 pounds. The double-barrel 12 gauge rifle used 7 drams of black powder, a 750-grain bullet at a muzzle velocity of 1,550 with 4,000 foot-pounds of energy and the rifles weighed around 11 pounds. Even in rifles of that weight the recoil, particularly of the 4-bore and 8-bore must have been something!

A somewhat more modern cartridge and one which was possibly the direct ancestor of the Nitro-Express cartridges was the .450 black-powder Express, a cartridge on the order of the big Sharps "Buffalo" cartridges. It used 120 grains of black powder with a 270-grain bullet for a velocity of 1,875 and 2,110 foot-pounds of muzzle energy.

Because there were many old .45 caliber black-powder military rifles floating around in India and much of that ammunition was in the possession of rebellious tribesmen on the Indian frontier, importation of .45 caliber rifles and ammunition into India was prohibited by the British government. As a result, the British gun makers pretty well abandoned the .45 caliber Nitro-Express cartridges and developed elephant cartridges above and below .45, usually above.

An example is the .470 Nitro-Express, which is probably the most widely used of the big British elephant cartridges. It is loaded with 75 grains of Cordite to drive a 500-grain full-metal cased or soft-nosed bullet at a velocity of 2,125 with 5,030 foot-pounds of muzzle energy. Another is the .475 No. 2 Nitro-Ex-

RIFLES FOR THICK-SKINNED, DANGEROUS GAME

press which uses a 480-grain bullet which is given a muzzle velocity of 2,200 f.p.s., with 85 grains of Cordite and 5,170 foot-pounds of muzzle energy. For their heaviest cartridge, the famous firm of Holland & Holland developed the .465 "India," which uses a 480-grain bullet at a muzzle velocity of 2,150 f.p.s., with a muzzle energy of 4,930 foot-pounds. Holland & Holland rifles for that cartridge weigh from 9½ to 10¼ pounds, according to the Holland & Holland catalog.

As we have seen, the typical British cartridge for double rifles, a cartridge designed to stop the very heaviest and most dangerous of game, uses a bullet weighing in the neighborhood of 500 grains with a velocity around 2,150 and with something like 5,000 foot-pounds of muzzle energy.

Even more powerful cartridges are made. The heaviest of the lot is the .600 Nitro-Express which uses a 900-grain bullet at a muzzle velocity of 1,950 f.p.s. with 7,610 foot-pounds of muzzle energy. Rifles made to fire this terrific cartridge weigh between 16 and 17 pounds. The .577 Nitro Express drives a 750-grain bullet at 2,050 and delivers 7,020 foot-pounds of muzzle energy.

As will be seen in the ballistics table (on page 222), however, there is no vast amount of difference in velocity, bullet weight, and striking power of the majority of these big cartridges. There are undoubtedly too many of them, as the British rifle makers are individualists and they have developed cartridges bearing their names and only slightly different from many others. Being a manufacturer of center-fire metallic ammunition in Great Britain must be full of headaches. Sales of cartridges in these various calibers must be incredibly small and even at the high cost of the ammunition there probably isn't any profit in it. No one goes around touching off a rifle which carries with it from 60 to 100 pounds of free recoil just for the heck of it. I have seen second-hand double-barrel British Nitro Express rifles twenty years old or more that have been carried on four or five African hunting trips with barrels which still look as good as new in spite of the highly erosive effect of British Cordite powder. Surely one does not shoot them for fun and there cannot be any profit in making ammunition for such rifles.

I have mentioned the recoil of those rifles. Shot at a target in cold blood, the only way that I have ever shot such a rifle, the recoil is formidable indeed and after about five shots a man shooting one is apt to develop a headache. I read pieces by stout fellows who are not bothered in the slightest by such massive recoil. I am inclined to believe that they are talking through their hats. They are probably not bothered by recoil when they are shooting at elephants or charging rhinos or something of the sort, but I seriously doubt if they do much target shooting with them. The rifle with a recoil of that order cannot be fired prone because it might break the shoulder. However, my friend, Kristen Sergel, who is a slender, svelte, and I might add, exceedingly good looking young woman, owns a beautiful .465 Purdey weighing only about 9½ pounds. I have hefted the weapon. It points like a fine shotgun. Kristen tells me that when she shoots at game with it she never notices the recoil at all. She has killed a lot of big stuff with it, including record elephants, and she has gone out after them all by her lonesome without a white hunter to back her up. She tells me that in Africa rifles just don't kick, no matter how powerful the cartridge, and since she is in one piece, I think she has something there.

Powerful Cartridges for Mauser Magazine Rifles

Because there was considerable demand on the part of British colonists in Africa, and to some extent in India, for rifles using cartridges with power equivalent to the big doubles and yet at less cost, the British developed cartridges comparable in power for magazine rifles built on Mauser actions. Probably the best known of these in the United States is the .505 Gibbs, which was developed by the firm of George Gibbs of Bristol. It uses a 550-grain bullet at a muzzle velocity of 2,250 with 6,200 foot-

RIFLES FOR THICK-SKINNED, DANGEROUS GAME

pounds of muzzle energy and the rifles firing that terrific cartridge, as built in England, weighed from 10 to 11 pounds. Back in the 1920's, the Hoffman Arms Co. built some rifles in this caliber (just how many I do not know, but surely not many). Some were probably taken to Africa by Americans and some American gun nuts used them on such game as elk, moose, and on grizzly bear. There isn't any doubt that that is a tremendous cartridge. British colonists also used them, since they had plenty of authority and cost less than comparable doubles.

The firm of W. J. Jeffery & Co. at one time made rifles for the .500 Jeffery cartridge, which used a 535-grain bullet at a muzzle velocity of 2,400 and a muzzle energy of 6,800 foot-pounds. Apparently the cartridge is obsolete. I cannot find it listed in the Imperial Chemical Industries catalog and Jeffery no longer builds rifles for it—but it was a killer-diller.

In his book, "African Rifles and Cartridges," John Taylor writes that no normally constituted hunter should be bothered by the recoil of either cartridge. Those British must be made of stern stuff indeed.

The .425 Magnum Express uses a 410-grain bullet at a muzzle velocity of 2,350 with 5,010 foot-pounds of muzzle energy. The firm of Westley Richards still builds rifles for it.

In the United States there has never been enough demand for ultra-powerful cartridges for magazine rifles to warrant their mass production. There have been, however, some wildcat experiments along that line.

The New York firm of Griffin & Howe for a time made the .400 Whelen cartridge which was the .30/06 case necked up to .40 caliber and using a 350-grain bullet at 2,200 f.p.s., with 3,760 foot-pounds of muzzle energy. It was also loaded with the 300-grain bullet at 2,375 with also 3,760 foot-pounds of muzzle energy. The cartridge, however, would hardly be considered in the elephant class but more in the class of the all-around African plains rifle. It was never very successful because it was a rimless cartridge and the very slight shoulder on the case was not suffi-

THE BIG-GAME RIFLE

BALLISTICS OF CARTRIDGES SUITABLE FOR DANGEROUS, THICK-SKINNED GAME

CARTRIDGE	BULLET WEIGHT	VELOCITY	ENERGY
.450/.400 Magnum Nitro Express	400	2150	4110
.450 Nitro Express	480	2150	4930
.450 Black Powder Express	365	1700	2340
.500/.450 Magnum Nitro Express	480	2175	5050
.577/450 Black Powder	325	1600	1850
.465 Nitro Express	480	2150	4930
.470 Nitro Express	500	2125	5030
.475 Nitro Express	480	2175	5050
.475 No. 2	480	2200	5170
.500 Nitro Express	570	2150	5850
.577 Nitro Express	750	1800	5400
.600 Nitro Express	900	1950	7600

NOTE: Some of the older black-powder cartridges are included in the above table for the sake of comparison. Some hunters prefer magazine rifles to the big doubles for dangerous game, and they can use the .404 Rimless Nitro-Express and the .416 Rigby cartridges listed in the table for the use of heavy soft-skinned game, as they turn up energy between 4,000 and 5,000 pounds. The .505 Gibbs cartridge, which is also used in magazine rifles, gives a 535-grain bullet a muzzle velocity of 2400 f.p.s. with 6,800 foot-pounds of muzzle energy.

cient to maintain headspace. Another experiment of the sort was the wildcat .400 Neidner cartridge developed by Neidner Arms Corp., of Dowagiac, Michigan. It employed the .35 Newton case necked up to .40 and using the same bullets as the .400 Whelen except at considerably higher velocity.

A late and very interesting experiment is the .450 Watts Magnum developed by H. B. Anderson of Yakima, Washington. It employs the .375 Magnum case necked to .45 with a perfectly straight taper. This is, after a fashion, sort of an American version of, let us say, the .505 Gibbs and it is really in the elephant class because, loaded with a case full of Government No. 4895

RIFLES FOR THICK-SKINNED, DANGEROUS GAME

Ballistics of Holland & Holland Double Rifles

		MUZZLE VELOCITY FT. PER SEC.	MUZZLE ENERGY FT.-LB.	100 YARDS VELOCITY IN FT. PER SEC.	100 YARDS ENERGY IN FT.-LB.
.240 Flanged	100 gr.	2775	1711	2537	1430
.275 Magnum Flanged	160 gr.	2575	2357	2342	1950
7 m/m. H. & H. Magnum Flanged	140 gr.	2650	2184	2450	1867
.30 Super Flanged	150 gr.	2875	2755	2581	2225
" " "	180 gr.	2575	2653	2309	2131
" " "	220 gr.	2250	2475	2045	2045
.375 Magnum Flanged	235 gr.	2750	3950	2489	3240
" " "	270 gr.	2600	4060	2367	3362
" " "	300 gr.	2425	3930	2183	3180
.375 Flanged Nitro-Express 2½ inch case	270 gr.	1975	2340	1760	1860
.500/.465 Nitro-Express 3¼ inch case	480 gr.	2150	4930	1862	4100
.475 No. 2 Nitro-Express 3½ inch case	480 gr.	2200	5170	1974	4160
.500 Nitro-Express 3 inch case	570 gr.	2150	5850	1948	4800
.500 Nitro-Express 3 inch case	750 gr.	2050	7010	1874	5860
.600 Nitro-Express	900 gr.	1950	7600	1676	5620

powder, the cartridge turns up what seems to be the British requirement for an elephant rifle—around 5,000 foot-pounds of muzzle energy giving bullets weighing from 400 to 500 grains high velocity and a tremendous striking power. One can also say that the recoil is plenty husky too. I have shot a .450 Watts Magnum and I can testify that it kicks. Because the cartridge is a long one, Anderson builds rifles on the 1917 Enfield action and prefers that they weigh 10–10½ pounds to help cut down on the recoil. Anderson himself, stands recoil well and even shoots this cannon on jackrabbits. Ralph Hammer of Redlands, California

THE BIG-GAME RIFLE

carried a Watts Magnum on an African trip and found it entirely adequate for elephant, rhino and other dangerous game.

These great elephant cartridges have their place in the scheme of things. It may be a minor place and it may be a place which is only of academic interest to the American hunter. The cartridges will usually turn a charging elephant. The tremendous momentum of their heavy bullets will knock down a charging lion in his tracks, throw a charging buffalo back on his haunches. With their heavy bullets of large diameter and their tremendous shock power, they give penetration and otherwise do a job that no ultra high-velocity small-bore rifle can do, and if a man gets himself in a jackpot with dangerous game, they are the things which will get him out of it.

CHAPTER XII

The Construction of Hunting Bullets

MANY different effects are demanded of bullets used in the hunting of big game. If we are to shoot small, thin-shelled animals at long range what we want is a bullet that will expand readily against light resistance—a large caliber varmint bullet, in other words. If we are shooting large animals like elk at moderate ranges, a bullet of the first type, which would be ideal for antelope, might go to pieces too quickly, particularly if it had to penetrate much meat in order to strike a vital area, or had to break large bones. At the other extreme, there are bullets designed for the deepest possible penetration against enormous animals with massive bones and thick hides—creatures like rhino, elephant, and the various wild cattle such as the African Cape buffalo.

Back in the days of muzzle-loaders using spherical bullets, there was only one thing to do if the rifleman wanted deeper penetration, and that was to use a larger ball, since all bullets were spherical and were of relatively pure lead. The larger the animal hunted the larger the hole had to be in the end of the barrel. In those days elephants and other dangerous game were shot with ponderous 4-, 8-, and 10-bore guns with bullets that weighed ¼, ⅛, and ⅒ pound! Curiously some people still judge the killing power of a rifle by the hole in the end of the barrel, and consider a .45/70 a better elk cartridge than a .30/06 and an 8 mm. Mauser a better deer cartridge than the .270.

When smokeless powders, long bullets, and high velocity came in, the ballisticians discovered that, if they were to function, the lead bullets had to wear overcoats of some stronger and tougher metal, so they put "jackets" on them, as we call them in the United States, or "envelopes" as they call them in England. Various materials were used—cupro-nickel, gilding metal, pure copper, mild steel, or a layer of gilding metal over a layer of mild steel.

Early jacketed hunting bullets were all round-nosed jobs like the 220-grain .30/40 bullet and the 175-grain 7 x 57 Mauser. Most were driven at a velocity of 2,000–2,200 f.p.s. Expansion was obtained by leaving the jacket off the forward portion of the bullet to form what was called a soft nose. The more lead exposed, the quicker the expansion was, and the less lead the slower the expansion. At those relatively low velocities such bullets were all right on soft-skinned game. The boys who wanted very deep penetration were given bullets that were reversed. With the soft-point the forward portion of the bullet was open, the base enclosed. The full-metal cased bullet, or "solid," as the British call it, had an open base and the forward portion was enclosed in metal.

For velocities of around 2,000 f.p.s., such bullets were satisfactory, and still are. For ordinary use, the most killing 170-grain .30/30 bullet on light game like deer is still the old-fashioned soft-point, with plenty of lead exposed at the tip.

Then in the early part of this century, it was discovered that a bullet with a sharp (spitzer) point shot much flatter than a round-nosed job. The Germans loaded their Mod. 1905 7.9 x 57 cartridge with a spitzer 154-grain bullet at about 2,900. Americans brought out the .30/06 with a 150-grain bullet at 2,700 f.p.s. The .280 Ross came along with a 145-grain bullet at 3,060, the .22 Savage High Power with a 70-grain bullet at 2,800, and the .250/3000 Savage with an 87-grain bullet at 3,000. The late

THE CONSTRUCTION OF HUNTING BULLETS

Charles Newton introduced a whole flock of hot-shot big-game calibers from .256 to .35 with velocities of around 3,000 f.p.s.

Right away the boys started having bullet troubles. First effort to put out spitzer bullets to be fired at high velocity was simply to make a spitzer soft-point with the same thin jacket as the old bullets that were shot at around 2,000 f.p.s., with the same soft lead core. Quickly the hunters started screaming. The soft, fragile points battered in the magazine until they looked like

Typical bullets manufactured by the conservative British. Left to right: soft nose, full metal cased or "solid" for deepest penetration on thick skinned game, soft nose split.

miniature mushrooms, the users declared, and instead of penetrating into the boiler room, they often flew to pieces on the surface.

Lads who slave for the ammunition factories started battling this bullet design business in a serious way almost 50 years ago, and they are still at it. Their task is complicated by the fact that the average rifle user wants an all-around bullet and there ain't no such animal and never will be. Let's see why.

The sharp-point, which is the best form for getting through the air rapidly without losing its velocity rapidly as it barges along, is the poorest possible form for getting through brush without deflection, and also the poorest possible form to build an expanding device into. The round-nose, which gets through brush well and which is easy to make expand, sheds velocity in great hunks and therefore isn't so hot for long-range shooting.

BUT all our boys who use bullets want is one that will retain its velocity with maximum efficiency, shoot like a match bullet, get through brush, expand properly on a whitetail deer weighing on the hoof about 125–165 pounds or on a moose weighing 1,000–1,500 pounds. No wonder the designers climb trees!

In well over 30 years as a practicing gun nut, I have watched the pendulum swing back and forth. A certain bullet comes out and the taxpayers scream that it goes to pieces like smoke. The factory makes another and they yell that it goes through without expansion.

Let's see what can be done to control rapidity of expansion, the other side of which is depth of penetration.

Expansion on game is dependent on many things: (1) the velocity at time of impact. The faster a bullet is traveling when it hits, the more violently it expands. A bullet that may be entirely satisfactory at 100 yards may slip on through almost without expansion at 300. (2) The thickness of the jacket, particularly toward the point; (3) the hardness and toughness of the jacket; (4) the hardness of the lead core. I knew a small bullet maker who tried to save a buck by reclaiming and using shot from a trap layout. Next season most of his customers reported shooting through bucks from stem to stern without much result. (5) The amount of lead exposed at the tip; (6) reinforcement of jacket with folds, belts, solid bases, etc.; (7) weakening of jacket with canelures (American practice) or splits (British practice); (8) character of device at forward end to promote expansion—hollow points, capped soft point, wedge, etc.

At one extreme we have a bullet with a core of pure soft lead covered with a soft thin jacket. For a time I used a 120-grain spitzer soft-point of that sort loaded to about 3,200 f.p.s. in a .270, on jackrabbits, coyotes, javelinas, and little Southwestern whitetail deer. The bullet would go completely to pieces in the chest cavity of a little deer weighing, field-dressed, about 100 pounds. No portion would go through, and the whole chest cavity would be a mush filled with little pieces of lead and tiny hunks of jacket. On *light* game shot *broadside* the bullet killed instantly. Such a bullet would be worthless for heavier game.

THE CONSTRUCTION OF HUNTING BULLETS

At the other extreme, we have a full-metal cased round-nosed bullet weighing around 500 grains and designed for the very deepest penetration on elephant and rhino—bullets that will break both shoulders of a rhino, drive through the heavy frontal bones of an elephant's head into the brain. The business end of those bullets is heavy reinforced *steel*, almost flat in contour, with hard lead core and heavy walls.

The best *compromise* bullet is one so constructed that it will open up the forward portion at relatively low velocity at long range against light resistance, yet hold together at the high velocity of short range against heavy resistance. Examples of this type of construction are the Silvertip, with its reinforced multiple jacket and soft point protected by metal, and the Core-Lokt which has the jacket locked around the core.

Results with even the best bullets vary. One hunter will shoot an animal and claim a certain bullet goes to pieces too quickly. Another hunter will shoot the same sort of animal with the same bullet and scream that the damned bullet didn't open up at all. Bullet effect is governed not only by the construction but by the impact velocity. (It makes a lot of difference whether you shoot an animal at 50 yards or at 400.) It is also governed by where you hit it—in the rump (relatively soft muscles), rib cage (relatively thin bone and cartilage), shoulder (relatively heavy bone in case of a large animal), or stomach (thin layer of skin over moisture-filled bag).

A pal of mine named Jack Holliday, when we were hunting in Alberta in 1943, took a pop at a grizzly with a .22/250 with a 41-grain Sisk bullet loaded to about 4,200 f.p.s. The first bullet hit the relatively massive shoulder blade, cracked the shoulder but flew to pieces. The second bullet struck between ribs, penetrated the relatively thin cartilage, and blew up in one lung. The grizzly fell in its tracks. Conclusion from the first bullet would be that the .22/250 was no good on grizzly, and from the second bullet that it was poison!

The picture is further complicated by occasional freak performance which comes, evidently, from a defective bullet. I once shot a mule deer broadside through the rib cage with a certain 150-grain .30 caliber bullet at about 75 yards. The bullet blew up on a rib, killed the deer with the debris, but *made a hole where it went in the size of a saucer.* I shot a big heavy ram at about the same range with the same make and weight of bullet as it ran directly away from me. The bullet struck in the ham, went through the abdomen, through the lungs, out through the brisket and made a hole but little larger where it came out than where it went in. How come? You've got me! Only explanation, I believe, is that something had slipped up in the manufacture and both bullets were haywire.

I am inclined to believe that bullet action is a whipping boy for many hunters and that bullets get the blame for a lot of lousy shooting. A guy I knew came to me about 10 years ago and asked me what to use on an antelope hunt. I had just returned from a successful one, told him I had used a .270 with the 130-grain Winchester pointed expanding bullet. He came back empty-handed and with his nose out of joint to report that he had hit an antelope four times right through the lungs at 100 yards or so and that the antelope had kept going. The bullets, he said, hadn't opened up at all. I cross-questioned the guy. The antelope, he told me, got away. Had he seen blood? No. Had he seen hair fly? No. Did the antelope stumble, go down, or otherwise show it was hit? No. I could draw no conclusion but that he had simply missed the antelope four times and was trying to salve his ego by blaming the bullet.

It is a fact, though, that with light, fragile game like antelope and small deer the problem of bullet construction is not deep penetration but speed in expansion. Around 15 years ago I took a .257 on a month's hunting trip into Mexico. Bullets I used had very thick jackets and small open points with shallow cavities. I had a heck of a time with them, and the only deer I killed cleanly was one that was standing behind a tree. The bullet went through the tree and was pretty well expanded by the time it

THE CONSTRUCTION OF HUNTING BULLETS

hit the deer. The others I shot (and that a Mexican rancher friend shot with the same rifle) ran merrily on and had to be whittled down. One buck was shot precisely through the heart, and there was no sign of expansion at all. Since it was hardly feasible to carry a tree around to shoot a deer through, I came back pretty sour on that bullet.

Sectional density of a bullet (relationship of weight to area of cross section) is an important factor in securing penetration. The relatively light 160-grain bullet used in the 6.5 Mannlicher-Schoenauer has an excellent reputation for deep penetration. With soft points it has been used successfully on lions and with full-metal cased bullets even for head shots on elephants. Likewise the 175-grain bullet for the 7 x 57. Neither the 6.5 or 7 mm. bullet was particularly heavily constructed, and the results obtained were due entirely to the length in relation to caliber.

If deep penetration is wanted, construction can to some extent be substituted for sectional density. Example is the 180-grain Remington pointed soft-point Core-Lokt bullet, which will go through a grizzly, elk, or caribou like a chorus girl through a C-note. Unless my somewhat foggy memory is wrong, I have shot with that bullet two grizzlies and three big bull caribou. I have never recovered one yet since they have all gone through to crack rocks and blast down timber on the far side. In two cases the bullets, incidentally, broke shoulders of grizzlies while they were about it and in one case broke the off shoulder of a caribou.

Most experienced brown bear hunters recommend the 220-grain bullet in .30 caliber rifles for Alaska brown bear (if indeed they don't demand that the hunter fetch along a .375), but my pal, Herb Klein, called me up from Dallas the other day to tell me about killing a brownie with the 180-grain Nosler bullet driven at very high velocity in his .300 Weatherby Magnum. The bullet struck the bruin behind one shoulder, broke the one on the far side, drove on through leaving about a .40 caliber hole, sailed on across Bering Strait into Siberia where it killed two

THE BIG-GAME RIFLE

commissars and a Kalmuck. Only a lousy little 180-grain bullet on North America's largest and most dangerous bear, yet if it does not have ample penetration *because of its construction*, then my name is Molotov!

Once Roy Weatherby sent me over a .257 Weatherby Magnum to do a bit of shooting with the hope that I would write something kind about it. I had some 117-grain full-metal cased .25/35 bullets around, so I loaded them up to a velocity of probably around 3,100 f.p.s., and took the rifle out on a jackrabbit hunt. One would think that a full jacketed bullet of this sort would not expand at all. But, we forget the joker. That bullet was designed to be driven at around 2,200 f.p.s. Jacket was thin, core soft. At over 3,000 f.p.s. it exploded jacks like a bomb. I blundered into a coyote when I had the rifle, leveled down on him, and blew the far side off!

Just because a bullet is a "solid," as the English say, there is no sign that it will hold together. Many a time the British hunters in Africa have found that such bullets will break up on the heavy skull and shoulder bones of rhino, buffalo, and elephant. To be sure of results on such game one needs the very heaviest type of jacket so the bullet will not only hold together but keep its shape and drive through to the vitals.

Preserving the spitzer shape of a bullet, yet constructing it so that it will expand, is a tough assignment which has been met in various ways. Cheap and simple way to cut it is to swage jacket and bullet to spitzer shape and let it go at that. Expansion can be controlled by the amount of lead exposed at the point, the hardness of the lead, and the thickness of jacket toward the point. Joker there, though, is that the point batters and flattens in the magazine from recoil. Furthermore, the bullet often upsets or becomes foreshortened in the bore from the impact of the gasses on the base in starting it out, so when it leaves the base it does not have the beautiful spitzer shape it started out with. What happens is that the base of the bullet starts moving before the front and the phenomenon is called "slugging in the bore."

THE CONSTRUCTION OF HUNTING BULLETS

Another stunt is to use an open point, controlling expansion by the diameter of the open point, the depth of the cavity, thickness of metal toward the point, and hardness of the core. Particularly for quick expansion, the open-point bullet is excellent, and no bullet ever manufactured has had more friends than the famous 180-grain Western open point for the .30/06. Rub is, though, that with open-point construction it is impossible to get a true spitzer shape.

The Remington Bronze Point bullet obtains true spitzer shape and fine ranging qualities by the use of a bronze wedge over a cavity. When the point hits, the wedge drives back, splitting the jacket, and letting the cavity get in its work. I like the bullet very much. It is my favorite deer medicine in the 150-grain version in the .30/06, and it is a very fine bullet in the 130-grain version in the .270. Expansion is good but not too violent and I have never had any trouble in getting sufficient penetration. I killed a very big moose with the 130-grain B.P., shot him three times through the lungs, and found all the funny little bronze points stuck in the hide on the far side. I shot a grizzly in 1949 with the 180-grain B.P., loaded to about 3,200 f.p.s, in a .300 Weatherby Magnum. Range was about 125 yards. Grizzly pitched over on his nose and that was that. The hole behind the shoulder on the far side was the size of a saucer and there was a fan-shaped spray of blood, rib fragments, and bits of lung 3 feet long and 3 feet wide. With that combination the hunter can go after grizzly with about as much risk as hunting woodchucks with a Swift.

Western-Winchester preserves semi-spitzer shape with the Silvertip by protecting the soft lead point by a thin jacket of tin. Same stunt was used on the now obsolete Winchester protected soft-point bullets in .25, .270, and .30 caliber. They are now obsolete, but the 130-grain .270 bullet of that construction with its sharp point and heavy reinforced base was largely responsible for making the reputation of the .270 cartridge. It was an expensive bullet to manufacture, but so are the Bronze Points and the Silvertips.

THE BIG-GAME RIFLE

The Germans made many very fine and elaborate bullets and have greatly influenced American bullet design. One of the most intricate is the famous R.W.S. Torpedo jacket bullet made by the Rheinisch-Westfalische Sprengstoff-Actien-Gesellschaft in Nürnberg. I am illustrating one sectioned—a 177-grain job for the 7 x 64. It is built as follows: a hollow copper cap over a round soft point; jacket is mild steel, very thin at the forward portion; forward two-thirds or so of the core is soft, unhardened lead; then there is a heavy fold to strengthen the jacket so the rear third will remain intact; last third or so of the core is very *hard*

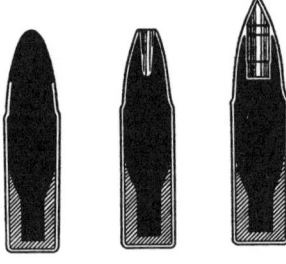

The Germans made some of the finest and most elaborate bullets in the world and generally led the field. Here are three examples of the D.W.M. Stark Mantelgeschosse or strong jacket bullets in soft point, hollow point, and hollow metal cap styles, all in 7 mm. Outfit is Deutsche Waffen und Munitionsfabriken A.G. Werk Karlsruhe.

alloyed lead. I showed that bullet to a manufacturer. He turned pale and said: "Great Scott! If I made those I'd have to peddle them for two bits apiece!"

It begins to look as if this bullet business were a bit complicated, then, and that instead of just walking in and demanding some .30/06 fodder, the customer should do a little thinking about what results he wants and on what!

CHAPTER XIII

Iron and Glass Sights for the Big-Game Rifle

No MATTER how excellently made the rifle is or how powerful and how potentially accurate the cartridge fired in it, the combination is no good unless the rifle is equipped with the suitable sights properly adjusted. It is axiomatic that no one can shoot any better than he can see. The best marksman in the world with the finest rifle will yet shoot poorly with crude, poorly adjusted sights. Any big-game hunter should give as much thought to the proper selection and adjustment of sights as he does to the selection of the caliber of his rifle.

The first sight most shooters become acquainted with is the open sight—usually some form of a U or of a V, but sometimes a flat bar. The open sight must be positioned on the rear portion of the barrel far enough from the eyes so that a man with good vision can make a stab at bringing rear sight, front sight, and target into something like the same focus. Most American factory rifles come equipped with some sort of an open sight. This is not because the factories think that the open sight is the best but because the open sight is the cheapest of all sights to manufacture and the sales departments believe, undoubtedly correctly, that a rifle should go out of the factory equipped with some sort of a sight. Then the customer can take it out of the rack of a sporting goods store and go out and shoot at something with it with some chance of hitting it. If the factory rifle were equipped with a more expensive type of sight it would raise the selling price to the consumer and make the rifle more difficult to sell.

Like practically everyone else, I grew up with open sights. I did not own my first rifle equipped with a good aperture receiver sight until I was in my twenties. I am now, however, convinced that there is no such thing as a good open sight, although some open sights are better than others. Open sights have many grave faults. Let's take a look at them:

In the first place, the optical principle of the open sight is all wrong. It asks the eye to do the impossible—to focus on the rear sight which is 16 or 17 inches from the eye and then on the front sight which is from 30 to 40 inches from the eye, depending on the length of the barrel, and then on the game which may be anywhere from 10 yards to 400 yards from the eye. That is a job that can be done only fairly well even by young, flexible eyes. It is a job that cannot be done at all by middle-aged eyes that have lost their powers of adaptation. As the rifleman's eyes enter the bi-focal stage, the rear sight fuzzes up until he cannot see it plainly, and in some cases of extreme far-sightedness the same thing holds true even of the front sight.

The second thing wrong with the iron sight is that even the best of open iron sights blot out half of the game—and the best type of open sight is the shallow U or V on a flat bar. The worst open sight is the Rocky Mountain buckhorn or semi-buckhorn sight which blots out about three-fourths of the game, as these sights have big "horns" or "ears" sticking up on either side of the U or V. Exactly what the function of those horns was supposed to have been in the first place, except possibly to look fancy, I have not been able to dope out in forty years of melancholy brooding.

This fact that even the best open sights blot out half of the game, coupled with the fact that a great many open sights have U's or V's that are too deep, is responsible for the old warning to the deer hunter—always shoot low on a deer. The hunter wants to see his front sight and he also wants to see the game.

The fact that seeing game and front sight is difficult with the open sight makes the hunter tend to see too much of his front bead in order to get it against the target. This causes over-shooting. With the deep U or V the light grows dimmer the finer one draws his bead. Many a hunter will sight in his rifle with a "fine bead"—or the bead drawn right into the bottom of the notch—and then under the stress of excitement, in the poor light often encountered in hunting, he will fail to get the bead down fine and will overshoot.

The last indictment of the open sight is that most of them on the market are hard to adjust. The overwhelming majority of them have no provision whatsoever for lateral adjustment or windage and any such adjustment has to be made by knocking the sight back and forth in a dovetail slot. Elevation on the average factory sight is obtained by crude steps in a bar incapable of finer adjustment than from 4 to 6 minutes of angle. In many cases factory rifles are properly and conscientiously sighted in by good shots with factory open sights. One of the sad and depressing facts of life is, though, that, particularly with open sights, no man can sight in a rifle correctly for another because people's eyes differ, the ways of holding a rifle differ, guns shoot differently with different brands of ammunition and bullet weight. The factory, let us say, may sight in for 100 yards, whereas the man who buys the rifle may want it sighted in to hit on the button at 250 yards.

I have carefully sighted in rifles with open factory sights so that I could stay from a hunting position pretty well inside a 10-inch bull at 200 yards. It is, however, a job to try the patience of the gods as well as a great expenditure of time and ammunition. Often, to get the elevation right, one has to file down one of the steps on the elevation bar.

The British equip magazine and double-barrel rifles with from one to four leaf sights on a short rib. A favorite type with them is the shallow V with a platinum line making more conspicuous the center of the V. A rifle so equipped is carefully "regulated"

THE BIG-GAME RIFLE

or sighted in by the maker. Usually the job is done for 100, 200, or 300 yards in the case of a plains rifle, or possibly at 50 and 100 yards for the big-bore jungle rifle. Presumably then, these British hunters use these rifles with perfect satisfaction the rest of their lives and, unlike other rifles, they never change point of impact. They shoot to the same point of impact with all brands of ammunition in all temperatures. The stock never warps up against the forend and all the British hunters have eyes and holds exactly like those of the factory experts who regulate the sights.

The adjustment of one of these parades of open sights is quite a chore. One time a custom maker had finished up a .375 Magnum which was equipped with a 2½-x scope on a side mount and as an auxiliary sight three open sights on a half rib. Like a great many custom gunsmiths, the chap who finished up the rifle had got behind on his delivery date. The man who had ordered the weapon was bombarding him with telegrams because he was all in a swivet to take off on an Alaska brown bear hunt. Apparently he wasn't the only impatient customer, since the gunsmith was tearing his hair. He asked me if I would take the rifle out and sight it in with the 300-grain factory load with the scope and also with the three open sights respectively for 100, 200, and 300 yards. He gave me a hundred rounds of ammunition and a file to deepen the V's to the proper amount. Then when I got back he planned to finish shaping up the V's in an artistic and workmanlike manner, blue the whole rifle, which was then in the white, and ship it. I finally got the job done but, believe me, it was a headache, both figuratively and literally, as anyone who has ever fired one hundred rounds from a .375 Magnum in an afternoon can testify. Apparently the job worked out because the customer was happy and wrote the gun maker that he had killed a brownie with the 200-yard leaf turned up.

I have no doubt that the open sights used on the big British doubles for short-range shooting at very large and very dangerous game work out all right because no very high degree of accuracy is demanded for such work. However, for shooting at the longer ranges from 200 to 350 or 400 yards, I should think such sights would be very sorry indeed.

Doing a good job of sighting in with ordinary open sights will almost always result in the expenditure of enough ammunition to pay for a sight that would have been easier to adjust in the first place.

A much more logical type of iron sight is the peep or aperture. The principle of looking through a hole at the front sight is a very old one, as aperture sights were found on European crossbows made in the Middle Ages. The idea, however, was popularized by the Lyman Gun Sight Company. The principle is quite simple—that the eye naturally centers the front bead at the point of strongest light, which is the middle of the aperture. To use a peep sight correctly, one should forget all about centering the bead but simply look *through* the aperture, put the front bead on what one wants to hit, and touch her off. For game hunting one needs a large aperture which gives a wide field of view and lets through plenty of light. It is difficult for most beginners with a peep sight to realize this. They almost always use the supplementary discs with small holes for sighting. They are appalled by the fact that they can look through a wide peep and see the whole world in it. These little target discs have certain advantages on the target range. They sharpen up the front sight and the target and bring them more or less into the same focus. They are slightly more accurate than the large aperture.

When I obtained my first receiver sight I was shocked by the fact that I could see so much through it without the disc. I screwed the disc in and went hunting. In late evening I saw a very handsome buck mule deer standing looking at me right at the edge of the timber in a mountain meadow. I could see him nicely with the naked eye but when I lifted my rifle I could not see the deer and the front sight through that miserable little aperture. Frantically I lowered the rifle and tried to screw the disc out. The buck jumped into the timber and that was that.

This mishap caused me to do some experimenting. I tried

shooting groups from a rest and from the sitting position with and without the disc. From the rest I could ascertain that I could shoot very slightly smaller groups with the disc. From the sitting position I could discover no difference whatsoever. From any practical hunting position one can get as good accuracy with a large aperture as he can with a small one.

The first popular aperture sights were of the tang variety mounted on a stem attached to the tang of the rifle. All were adjustable for elevation. Some were adjustable for both elevation and windage. Placement of an aperture sight on the tang has the advantage in that it is close to the eye and is very fast to use. It also has a very real disadvantage in that it is so close to the eye that under certain conditions it is possible for the rear sight to be driven into the eye. Aperture sights are also attached to the cocking piece, which in some instances is not a bad idea. It is much safer on a rifle of heavy recoil than the tang sight because although the aperture is close to the eye at the time the trigger is pressed, the sight jumps away from the eye as the firing pin falls. It is not a very good idea, though, from the standpoint of accuracy, since there is always a certain amount of wobble in the cocking piece. Accuracy is, however, good enough for short and medium-range shooting.

When the bolt-action rifle came into general use the receiver sight, like the famous Lyman No. 48, became the most popular type. It is made in one form or other for all bolt-action rifles of the Mauser type—Model 70 Winchester, Model 721 Remington, Mauser, Springfield, Enfield, etc. All of these sights are easily and quickly adjusted for both windage and elevation and click in from $\frac{1}{4}$ to 1 minute of angle.

With them one can fire a group at 100 yards, let us say, and then be right on the button after adjusting his sights. Let us say that he fires a group and discovers that his bullets averaged striking 6 inches high and 4 inches to the right. He knows that his sight clicks in $\frac{1}{4}$ minute of angle and each click changes the point of impact $\frac{1}{4}$ inch at 100 yards. Therefore, he turns the

IRON AND GLASS SIGHTS FOR THE BIG-GAME RIFLE

adjustment knob 24 clicks in the down direction and the windage 16 clicks in the left direction and he is set. If he fires two 5-shot groups, he is sighted in at the expenditure of half a box of ammunition. With difficult-to-adjust open sights he would be lucky to be reasonably well adjusted with two boxes of ammunition and at today's cost of ammunition he would just about save the difference in the sights at the first sighting in. Excellent receiver sights are the Lyman 57, 48, the Redfield Series 102 and 70, the Williams Foolproof receiver sights, etc.

The Lyman 48 has had an advantage over the competition in one respect and that is that it has a quick removable slide which can be got out of the way so a quick detachable scope can be slipped into the side mount. The same feature is now incorporated into the Lyman 57 and as I write this I understand that the Redfield Gun Sight Company is coming out with a modification of their excellent Series 70 sight which will also incorporate the quick removable slide.

Hunting Telescope Sights and Mounts

The enormous and growing popularity of the telescope sight for hunting has been an interesting phenomenon of the past twenty years. So popular is the scope sight that a very high proportion of first-rate big-game rifles purchased annually in the United States are fitted very quickly after purchase with a scope of some sort or another.

For about ninety per cent of all hunting conditions the scope is the finest of all sights because with a scope one can see better, *and no one can shoot any better than he can see.*

The use of the wide-angle hunting scope of relatively low power began in the United States prior to the first World War when a few daring and enterprising hunters imported Zeiss and Hensoldt scopes made in Germany, usually with German mounts. In Continental Europe the sportsmen have always been content with the strange mounts which they use, but although the American sportsmen found the scope satisfactory, they found the mounts very poor. The outdoor writers like the late Captain E. C. Crossman, the late Paul Curtis, and Colonel Townsend Whelen are pretty largely responsible for the early popularity of the scope sight. They praised the scope and created enough interest so that a good many scopes began to be imported, and American gunsmiths and mechanics tried their hand at making mounts. The first successful mount was the Noske side mount, a side-bracket job. The base is attached to the left of the receiver by screws and pins. It has a male dovetail. The detachable portion of the mount has rings of the diameter of the scope tube and is attached to the base by a female dovetail. Since the German scopes did not have any provision for internal adjustment and windage, these early Noske mounts incorporated windage.

The Griffin & Howe side mount was a modification of the Noske, but the basic principles are the same. Like the Noske, the early Griffin & Howe mounts incorporated windage adjustments. Some Griffin & Howe mounts for foreign scopes are still so made.

In the early days the customers were pretty suspicious of scopes and used them principally as auxiliary sights. They mounted them high enough so that iron sights could be seen underneath them and they made a virtue of this. Actually with the scopes so mounted it was difficult to shoot the scope-sighted rifle accurately because the cheek was up above the comb and the rifleman could not get a good steady hold.

Presently, gunsmiths learned to alter the bolts of Springfields and Mausers for low-scope mounting by cutting them off and welding them on at another angle. Then scopes were brought down so that the line of sight was not much higher than that of iron sights. Some daring fellows went so far as to have no iron sights on their rifles at all. The revolution was under way.

The next step in the revolution was also engineered by R. Noske. He brought out scopes with very long eye relief so that the eye piece could be mounted forward of the lift of the bolt handle. He also designed scopes with internal adjustments for both windage and elevation—did away with the necessity for windage adjustments in the base.

Practical hunting scopes and practical hunting mounts were there. The only thing which held up their greater use was the price. Back in the '20's a Zeiss 2½-x Zeilklein scope cost about $36. The Griffin & Howe mount or Neidner mount cost about $30. Side mounts are rather difficult to put on, so most gunsmiths charged about $10 for the mounting job. All of that added up to $76 in the days when dollars were dollars. If a man wanted one of the more expensive scopes like the 4-x Zeiss Zielvier the mount cost a little more and the total bite was about $90. This was in the day when one could purchase a good Winchester Model 54 and later a Model 70 for from $55 to $65. The sights cost more than the rifle and, as a consequence, this seemed to many like putting a $300 saddle on a $25 horse.

The man who popularized the scope sight was Bill Weaver, of El Paso, Texas. He brought out what was, in those days, an absolutely first-rate scope, the Model 330, which was about a 2-x with a good, clear field and internal adjustments for windage and elevation. He also brought out an inexpensive but satisfactory side mount of pressed steel. First price for the scope, I believe, was $27.50, the mount cost about $3.50, and all a gunsmith had to do to put the mount on was to drill and tap two holes. Usual mounting charge was about 3 bucks. Here was a perfectly satisfactory scope for the big-game rifle at about half the price of a good factory rifle and much less than half the price that had heretofore been obtained for a satisfactory scope, mount, and mounting job.

The 330 and a 4-x job known as the 440 immediately sold very well and scopes began to blossom on rifles all over the country.

The Lyman Gun Sight Company, of Middlefield, Connecticut got into the hunting scope business with the excellent 2½-x Lyman Alaskan, which was and is about as good a low-power

THE BIG-GAME RIFLE

hunting scope as one can obtain. After the war Bill Weaver brought out the most excellent and relatively inexpensive series of K scopes, the K-2.5, K-4, K-6, K-8, etc. The Kollmorgen Optical Corporation, of Brooklyn, a fine precision manufacturer of optical instruments, got into the scope business with the beautiful line of 2½-x, 2¾-x, 4-x and 6-x scopes sold by Stith Mounts of San Antonio, Texas, and known as the Stith Bear Cubs. The Leupold-Stevens Instrument Co., of Portland, also brought out 2 and 4-x scopes and so did Norman-Ford & Co., of Tyler, Texas, with a 2½-x and a 4-x. Lyman added a 4-x Challenger scope to its line.

From my experiences as a gun editor I would say that about half of the practicing gunsmiths in the country have invented scope mounts. Hardly a week goes by that I don't hear from one who has a new mount that will make his fortune.

The hunting scope has many advantages. Most obvious of all is that the scope can be focused to the individual eye, and since scope and reticule are in the same optical plane there is no problem whatsoever of adapting the eyes. This gives the middle-aged or elderly shooter a new lease on life because he can see like a kid again. The second great advantage of the scope is that the magnification as well as the clarity of the field and the great light-gathering power enable any shooter to see much better, particularly in poor light and in timber where the view is partially obscured by brush. The hunter with a good scope properly focused can tell the difference between a doe and a buck, between a deer and a man or a domestic animal. Like the receiver sight the scope is easy to adjust for both windage and elevation, and some of the cost of the scope can be charged off to the saving in ammunition over the more simple and difficult to adjust open sight.

The scope has its disadvantages too. It is more expensive than an iron sight. It is also somewhat more fragile than an iron sight, although not as fragile as some people might believe. I actually believe that the scope is less fragile than the average front sight which is always getting bent or always getting an ivory or plastic bead knocked off. With certain mounts, the scope is quite strong and rugged and can take very hard knocks. On many occasions scopes have taken beatings that have broken the stocks on rifles.

All the scope does is to enable the rifleman to see better. It does not hold the rifle steady and it does not squeeze the trigger. The scope apparently increases the wobble of the rifle if it is not held steady. This annoys the poor shot. When the rifleman first begins to use the scope he often shoots behind a running game animal, because the animal looks larger, and tends not to lead enough. I had that experience when I first started shooting running jackrabbits with scope-sighted rifles. However, I quickly discovered the error of my ways and found I could hit running game even at fairly close range far better with a scope than I could with iron sights—again because I could see better.

The Choice of a Hunting Scope

The first successful American hunting scopes were built with power of from 2 to 2½, and all the gun writers in those days assured us that for big-game hunting one did not need a scope of higher power. This is not wholly true because the greater the magnification (all things being equal) the better we can see and the better we can hold. However, for the great majority of shots at big game a scope of around 2–2½-x is entirely satisfactory. With modern scopes the field of view is very wide—40 feet at 100 yards. With such a wide field one can shoot rapidly and get on quickly even at short range. Scopes of low power have greater latitude of eye relief and, hence, are faster.

For woods shooting, then, where shots are mostly under 100 yards, and very seldom over 200 yards, the 2½-x scope like the Lyman Alaskan, Weaver K-2.5, Stith 2½-x Bear Cub, etc., is perfectly all right, and probably is the wisest choice. Actually such a scope enables good aim to be taken on the animal the size of a deer or sheep to 300 yards, or one the size of an elk or caribou to over 400 yards. As I mentioned before, I killed an elk once at about 600 yards, using a 2½-x scope with Lee dot reticule. With the same rifle and scope I once killed an antelope at about 450. I also shot, with that 2½-x scope, coyotes at 300 yards or over. In spite of this I would not consider, however, a 2½-x scope to be very satisfactory for such long-range shooting.

For the plains and mountain hunter the 4-x scope is far better. It is also better for the man who wants to use the same rifle on varmints as on big game. Good modern 4-x scopes have fields of view of about 30 feet at 100 yards or 15 feet at 50 yards. If the scope has proper latitude of eye relief and is correctly placed to give a maximum field for the eye of the individual shooter, then perfectly respectable jump shooting at close range and in brush can be done with the 4-x. There isn't any doubt about it. A good 4-x will also give sufficient definition to kill a large woodchuck or jackrabbit in the open at around 200 yards and often hits can be obtained even farther. The 4-x, then, is the best bet for open country shooting and for all-around shooting—at antelope, mule deer, jackrabbits, and coyotes in the West, and for whitetail deer and chucks in the East. Some very fine 4-x scopes are now made. The cheapest, and a very satisfactory one, is the Weaver K-4 which is actually about a 3.8 in power. It is a bright scope with a clear, flat field and one which I have used on several rifles with entire satisfaction. It is so much cheaper than the other good 4-x scopes that the scope user will do some plain and fancy thinking before he puts out the extra money for a little greater power and perhaps slightly superior optical qualities and interior construction.

The two top-quality scopes in 4-x are the Stith 4-x Bear Cub with internal adjustments for windage and elevation, and the Lyman Challenger. Both are superb. The Challenger is a true 4-x and the Stith about a 4.3-x. The Challenger is probably the stronger scope which would stand up to a greater beating on a rifle of extremely heavy recoil like the .375 Magnum or .300 Weatherby Magnum. It is also a very heavy scope and for that reason should never be chosen if a man wants a featherweight rifle. The power of the Leupold and the Texan 4-x is about like that of the Weaver and, optically, I don't think either of them is comparable to the Bear Cub and the Challenger. The 4-x Bausch & Lomb is apparently not a true 4-x and since it is made without internal adjustments it has to be mounted on a special mount, like that turned out by Bausch & Lomb, which incorporates adjustments. The Stith-Kollmorgen scopes in 4 and 6-x are made with and without internal adjustments. The 2½ is with elevation only and the 2¾ with double adjustments only. The 2½ and 4-x Leupold scopes are available with or without internal adjustments.

A good 6-x scope is a beautiful optical instrument. For all except the very longest shots at varmints it is perfectly satisfactory, but no 6-x will give definition sufficient for 300 or 400 yard shots at woodchucks. However, a good 6-x is perfectly satisfactory for chucks to 225–250 yards and in some lights it can be used at 300 yards.

The outstanding 6-x hunting-type scope is the superb 6-x Stith Bear Cub which, as this is written, sells for $100 with double adjustments. Optics of this scope are so good that one can, under good conditions, spot .30 caliber bullet holes at 200 yards with it. Another good 6-x is the Unertl 6-x Condor made by the John Unertl Optical Co., of Pittsburgh, Pa. Unertl also makes a very good 2¾-x hunting scope which actually is a 2¾-x and not a 2-x and he makes the fine 4-x Hawk which is beautiful optically but is not a true 4-x. The Unertl hunting scopes sell in the price range of the Weaver scopes and are good buys.

Weaver makes a scope of variable power from 2¾ to 5-x and Bausch & Lomb makes a variable power scope of from 2½ to 4-x. The idea of instant power variation has a great deal of sales appeal, but it has been my experience that the man who buys a KV leaves it set at 5-power and the man who buys the Bausch & Lomb job leaves it set at 4. There is one sour aspect to the varia-

THE BIG-GAME RIFLE

ble power idea and that is that as the power is reduced so is the apparent size of the reticule. In other words, the reticule looks coarser at high power and finer at low power whereas the scope at low power would be used in poor light in thick woods and a coarse reticule would be needed; set at higher power, it would tend to be used on small objects at long range, and in good light, and the fine crosshair would be more useful.

In the future I think the tendency is going to be more toward the 6-x scope for certain purposes, just as the tendency has been away from the 2½-x scope to the 4-x. As this is written, the Weaver K-4 greatly outsells the 2½-x K-2.5 in the West. The 4 and 6-x Stiths far outsell the 2½-x Stith. As hunters become more used to the scope, they see the advantage of power and the good definition it gives. For long-range big-game shooting, such as antelope shooting, on the plains of Wyoming, a 6-x is unsurpassed. In the Southwest where many hunters go after the little whitetail deer with small antlers which are often difficult to see, the 6-x scope is becoming increasingly popular. The hunter does not have to see the antlers with a binocular, then drop the binocular and find the deer in the scope. Instead a good 6-x gives sufficient definition so the man can lift his rifle when the deer jumps, see the antlers in the scope and at the same time get the reticule on the buck and touch her off!

I seriously doubt if a scope higher than 6-x has any real use in the big-game hunting field. Scopes of 8 and even 10-x are very useful on varmints and some are using target-type scopes with power as high as 15-x. However, the target must be stationary as even an 8-x scope is useless on running game, because the field is too small and the latitude of eye relief is too critical.

Another great advantage of the telescope sight is that it turns the user into a better shot. The scope-using rifleman can see better and call his shots better. Because he can see better he learns to hold steadier and develops better trigger control. Riflemen who habitually use scopes of high power and can see exactly what their rifles do, are able to realize the potentials of accuracy built

IRON AND GLASS SIGHTS FOR THE BIG-GAME RIFLE

into fine modern rifles and fine ammunition as well as to develop their skill as marksmen. Actually no one without a good scope sight can realize the virtues built into his rifle, and for modern big-game hunting a good scope, properly selected, properly mounted, and properly adjusted is practically a necessity.

Mounts for Hunting Scopes

If I were to describe in detail all of the mounts for hunting scopes available on the American market today, this chapter would be endless, so I shall take up only the proved and popular types of mounts and individual makes.

Choice of mount depends primarily on one thing. That is whether the hunter plans to leave his scope on his rifle on all occasions or whether he wants to be able to remove it quickly and use a good iron sight as an auxiliary sight.

For about 80 per cent of all hunting the best deal is to mount a scope securely on a rifle and leave it there, come hell or high water. However, it is a pious idea in certain instances to have iron sights available. If the hunter goes on a long wilderness trip, particularly if he has but one rifle, he should have iron sights in addition to the scope, so that if something should go haywire with the scope his rifle would not be useless. The rifle to be used in a land of wet brush and much rain should also have iron sights available. I have just heard, as this is written, from a friend who recently returned from a brown bear hunt on Kodiak Island, a land of rain, fog, mist, and high, wet brush. He carried a rifle with a scope attached with a permanent bridge mount. He said he had a heck of a time. Even with scope covers on, he was always getting moisture on the lenses and having to stop and wipe them off.

One time at the head of the Muskwa River up in the Stone sheep country of northern British Columbia, I was carrying a scope-sighted .270 with no iron sights. A heavy rain came on when we were about 3,000 feet above camp and about four or five miles away. Anyone who has hunted in that country knows that the willows and buck brush grow as high as a man's shoulders and that they have a wonderful affinity for water. When we finally got down that mountain my scope was completely water-logged. There was moisture between the lens elements of the ocular and it actually took me almost a week to dry it out. The scope would look clear and bright, but if the temperature would change the moisture would condense, and one could no more see through it than through a London fog. Scopes today are more nearly waterproof than they used to be, but a good many of them can take in moisture, and rain can fog up the lenses.

This will seldom happen even on the long trip into the Canadian Rockies or in the mountains of the Yukon or Alaska, but when it does it is a pretty embarrassing condition and a dangerous one in case a man should blunder onto a truculent grizzly.

There are various ways of licking this problem. Some bridge mounts are made with auxiliary peeps that can be slipped in, but these usually take a higher front sight and the higher the front sight is the more liable it is to get bent and damaged.

I think the best way to solve the problem is to have the scope mounted as low as possible on a good quick detachable side mount like the Griffin & Howe or Mykrom. Then one can put on a receiver sight with a quick detachable slide like the Lyman 48. He can carry it on his belt and then slip in the slide of the receiver sight. He is then set. I have a .30/06 and a .270 especially built for far Northern hunting and so equipped. Both have Lyman 48's and both have Griffin & Howe side mounts. In one case the scope is a Lyman Alaskan; in the other case it is a Stith 4-x Bear Cub.

I would not recommend a quick detachable side mount for saddle use where a man will jump off his horse, grab the rifle out of the scabbard and cut loose. Because of the construction, any side mount lets the scope have considerable overhang and

IRON AND GLASS SIGHTS FOR THE BIG-GAME RIFLE

there is always the possibility that a man can drop his scope and bend one end or the other. The saddle scabbard has to fit exactly or there is the possibility that the front end of the scope tube can be wedged into the scabbard and the entire weight of the rifle will be carried by the scope tube itself, and the scope will be bent as it is jounced around by the horse. One time I took a .30/06 equipped with a quick detachable side mount in a poorly fitting scabbard on a mule deer hunt in the Salmon River in Idaho. When I started out that morning I very neatly killed a coyote at about 250 yards. My rancher-guide told me that his troubles were over. He knew that if I saw a nice buck that it was mine. Then we saw a handsome buck and I shot over it four times. I also shot over another four times. As luck would have it, I got a crack at a third buck and by holding below the bottom line of the belly I managed to kill it. When I got home I discovered that the rifle was shooting well over a foot high at 100 yards and what had happened was that the arms of the mount had been bent. They were of aluminum construction. Wedging down into the saddle scabbard was the villain in this case.

When a man is allergic to hunting in the rain as most of us are, when a man lives in a country that is dry during the big-game season, and when he carries his rifle with a scope on it much in a saddle scabbard, far and away the best way to mount a scope is with a low, permanent bridge-type mount with the bases of the mount attached to the receiver ring and the receiver bridge. This is the most popular type of hunting scope mount and properly so. It gives lower line of sight, maximum protection to the scope and minimum overhang. A very satisfactory type of bridge mount is the two-piece Redfield Senior which is now no longer made and the very similar Tilden made by the Tilden Manufacturing Co., 2750 North Speer Blvd., Denver 11, Colorado. Another very good mount is the famous Redfield Jr.. which is one of the most popular of all American scope mounts. The similar Buehler mount has also proved to be highly satisfactory.

THE BIG-GAME RIFLE

Another very good mount which I have used on several rifles and on many trips, is the Stith Streamline mount, a combination of side mount and bridge mount. The rear portion is attached to the side of the receiver. The front portion is attached to the barrel on a block. The front end of the scope tube is held in a sleeve which protects the scope from water and from side lights. It gives maximum scope protection because at the front end, anyway, there is absolutely no overhang. The Stith Streamline mount is a custom made proposition and rifles have to be sent to Stith Mounts in San Antonio, to have scopes mounted. However, for the very strongest type of mount, I think it is worthwhile. I have carried Stith-mounted scopes all over North America on horseback and on foot and have never had any trouble with them.

I remember one day when I was carrying the head of the best Stone sheep I have ever shot down a very steep mountainside off the Prophet River in British Columbia. I was heavily laden with my rifle, a 45-pound sheep head, cartridge box, binoculars, camera, sheep feet to make a gun rack from, and a couple of back straps to devour. All of a sudden, one of my heels came down on a perfectly round rock about the size of a baseball buried in the soft moss and lichens of the hillside. My feet shot out from under me and I landed with a terrific crash. In a moment sheep head, rifle, sheep feet, and O'Connor were all rolling down the hillside. With a lot of misgivings I picked up my rifle. The stock had some very bad and ugly nicks in it, and it had hit so hard that the rocks had even made nicks in the barrel, but the scope was intact and the next day when I tore a piece of paper out of a notebook, tacked it to a tree, and shot at it from a rest over a bedroll, the rifle had not changed the point of impact in the slightest.

The bridge-type mount also has other advantages. Most factory rifles are tapped and drilled for that type of mount, with two holes in the receiver ring and one in the receiver bridge.

IRON AND GLASS SIGHTS FOR THE BIG-GAME RIFLE

One can put such a mount on with no more elaborate equipment than a screwdriver. The bridge mount like the Redfield and Buehler is useful if a man wants to use two scopes on one rifle or the same scope on two or more rifles. All he needs is bases for each rifle. Then he can quickly remove the scope from one rifle, put it in place on another rifle equipped with the same base, sight it in, and he is set. He might use, let us say, a 6-x Stith Bear Cub on a .220 Swift for his spring and summer varmint shooting, then when fall came he might put it on a .30/06 or .270 for a mountain hunt.

There are many other types of mounts. Some are made on a V-block principle by which the scope lies either in a regular V-block or in V-blocks formed by cones. The Bausch & Lomb and Stith Master Mounts are built on this principle. Those mounts are satisfactory enough, but I do not think any of them improve the looks of the rifle and for esthetic reasons I have never cared for them.

There have been many attempts to sell the American big-game hunter on scopes with no provision for windage and elevation but with adjustments in the mount. They have not been particularly successful. I happen to know that the Stith scopes with double adjustments by far outsell those without them. As this is written Leupold-Stevens Co., of Portland, has seen the handwriting on the wall and has brought out a good 4-x with adjustment for windage. Elevation can be obtained in a mount. Theoretically perhaps, the adjustments are stronger and possibly more reliable in a base. Actually, in my experience, I have found it easier and quicker to adjust the scope with internal adjustments. If windage and elevation are in the scope it also makes it possible to produce a lighter, simpler, and cheaper mount. It is very true that the scope with no internal adjustments is cheaper to make, more nearly waterproof, and able to stand up under more recoil. Nevertheless, I will string along with the majority of American sportsmen and pick a scope with internal adjustments.

Anyone is, I believe, bucking the current if he tries to sell the American big-game hunter a scope with no internal adjustments.

In spite of its manifold virtues, the scope is not the answer to everything. Very heavy recoil will shake even the best scopes to pieces. The scope on a .375 Magnum should, for instance, be carefully chosen and so should the mount because over thirty pounds of free recoil is a tough proposition to buck. I shook three scopes to pieces on the first .375 I had. Phil Johnstone, of Griffin & Howe, writes that the Lyman Alaskan has never given them any trouble on .375's and the firm usually recommends that scope for rifles of heavy recoil. How the others stand up I cannot say. That is the heaviest rifle that a scope should be put on. A scope is out of the question for the heavy magazine rifles like the .404 and the .505 Gibbs. A scope would also be out of the question on one of the even more potent doubles for the very heaviest and most dangerous game.

Because of the higher line of sight I wouldn't care for a scope on a rifle to be used on heavy game in the brush. Elephants and Cape buffalo are often killed at ranges which are actually measured in feet rather than yards and often, to stop a charge, one has to point his rifle as he would a shotgun rather than aim. A scope would complicate matters because of this higher line of sight and restricted field of view.

In open country a scope of about 2½-x would be fast to use and excellent even for stopping the charge of a lion because of its great depth of focus and its wide field. I believe the African rifle, like the rifle to be used on the big Alaska brown bear, if it is going to be scope-equipped, should always be equipped with a quick detachable side mount and with receiver sight with a large aperture attached.

Nor is the scope of any use to the dumbbell or careless man who treats his rifle as he would an old rusty axe or a hoe. I knew one chap who bought himself a new Model 70 Winchester and had it equipped with a good scope on a good mount. He habitually carried the rifle by throwing it in the trunk of his car along

IRON AND GLASS SIGHTS FOR THE BIG-GAME RIFLE

with the chains and the tire tools. When I say throwing it, I mean throwing it. Presently he was squawking to me that scopes were no good because they wouldn't hold their adjustment.

For most purposes, though, a good scope on a good mount is the finest sight the big-game hunter can buy. If he chooses a good scope of the right power, puts it on a satisfactory mount, sights it in correctly for the proper range, and learns how to handle his outfit he will do big-game shooting with his modern high-intensity rifle that a few years ago would have been considered impossible.

Reticules for the Scope Sight

Almost as important as the choice of the scope and the mount is the choice of the reticule. There are a few good ones and many bad ones. Some European scopes have come over with the doggondest collection of bars, crosshairs, dots, and picket posts that you ever saw. They clutter up the field so much that it is difficult to pay any attention to the game because there is so much other stuff to look at.

A most universally useful reticule is the plain crosshair or crosswire of the medium fine or medium variety. The eye naturally finds the center of the crossed wires and even if he cannot see the intersection he will know almost precisely where it is because the wires will lead him to it. With a crosshair one can also hold over for a long shot without blotting out the game. I use crosshairs almost exclusively in all my scopes.

The next most popular type of reticule is a flat-top post. It is the most conspicuous reticule and probably a bit the fastest to use. It is probably the best reticule to use if one is to hunt in very poor light in heavily forested country, because it is a fact that under certain conditions the post with the wide, flat top can be seen when the crosshair cannot be seen at all. This does not happen very often, but it happens, and particularly for shooting in

THE BIG-GAME RIFLE

the first few minutes at dawn and the last few minutes at dusk before things fade out completely the flat-topped post is the business. I would rather forego those shots in the very poorest light to obtain greater accuracy with long shots on small objects with the crosshair, but it is up to every man to name his poison. For my part I have almost never run into an occasion when I couldn't see the crosshairs perfectly even when I was hunting in timber in the far North in the sub-arctic. The first moose I ever shot was taken with a scope-sighted rifle with crosshair reticule in timber just about as heavy, thick, and dark as any I have ever seen and I had no difficulty in getting the crosshair on the target.

The crosshair has another advantage over the post and that is that it is more accurate on running game. I very quickly found that out. The horizontal crosshair is excellent at maintaining elevation. All one has to do is to drag the horizontal hair along the running animal's body, then put the vertical hair the right distance ahead and touch 'er off. I have done far better running shooting on jackrabbits and coyotes with crosshair reticule than with post. The advantage is distinctly noticeable on short use.

Another excellent reticule is the dot which was originated by Capt. T. K. Lee, Box 2123, Birmingham, Alabama. It is suspended on spider web so fine as to be invisible and can be ordered to subtend anything from a quarter-minute on up. The dot has many advantages. For one thing it is excellent to hold over with since the web is so fine as to be invisible and the dot appears to float in the field of the scope. For another it is a fine range-finding reticule. I found a 4-minute dot in a 2½-x scope to be particularly useful for that purpose. Let us say that our average antelope will be from the bottom of the brisket to the top of the shoulders about 16–18 inches deep. Suppose that you put the dot on the antelope and you find that you can see antelope both above and below the dot. Your antelope would then be about 300 yards away. I remember one time when I killed an antelope in Wyoming which the guide said was 450 or 500 yards away. The dot told me that the antelope was actually about 300 yards

IRON AND GLASS SIGHTS FOR THE BIG-GAME RIFLE

away and I hit it squarely with the first shot. Another time I was hunting Dall sheep in the Yukon and a ram popped up above me on a cliff. Because objects above or below one look smaller, I would have judged that ram to be about 400 yards away or thereabouts. As a matter of curiosity I put the dot on it and figured it out and the ram was actually only something over 200.

For all-around use in a scope of about 2½-x a 4-minute dot is about right. For use in heavy woods a dot subtending 5 or 6 minutes is even better, but too big for open country shooting. In a scope of 4-x a dot subtending about 2½ minutes is sufficiently conspicuous to be very fast and very effective. As the power of the scope is increased the value of the dot will be decreased because the dot is magnified.

There are many other reticules. One favorite is the crosshair combined with the post. Presumably the crosshair keeps the rifleman from canting his piece, but although I have used such reticules I never notice the crosshair at all but instead focus my eye on the top of the post. A reticule consisting of four bars and a crosshair is an excellent one for moonlight shooting, but it is a special reticule with a very limited use.

The simple reticules are the best and the crosshair, the flat-topped post, and the dot are the ones to be selected.

CHAPTER XIV

Sight Adjustment for Big-Game Hunting

A THING which has always astounded me about hunters of big game is how few of them give much thought to the subject of sighting in a rifle perfectly for the conditions under which they are planning to hunt. With many hunters, sight adjustment is very casual. They assume that the rifle was sighted in at the factory and that the workers who do the job there are experts and that they are not. If they "check" their sights it is by taking a pop at a stone at some undetermined distance. If they hear a pop of bullet against something hard and see dust fly all is well with the world.

The good big-game hunter should *know* where his particular rifle puts a particular bullet at various ranges and under various conditions—with tight sling, with no sling. He shouldn't guess, he should *know*, and the only way he can find out is by shooting.

The best way to line up sights with the big-game rifle is by shooting at short range and making preliminary sight adjustments there. Many scope-sighted rifles are received from custom makers with the scope bore sighted only—and "bore sighting" is a term which means a preliminary lining up of sights and bore by putting the rifle in a vice, training it so that some object can be seen through the bore and then adjusting the scope or other sight so that the same object can be seen with the reticule superimposed upon it. This is a good *preliminary* way of sighting a

SIGHT ADJUSTMENT FOR BIG-GAME HUNTING

rifle in but by no means a final way. Shooting is the only thing that really tells the story.

Short-range preliminary shooting is to be preferred, because then the bullets will strike somewhere on the target, whereas if the rifle is shot, let us say, at 200 yards the bullets may strike off the target and the rifleman will be no wiser than when he started.

It is a good stunt to shoot an iron-sighted rifle at 12½ yards and a scope-sighted rifle at 25 yards, in each case making tentative sight adjustment to put the bullets at point of aim at that distance. When this is done, bullets are not going to hit so far off at 100 yards.

The joker, though, is that every error at 12½ yards will be multiplied by 8 at 100 yards and every error at 25 yards will be multiplied by four. That is why no one should ever depend wholly on short-range sighting.

Good scope and iron sights today are marked in minutes of angle or fractions thereof, and a minute changes the point of impact 1 inch at 100 yards, ½ inch at 50 yards, ¼ inch at 25 yards. Likewise, a minute equals 2 inches at 200 yards, 3 inches at 300 yards, etc. If, for example, our bullets *average* striking, 6 inches too high and 4 inches to the left of where we want them to strike at 100 yards, the sights should be moved 6 minutes in the down direction as marked on the adjustment dial of the scope or on the slide of the receiver sight and 4 minutes to the right. One should never attempt to adjust sights from one shot. Instead he should shoot a group of at least 3 shots, and better 5 shots, and then determine the average point of impact and make adjustment from it. Shooting should always be from a bench rest, a sandbag, a bedroll or something of the sort.

Sight adjustment with either scope or receiver sight marked in minutes of angle is simple, but with almost all open sights without these fine adjustments, it is a headache. Now and then it will be discovered that with the scope properly adjusted the reticule is out of the center of the field. When this happens the

THE BIG-GAME RIFLE

fault lies with the mounting and the rifle should be returned to whoever mounted it for correction.

Upon occasion one will run into a rifle which will still shoot high with the lowest adjustment of the rear sight. In that case, the only cure (except possibly rebedding of the barrel in the forend) is a higher front sight. At other times a rifle pops up that when sighted in has the slide of the receiver sight boosted high in the air. Then the cure is a lower front sight. If a rifle with open iron sights shoots to the right, one can only knock the rear sight over to the left in the dovetail slot.

The rifleman should always remember that his bullets never fly in a straight line, and that sighting in only consists of pointing the barrel up so that the path of the bullet's flight will rise above the line of sight at some point and then fall across it at some other point. Even though the bullet is rising in relation to line of sight, it is always falling in relation to the line of bore.

Thorough knowledge of this curved bullet path called trajectory and its relationship to the line of sight is of utmost importance to the rifleman, whether he has to knock off an antelope at 500 yards or wants to shoot the head off a rattlesnake at 10 feet.

Up in northern British Columbia one fall, my guide and I were coming down the steep trail after a day of caribou hunting when a flock of a half dozen plump blue grouse flew up out of the brush and perched in a spruce. I had no compunctions about making a racket, since we were on our way out and my big-game hunting was about over. Furthermore, I was hungry for grouse.

What to do? I had no shotgun, no .22 target pistol, and my .22 rifle was back in camp. The only thing I had to collect those grouse with was a .30/06 loaded with 180-grain Remington Core-Lokt bullets and sighted with a scope.

The thing that made a grouse rifle out of the .30/06 was the fact that I knew something about the trajectory. I had sighted in to put the bullet to the point of aim at 225 yards. BUT the bullet first crossed the line of scope sight at 25 yards. Because of

SIGHT ADJUSTMENT FOR BIG-GAME HUNTING

the trajectory curve, the rifle was sighted in for *two* distances, 25 and 225 yards.

Anyway, I put the crosshairs of the Weaver K-2.5 scope right at the point where the neck of the grouse joins the body and touched her off. The grouse hit the ground with a thump, his head hanging by a bit of skin. Believe it or not, I knocked off 5 of those 6 grouse, all with neck shots. The sixth bird finally decided something pretty fishy was going on and flew off.

When I lined up on my first bird, my guide thought I was nuts, he told me later, as he was sure the .30/06 would blow them to shreds. The fact that I had been able to break their necks had seemed like nothing less than black magic. Yet the guide had done the same thing time after time on a trapline with a .22. Only the fact that it was done at short range with a "long-range" rifle made it seem mysterious.

Knowing a few facts about trajectory curves has paid off for me many times—in picking off meat for the pot at short range with big-game rifles and also in making hits at long range on big game. Everyone should know, for instance, that his big-game rifle is actually sighted to hit the point of aim at *two* distances, the first at from 10 to 25 yards, depending on several factors which we shall go into later, and the second at from 150 to 250 yards or so.

When a bullet leaves the barrel of a rifle it immediately begins to fall from the *line of bore*, although at the same time it is rising toward the line of *sight*. All bullets are acted on by the same force, gravity. A 130-grain .270 bullet dropped from the hand will hit the ground at exactly the same time as the same bullet fired from a rifle with a muzzle velocity of 3,140 f.p.s., as both are free-falling bodies of the same weight and shape. If the same .270 bullet could be speeded up to 4,000 or even to 5,000 f.p.s., it would also hit the ground at the same time. However, the faster the bullet travels the farther it goes in the interval that gravity is acting upon it.

The faster a bullet is traveling, the "flatter" the path of travel, or the less it falls for every foot of forward travel. No bullet flies flat, no matter how fast it is traveling because it is being acted upon by gravity.

The answer to the often-asked question: "How far will such and such a bullet travel without dropping?" is, then, "No distance at all." Near the muzzle where velocity is high the drop doesn't amount to much, but it is there just the same.

The "flatness" of trajectory depends on the initial velocity coupled with the shape and sectional density of the bullet. The long sharp-pointed bullet loses its velocity more slowly than a short round-nosed bullet and hence shoots "flatter." And that word, by the way, should read "more nearly flat" or "with a less pronounced curve." To employ another popular term which doesn't mean much, such a bullet "carries up" better.

To get down to concrete instances, let's take the round-nosed 110-grain bullet in the .30/06 at a velocity of 3,350. In spite of the high velocity this bullet has a more curved trajectory over 300 yards than does a 150-grain spitzer bullet which left the muzzle with about 400 f.p.s. less velocity. The answer, of course, lay in better shape and sectional density or, to employ a fancy term, in a better ballistic coefficient. This is why using a lighter but faster bullet of the same caliber does not always pay off. The shorter the bullet is for the caliber, the faster it loses its velocity and the more pronounced the trajectory curve is.

Because gravity remains constant whereas velocity is always falling off, the path of a bullet is a curve known as a parabola. It is irregular and NOT a segment of a circle as is often imagined. Consequently, the height of the trajectory over any given range is not at the point midway, but somewhat beyond. Over a 200-yard range the high point is at about 110 yards; over 300 yards at about 165 yards, etc. The farther the bullet travels, the greater the drop per 100 yards of flight. If the bullet were to travel so far that all forward motion would be lost, the bullet would drop straight down just like the bullet we mentioned dropped from the hand.

SIGHT ADJUSTMENT FOR BIG-GAME HUNTING

This all may be on the technical side, but we bring it in to show: (1) that bullets are always falling; (2) that, strictly speaking, there isn't any such thing as a "flat shooting" rifle; and (3) to show that muzzle velocity is just one of the factors in a comparatively flat trajectory.

In order to compensate for the drop of the bullet, the properly sighted in rifle has the bore pointed *up*, as the rear sight is higher than the front sight. The line of sight, then, is an imaginary line running straight to the target. The line of bore is another imaginary line which intersects the line of sight and continues on. The trajectory curve is the path followed by the bullet. It intersects the line of sight once near the muzzle and once again at a considerable distance, but never cross the line of bore because the bullet falls continuously after it leaves the muzzle.

If the line of bore of a rifle is pointed parallel to the earth, the bullet drop at 100 yards is amazing, since the bullet does not have a chance to rise above the line of bore at all.

Here are some figures: the .22 long rifle bullet at standard velocity of 1,180 has a drop, or total fall, over 100 yards of 15 inches; the high velocity version of the same bullet at 1,375 f.p.s. has a total fall of 12 inches; even the 170-grain .30/30 bullet, which steps along at the much faster rate of 2,200 f.p.s., falls 4 inches below the line of bore at 100 yards. The 180-grain .30/06 bullet is traveling at 2,700 f.p.s. when it leaves the muzzle and drops 1 inch less or 3 inches below the line of bore; speed the bullet up to 3,140 as in the case with the 130-grain .270 and the drop is only 2 inches; speed it up still more until it is traveling like the Swift or the 100-grain .270 and the total fall is only about 1 inch. *The faster a bullet travels the less it falls over a given range because the less time old man gravity has to work on it.*

Now let's look at the total fall from line of bore of those bullets over 200 yards where they are slowing up more and where gravity has more chance to get in his dirty work:

THE BIG-GAME RIFLE

22 long rifle (standard speed)	55 inches
.22 high velocity	50 inches
.30/30	18 inches
.30/06 190-grain	11 inches
.270 130-grain	8 inches
.220 Swift 48-grain	4 inches

The thing to do in sighting a rifle in, then, is to jockey these figures of total fall, line of sight, and line of bore around until we have a workable combination. We tame this trajectory business and *learn* it.

In the case of a load with the trajectory of the .22 with high speed ammunition—and that includes most black-powder jobs—we learn that we tame the trajectory curve a bit by hoisting it above the line of sight, then letting it drop again. Whereas, at only 50 yards, the total fall of the high velocity .22 bullet is 3 inches and the bore sighted .22 would miss the head of a squirrel, if we sight in the .22 to hit the point of aim at 50 yards, the bullet will rise only about ½ inch above the line of sight at 30 yards. Even sighted in for 75 yards, we find that the bullet from an iron-sighted .22 will cross the line of aim *first* at 10 yards, climb 1.3 inches above the line of aim at 50 yards, cross the line of aim again at 75 yards (the distance at which it is said to be sighted in for), and fall 3 inches below the line of aim at 100 yards, a very far cry indeed from the appalling total fall of 12 inches at that distance. Anywhere along the way from the muzzle to 85 yards, the bullet would not deviate from line of aim enough to miss the head of a cottontail, or for that matter the head of a squirrel with a very little bit of allowance. With the scope-sighted .22, the range can be stretched a bit with the same maximum trajectory height of 1.3 inches. In this case the bullet will first cross the line of aim at 25 yards, cross again at 85 yards, and be only 2 inches low at 100. Even with that sighting, though, the .22 bullet, because of its low velocity, is 7 inches low at 125 yards, and 13 inches low at 150 yards. All of which explains why the finest scope in the world won't make a .22 rim-fire a long-

SIGHT ADJUSTMENT FOR BIG-GAME HUNTING

range varmint rifle! Gravity simply has too much time to work on a .22 bullet.

To me it has seemed like sheer folly to sight a rifle in for some short distance simply because most game is killed at that range. Not long ago I read a very good hunting tale by a man who used a scope-sighted .270 which he had sighted in for 100 yards because he had it doped out that he would probably shoot his deer at 100 yards. Now suppose our hunter had got a quick shot at 250 yards and he had held dead on. The 150-grain bullet would have fallen 10 inches below point of aim, and he probably would have missed the buck. On the other hand, if he had sighted in for 225 yards, the bullet would have been only 3 inches high at 100 and 150 yards and only 2 inches low at 250. Unless he planned to go around shooting deer in the eye, a 3-inch deviation from line of aim surely is not excessive!

This lesson *to sight in for the longest possible range that will not cause mid-range misses* was very nicely impressed on me down in Mexico a good many years ago. Carrying a .270 sighted with the 130-grain bullet to hit at the conventional 200-yard range, I came over the rim of a big, open *rincon*, or basin, and just as I got set to glass it, a fine whitetail buck got up and took off, traveling around the basin in a semi-circle.

I didn't give much thought as to how far he was and didn't hold high. I emptied the rifle, rammed in some more cartridges, and finally knocked him off on the eighth or ninth shot. When I got to him, I found four bullet burns on the lower edge of his body. Instead of being around 200 yards away, he was probably over 300 yards. Because of the 200-yard sighting, the drop below line of aim at that distance was 8 or 9 inches. The high shots in the group were just chewing at the edges of the buck and the shot that killed him was actually a poorly pulled one that was well out of the group. A great light dawned on me then, and from that time on I have always sighted a .270 in for a much longer range.

With the .270 Winchester-Western factory load with the

130-grain Silvertip bullet I do the preliminary sighting at 25 yards, and adjust the scope to hit the point of aim at that distance. The bullet then strikes 3 inches high at 100 yards, 4 inches high at 150 and 200 yards, at point of aim the second time at 275, and only 2 inches low at 300. At 325 yards, the bullet is 4 inches below the point of aim. For big-game shooting, even smallish deer and antelope which run from 14 to 17 inches from top of shoulder to bottom of chest, this is not excessive deviation, and the point-blank range of a .270 so sighted is 325 yards. Sighted for 200 yards, on the other hand, the point-blank range is only about 260 yards, because at that distance the bullet falls 4 inches below point of aim.

Let's apply the same formula to the 30/06 with the factory 150-grain load at 2,960 f.p.s., and sight in so the path of the bullet first crosses the line of aim at 25 yards and strikes 3 inches high at 100 yards. At 150 yards, the bullet strikes 4 inches high; at 200 yards, 3 inches high; at 250 yards, it is at point of aim the second time, and the bullet does not fall more than 4 inches below point of aim until it has pressed the 290-yard mark. Such a sighting makes the old .30/06 a pretty doggoned good long-range sheep and antelope rifle!

With the slower 180-grain bullet at 2,700 f.p.s. and the same formula of the scope-sighted rifle laying them at point of aim at 25 yards the first time and putting them 3 inches high at 100 yards, the range is stretched to 225 yards, where the bullet crosses the line of aim the second time. It does not drop more than 4 inches until it has passed the 260-yard mark.

Now let's take a look at the ordinary deer rifle of the 2,000 f.p.s. class, and with iron sights. If you sight one of these babies in for 100 yards, the bullet fall at 200 will be about 10 inches,—enough to miss even a big whitetail buck with a center-of-the-chest hold. On the other hand, if the rifle is sighted for 150 yards, the bullet will fall only 5 inches at 200 yards and a hit with no allowance for drop is probable. With a 150-yard sighting the bullet is only 2 inches above the point of aim at 100 yards, and

SIGHT ADJUSTMENT FOR BIG-GAME HUNTING

that is so little deviation from line of aim as to be negligible. An iron-sighted .30/30 so sighted lays the bullet across the line of aim the first time at about 12½ yards, a handy thing to remember when a grouse perches up in the tree. The same trajectory applies to any of the so-called deer cartridges, the .32 Special, .25/35, .35 Remington, .30 Remington, etc., and also to the big Nitro-Express elephant cartridges.

The iron-sighted rifle using a cartridge with a velocity of 2,400–2,500 f.p.s. can well be sighted in for 175 yards. This will include the .300 Savage with the 180-grain bullet, the .348 with the 200-grain bullet, the .30/40 Krag with the 180-grain, or the .303 British as loaded in Canada with a similar bullet, the .30/06 with the 220-grain bullet, and the 7 mm. Mauser with the 175-grain. With any of these the bullet will first cross the line of iron sight at 10–12½ yards. At 100 yards, it will be 2½–3 inches high, at point of aim again at 175 yards, and only 2 or 3 inches low at 200 yards.

When such rifles are scope-sighted, the trajectory is apparently flattened out a bit, and they can be sighted for 200 yards. In that case, the bullet will first cross the line of sight at 25 yards. At 100 yards, it will be 3 inches high, and at 250 only about 5 inches low—all of which means that with the 180-grain bullet and a scope sight, even the old .30/40 can stretch right out there.

How high a mid-range trajectory to allow depends on many factors: the size of the game, the size of the portion on the game you want to hit, the type of country you are to hunt in, and so on. A squirrel hunter who wants to hit his game in the head can't have much deviation from line of aim or he'll register misses with good holds. On the other hand, pretty much the same thing applies to the man who hunts heavy and dangerous game in brush and jungle at short range. The elephant hunter wants to put his bullet very close to point of aim at from 20 feet to 50 yards and if he has a chance he tries to aim midway between the eye and the orifice of the ear. Very much deviation from line of aim in his case might be fatal. For this reason the big "stopping rifle" prob-

THE BIG-GAME RIFLE

ably should be sighted in to hit the point of aim at 100 yards. The bullet will then first cross the line of iron sight at about 20 yards, which should be about right for use on dangerous game in the brush, and at 50 yards, the bullet will be only 1 inch high, something which should not be fatal even in the case of a charging lion or Cape buffalo.

The hunter of non-dangerous big game, on the other hand, has much larger marks, from the small deer measuring 14 inches from chest to withers, to the enormous moose measuring from 35–40 inches. A 4-inch deviation is peanuts even on a medium-sized animal like a bighorn ram or a mule deer, either of which will average around 20 inches.

For those who haven't got the trajectory of their rifles memorized, it wouldn't be a bad idea to copy the dope in the accompanying table and affix it to the buttstock of their rifle with scotch tape. Then it is right there when it is needed.

Trajectory Dope and Suggested Ranges for Sighting in

.22 Long Rifle low velocity with iron sights.

Bullet first crosses line of aim at 10 yards. At 25 yards, 1 inch high; at 50 yards, 1.3 inches high; at 75 yards, crosses line of sight second time; at 100 yards, 2 inches low; at 125 yards, 10 inches low, at 150 yards, 18 inches low.

.22 Long Rifle high speed with scope sight.

First crosses line of sight at 20 yards; at 50 yards, 1.3 inches high; at 85 yards, at point of aim again; at 100 yards, 2 inches low; at 125 yards, 6.5 inches low; at 150 yards, 12 inches low.

Big Nitro Express "Stopping Rifles"—.465, .470, .475 No. 2, with heavy bullets at velocities of something above 2,000 f.p.s.

Bullet first crosses line of sight at about 20 yards; at 50 yards, about 1 inch high; at 100 yards, at point of aim; at 150 yards, about 3 inches low.

.30/30 with 170-grain bullet at 2,200 f.p.s., iron sights. (Also applicable with slight error to .25/35, .32 Special, .30 and .32 Remington, .303 Savage, .35 Remington, etc.)

SIGHT ADJUSTMENT FOR BIG-GAME HUNTING

Bullet first crosses line of aim at 12½ yards; at 50 yards; 1½ inches high; at 100 yards, 2 inches high; at 150 yards, crosses line of aim second time; at 200 yards, 5 inches low; at 250 yards, 14 inches low; at 300 yards, 28 inches low.

.30/40 Krag 180-grain bullet at 2,500 f.p.s., iron sights. (Also applicable with slight error to all calibers of the 2400–2500 f.p.s. class— .300 Savage 180-grain, .30/06 220-grain, .348 W.C.F. 200-grain, .22 Hornet, etc.)

Bullet first crosses line of sight at 12½ yards; at 50 yards, 1 inch high; at 100 yards, 2½ inches high; point of aim second time at 175; 2 inches low at 200; 8 inches low at 250; 16 inches low at 300.

.30/06 180-grain bullet at 2,700 f.p.s., scope sight.

Bullet first crosses line of sight at 25 yards; 1 inch high at 50 yards; 3 inches high at 100 and 150 yards; at point of aim again at 225; 9 inches low at 300; 18 inches low at 350; 32 inches low at 400; and 72 inches low at 500.

.30/06 150-grain bullet at 2,960 f.p.s., scope sight. (Also applicable to other 2,900–3,000 f.p.s. loads such as the 180-grain .300 Magnum, 87-grain .250/3000, 100-grain .257.)

Bullet crosses line of sight at 25 yards; 1½ inches high at 50 yards; 3 inches high at 100 yards; 4 inches high at 150; at point of aim again at 250 yards; 5 inches low at 300; 12 inches low at 350; 18 inches low at 400; 55 inches low at 500.

.270 130-grain bullet at 3,140 f.p.s., scope sight.

Bullet crosses line of sight at 25 yards; 1 inch high at 50 yards; 3 inches high at 100 yards; 4 inches high at 150 yards; 3 inches high at 200; point of aim again at 275; 3 inches low at 300; 8 inches low at 350; 15 inches low at 400; 40 inches low at 500.

Wildcat Big Game Rifles of Ultra High Velocity, scope-sighted. (This table applies to such ultra high velocity wildcats as the Weatherby series with the 100-grain bullet in the .257 Magnum, the 130-grain in the .270 Magnum, 145-grain bullet in the 7mm. Magnum, 180-grain bullet in the .300 Magnum.)

Bullet first crosses line of sight at 25 yards; 3 inches high at 100 yards; 4 inches high at 200 yards; 3 inches high at 250 yards; at point of aim at 325 yards; and about 2 inches low at 350 yards.

CHAPTER XV

Becoming a Good Game Shot

IN THE outskirts of the Idaho city where I live, there is a grassy basin which is an ideal spot for a rifle range, since any bullets fired therein are stopped by a solid background of hillside. I discovered the basin when I first moved to the city. A friend and I built a bench rest in it and erected some target frames. It is there that I do my testing and my practicing. Most of the year I just about have the place to myself, and the only other shooters who use it are a few rifle nuts and handloaders, possibly a dozen or so in a community of about 25,000.

Then come the last days of September, just before the elk and deer season opens. All at once this lonely little basin is as crowded as Coney Island on a hot Sunday in July. The "practical hunters" are doing their annual practicing. Volleys of rifle fire echo and re-echo. Fired .30/30, .300 Savage, and .30/06 cases litter the ground. Comes the opening day and all is quiet again. The pheasants and Hungarian partridges come back. Again the rifle nut appears with his leather bags for the bench rest, with his spotting scope, with his 200-yard small-bore targets.

The world is not exactly full of good game shots because most casual hunters never practice, except possibly to run a box of cartridges through their rifles once a year. People become good shots just as they become good tennis players, good golfers, good baseball players, or anything else—by intelligent practice. The man who would enter a golf tournament with only one round of

BECOMING A GOOD GAME SHOT

practice behind him in a year would be considered eccentric if not actually off the beam, but many a hunter goes off on a long and expensive big-game hunt with only the most casual practice, and this to "sight his rifle in." Many very bum shots bring home game, of course, but it is because game animals are large, often not very far away, and relatively plentiful.

Varmint shooting is excellent practice for big-game hunting, but any genuinely good shot has almost always acquired his skill by shooting at paper targets. Don't let anyone tell you different.

There is a myth to the effect that there is such a thing as a man who is a deadly big-game shot but who cannot hit paper to save his life. I do not believe it. A target is at a known distance. It is sharply defined. It stays put. The game animal is at an unknown distance, is moving or apt to move, and often it blends in with the surroundings and is not easy to see. Actually, the target is much easier to hit.

The man who shoots only at game can kid himself. He knocks over a deer at 150 yards. Presently the distance has become 400 yards. He shoots at the whole deer, happens to yank his trigger in such a manner that the shot hits the deer in the head. Presently he makes himself believe that he actually aimed at the head and is capable of shooting a deer in the head at 300 or 400 yards. He remembers his hits and forgets his misses.

Then he goes out to a target range. He is shocked to find he cannot stay in the 4-ring at 200 yards. "To hell with it!" he says. He is not a paper puncher but a "practical" shot. He will admit that he cannot do a thing on a target but there is just something about him which makes him poison on game.

Any good game shot is also a good target shot. He may not be the best target shot that ever lived, but he is not a poor one. Actually, targets may give some good game shots "target fever," just as game will give target shots buck fever. Nevertheless the same principles of good position, trigger squeeze, and shot calling apply to game shooting as well as to target shooting.

THE BIG-GAME RIFLE

There are such things as target shots who have progressed so far in their specialization that practice does them little further good for game shooting. The prone 100-yard small-bore shooter who practices in no other position is an example. So is the chap who never fires a shot without wearing his shooting coat and his mitt and without being wrapped up in a sling. These specialists are fine shots in a limited field. Since they have mastered the principles of holding and squeezing, however, they can very quickly become good game shots.

The game shot has to improvise. He often has to shoot quickly from unorthodox positions. He has to be able to shoot from any position and to make up his mind quickly what position he is going to use. He must learn to finish his trigger squeeze the instant his sights are correctly aligned the first time, even though on a target his shot would be a 9 rather than a 10, as a 9 will kill a mountain sheep, let us say, just as dead as will a 10.

He has to learn to hold over for long shots instead of adjusting his sights and, if he is to be an all-around game shot, he has to learn to hit running game.

Anyone with ambition to become a deadly big-game shot should, if he lives in a community where it is possible, join a rifle club and do regular shooting with anything from the .22 to a .300 Magnum. The club member meets good shots, picks up information on shooting, keeps his hand in. He should never forget, though, that his primary ambition is to become a game shot and that target shooting is but a means to an end.

The man who wants to become a crack big-game shot should hunt varmints regularly in season if he finds it at all possible, as varmint shooting is a sort of a postgraduate course for the big-game hunter, since he has to shoot at small, neutral-colored marks against poor backgrounds at unknown ranges. Shooting woodchucks is fine practice for the hunter, but the best of all varmints for training the game shot is the Western jackrabbit of the whitetail, blacktail, or antelope variety. He can be shot at 50 yards or at 400, on the sit or on the run, from offhand, kneeling, or sit-

BECOMING A GOOD GAME SHOT

ting. Any skill that I have in the shooting of running game I owe to the jackrabbit.

In this day and age, no one becomes a crack big-game shot by the shooting of big game only. The man who confines his big-game hunting to deer in one state can kill but one annually if he obeys the law. If he is particularly fortunate he may live where he can hunt both deer and elk. No one becomes an expert by shooting at one animal a year—or even at two, three, four or five. Once, many years ago, I hunted in two Canadian provinces and I shot two bighorn rams, two caribou, one grizzly, one moose, one goat, one mule deer, and one black bear on the trip. That is a lot of game for this continent and for one trip and more than I have ever shot on a trip since. As an opportunity for practice, though, this was relatively picayune. On many occasions I have shot 25 or 30 jackrabbits, half of them running, in a single afternoon, and the practice was worth several times as much as that of a 30-day trip into the big mountains. The jacks were smaller, less sharply defined, moving faster. Anyone who becomes a good varmint shot—particularly a good jackrabbit shot—will find the average shooting of big game almost ridiculously easy.

Intelligent practice is the only thing which makes a man a good shot. I say intelligent practice because poor practice simply fixes bad habits. No one can become a good shot without practice and lots of it. Nothing helps the shooter if he does not practice. He may be the grandson of a Western sheriff who fought and won 75 gun battles. He may own a library of 800 books on shooting and a battery of rifles containing everything from a .22 rim-fire to a .600 Nitro-Express. He may be able to quote ballistics by the yard. He still cannot be a good shot without *practice*. The poorest shot of all is the once-a-year hunter who never pops a primer except on his annual deer hunt. He may kill quite a few deer, but no one counts the empty cartridge cases per deer that he leaves in the woods.

Again, let no one kid himself that he is a good game shot but

THE BIG-GAME RIFLE

can't hit targets. There is nothing about game that suddenly turns the poor shot into a good one, that steadies his aim and causes him to squeeze the trigger instead of jerking it.

Getting the necessary practice is not too easy for many of us. Far better than nothing is dry firing. Anyone can put up a small bullseye in his room and practice holding, squeezing, and calling them for 15 minutes a day. A regime of this, coupled with a little actual shooting, will make anyone a far better-than-average shot in a short time.

Muscular co-ordination is important in rifle shooting. So is good eyesight, but the man who practices intelligently in good, steady positions will be a far better shot than the gifted athlete, with steel muscles and eyes like a hawk, who doesn't practice. There isn't such a thing as a born good shot. There are only good shots who learned by holding, squeezing, and calling!

A.B.C.'s of Rifle Shooting

But let's get down to essentials. . . . In its essence, nine-tenths of all rifle shooting is very simple. All the rifleman has to do is to put his sights on what he wants to hit, hold steadily, then get off his shot without disturbing his aim. If the rifle is correctly sighted and sufficiently accurate, and if trajectory does not have to be taken into consideration (as is the case with a long shot) or lead (as is the case with a running shot) that is all there is to it.

If it is all as easy as that, then, why isn't everyone a good shot?

A few little facts louse up this beautiful picture. In the first place, strictly speaking, there isn't such a thing as holding a rifle absolutely steady. Even from a bench rest, with the forend and butt rested on sandbags, a 20-x scope will show the keen-eyed that there is still a wobble, a very slight one but a wobble none the less, from the pulsations of the heart, from the blood flowing through the veins, perhaps. In the second place, letting the shot off without disturbing the aim is almost as difficult as holding the rifle steady. Even under ideal conditions with a heavy rifle and a light pull delicately squeezed, letting her off undoubtedly causes some slight movement.

Knowing all this, then, acquiring skill in shooting a rifle consists largely in learning to assume quickly the steadiest position feasible under the circumstances and then controlling the trigger to get the shot off properly.

It is unfortunate, perhaps, that most people who shoot rifles are self-taught. Most of us began with a rifle by getting hold of a .22 somehow, buying some ammunition, then going out and pecking away at tin cans, sparrows, rocks, or what have you. Our rifles were not properly sighted in. We knew nothing about correct positions and, for that reason, we couldn't hold a rifle even fairly steady. This exaggerated wobble gave us the tendency to yank the trigger. Most of us began in the offhand position, which is the most difficult of all positions. Some of us became fairly good shots, through a long process of trial and error, and through unlearning a lot of the bad habits we had picked up. Some of us did not.

The first step in learning to become a good shot is *wanting* to become one. In my own years as a professor of journalism, I found that the very first requirement for learning was enthusiasm. If I could make whatever skill or knowledge I wanted to impart seem interesting, dramatic, and important, I could teach anything, but if I couldn't arouse enthusiasm I was sunk.

So it is with starting anyone out with a rifle. Punching holes in black and white targets is a dull business to the beginner. He wants to see things break, watch feathers fly, hear bells ring. Practice with the rifle is far less dramatic than practice with a shotgun. Busting a clay target with a shot charge is spectacular. It gives a man something for his effort. Sad to relate, punching a little hole in a piece of paper is not.

The ideal combination for arousing enthusiasm in the beginner would be a shooting gallery crossed with a bench rest. Our tyro should be seated with his rifle rested solidly so an unsteady aim would not tempt him to yank the trigger, and allowed to shoot at iron bunnies, ducks, and what not. Lacking that, he can be started on lumps of clay, tin cans filled with water—anything that would give him a little drama.

At any rate, the beginner should start from the steadiest possible position. Since bench rests aren't too common, the next best bet is to use a sandbag from the prone position. Granted that the rifle is correctly sighted in, the problem is the let-off of the trigger. It sounds very simple indeed. All one has to do is to keep the sights correctly aligned and then squeeze off the shot.

It is much easier to learn trigger control from a steady position like shooting over a sandbag than it is from an unsteady position like offhand. When the sights are on and the rifle does not wobble about, the beginner can concentrate on squeezing the trigger, whereas if the rifle is unsteady the temptation is to yank and jerk in the vain hope of getting the shot off when the sights are right.

For many years it has been taught that the way to shoot is to increase the squeeze when the sights look right, hold it when they don't. Then, according to the theory, the gun goes off *unexpectedly when the sights are right* because that is the only time the trigger is being pressed. Theoretically this method of trigger control does not allow a man to flinch because he does not know when the gun is going off. Often this method is known as "surprise fire" because presumably our shooter is astonished each time he hears a bang.

I have been shooting a rifle for around 40 years, and I still am not certain if there is such a thing as surprise fire or not. Many good shots say they always know when a rifle is going off. Equally good shots claim they *never* know. My own notion is that the good shot knows *about* when his rifle is going to fire but not *exactly*. The difference would be in minute fractions of a second, perhaps perceptible to some but not to others.

The ideal, then, is to squeeze that trigger with the utmost gentleness and to concentrate on the squeeze and NOT on when the

BECOMING A GOOD GAME SHOT

gun is going off. The wild shots are caused not by poor aim, not by wobble, but by anticipating the recoil, yanking the trigger and jumping. It is far better to concentrate on trigger squeeze than on aim, although both are important, as aim, I am convinced, comes more naturally than squeeze. At first, then, the beginning rifle shot should form correct habits of trigger squeeze and sight picture. Learning to hold the rifle with a fair degree of steadiness can wait. He learns that when his rifle goes off as the sights look right something happens. A clod dissolves into dust, a bottle breaks, or a tin can filled with water flies into the air.

He should quickly be taught to call his shot, to know exactly where his sights rested when the gun went off. No one who does not habitually call his shots can ever become a good shot—on targets, game, or anything else. If the beginner calls a bullseye or a broken bottle and gets a miss, the answer is that he is yanking the trigger or flinching—more or less the same thing.

If our lad begins right by shooting from the steadiest possible rest where he can concentrate on sight picture and trigger squeeze rather than on trying to hold his rifle steady, he will never get into the habit of yanking the trigger, and if he starts with a .22 and gets his habits properly formed he will never develop a flinch. Proper reflexes are on the way to being formed. He has developed the habit of increasing the pressure on the trigger when the sight picture looks right, slacking up when it doesn't. He has learned to call his shots.

By this time, if he has the makings of a rifle shooter in him, he should have developed enough enthusiasm to progress to a black and white paper target, a more revealing but less dramatic mark than a tin can filled with water. Here he can align his sights more exactly because he has a more definite aiming point. Because the paper will leave a record of his shots, he can develop more skill in calling them. He begins to learn that the small group is the test of the rifleman's skill, not the occasional spectacular hit.

By now he is ready to master the shooting positions, those arrangements of the human anatomy by which a mass of wobbling joints, quivering muscles, and throbbing veins can become a fairly satisfactory shooting platform.

Because prone is the steadiest of all positions, he should be introduced to it first. A picture of the position will show the beginner more than a detailed description here, and of course personal coaching from a skilled rifle shot will be even better. Principal things to remember, though, are to get the left elbow under the rifle so that it supports the weight in a straight line like the pillar of a building and not at an angle. It should also be remembered that the body should not be in a line with the rifle but at an angle of about 45 degrees to the left.

Much target shooting, probably too much, is done from prone, and many a .22 caliber "small-bore" shooter does competitive shooting in no other position. Some of those lads are so skilled as to be human machine rests.

We are assuming in this modest chapter, that our beginner is not ambitious to become a hot target shot but to become a good game shot, and in game shooting, alas, the prone position is the least useful of all. In game country it is rare to find a piece of ground level enough to lie down on or free enough from high grass or brush so that the prone position can be used.

However, even the man who wants only to be a good game shot should do some practicing from prone because occasionally he will use it. In the high Rockies above timberline the hunter can often assume a good prone position on a rounded, grassy ridge to shoot caribou, sheep, goats or grizzlies in a basin below. In the prone position one can shoot up a slope whereas he cannot do it from sitting. The first two Canadian bighorns I ever shot were both from prone—one from a grassy ridge across the head of a little canyon, and the other from a basin at a ram a bit above me. Antelope are usually found in open, rolling country, and since they are usually shot at rather long range, prone is a natural for them. Prone is also one of the most useful positions for the varmint shot because it is the steadiest of all positions and varmints are small marks.

BECOMING A GOOD GAME SHOT

The Sitting Position

The sitting position is, for plains and mountain country, the most useful of all positions for the shooting of big game. It isn't quite as steady as prone and not quite as accurate shooting can be done from it. It isn't quite as fast to get off an *easy* shot from as offhand, but it is a lot faster than offhand for a *precise* shot at a difficult mark. It doesn't put the line of sight quite as high above the ground as kneeling, but it is one heck of a lot steadier. It can be used, though, under more different conditions than any other reasonably steady position.

If I had to make an estimate, I'd guess that I had killed about 70 per cent of the big game I have shot from the sitting position, about 20 per cent offhand, and 5 per cent each from kneeling and from prone.

I do about three-fourths of my practicing from the sitting position, the rest from offhand. I use kneeling very rarely, and when I shoot prone at game it is usually not from the conventional prone position but with the rifle rested with the forearm on a rolled-up jacket over a stone, a little bush, a log, or something of the sort.

I mentioned this business of speed of getting off a quick *accurately* aimed shot from sitting as compared to offhand. In the mountain and canyon country of the Southwest, where I grew up, shots at deer are usually from one side to the other of a canyon that may be from 150 to 400 yards wide. The minute game pops into view, the thing to do is to sit down, get on, and touch her off. But *sit!* I remember sitting down and getting off a shot at a running deer in plain sight so fast one time that my companion, who was looking the other way when the buck jumped out from his bed behind a little tree, didn't see it and thought the gun had gone off by accident. From the time I saw the deer until it lay dead, three seconds may have elapsed.

On the other hand, I remember taking an offhand shot at a

THE BIG-GAME RIFLE

buck drowsing under a tree like a sleepy horse. I was in waist-high chaparral and, of course, I could not see if I sat down. The buck was somewhere between 250 and 300 yards away. I assumed my best target stance, but my sights wavered all over the buck and 20 or 30 feet into the surrounding territory. It must have taken me a good minute, or 20 times as long, to get off the shot from my hind legs. If I had been able to sit down I could have got off an accurate shot within seconds.

When I used to shoot a lot of running antelope and blacktail jacks I always sat if the targets were much more than 100 yards or so away. Sitting is not as flexible as offhand or even kneeling, but it is flexible enough for most running shooting in open country. The major hazard in assuming the position quickly is what you're going to sit on, something which seems of small consequence when a buck mule deer with 10 points and a 38-inch spread is taking up the opposite side of the canyon. I have carried home many a bruise from sharp rocks, sharp sticks and other hazards, but the worst jackpot I ever got into came, not from spotting a lordly buck or a big ram, but from running into a whole flock of jackrabbits. My oldest boy and I were out hunting when we came over a ridge and there on the opposite side was a herd of five or six big, juicy antelope jacks. Automatically I went into a sit, but on the doggondest pile of *cholla* balls you ever laid your eyes on. In case you have never seen one, imagine a package of about 10,000 No. 10 fish-hooks sticking out of an egg and you have it. I had 7,692 thorns in my rear end and I slept on my stomach for a week.

Sitting is not only fast and fairly steady, but, best of all, it can be used from a hillside to shoot across or down, whereas prone and kneeling cannot. For mountain hunting it is the business. Even for plains hunting it is very useful for a steady shot when no rest is available, as even in open, level plains a prone shot is often impossible because grass and weeds are too high or because cactus, thorns, or sharp rocks make lying down full-length hazardous.

BECOMING A GOOD GAME SHOT

Just how accurately can a lightweight, scope-sighted hunting rifle be shot from the sitting position? A good shot should be able to keep three-fourths of his shots from that position in a 10-inch bull at 300 yards. Now and then he'll score a possible, but ordinarily from one to three or four shots will wander out of the black when a shot gets away from him. They should not, however, be *far* out of the black. Holding an 8–9½-pound hunting rifle steady is a more difficult job than holding down a 10½–11½-pound target rifle. At 200 yards, if our boy is holding and squeezing them well, practically *all* the shots should be in the 10-inch black pretty well centered in the middle. On some occasions, when I have been holding steadily and squeezing them off just right, I have shot groups running around 4 inches. There is always a lot of luck connected with an extra small group shot from such a position, however. Once I shot a 5-shot group with a scope-sighted .270 at 200 yards which measured only about 2¾ inches. I cut the thing out and filed it, but I don't kid myself that it wasn't about 85 per cent luck. Be that as it may, though, a good shot with a 4-x scope on an accurate rifle will kill *more* jackrabbits and woodchucks at 200 yards from the sit than he will miss, and even at 300 yards, with a scope of 8 or 10-x, he will make a surprising proportion of one-shot kills. Since, from the sitting position, errors of aim tend to be horizontal rather than vertical, there is more leeway on a big-game animal than on a varmint, and it is no astounding feat to keep all shots on the forward half of an elk or caribou at 400 yards.

In shooting game, be it jackrabbit, woodchuck, whitetail deer, grizzly bear, or what have you, there are no close 4's; only the 5's count. It is better by far to get in one well aimed, well held, well placed shot from a relatively steady position like sitting than to get in three or four poorly aimed, poorly held, poorly placed shots or misses from offhand. I have seen many a man who felt he didn't have time to get down into the sit, miss three or four shots at standing game that he could have killed dead if he had taken a second longer to plant his posterior on the earth.

THE BIG-GAME RIFLE

I recently read a book by an African lion hunter, who, when he was faced with a charge, always sat down if the grass was not too high. Then he figured on getting off one well held, well aimed shot and knocking the lion for a loop.

I remember one very sad occasion when I elected to shoot from offhand rather than taking a second longer and dropping into the sit. I was hunting deer and came around a point to see, about 200 yards away, a beautiful buck that had apparently heard me and had just got out of his bed. He was poised there, alert, beautiful, his gray body outlines sharp against a dark timber background, the sun glittering on the polished points of his antlers. The ones that get away usually look big, but I'll swear that that buck must have had 18 points. He saw me just as I saw him, and he was set to jump into the timber and out of sight. I was afraid he'd scram before I could drop down into the sit, so I slowly lifted my rifle, and shot right over the top of his back. On the target range, I would have got a close 4 for that one, but he got away just as cleanly as if I'd missed him by 50 feet.

When the uninstructed beginner first tries the sitting position, he almost always makes one principal mistake. He sits up too straight, and he almost always puts his wobbly elbows right on his wobbly knee-caps, with the result that he has a position little, if any, steadier than offhand. The secret of a good sitting position is to lean forward and put the flat of the left arm *above* the elbow against the flat of the shin *below* the left knee. Feet should be well apart and feet and ankles should be relaxed. I have often read that "the heels should be dug into the ground." That is the poorest advice I know of when one is shooting from level ground, since the digging introduces a tremor. The only time the rifleman should dig his heels into the ground is when he is shooting from a steep hillside and has to dig in to keep from sliding down hill.

Everyone, I believe, has to work out the minor details of his own sitting position for himself. A character with much of a paunch cannot, for instance, get over as far as can a flat-bellied

BECOMING A GOOD GAME SHOT

youth. Some prefer crossed rather than outstretched legs. For me, though, the key to a good solid sitting position is the relationship of the bottom of the left upper arm with the upper portion of the left shin. What happens to the right arm is relatively unimportant, just so the position feels comfortable and *relaxed*. The natural tension of the back muscles will pull the upper arms against the shin and result in a state of equilibrium and relative steadiness. In no position should a rifleman try to hold by main strength and awkwardness. He should at all times feel relaxed, because the harder he tries to hold, the more tense he is, and the more tense he is, the greater the wobble. My own besetting sin is tenseness. I often catch myself bearing down, determined to hold that damned rifle steady if I have to squeeze it in two at the grip, and when I do, the old musket wobbles all over the paper. I then have to loosen up *deliberately*. The difference, I am convinced, between the ordinary good rifle shot and the superlative shot is not that the superlative shot has better eyes, muscles, or that he is smarter or better looking, but simply that he can relax under all conditions, including picking off the biggest buck he ever saw at 350 yards, or firing the last shot in a string when a 5 will mean a win and a 4 a tie. The more relaxed the rifle shot is, the steadier he tends to be and the more he can concentrate on a gentle squeeze of the trigger. Let it be said right now that if a man misses a standing buck from the sitting position up to 250 yards, it is not because he could not hold but because he yanked his shot. Really wild shots always come from a yank. A shot may "get away" from a shooter, which means that the rifle goes off when the squeeze is in progress but not at the precise moment the shooter would will it. The shot that gets away will result in a hit out of the black on the target range or one out of the vital area on game, but it won't result in a very wide one. The lad who misses his game by feet or who knocks out 3's, 2's, and clean misses of the whole target does so NOT because he cannot hold steady but because he is yanking the trigger. With any rifled arm, under any conditions, the trigger must

THE BIG-GAME RIFLE

always be squeezed gently. A good rifleman may squeeze it *fast*, but he squeezes it, never yanks it!

Years ago another citizen and I were doing some handgun shooting and I was pretty sour. I protested that I couldn't hold the lousy roscoe steady. "That's not the trouble!" quoth my companion. "You're yanking the trigger, trying to catch the 10's as they go by. You can't shoot a handgun like that. You are jerking the whole revolver."

Then he demonstrated. He took the revolver, deliberately wobbled it, far more than even the poorest holder would. *But he squeezed his shots off*. He didn't get all of them in the black by any means, but he had no wild shots such as I had been getting. My trouble had not been holding, but squeezing!

Using the Sling

A good shooting gun sling properly adjusted is one of the great inventions of the human race, along with fire, the wheel, good-looking dames. Particularly is it a wonderful aid to the rifleman, in the sitting position, who wants to polish off some self-satisfied woodchuck perched insolently on a rock at 200 yards, or to nail a fine buck poised for flight high on some lofty ridge and way out yonder. Every game shot who takes his shooting seriously owes it to himself to get a good sling, learn how to adjust it, and how to use it. Not only is the sling a wonderful aid to holding, but it takes the curse off of lugging a heavy rifle around, which without a sling is one of the most awkward burdens known to man. You couldn't run fast enough to present me with a rifle to which a sling could not be attached, even if it were done up in 20-dollar bills.

The best type of sling for the hunter is one ⅞ inches wide of the one-piece Whelen type, much better for our purposes than the 1¼-inch two-piece military and target sling. For use in carrying and for sling adjustment for the sitting position, the front swivel should be about 15 inches forward of the center of the trigger. Short-armed characters would want the swivel farther back, and target shooters using a low prone position would want it farther forward—one reason why swivels on target arms are adjustable for position.

The sling can be permanently adjusted for use in the sitting position and for carrying. The one-piece sling is a single strip of leather 52 inches in length with a claw hook at one end and with holes punched into the strap for the hook. The sling also has two keepers and a stout leather lacing.

The whole key to successful adjustment of the sling for the sitting position in hunting use is the loop, which is formed by the placement of the leather lacing. I like the lacing to form the loop placed 18 inches from the base of the swivel or, in the case of Winchester quick detachable swivels, about 17 inches from where the sling joins the swivel bow. I also like to have the two keepers on the loop, as when both are drawn down against the arm, one keeper helps keep the other in place. Total length of the sling for comfortable carrying is determined by the placement of the claw hook. If, for instance, your boy wants to use both hands for climbing and carry the rifle slung over his back, he can put the claw hook into another set of holes.

The so-called "hasty" sling is a snare and a delusion. After years of solitary and melancholy brooding and endless experiments, I am convinced that the use of the hasty sling is a waste of time and a handicap to the shooter.

No sling without a correctly adjusted *loop* is worth a hoot. Proper adjustment can be arrived at only by experiment. If the loop is too short or too long, it loses its value and introduces shakes and tremors.

To get into the sling, sit down, with the feet widespread and relaxed facing away from the target at an angle of about 45 degrees. Then turn the loop a half turn to the left, put the arm through it, and draw the loop high against the upper arm. Then pull the keepers up tight so that you can feel the pressure of the loop against the arm muscles. The loop should be so tight that in the sitting position the left hand is hard against the swivel after it has gone *over and then under* the sling strap. The butt should be low enough on the shoulder so that the shooter has the feeling of holding down the rifle and pressing it against his left hand with his cheek. The sling should be so tight that the butt has to be placed on the shoulder with the right hand. The right hand has no work to do, if the sling is adjusted properly and the position is good, except to grasp the grip gently, with the trigger finger free to squeeze off that shot.

Except for prone with tight sling, or prone with the forend of the rifle rested on some object, this is the steadiest of all hunting positions and the easiest to shoot accurately from.

The rough and ready "practical" hunter should not sneer at this sitting position with tight sling as being just a lot of impractical target stuff, as it is a wonderfully practical and helpful position for the game shot, a position which enables him to place his bullets humanely on big game and to knock off varmints at long ranges when he cannot lie down, and could make a hit on the button from any other position only through luck.

In the summer of 1951, George Pfeffer, Doc Braddock, and I were walking across a field of high grass headed for a big canyon full of rockchucks when George spotted, with a glass, a voluptuous and patriarchal chuck perched on a rock, gleaming russet against the blue sky, and a good 300 yards away. I was nominated to take the shot. I dropped into the sit, but did not get into the sling and could not hold the Swift with its 10-x Unertl scope steady enough on the small mark. I tried to catch him as the crosshairs swung by and apparently missed the chuck so far the crack of the bullet didn't bother him. I paused then, slipped my arm into the loop of the sling, pulled up the keepers. The difference was wonderful. With the magnificent definition of that big scope I could hold right on the chuck's head to allow for a little bullet drop. As I put the last fraction of an ounce of pressure on the trigger, the crosshairs were glued momentarily right on the chuck's head. The bullet landed right in his chest and he flattened.

Best group I ever shot on a big-game animal from the sitting position with a tight sling was on a grizzly at about 200 yards with a .30/06 and 180-grain bullets. First shot was at him standing, second and third were when he was trying to get out of the open and into the timber, fourth was when he was lying on the ground and I shot again for luck. A good deal of luck went into the shooting, but the four shots could be covered by the palm of the hand. The tight sling from a good sitting position had a lot to do with it. In case that's a hard one to take, it was witnessed by Field Johnson of Champagne, Yukon Territory.

The sitting position, then, is one to cultivate, both with and without sling, if you aspire to be a good game shot. If you practice it, you will be rewarded by shots that will warm your heart and by trophies you couldn't otherwise have got. It's the queen of the hunting positions!

Shooting from the Hind Legs

Prone is the easiest position from which to shoot accurately; sitting is next. Fairly tough is kneeling, and offhand is the toughest of all. It is the position for the expert, and yet it is the one that the beginner will instinctively try if he does not have the advice of a more experienced shooter.

Offhand, then, is the position of the slicker, the cool, precise, skillful shot, and it is also the position of the tyro. A man is usually pretty good at offhand, or else pretty bad.

I have seen some strange things in the way of offhand shooting. I remember one time at a rifle range, a chap came out to sight in his rifle, *and he was trying to sight it in offhand.* He had brought with him a home-made target, a piece of cardboard about 4 feet square, with a 6-inch black bull painted in the middle. When he had put it up at 100 yards, he would shoot one shot, see where it went, adjust his sight, then shoot another only to find he was a couple of feet off in another direction. He was just about staying on the target. Finally, whether by accident or design, he got one in the bull and another a couple of inches away in successive shot. He said that was good enough for him and went home. He told me that if he was going to do all his shooting offhand, he might as well sight in that way and perhaps he was right.

Many men hunt deer annually and never do any shooting in the meantime. Their sighting in consists of standing up and blazing away at a rock on a hillside at some undetermined distance. If they hear the smack of a bullet on stone, they think they hit the rock they shot at and are happy. If the dust flies somewhere near the rock they are also happy. They have not learned that stones are usually surrounded by other stones and that a high speed bullet anywhere in the general vicinity will make a shot sound and look deceptively close.

One year, just before the hunting season opened, I was sighting in a rifle at a bench rest with a new load I intended to use. When I got it hitting on the button, I tried 5 shots sitting without sling as that is the way I'd probably shoot at game. About the time I wound up, I was joined by a chap with a .348 Winchester and open sights. He told me that he did his shooting on his hind legs like a man, and that shooting from a rest was a lot of fancy fol-de-rol; likewise shooting from the sitting position. Then he asked me if he could take a few shots at my target—a 200-yard small-bore target which I had tacked up on a frame. He fired 5 shots, missed the whole target every time. He then fired 5 more, hit it once. Then he told me that he had never been any good at paper targets, but just show him anything with blood on the inside and hair on the outside and he was dynamite.

A *good* offhand shot should kill a standing deer three times out of four at 200 yards. A poor offhand shot can miss one, three out of four at 100 yards. At a recent turkey shoot, I watched 7 men shoot offhand at 100 yards, at the 100-yard small-bore target with its 6-inch bull. One was in the bull, one on the paper, and

BECOMING A GOOD GAME SHOT

five off the paper. Once I was hunting deer in Arizona and saw four men shooting *offhand* at a doe across a canyon about 400 yards away. I watched the intended victim with a good 9-x glass and some of the shots missed her by at least 100 feet. None hit her.

On the old army A target, the bull measures 10 inches, the 4-ring 26 inches. The offhand shot who can keep half of his shots in the 10-inch bull offhand and the rest of them in the 4-ring is a crack shot. Actually, the man who can average 3 in the bull and none out of the 4-ring is good. An old offhand shot many years ago gave this sage advice: "If you don't get out of the 4-ring, the 5's will take care of themselves!"

Now superimpose a 26-inch circle on a buck's shoulder and you'll find that you could still stay in the 4-ring and yet miss your buck, as bucks come in assorted sizes and run from 14 to occasionally 20 inches from the top of the shoulder to the bottom of the brisket.

Some time ago, a club advertised a turkey shoot and one of the events was to shoot at a clay target, which measured 4¼ inches, at 120 yards. If you hit the saucer, you got a turkey. Shots cost a buck. Now that is a tough one, but it was a sort of a challenge to me so I decided to practice up for it. First thing I did was to sight in a very accurate .257 with a sweet trigger pull to put the bullet exactly where the crosshairs in the Weaver K-4 rested at 120 yards. Then I made myself a target with a 4¼-inch bull and did some practicing, shooting in strings of 5. Best I did was 3 bulls out of 5. Poorest I did was 1 out of 5. The last day I practiced my average was about 2.5 out of 5. I figured that even if I had to pay 5 bucks for a turkey it was still a cheap turkey and unless I got jumpy I had a good chance to get a couple of birds for 5 smackers. As it happened I came out all loaded for bear, but didn't get to compete, as the match had been postponed until afternoon and I was there in the morning. I got itchy fingers and picked up a bird at the running deer and went home. Later I heard that members of the club found this clay-saucer event

THE BIG-GAME RIFLE

their biggest money maker. They gathered in about $18 per bird!

Shooting on the hind legs is a tough position, but no one who cannot do pretty well in it can be classed as a good all-around shot. On one hand it is a highly specialized position for competitive target shooting and, on the other, an exceedingly useful position for the big-game hunter. I am a firm believer in never taking a shot at game offhand if it is possible to plant the posterior firmly on mother earth and take a shot from the much steadier sitting position. Nevertheless, mixed big-game hunting abounds in situations where the shot must be taken from the hind legs or not at all. In many cases there is no time to get into a steadier position. Very often high grass or low brush makes it impossible to see from sitting or even kneeling. In forest and jungle hunting, the great majority of shots are taken from the hind legs. Even on the plains, and in relatively open mountain and canyon country, situations often arise where the hunter has no choice but to shoot offhand. It is in order, then, for anyone who wants to be an adequate game shot to learn to shoot on his hind legs.

The offhand shot finds that he faces two tough problems. The first, of course, is holding his rifle with some degree of steadiness. Obviously the steadier a rifle is, the easier it is to shoot. If a rifle did not wobble at all and if the trigger could be let off without introducing any movement, accurate shooting would be very easy. Sad to say, though, no one can hold a rifle with absolute steadiness, even from a good prone position with tight sling, or even with a 15-pound rifle from a bench rest. I said *absolute* steadiness.

Offhand is the least steady of all positions because the rifle has from 4 to 5 feet of wobbling, quivering, throbbing human muscles and nerves between it and the ground. Anyone who begins offhand practice under the illusion that he can hold a rifle still offhand is in for some bitter disillusion, as he will soon find that his sights wobble and sway like a tree in the wind.

The best the offhand shot can do is to hold his rifle *fairly* steady, to slow down and tame the oscillations of the muzzle, because, obviously, the narrower the arc of the swing is, the smaller the group on the target will be.

The old-time scheutzen and present free rifle shooter licked this swinging muzzle business by using a very heavy (and also muzzle-heavy) rifle and firing it from a hip rest. The rifle with the long heavy barrel swings more slowly and in a smaller arc, of course, than the light sporting rifle that is also muzzle-light. Some of the old-time scheutzen shots with their ponderous .32/40's, and .38/55's with their palm rests and special offhand stocks, shot groups at 200 yards that would knock your eye out. I have seen such groups shot with iron sights that would compare favorably with the best groups shot from the sitting position with a modern scope-sighted big-game rifle fired with tight sling by a crack shot.

However, no hunter will want to lug around a 12- or 14-pound free rifle equipped with palm rest, nor will he favor the old hip rest position which is still used in free rifle shooting and three-position small-bore shooting, but which was outlawed a good many years ago in .30 caliber military shooting. The hip rest position might be used once in a blue moon for a long offhand shot at game, but it is an exceedingly unflexible position, unless for a moving target. I'd call the hip rest position strictly for targets, and the game shot without target ambitions should not spend much time practicing it.

Beginning offhand shots make two principal mistakes. For one thing, they hold the left hand too far out on the forend and usually to one side instead of underneath. Holding the left hand out toward the forend is like trying to carry a tray of dishes at arm's length. It is tiring, unsteady, even painful. The steadiest offhand position is with the *heel* of the palm just forward of the trigger guard on the magazine floor plate with the left elbow under the rifle. That way the weight of the rifle is supported on a straight line, in much the same position as a waiter carries a heavy tray. Such a position supports the rifle as steadily as it is possible to support it *offhand*, makes the weight hang forward and slows down the rate of oscillation. For quick shooting at nearby game and for any running shooting the left hand should be moved farther out—perhaps 9 or 10 inches in front of the trigger guard—and it is not necessary to get the elbow clear under the forend. Such a hold gives more leverage, enables the shooter to swing faster. It is *never* necessary for the left hand to grasp the rifle clear out near the forend tip, any more than it is necessary or advisable to carry a tray of dishes at arm's length.

The upper right arm should be horizontal, with the elbow level with top of the shoulder. The exaggerated position effected by many military shots, with the right elbow as high as the head is unnecessary and to many, clumsy. The butt should rest on the pad of muscle formed at the junction of the shoulder and the upper arm when the arm is lifted, and not down on the collar bone. Weight should be evenly distributed on the two feet, and a line drawn across the toes should point slightly to the left of the target. The rifle merely rests on the left hand, and the right hand at the pistol grip holds the butt firmly against the shoulder.

The rifleman should stand in an easy and *relaxed* position with his weight balanced against that of the rifle. If he is tense, if he tries to stop the swing and the wobble of the rifle by main strength, he will introduce new shakes and tremors. This business of being relaxed is of utmost importance in any position, and in no position is it more important than in offhand.

Secondly, many uninstructed rifle shots make the mistake of trying to let the shot off with the *tip* of the index finger. This is OK with a hair or set trigger, but with the ordinary single trigger the portion of the finger to use is the pad of muscle between the first and second joint. Trying to *squeeze* off a shot with the tip of the finger is another example of trying to carry our tray of dishes at arm's length.

Good offhand shooting is half good position and half good trigger control. If a man could hold his rifle with absolute steadiness, the control of his trigger would not be of much importance so long as he could get the shot off without disturbing the aim.

On the other hand, if a man had perfect trigger control and could let his shot off *exactly* when he wished, position would not be so important, as the sights could swing all over hell's half acre, but he would shoot only when they were right.

I have a pal of many years' standing whose form in offhand shooting would make your blood run cold. He does everything exactly wrong, and even if you watch him from 50 yards away you can tell his muzzle is describing arcs and circles like a kid with a sparkler the night of July 4. Why can he shoot? Because he has the most fantastic muscular co-ordination I have ever seen. He simply touches off his shots at the right moment. I can't do it with a rifle that wanders around that much. You probably can't. He *can!*

But he is an exception. Most of us, if we are ever going to hit anything offhand, have to stand properly, hold our rifles properly, avoid tensions, and learn to control the trigger.

The beginning shot should squeeze his trigger so gradually that he doesn't know when his rifle is going off; so should the lad with the tendency to flinch. Many fine shots claim they are always surprised when their rifles go off, even from the offhand position, that they simply increase the pressure when the sights look right, and hold it when they don't. One army training manual says that the man who doesn't know when his rifle is going off is always a good shot, the man who does know is a bum shot and a flincher.

A great many are skeptical about this. In the first place, the free rifle shots, the world's greatest target shots, use set triggers that can almost be touched off by a light breeze. It's a cinch that they know when their rifles are going off. In the second place, I believe most people who do much shooting can quickly feel out a trigger so that about the third time they let it off they *know* the exact amount of pressure required to make it let go. For my part, I cannot shoot offhand worth a hoot unless I know when the rifle's going off.

The good offhand shot is the lad who can squeeze out all the pull but two or three ounces and then when his sights hang momentarily in the right place can let off the balance. This fine trigger control, this ability to make the rifle go off at the right moment without disturbing the aim is what distinguishes the crack offhand shot from the ordinary offhand shot. It is something which can be acquired only by practice, by constantly squeezing off from a good position, and *calling the shot*—remembering exactly where the sights rested when the trigger let go and the firing pin fell.

The nice part of it is that about 90 per cent of this skill can be obtained by dry firing. I have a little target with a ⅜-inch bull on the wall of my office, and two or three times a week, I practice for 10 or 15 minutes "shooting" offhand, calling my shots, and keeping score. This dry practice keeps my co-ordination in good enough shape so that I am never too lousy at offhand, even though circumstances may keep me from firing a "wet" string for months. If I did this every day without fail, I would probably shoot as well on the average as I ever have. Because a man is practicing to shoot on his hind legs at big game, it is no sign that he has to do it with a big-game rifle. A lot of good can be had with a .22 of sporting weight and balance outdoors at 50 yards, or even indoors.

It is a mistake for the man who wants primarily to be a good big-game shot to do all his practice slow fire at targets. If he hunts chucks or jackrabbits he can make it a rule to take all shots at 100 yards or under, offhand. If he hunts squirrel and cottontails with a rifle he should plan to shoot only for the head.

He should shoot rapid fire at targets, getting up some degree of skill in working the bolt or the lever with the butt at his shoulder. Once I shot in a place that had a string of six rocks, the last about 175 yards away, the first about 25 yards away. I would try starting at the farthest rock and working up to the closest, shooting as fast as I could with accuracy. Stones were about 12 or 14 inches in diameter. In shooting like this, accuracy should come first and the speed should come gradually. It teaches the game shot to fire the instant his sights are approximately right without dawdling and double checking to see that they are *exactly* right.

For interest and realism one can practice by shooting at the colored picture of a game animal, something which may sound a bit like playing with paper dolls but which actually helps make proper aim and bullet placement subconscious. The man so trained does not stop to think how he is going to shoot the buck that walks out in the clearing 75 yards away or where he is going to shoot him. He just shoots him—and in the right place.

Most of the game I have shot has been from the sitting position since the bulk of my hunting has been in open and semi-open mountain country where the shots tend to be fairly long and where the game is in sight for a considerable period. I have done a fair amount of prone shooting on game, too; but even in open country a fair degree of skill in offhand pays off.

One would think that sheep would seldom be shot from offhand, yet the first desert ram I ever killed was taken offhand, at a distance of not more than 75 yards, and maybe as little as 50. The last Mexican ram I shot was also shot offhand at probably no more than 40 yards at most. Antelope are animals of the open plains, but I have shot several from my hind legs, mostly when they were running like the devil and at no great range.

The offhand shot at game that I think of most smugly was at an elk. I had found it with glasses bedded down about a mile away across a great canyon. I cut back into some timber, went clear around the head of the canyon as fast as I could travel. When I finally got within 150 yards of the bull I was winded, shaking with weariness, and trembling with elk fever. I started cautiously up the slope of the last draw and the moment I poked my head over I found myself staring right into the bull's eyes. He had seen me the moment my head popped up. He knew I was something strange, but he could not identify me from my head alone and the wind was in my favor. He was suspicious, though, and after watching me a moment he got to his feet. I couldn't lie down, I couldn't sit. The only way I could get the rifle high enough to shoot across the intervening rise was to shoot on my hind legs.

I hoisted the rifle up and tried to hold the dot in the scope on him as he stood facing me. I was winded and shaky and my dot was wandering all over the landscape. Finally the swings and wobbles slowed down a little. I squeezed out all but the last few ounces of the pull, and as the wobbling rifle swung from left to right on the bull's chest I touched her off. Leaning sidewise, the bull ran in a narrow circle and fell on his nose. The 160-grain Barnes .270 bullet had gone almost the length of the body cavity. Because I was winded I couldn't hold the rifle steady, but trigger control paid off.

The snapper on this story is that the bull I shot was a 5-pointer, just a cooking bull, not a trophy. He had hardly fallen when I heard the brush popping and an enormous 6-pointer with antlers as long as a dictator's dream came pouring out of the timber and ran past me at about 20 feet.

The woods hunter will do 90 per cent of his game shooting from offhand, and as we have seen, even the mountain hunter often has to shoot on his hind legs, this most difficult of all positions. Anyone with ambitions to be a good game shot would do well to practice it!

CHAPTER XVI

The Rifle in the Field

PRACTICE at conventional black and white targets is available to most riflemen without too much trouble, even to those who live in large cities. No one can become a good shot without a great deal of such practice. The foundation of all good rifle shooting consists of those fundamentals of good hold, careful trigger squeeze, and the calling of the shot. However, no one can become a crack big-game shot on targets alone, or at least I have never seen one who has. The good target shot has mastered the fundamentals and with experience he soon becomes expert on game. He must, though, get field experience.

How to do it?

Probably the best way, without actually hunting big game, is to try some varmint shooting. Roy Hargreaves, the famous Alberta and British Columbia guide and outfitter, with whom I hunted around the Big Smoky in Alberta back in 1943, told me that the finest long-range big-game shots he took out were Eastern woodchuck hunters. Many of them had never shot any big game but whitetail deer in their lives and not too many of them, but on sheep, caribou, goat, and grizzly they were poison. Why? Because their chuck hunting had taught them to use steady, if unorthodox, positions, to shoot at unknown ranges, to squeeze off the shot quickly instead of dawdling about it the way many slow fire target shots do, to shoot at poorly defined marks under bad light conditions, and to shoot under pressure. The man who can settle down and knock a chuck off a rock at 300 yards isn't going to find shooting his ram at the same range and under the same conditions difficult. In fact he is going to find it almost ridiculously easy. The man who has learned to hit his chuck, poised on the edge of its hole, quickly, before he drops out of sight, can do the same with the big buck standing on the edge of the timber.

The finest of all practice for running shooting is the hunting of the jackrabbits on the plains and deserts of the West—the whitetail jack of the Northwest, the blacktail, which is pretty well all over the Western states, and the antelope or whiteside jack of the Southwestern border states. What skill I have as a running shot I feel that I owe almost entirely to the jackrabbit. For the years when I lived in southern Arizona I must have averaged nearly a jackrabbit hunt a week and every day I hunted I probably shot at from five to twenty jacks on the run. A few days like that will give a man more practice at running shooting than he could get in a lifetime of legal deer hunting. In many sections coyotes are plentiful enough so that a rifleman who goes after them can shoot from five to thirty a year without working too hard, but as compared to the opportunities offered by the ever-present jackrabbit, the coyote is simply the frosting on the cake.

No one can become a first-rate big-game shot by shooting only at big game. The market hunters of the 70's and 80's could, but that day has passed. Even the trappers and mountain men of the far North, who live on game, do not shoot enough game to get really good from that alone. The rifleman becomes a good running shot by practice and a lot of it.

Shooting at a stationary mark is simply one phase of rifle shooting. No matter how good a man is on a black and white bullseye, at a sitting chuck, or a standing deer, he cannot be called an all-around rifleman unless he can hit them fairly well on the run.

About the first thing the man, ambitious to learn to hit running game, should get through his head is that it appears to be more difficult than it is. A running jackrabbit at 100 yards is just as large as it is when it is sitting. Likewise, a running antelope at 200 yards affords just as large a target as if he were standing still. Much of the difficulty is in the mind of the shooter. Any target one thinks of as a tough one is a tough one. Likewise any target one thinks of as easy *is* easy.

It would not surprise me if it were proved that the best of all ways to begin learning to be a running game shot, would be to start out with an empty rifle and to follow the game along in the sights without shooting. That way a man could prove to himself that he had more time than he thought. When a beginner at running game first tries to hit them on the move, he feels excited and inadequate. Because of his mental turmoil, a buck bouncing along at 15 miles an hour looks like a cottontail doing 60. However, if our gunner can do some dry firing first, without the pressure of the necessity of making a hit, he'll find that actually there is no need to break his neck.

Most riflemen, starting out to shoot running game, try holding right on the mark, a method as unproductive of results as the same stunt would be on a flying bird. Even the .220 Swift isn't fast enough to enable the hunter to hold dead on a crossing jackrabbit at even 100 yards and kill it. One cannot hold where they are. Instead he has to put the bullet where they are going to be!

The simplest type of running shooting and the one exception to this rule, like the simplest type of wing shooting, is at a straightaway animal. This is the one instance when a dead-on hold works, and hitting an antelope running directly away from the rifle is no more difficult than hitting one standing with his rump toward the hunter. Aiming exactly and shooting quickly is all that is required.

Some years ago, Tom Ellinwood and I were hunting whitetails in southern Arizona near the Mexican border when I saw a good buck jump from his bed and take off running directly away up a ridge and about 250 yards away. I sat down, got the Lee dot in the scope of the .270 I was using right in the middle of his rump just as he topped the ridge. I pressed the trigger and a fraction of a second later I saw all four feet in the air. Tom had happened to be looking the other way when the buck jumped and when he heard the shot he thought my rifle had gone off by accident.

A couple of years later, I got the same sort of shot. Bill Everhart and I were hunting in the Tortolita mountains with a cow puncher, when a big whitetail took off along the side of a canyon about 200 yards away, running broadside. Bill was using a .30/30 and the cowboy a short .35 Remington pump. Neither ever caught up with the buck. After the big whitetail had run perhaps 100 yards broadside, he turned to cut up through a gap and for a moment he was running directly away from me. Until then I had been watching the fireworks and getting set. The crosshairs were right in the middle of his rump when I pressed the trigger, and he went down. I shot from the sit whereas Bill and the vaquero were pumping lead at him offhand, but more of that later. If a hunter gets over the mental hazards, such a shot is actually easy.

The next simplest shot on running game is the slightly quartering shot. Then the rifleman simply holds off the right amount in the direction the animal is running, shoots with a stationary rifle, and lets the animal run into the bullet. If an animal is slightly quartering one can hold on the side toward which he is running. If he is quartering at more of an angle, one can hold off a foot or two. I cannot remember just now of ever making such a shot at anything but short range at big game, but I do remember killing a coyote like that. I had missed a running shot at him in the brush and had then run about 150 yards, hoping to get another crack at him as he went over a ridge. I got up on one ridge just as he was topping out on another, quartering away from me and around 200 yards away. I slid into a sitting position, put the crosshair of the scope about 1 foot to the right, and pressed the trigger. Down went the coyote. I had almost missed him, as the bullet had entered just behind the last rib and had

THE RIFLE IN THE FIELD

practically taken one side off. Such shooting is like "spot" shooting with a shotgun. You shoot at a spot where the animal isn't but where you hope he will be when the bullet gets there.

A sort of variation of this spot shooting at a quartering animal is one which is very common in open mountain country—at an animal that is climbing out of a canyon or going up a hill directly away from the hunter. Then all one needs is to hold high, either on the animal if he is at close range or moving slowly, or above him if he is a long way off or moving rapidly.

I killed a Dall ram in the Yukon with a shot like that. He was going out of a basin up the opposite ridge. The range wouldn't have missed 375 yards by much. I touched my first shot off with the aim right between his horns. The Indian guide who had the binoculars, told me I had broken its left hind leg. Thinking I had undershot I held my next two shots well above the horns. In each case I nicked a horn. The head is now in my trophy room and the first thing a visiting fireman notices is those old bullet burns on the horns. The last two shots, which did no good anyway, were unnecessary, since I had actually hit the ram at the first shot in the hip joint, and the 180-grain .30/06 bullet had gone clear through and had come out behind the right foreleg. The ram was down and out in the next canyon about 100 yards from where he had gone over the ridge.

For the slightly quartering shot, spot shooting works; but for the sharper angle the system is worthless, just as it is with a crossing bird. The spot shooter may kill an occasional crossing antelope or deer by that method, but he can never work up a good average. In still hunting deer in brush and woods, though, one gets quite a few opportunities to spot shoot, as the animal is running away from the hunter, often straightaway or at a slight angle.

For crossing shots, the hunter has to swing his rifle and to get well ahead. There are two methods of swing with the rifle, just as there are with a shotgun—the fast swing and the sustained lead. The fast swing simply means that the hunter starts with his

THE BIG-GAME RIFLE

sights behind the animal, then swings apparently faster than the animal is moving, gets ahead what he considers the proper distance, and touches off the shot instantly with the rifle still moving faster than the animal. The man who uses this method has to have good eyes and fine muscular co-ordination and he also has to be practicing constantly. He can, though, get by with less apparent lead than can the practitioner of the sustained lead method.

This is genuine art as far as rifle shooting goes. But the man using it is apt to be wonderful or sour. Few people have the split-second muscular co-ordination to use it successfully.

For crossing shots on running game I am convinced that the most reliable method is the sustained lead, just as it is for pass shooting at waterfowl, crossing pheasant, doves, or what have you. The idea here is to swing the rifle apparently as fast as the animal is moving, keeping the intersection of the crosshairs, the bead, the dot, or whatever it is, the right distance ahead for a few yards and then squeezing the trigger without stopping the swing.

The method has many advantages. For one thing it makes such shooting more of a science, less of an art, than the fast swing. It lends itself more to analysis. It is less dependent on split-second timing because with the fast swing success depends on letting off the shot at the precise moment.

With the sustained lead, it is absolutely necessary to keep swinging while the trigger is being squeezed. Any tendency to jerk the trigger is as fatal as it is when shooting at a black and white target, and any tendency to slow or stop the swing is as fatal as it is when a man is pass shooting ducks. Keep the rifle swinging the proper distance ahead, squeeze the trigger!

Then, if the lead is correct, something's going to get hit. If it is not correct, one can very often spot a puff of dust as the bullet strikes rock or soil and make the proper correction.

But to hit anything this way, you have to lead it.

Next question is: how far do you lead it?

That *is* a question, as the answer varies with the average velocity over that certain range of the rifle bullet, the speed at which the hunter is swinging the rifle, the distance, the angle, and what not.

At best any such lead is an approximation. Because of the long body, there is considerable leeway on a deer, a sheep, an antelope, and, of course, much more on an elk or a moose. A coyote or a bobcat offers less leeway and a galloping jackrabbit still less. However, any shot that is a hit no matter where on a jack, is practically a pinwheel 5 on a larger animal, and the finest of all ways to learn to shoot them running is to go after those galloping bunnies.

On big game that is really scared, and picking them up and laying them down at right angles and about 100 yards away, I try to swing with the animal with the front sight or scope reticule slightly ahead of the brisket. If there are no mis-cues this will usually result in a hit in the chest cavity. If the animal is around 150 yards away and stepping on it, I try to shoot with the reticule about ¾ of a length ahead, and if it is at 200 I try to reach out 1½ lengths ahead, or, in the case of a running jack, somewhere around 6 or 7 feet.

A scared jackrabbit can run 35 miles an hour for a little way but soon tires, and I imagine the average jack shot at is traveling between 15 and 20. A mule deer may be able to make 35 miles an hour on the level, but one ordinarily does not travel that fast and a good, speedy cow horse can usually run one down. I'd say that 20 miles an hour is a good gait for a trotting elk or moose. Once in the Yukon, when hunting with Myles Brown, I put three shots behind the shoulder of a trotting moose at about 125–150 yards, and I was leading the point I wanted to hit only about a foot. On level country a bighorn ram cannot run very fast, and that is no doubt one of the reasons mountain sheep like the hills. The real speed demon is the antelope, which, under the best conditions, has been clocked by reliable men at between 50 and 60.

As far as sights for running shooting are concerned, the scope has it all over any iron sight because of the sharpness of detail.

THE BIG-GAME RIFLE

A good peep comes next, and the open sight isn't even in the running because the best of them blot out half the view of the target. For woods shooting the 2½-x scope is the best, but for open country a good 4-x is better. For long-range running shooting, a hunting-type 6-x can be used, but such a scope is no good for the brush because the field is too small.

The crosshair reticule is the best for running shots because it gives good elevation control. The hunter can have the animal on the horizontal crosshair while he keeps the vertical crosshair the proper distance ahead. The floating dot is also excellent, but it does not have the advantage of the conspicuous horizontal crosshair to control elevation. The post is the worst of the lot.

The closest running shots can be handled offhand, but if the game is at any distance, I always sit. Sufficient flexibility for the swing can be obtained by rotating the shoulders. For very long range, one can even swing the rifle sufficiently from prone, although for my part I have seldom shot that way. One of the best running game shots I ever knew almost always shot from the kneeling position.

On many occasions I have read the advice to shoot only at standing game and to place the shots exactly. I am fully in agreement that when this is possible it is a very pious idea.

But often the hunter has to shoot at running game or go home empty-handed. This is especially true of whitetail deer. Under modern hunting conditions it is apt to be true of antelope and mule deer. Most of the sheep I have shot have been standing, but about 40 per cent, for one reason or the other, were taken on the run.

Although hitting them running is actually not as difficult as it might seem to one who has never tried it, it is more difficult than shooting them on the sit and harder to place shots exactly. For this reason, the man who plans to do much running shooting of big game should have a rifle with enough soup to knock the animal down and keep him there for a while with even a poorly placed shot. A rifle that is adequate for the well-placed shot at a standing animal, often isn't worth a hoot for running game because it will not knock the animal down with gut shots and ham shots. The man who uses a .30/06 or .270 on galloping antelope or Western deer is going to have fewer cripples than the man who uses a less powerful rifle, and the man who hunts in country where he must shoot at running grizzly, elk, or moose isn't making a mistake when he goes armed with a .300 H. & H. Magnum, a .300 Weatherby Magnum, or if he can shoot one and still hold on to his bridgework, even a .375 Magnum.

Hitting at Long Range

There are two very vocal schools of big-game hunters, the nonchalant long-range shots and those who belong to the get-close-and-shoot-them-in-the-eye school. The long-range experts tell about knocking off rams at 500 yards without batting an eye, and the get-close boys sneak up to ranges so short that their victims get powder burns.

Both schools strike me as unrealistic.

As a rule, particularly in the mountains, it is possible to stalk much closer than 500 yards, and there is usually little excuse for taking one of those long shots. Mountain sheep are almost always thought of, by those who have had limited or no sheep hunting experience, as being a long-range proposition, whereas they are not. I have hunted sheep from the desert mountains of northwest Sonora to the glaciers of the Alaska border and I can think of only two really long shots I have ever made on rams. Both were somewhere around 400 yards away. The largest Dall ram I ever shot fell exactly 85 paces from the muzzle of my .30/06, the largest bighorn at about 125, the largest Stone at around 225, and the largest desert sheep at somewhere around 75. Long-range shots at sheep or goats usually come from very bad luck, very poor management, or poor judgment. If the sheep hunter or the sheep hunter's guide knows his business, the typical shot at sheep is at from 100–200 yards, and at a standing animal. The same thing is true of any mountain game that stays in the open most of the time so it can be stalked—goats, caribou, grizzly, and often elk and mule deer. It is foolish indeed for any hunter to blaze away the instant game is sighted.

The other extreme is the shoot-them-in-the-eye school, the members of which believe that no one should take a 200-yard shot if he can get one at 100, or a 100-yard shot if he can sneak up to 25. To my way of thinking this is as dizzy as wanting to blast them down at a quarter of a mile. A rifle shot worthy of the name can place his shot just about as well at 150 yards, let us say, as he can at 25. Actually he is apt to do better shooting at 150 than he is at the closer range. If he passes up a 150-yard shot to get closer, he may frighten the game and have to shoot on the run, and a close look at the animal may give him buck fever. Many a stalk for grizzlies has been loused up because the guide has wanted to get his client so close he could ram the muzzle down the bear's throat. Getting right on top of a grizzly is apt to give the tyro bear hunter the buck fever and, furthermore, it is dangerous, because a grizzly is hard to kill and if the wounded bear happens to run the wrong way someone is apt to get hurt.

Legitimate shooting at long range requires the rather poorly distributed commodity called judgment. Before anyone takes a pop at any animal at beyond what is his sure hitting range he should pause and ask himself what will happen if he wounds the beast. Once I was riding back toward camp with a trigger happy friend, when we saw, standing on the far side of a muskeg meadow, about 400 yards away and right at the edge of heavy timber, a big bull moose with enormous snowy white antlers. My companion jumped off his horse and before you could say "boo" he had shot offhand. I heard the plunk of bullet on water-filled stomach, and the bull faded into the timber. We found no blood, but we did find some hairs cut off by the bullet. We tracked the bull about a quarter of a mile but it grew dark back in the timber

THE RIFLE IN THE FIELD

and we had to go back to our horses and ride to camp. As far as I could discover, our boy suffered no pangs of conscience, but all he had done was to donate some meat to the wolves.

It was no time to make a long-range shot. In the first place, the hunter couldn't get a steady position. In the second place, a moose is a big, tough animal which is very difficult to kill at 400 yards with a .30/06 or, for that matter, with any weapon short of a 37-mm. cannon. In the third place, the bull was standing at the edge of the timber and would be out of sight at one jump, and in the fourth place only a few minutes of light remained.

If our hunter had caught the bull in an open basin above timberline where it couldn't get out of sight until he had the opportunity to shoot a dozen shots, if he had been able to get into a steady position, and if he were desperate for a moose trophy, he might have been justified in taking a long shot.

Just what is a long-range shot on big game? Let us define it conservatively as being any shot that is beyond the ordinary point-blank range of the rifle being used, any shot where the bullet will fall more than 4 inches below the line of sight and where allowance for drop is necessary.

With an iron-sighted rifle of the .30/30 class sighted to put the bullet at point of aim at 150 yards (which is the usual practice), that would mean that anything over about 190 yards (at which point the bullet drops 4 inches) can be considered at long range. With a scope-sighted .30/06 using the 180-grain bullet and sighted to hit the point of aim at 200 yards, anything over 250 is a long-range shot. With a .30/06, scope-sighted for 250 yards, with the 150-grain bullet, anything over about 290 yards is a long-range shot; and the same figures apply to the .300 Magnum with the 180-grain bullet. With a .270 scope-sighted for 275 yards, anything beyond 325 is at long range. Big-game rifles of still higher velocity, like the Weatherby Magnum series, have a still longer point-blank range, where this bullet fall does not exceed 4 inches (and in this case the critical point is about 350) or 25 yards farther than with the .270.

THE BIG-GAME RIFLE

Never let it be said that, even with the flat-shooting .300 Weatherby Magnum at 350 yards, a shot isn't a good one unless it lands in the chest cavity, as the human being behind the rifle is still a human being, with human jerks and shakes and wobbles.

Great aids to long-range shooting are a flat-shooting, accurate rifle, a scope of good definition so the rifleman can see exactly where he is holding, and the combination sighted in for the longest possible distance so that the rise of the bullet above the line of sight will not cause mid-range misses. On a big-game animal that means that the bullet should not rise more than 4, or possibly 5, inches above the line of sight. The less guessing to holdover a man has to do the better off he is. Even the most experienced and skillful lay plenty of eggs. That is why a rifleman is a sucker, if there is any possibility at all of a shot at longer than the usual range, to sight in a .30/30 for 100 yards, or a .270 or .30/06 for 200.

The stunt then is to sight in for the longest possible range, if you're ever going to have to knock something over way off yonder, and to use a scope of good definition. A 4-x is a fine compromise, and for open country shooting exclusively, where a shot at under 150 yards is the exception, a lot of very shrewd riflemen are going to the 6-x scopes.

The lesson of sighting in for the longest possible range was impressed on me many years ago, when I did a lot of hunting for the smart and elusive little Arizona whitetail deer down in southern Arizona and northern Sonora. Most of my shots were from hillside to hillside or across canyons at longish and undetermined range. I found I could hit them better with a .270 than with the .30/06 because of the somewhat higher velocity and flatter trajectory, with a .270 sighted for 275 or 300 yards, than with one sighted for 200, and with 4-x scope rather than a 2½-x. The reason? When a buck bounces out across the canyon, my instinct (and I believe everyone's instinct) is to blast away directly at him instead of figuring the angles and holding over.

THE RIFLE IN THE FIELD

I remember very well the buck that made me a convert. He got up at undetermined range across a rough, rocky, and very steep canyon and started putting them down and picking them up. Because the terrain was so rough, he couldn't go very fast, and my lead was apparently perfect. I could see dust fly all around him. Finally he went down on about the ninth shot. I found several bullet burns on the bottom of the chest and belly. My .270 was sighted for 200, and the buck was probably over 300 yards away—beyond the point-blank range as I had sighted the musket. I had no business at all in killing the buck with a dead-on hold, and I wouldn't have done so at all if I hadn't jerked the trigger apparently and made the killing bullet fly high, wild, and out of the group.

Whereas it is usually possible to get close to many animals, particularly in open mountains where they can be located and stalked by approaching from behind a ridge, some have to be taken at long range. Those little Arizona whitetail are an example. Mule deer in many sections are found in open country where they often cannot be approached, and antelope almost always are. In many cases it is the better part of wisdom for the hunter to take a long shot at a standing animal than to attempt to get closer and run the risk of taking a running shot at an animal that is not too much closer.

If country is broken up, antelope, like wild sheep, can be closely approached, but if the country is flat and open or even gently rolling with the top of one gentle rise a half mile or more from another, antelope are a long-range proposition. In some areas the hunter will see ten elk at 300–400 yards for every one he sees at lesser range, and if he is going to fill the home freezer he is going to have to do some long-range shooting. Much of Idaho's Selway country is like that—great brushy ridges cut by enormous canyons.

Judgment of range is by no means easy. Animals look closer in good light than in poor, farther away when seen from above or below than when seen on the level, closer across a canyon with no intervening objects, closer across a perfectly flat, level plain with no vegetation.

I can remember some astonishingly bad guesses I have made. Once in the Yukon I came to a river bed and, across a perfectly flat bar glistening white in bright sunlight, I saw a wolf. I estimated the range to be about 300 yards and held accordingly. The bullet struck in the sand at least 100 yards short. Part of my error came from the bright light and the flat sand, but most of it came, I believe, from the fact that I was used to shooting at the much smaller coyote.

Another time I fired several shots at a black bear high above me on a northern British Columbia mountainside and never even came close enough to scare it particularly. The members of my party went into a huddle in an attempt to dope out the reason for the misses. The others came to the conclusion that the bear was much farther away than I thought—700 or 800 yards. I came to the conclusion that I was crossed up by the fact that the bear must have been a cub and that instead of underestimating the range as my pals thought, I was grossly *overestimating* it.

Now and then the hunter runs into a guide who is an experienced and expert rifle shot and a good judge of range. Such a guide is well worth listening to. Many guides, although they may have killed a lot of big game, have done so only at short range. They are often not particularly good rifle shots or particularly good judges of range. Because they usually take only short-range shots themselves, many chronically overestimate range, and I have seen many to whom anything over 150 yards immediately became "400 yards." I remember killing a ram once at what my guide swore was over "a quarter of a mile away." I held dead on with the .270 and hit about where I held. The ram was probably about 250–275 yards from the muzzle. An antelope which a guide swore was "500 or 600 yards away" was likewise killed with a dead-on hold and was no more than 300 yards away.

There are two methods of arriving at a fair estimate of range.

THE RIFLE IN THE FIELD

One, if the terrain will permit, is to divide the intervening country off in 100-yard units. Golf players are constantly in practice and are usually very good at guessing the range of game animals. The other is to use some sort of a range-finding reticule and compare it with the depth of the animal's chest. Sad to say, both methods are only approximate, but they will save the rifleman from the very worst errors. If game animals came in standard sizes, the use of the range-finder reticule would be quite positive, but, alas, they do not. Deer run from 14 to 20 inches from top of shoulder to bottom of brisket, adult antelope 16 or 17, a big ram or a goat 20 to 22, an elk 24 to 28, a bull moose from 30 to 40 with 36 being about the average of those I have measured, a coyote 8 or 9.

A range-finder reticule with two horizontal crosswires, with the space between them subtending 6 minutes of angle, is available in Weaver scopes. If a full-grown deer fills up the space between the crosswires, it is a pretty good guess that he is around 300 yards away. I have also used a 4-minute Lee dot in a 2½-x scope and I have found it useful, since very often it saved me from very poor snap judgments.

The last long-range shot I made was on an antelope. It was standing looking at my companions and me on the opposite slope across a wide, shallow basin in northeast Wyoming. I thought he was about 400 yards away, but when I divided the intervening ground into 100-yards units it looked more like 500 yards. At that distance the bullet I was using would drop about 3 feet. I got a good steady rest and attempted to hold the intersection of the crosswires 1½ times the depth of his body above his shoulder. I squeezed the trigger and the buck went down. My companions and I paced off the distance and it came out about 485 yards.

For genuinely long-range shots, the hunter should get into the steadiest possible position. Now and then the terrain is such that he can use prone with a tight sling, but such an opportunity is quite rare in big-game hunting. The long-range big-game shot faces exactly the same problem as the varmint hunter who likes to knock off chucks at from 300–400 yards, and he should follow his example of taking a rest at every opportunity, as few people can hold steady enough, even from a good, solid sitting position, to be certain of placing a bullet in the chest cavity of deer or antelope out at 400 yards or over. In the Canadian North I usually hunt in a down jacket, and many times I have rolled it up and used it over a stone or a moss hummock for a steady rest. In Wyoming antelope hunting I have used the same rolled-up down jacket laid over clumps of sage. It is also possible on occasion to put a 10-gallon hat in the crotch of a tree and use it as a rest. The rifleman should never lay the forend of the rifle on anything hard, because if he does the rifle will recoil away from the hard surface and the shot will fly high.

The longest shot I ever made on a mountain sheep was at a nice Dall ram in the White River country of the Yukon. My guide and I were behind a ridge almost sharp enough to shave with. I found a ledge on which I could sit, a notch in the sharp ridge which I could stick the rifle through rested on the down jacket. There was even a little ledge on which I could rest my right elbow. All in all, it was a crude, natural, but very effective bench rest. I could hold like a rock and the only problem I faced was that of judging range and dropping a bullet into a vital area of the ram. I hit him the first shot.

Just as the finest practice for the man who has to shoot running big game is popping away at galloping jackrabbits, the finest possible practice for the long-range big-game shot is long-range shooting of woodchucks, predatory hawks, crows, and coyotes.

This chapter is not an endorsement of promiscuous long-range shooting. From a humanitarian standpoint, the less of it even a good shot does the better. But the time will come when circumstances are right and when a good shot can save his bacon by making a hit at long range.

The animal, first of all, should be non-dangerous. He should

THE RIFLE IN THE FIELD

be in the open, so bullet effect can be judged and the first shot followed up with several others if it is not fatal. The hunter should have an accurate, flat-shooting rifle, sighted in for the longest possible range which will not cause mid-range misses. He should be able to judge range fairly well by mentally marking off the distances in 100-yard units, or by comparing the size of an animal with a reticule of known value. He should know the drop of the bullet he is using at various ranges, and if his memory is poor he should affix the data to the buttstock of his rifle with transparent, waterproof tape. He should shoot from the steadiest position possible to assume, then he should squeeze the trigger and hope for the best.

Never should he attempt a shot when the animal can get out of sight quickly, and never should he attempt a shot from an unsteady position. The sportsman should never try a shot at long range if it seems possible to get closer, to within his sure hitting range, even if he has to come back the next day. When he does try it, he should use every means at his command to do the job exactly right!

PLACEMENT OF SHOTS

An astute person does not have to do much big-game hunting before it dawns on him that the first thing in importance is for him to hit the game. The cartridge is yet to be invented that will kill game by concussion alone. A hit with a .25/35 does more damage than a miss with a .375 Magnum.

The second fact that gradually filters through his noodle is that *where* he hits his game is vastly more important than *what* he hits it with. A bullet from a .25/35 in the vital heart-lung area carries with it a lot more assurance of chops in the frying pan than the enormously heavier and more powerful slug from a .465 Nitro-Express that only breaks a leg.

There is no getting around the fact that the hunting and shooting skill of the man behind the rifle is of enormously greater importance than the rifle itself. One man who is a good and calm shot can hunt the largest and toughest of game with a relatively light rifle without leaving cripples in the woods. The same rifle in the hands of a less skillful and level-headed fellow would strew the woods with cripples. This is why there is so much contradictory testimony about the adequacy of various calibers. One man, let us say, hunts everything in North America with a 7 mm. and swears by it. Another comes along and declares under oath that the 7 mm. isn't even a good sheep or mule deer rifle. The difference, of course, lies not in the rifle itself but how it was used, by whom, and under what conditions.

The skillful woodsman who knows his game, and who gets close, can keep himself in venison or moose meat with a rifle which most of us would consider entirely inadequate. I know a homesteader in the Peace River block of Canada who fed his large and ravenous family on moose meat for twenty years with a beaten-up old Remington Model 14 slide-action in .30 Remington caliber. He did it because he knew his moose. He placed his shots carefully, and if he wounded a moose he had enough skill to follow it up. I knew another hunter, this time a Mexican, who for years hunted for a ritzy Mexican restaurant and kept its refrigerator bulging with whitetail deer. He used an old Model 92 Winchester in .32/20. Anyone knows that the .30 Remington is by no means an ideal moose cartridge and that the .32/20 is no deer cartridge. The difference was made up in both cases by skill in hunting and tracking and by the placement of the shots.

On the other hand, a great deal of vastly unrealistic stuff is written every day about the placement of shots by people who apparently assume that nothing but undisturbed deer are hunted, and only by cool and level-headed marksmen like our Canadian pioneer and our Mexican market hunter. These articles always come complete with diagrams of a cutaway buck showing how to reach the vitals from various angles. They don't do any harm and they may do some good, but they skip lightly over the fact that bucks are often very uncooperative and do not stand around waiting for someone to plink a bullet into them in the same calm and deliberate manner that the small-bore expert uses when he lays one in the middle of the X-ring.

The writers of these articles are fond of pointing out that, if the shots are exactly placed, even a .22 rim-fire will bring home the venison. With that very obvious statement no one can disagree. One consideration, though, is that under modern hunting conditions those brain and spine shots which make even a .22 effective are usually almost impossible to make. Another, which is seldom mentioned, is that if those small vital areas are missed, the result, all too often, is a wounded animal that escapes.

Of all the poor places to shoot a fine game animal, I cannot think of a worse one than the head. If the *brain* is struck, the animal is, of course, killed instantly. But the brain is a small mark. If it is missed, a broken jaw that dooms the animal to a slow death by starvation may result. Once a good many years ago, when hunting jackrabbits after the deer season was over, I found the carcass of a fine buck with the nose and the mouth shot away. It had died of starvation. Even if the brain is hit and the animal killed in its tracks, the resulting sight is one to turn the stomach. Once I pulled down on the head of a buck about 60 yards away and killed him. The light high-velocity bullet blew up in the skull. The sight of the pulpy shapeless head, the bulging eyes, the antlers askew, was almost enough to make a man stop hunting deer. A grand animal like a buck deserves a better end.

I cannot get too enthusiastic about the neck shot either. *If* the spinal vertebrae in the neck are broken, the deer is killed instantly. If the spine is missed, a neck shot is no more deadly than a shot in any other muscular tissue. I remember seeing a big bull caribou that was hit in the neck fall and then get up and run 300 yards until a lung shot brought it down. A fine mule deer I had occasion to track was hit in the neck. He fell at the shot, then got up and ran. My companion and I tracked him a full half mile. The bullet had severed a big artery, and it seemed incredible that an animal no larger than a deer could contain that much blood. Another time I was with a friend who took a very long shot at a whitetail across a basin. The buck staggered, recovered, then took off. When we went down to where he had been we found a few drops of blood that looked as if they had come from a muscle wound. We finally lost the trail over the rocks and concluded the deer had been merely scratched somewhere. A week later in the same basin my pal got another shot at the same buck and killed him. His first bullet had landed in the neck, but it had missed the spine and hadn't opened up well.

Head and neck shots are justified, however, at short range and under favorable conditions, particularly by the man who knows his anatomy and who wants to stop dangerous game in an emergency. For ordinary hunting, though, they are a long, long way from being a good idea.

About the only time a shoulder shot is justified is when the hunter wants to disable a potentially dangerous animal like a grizzly or Alaskan brown bear. Broken shoulders will put an animal down and render it helpless without killing it, and even with one shoulder broken a grizzly cannot manage a charge on a hillside. Old grizzly hunters try to break the shoulder on the downhill side on the first shot. Some hunters try for the shoulders on large animals like moose that are hard to kill in their tracks. However, the shoulder shot will wreck a lot of meat, fill it full of fragments of bone. If the shot goes low, a broken leg and an animal that can travel all day only to be pulled down by wolves is the result.

The best place of all to aim for is the lung area back of the shoulder. The advantages of this shot are many. A reasonably adequate bullet placed there almost always means a one-shot kill. Death is not always instantaneous, but it is usually quick. The rapid expansion of the bullet tears up the lungs, administers terrific shock to the whole nervous system, and very often ruptures or otherwise stops the heart action. The last grizzly I killed was below me about 125 yards away and walking slowly along in a big, open timberline basin. The .300 Magnum bullet went high through the left lung behind the shoulder and emerged low through the right lung. The bear fell to the shot, got up, took two steps, and fell dead. The only other grizzly I ever saw killed as quickly was one I shot in about the same place with the 130-grain Silvertip bullet in the .270.

For whatever the reason, a shot through the lungs near the heart usually kills quicker than a shot through the heart itself. The heart-shot animal will almost always run off frantically anywhere from 20 to 200 yards before it falls dead. In the late 1930's, Carroll Lemon and I were hunting mule deer in some Arizona desert mountains when a buck got up about 200 yards below us and took off in high gear. Each of us got one shot at him and shot at almost the same instant. I noticed that, when we shot, the buck ran even faster than he'd been going. He disappeared behind a low ridge. Then, 50 yards or so from where he had gone out of sight, I saw the tops of some cliff roses shake violently for a few seconds and then become still. We went over there and found that one of us had shot that buck squarely through the heart.

Another time I was painfully clambering down a high ridge toward camp, dead beat, thirsty, and footsore when a fine whitetail buck came out under the cliffs below and started running up the opposite side of the canyon. I just had time to throw a cartridge into the chamber of my .270, sit down, and get off a shot. The buck jumped about 5 feet into the air, lit, and disappeared over the top before I could shoot again.

In spite of the fact that the crosshairs were on the buck, I was inclined to believe I had missed him, probably with a shot at one side that hit a rock and stung him with the fragments. I should have gone over to look then, but I was weary and could look with no enthusiasm on climbing down over those cliffs and up the other side. I started on down the ridge, but the more I thought about that high and frantic jump, the more convinced I became that the buck was hit. Finally I retraced my steps, crossed the canyon, and climbed to where the buck had disappeared. There he lay, as dead as a mackerel. The bullet had gone in just behind the last rib, had ranged forward, and had blown the heart to pieces, and had emerged at the point of the brisket leaving a hole about 3 inches in diameter.

The lung shot is quickly if not always instantly deadly, as the ruptured lungs drown the animal in his own blood. The lung area is large and much easier to hit than the brain or spine. Furthermore, it will destroy no meat that is eaten. If the shot goes too high it will break the spine, if too far forward it may break the shoulders or land in the neck. Even if it is a bit too far to the rear and lands in the paunch, it may still kill or disable the game if the rifle is a powerful one.

However a standing animal is facing, the hunter should try to drive the bullet into this large lung area. If it is struck with a rifle of adequate power, the kill more often than not is instantaneous, and if the rifle can be called a deer rifle, the kill is almost always quick. Above all, the hunter should try to keep his shots out of the abdominal area. Now and then a paunch shot, particularly with a light, easily expanded bullet at very high velocity, will result in a very quick kill, but all too often, even with powerful rifles, a gut-shot animal can run for miles.

The heart and the lungs are *vital* tissue. Any serious interference with either means quick death. Stomach, intestines, and other organs back of the diaphragm are not immediately necessary to life or movement. An animal with a pair of broken shoulders cannot travel and an animal with a ruptured heart or torn-up lungs will quickly die; but animals have been known to travel a considerable distance with all organs back of the diaphragm gone.

Once, in northern Arizona, I took a shot at a big buck running away from me down a hill. The Remington 150-grain bronze-point .30/06 bullet struck him in the left ham, broke the bone high, and laid the whole abdominal cavity open. The buck went down, but when I got to him, he got to his feet and ran with his stomach bouncing along 30 feet behind him. He was almost completely clean back of the diaphragm.

In Sonora, a friend of mine took a shot at a desert ram running away from him down a canyon with the 150-grain bullet in the .300 Savage. The bullet opened up the abdominal cavity and the stomach protruded. The ram ran off the mountain and started to cross a flat to another mountain. When it jumped over a barrel cactus, the protruding stomach caught on the terrible thorns and everything back of the diaphragm was pulled out and lay on the ground. The hunter kept on the track across the sandy desert and found the ram dead after it had run a mile!

It is true that much game has been killed stone dead in its tracks with shots in the abdomen. Very often a bullet like the old 139-grain Western open point for the 7 mm. would do it. So would the 87-grain bullet in the .257 or the .250/3000, the 130-grain bullet in the .270, and the 150-grain bullet in the .30/06. I have also had many reports of quick kills with gut shots from the .220 Swift. The catch is, though, that *sometimes* such a shot results in a quick kill, but sometimes it doesn't, even with a rifle of high velocity and rapid bullet disintegration. Dressing an animal that has been gut shot is always a messy and disagreeable business. The good hunter tries to keep his bullets out of the abdominal cavity if he possibly can.

It is one thing to hunt plentiful and relatively tame game. It is quite another to hunt frightened and jittery game that often sees the hunter first and is on the move. In one case, exact placement of shots is relatively easy, and in the other, it is difficult. Over a half century ago, a famous deer hunter wrote that hitting a running deer anywhere at any distance was not a bad shot. In the course of a season the average hunter in average country does not see many bucks, and who can blame him too much if he takes his shots as they come. The deer may be on the move or hindend to or partly concealed by brush that may deflect the bullet. Under those conditions how many hunters will refrain from shooting? One in 10? I doubt it!

That is why I have always plugged reasonably powerful rifles for modern hunting, rifles that will knock down and disable animals even with relatively poorly placed shots. A man should always try to place his bullet so that it will drive up into the heart-lung area, but he should use a rifle with enough power so that if his shot mis-cues he still has a good chance for a dead or disabled animal.

A very typical shot today is at a frightened animal running directly away from the hunter. I have always refused to take such a shot at an elk, a moose, or a grizzly. I have either let the animal go its way unshot at or have waited for it to turn, as such an animal is too large and too tough for a rifle of the .270–.30/06 class with such bullet placement.

If the bullet goes between the hams, or approximately so, it will penetrate up into the lungs through the abdomen. If it goes high it will break the spine above the root of the tail. The thing to do is to keep the shot high and center. If it is low, it will disembowel the animal and may result in a long chase. If it is too far left or right it will strike in the hams. At best the result would be a lot of spoiled meat, and at the worst there would be a wounded animal to escape and become coyote meat.

In the case of a quartering animal at fairly close range, one can shoot past the hips to drive the bullet at an angle up into the lung area, but such a shot on a running target requires skill and coolness that I fear too many hunters do not have. Such a shot can be attempted on an animal the size of a deer, antelope, or sheep with a rifle of the power of a .270 or .30/06, but should never be attempted with less powerful rifles, even though under ideal conditions and with well-placed shots they will lay game of that size out as cold as kippered herring.

If a broadside running shot is offered and the hunter feels he cannot afford to pass it up, he should swing way ahead, as it is far better to miss in front than would behind the diaphragm. Actually, no one should attempt running shots unless he is armed with a rifle with enough power so that he would stand a good chance of disabling the game even with a fairly poorly placed shot. A shot in the abdominal cavity with a fast-opening bullet from a .270 or a .30/06, for instance, has a very good chance of knocking down the game and paralyzing it for sufficient time for the hunter to get to it, whereas a shot in the same area from a .25/35, let us say, will mean a wounded animal that keeps on going and escapes to die.

The power of the rifle is a poor substitute for calmness and for skill in the placement of shots, but it *is* to some extent a substitute. In the Canadian Rockies, the hunter usually shoots under very favorable circumstances. The game is in the open, undisturbed, and the hunter can almost always get into a good position, wait until the animal is turned right, and take time to get over his excitement and recover his wind. Consequently, a .270 or .30/06 is plenty of rifle under those conditions even for moose and grizzly, and a .257 or 7 mm. would nine times out of ten also be entirely adequate. Yet at the same time the .270 and .30/06 are not any too much gun for whitetail deer and antelope that weigh only a fraction of what a moose or grizzly weighs and have but a small part of the vitality. Why? Under modern hunting conditions it is often very tough indeed to place shots properly on the buck that is bouncing through the brush on the other side of the ravine or to tag that antelope just right when it has been spooked and is picking them up and laying them down on the opposite hillside.

The idea is, then, to place those bullets as well as you possibly can, to kill as cleanly as you can, to take advantage of every opportunity to get a one-shot kill. BUT, it is smart also to carry a rifle with enough power so that if something mis-cues, the chances are still good that you'll get the game instead of having it go away wounded.

THE BIG-GAME RIFLE

There isn't any doubt that where you hit the game, within limits, is more important than what you hit it with; and there also isn't any doubt that the man behind the rifle is far more important than the rifle itself. On the other hand, there also isn't any doubt that a good man with a powerful rifle is more deadly than a good man with an inadequate one!

CHAPTER XVII

Killing Power

THE PURPOSE of the big-game rifle is to kill mammals quickly, efficiently, as nearly painlessly as possible, and without danger to the hunter. Everything else is designed to that end. The most beautifully checkered, shaped, and finished stock is of no value unless it puts the eye quickly in line with the sights. The finest of scopes is no good unless it is properly adjusted to drive the lethal bullet home. The entire big-game rifle, with the cartridges for its use, is a precision instrument designed to perform a surgical operation at a distance, whereas the stone axe and the spear of the caveman were designed to perform the same operation at the very shortest range.

The moment we get into the subject of killing power we are in highly controversial territory. Evidence is clouded by prejudice, poor observation, downright falsehood. It is further complicated by the fact that life itself is a mysterious thing which will sometimes flee the body after a trivial wound, and yet will sometimes remain in a body horribly torn and mutilated. Individual animals differ in vitality. The same animal is harder to kill when he is frightened or enraged than he is when he is calm and unfrightened. A bullet may strike an organ when it is full or when it is empty.

Once, many years ago, I was hunting antelope when three bucks that had been lying down in some low bushes alongside a desert road jumped up and ran right into the sun. I piled out of the old Model A Ford to take a shot, but there was lint in the aperture of the receiver sight on my .30/06 and I could see nothing through it. I fired three times at one of the bucks when he was between 50 and 125 yards, pointing my rifle as if it were a shotgun.

All three bucks ran over a rise and disappeared, but my companion, who wasn't bothered so much by the glare of the sun in his eyes, told me he thought I'd hit the buck on the second shot. Just as he said that, two of the bucks appeared about a half mile away on a second ridge, and a logical conclusion would be that something had happened to the third one. We walked up to the top of the first ridge and below us in the valley lay an antelope as dead as dead could be. When we dressed him out we found that the bullet had gone squarely through the heart. He had run between 300 and 400 yards.

On another occasion I took a shot at a big mule deer with a very fine head as it bounded off below me at around 225–275 yards. Down he went in the sagebrush. I walked down, thinking him dead, but when I got within 30 or 40 yards, he staggered to his feet and took off. I shot him through the lungs and he went down, dead this time. The first shot, the one that had dropped him as if he had a broken neck, had gone through the joint of his right front leg. In one instance an animal ran almost a quarter of a mile with a hole in his heart, and in the other he went down with a trivial wound. In each case, precisely the same bullet was used—the 150-grain Remington bronze-point fired from a .30/06.

Suppose I had shot only two big-game animals and were basing my conclusions on my own experience! I would really be in a dilemma. The first kill would be evidence that the .30/06 was a poor cartridge even for antelope that weigh around 125 pounds on the hoof. The second experience would have convinced me that all one had to do to knock down a 275-pound mule deer was to nick it practically anywhere.

I have shot about a half dozen moose and I have never killed

KILLING POWER

one in his tracks with one shot with a .270 or .30/06. Every shot I have fired at a moose has driven into the lung area. My own conclusion from my own experience would be, then, that the man who expects to kill a moose with one shot through the lungs, as he would kill a deer or a sheep, is going to be disappointed. Yet I have had many letters from men who say they have killed many moose in their tracks with the same rifles, the same bullets, and the same placement of shots.

As a rule, though, the larger and heavier the animal is, the more difficult he is to kill. A mule deer weighing 250 pounds on the hoof is more difficult to kill than an Arizona whitetail or an antelope weighing 125 pounds. An elk weighing 600 pounds is more difficult to kill than a bighorn ram weighing 300 pounds. A 700-pound grizzly will carry more lead and survive than a 300-pound black bear, and a 1,000-pound Alaska brown bear will survive for a time a wound that would down a grizzly. Likewise, an elephant is more difficult to kill than the smaller rhino.

A frightened or angry animal is more difficult to kill than one that is undisturbed, as terror and rage pump an animal full of adrenalin that under some conditions seems to make him almost impervious to further wounds. As an example, I once saw a whitetail buck, that might weigh 135 pounds on the hoof, shot in the paunch and in the ham with a .348. It ran over a ridge and hid in the bottom of a canyon. When it was flushed out it was struck with 12 more bullets—150-grain .30/06, 100-grain .257, and 200-grain .348—before it went down. It was almost shot to pieces, and was still on its feet when the last bullet, a 150-grain .30/06, severed its neck vertebrae.

Not a few hunters have been killed or badly mauled in Africa by angry, charging lions and buffalo that have been shot through the heart, but which lived long enough to do damage.

Any discussion of killing power is complicated by the use of rather vague terms by hunters themselves. Witness the terms *hot-blooded* and *cold-blooded*. The hot-blooded, high-strung animal is supposed to be fairly easy to kill and sensitive to what hunters call *shock*, another term which takes some defining. The cold-blooded, phlegmatic animal is not supposed to be subject to this mysterious thing called shock.

These terms may make the scientist chortle in his beard, but they represent something which most hunters of experience have noticed. Some species of animals *are* easier to kill, as a rule, than others. A rabbit, for example, will be killed stone dead by a wound that would leave a member of the weasel family, of approximately the same size, full of life and fight. I have seen badgers shot with .22 rim-fire rifles and all have taken a lot of lead before they gave up the ghost. A wolverine is a tough nut, too. A woodchuck is enormously harder to kill than a jackrabbit (another rodent) of equal weight. Bob-cats, on the other hand, have always seemed to me to be creatures of very little vitality. In knocking around the desert for many years, I have killed perhaps 15 or 20, and they always struck me as being almost as easy to lay low as rabbits.

Among larger game animals, the Rocky Mountain goat bears a reputation of being as hard to kill as the much larger grizzly, much harder to kill than a bighorn ram, which is about the same size. Will he actually absorb more lead or are hunters kidding themselves?

Riflemen have invented a term, "shock," which means the reaction of an animal to bullet wounds in non-vital places, and the term is usually, but not always, associated with great tissue destruction. Medically, the term means a state of low blood pressure, rapid pulse, rapid respiration, unconsciousness—a condition following loss of blood after a wound or a long operation. The medical term "shock" then, and the hunter's term, are not the same thing.

Is the term "shock" as used by the hunter a misnomer or simply a piece of superstition? That is for a better scientist than I am to say.

One time I was jackrabbit hunting with Carroll Lemon of Tucson, Arizona, and took a shot at a running jackrabbit. Down it went. When we reached it, we found one front foot shot off and no other wound. What killed it? On still another occasion, I took a shot at a bighorn ram just as it was about to top a ridge at very close range, somewhere between 40 and 75 yards. As I fired, I could see one side of the ram's rump instantly change from dingy white to crimson—and then he was over the ridge. He was dead when I came up to him, yet the 139-grain Western 7-mm. bullet had blown up in the rump like a bomb and had not penetrated the body cavity at all. What does one call whatever it was that killed those animals?

In 1950, I hunted with friends in Wyoming and one of them shot a big buck antelope running at about 225 yards. The 130-grain .270 bullet struck the animal across the fleshy part of the rump—a long, long way from any vital area—BUT that buck was killed instantly in mid-air and before six witnesses. What killed him?

The killing power of any particular bullet is determined by two factors: where it hits and how large a wound it makes. Even the most unsophisticated know that a shot through the brain, or a shot that breaks the spinal column forward of the shoulders means instant death. It takes no physiologist to know that a broken back anywhere means paralyzed hind quarters and a disabled animal, that a heart shot means quick and sometimes instant death, and that the destruction of much lung tissue also means quick death.

I don't believe, either, that there can be much argument when I say that the larger the wound area in proportion to the size of the animal the quicker the death, or that if the wound area is large enough it will kill an animal no matter where located. The abdominal area back of the diaphragm is non-vital tissue. By that I mean it is not *immediately* necessary for life. However, if the whole hind end of an animal is blown off, be it a mouse or a moose, the animal will be quickly dead, as anyone who has shot woodchucks and jackrabbits knows.

The difference in vitality of various animals is pretty much in proportion to size, because a wound area that would destroy half a woodchuck would destroy a much smaller portion of a coyote, still less of a deer, etc. All things being equal, then, the larger the animal the harder it is to kill. For the sake of illustration, let us suppose that a certain bullet will destroy a pound of tissue. That would be $1/100$ of the dressed weight of an antelope or small whitetail deer, but $1/500$ of the dressed weight of a grizzly, caribou, or elk, and $1/1000$ of the weight of a moose or a large Alaska brown bear.

Most of my hunting has been done with the 130-grain bullet in the .270, and the 150-grain bullet in the .30/06. With either of those bullets, and a chest cavity hit at a range up to about 250 yards, I have almost always got instant kills on coyotes, antelope, whitetails, mule deer, and sheep. On elk and caribou I have got instant kills about half the time. I have never got a one-shot kill on a moose with either of those cartridges and I have made only one instant kill on a grizzly with them.

My own experience would tend to indicate, then, that the good shot with a .270 or .30/06 who places his shots in the lung area can expect very quick kills on animals that weigh up to about 500 pounds on the hoof; but that if the animal weighs more he cannot expect *instant* kills with shots in the lung-heart area.

It begins to look, then, as if the boys who want a bullet that kills quickly but doesn't destroy meat are talking through their hats, since killing power and destruction of tissue go hand in hand. The thing to do is to confine the tissue destruction to non-edible areas in the animal, such as the lungs.

What is it that gives a bullet this power to destroy tissue? The weight, the caliber, the sectional density, the construction, and the velocity. All things being equal, a bullet weighing 300 grains and traveling at, let us say, 2,000 f.p.s. is a better killer than one weighing 100 grains and traveling at the same velocity. A bullet of .35 caliber is a better killer than one of .25 caliber, a long bullet (one of great sectional density) is a better killer than a short one, and a fast bullet a better killer than a slow one.

KILLING POWER

The large caliber bullet kills better because it displaces more tissue, just as a dagger displaces more tissue than a needle. A heavier bullet will strike a harder blow, just as getting conked with a baseball is tougher on a victim than getting hit with a tennis ball. The long bullet (all things being equal) will penetrate deeper and make a deeper (and larger) wound than would the short one.

However, bullet construction makes up for a lot of this. A light, relatively short bullet can be so strongly constructed that it will penetrate deeper than a longer, heavier, but weaker bullet, and a small caliber bullet can be so constructed that it will open up to large caliber. Some bullets for hunting are made with heavy full jackets so they will not expand at all, but will drive through heavy hide and heavy bone of rhinos and elephants. Some are made to blow up in the fragile bodies of crows and woodchucks.

The bullet constructed to drive clear through a rhino and break massive leg bones on the far side isn't worth much as a deer bullet, and one made to explode inside a woodchuck is poor medicine for moose. On the other hand, a bullet that will drive through an elk's rump up into his paunch and on through into his lungs is a very poor killer on the same animal with broadside lung shots.

The function of the bullet is to get *inside* an animal and then to transmit its energy to the animal's vital tissues. Theoretically, the ideal bullet would remain within the animal so that every ounce of energy is absorbed. Actually, I like a bit of leeway in the way of penetration and I prefer a bullet that will go on through the animal I am hunting *on a broadside shot*. Such a bullet will waste some energy on the landscape, but it will have enough reserve of penetrating power to get into the vitals at an angle or break a heavy bone.

In the days of black powder and lead bullets, the only way killing power could be increased was by increasing caliber and bullet weight. Hunters of the largest game used tremendous 4-,

6-, 8-, and 10-bore rifles, and many unsophisticated hunters still judge the killing power of a rifle by the size of the hole in the end of the barrel, just as they judge the effectiveness of a shotgun by the length of the barrel. Since the advent of smokeless powder, killing power has been stepped up by increasing the sectional density of bullets, by controlling penetration and expansion by jacket thickness, jacket hardness, hardness of core, and by various mechanical schemes. It is possible to make a game bullet that will blow up like a bomb or will penetrate deeply, that will maintain its original caliber or expand to give it a cross-sectional area at the point double or triple the original. But, of all the means of securing greater killing power, stepping up velocity has been the most effective. If the bullet is so constructed that it will get into the vitals, velocity is the most important factor in killing power. This is the opinion of a pretty high proportion of all big-game hunters, and also of such an authority as the "British Textbook of Small Arms" and of surgeons who have studied battle casualties.

For many years there has been a running battle, with a lot of shooting but with few casualties, between the advocates of the heavy, large-caliber bullet at moderate velocity, and the lighter bullet of smaller caliber at high velocity. Some of the heavy-bullet boys have gone so far as to say that no modern high-velocity cartridge has as much actual killing power as the old black-powder cartridges like the .45/70—a statement which to me is utterly silly.

One chap wrote me as follows: "Why is it that no modern cartridge has the killing power of the .50/110, and why is it that no cartridge can kill game at 1,200 yards as the buffalo hunters habitually killed buffalo?"

The question is about like the one that goes: "When did you stop beating your wife with a tackhammer?"

The answer is, of course, that (a) there are a lot of modern cartridges with more killing power than the .50/110, and that (b) the buffalo hunters didn't shoot buffalo at 1,200 yards.

KILLING POWER

For a long time, the big-bullet boys have been shooting at published figures listing energy produced. It is valueless, they say. Instead, they have invented their own terms. One writer has invented the term "pounds feet." Another uses mysterious killing power units and rates cartridges accordingly.

Actually, extensive tests made at Princeton University during the last war show that the relationship between energy and wound severity is very close, and that this often noted "shock effect" of impact velocities of much over 2,000 f.p.s. comes because at velocities over 2,000 f.p.s. energies go up very rapidly.

When the .270 with its 130-grain bullet at 3,140 f.p.s. came out, the conservatives looked down their noses at it because it had a light bullet. Yet at 200 yards, it delivers 1,850 foot-pounds of energy, almost exactly that delivered by the 180-grain .30/06 bullet fired at a muzzle velocity of 2,720 f.p.s. Experience has proved that it kills just as well as the .30/06 and that often it kills better because on light, thin-shelled game the .270 bullet is apt to shed all or most of its energy within the animal, whereas the heavier .30/06 bullet is apt to go on through and shed only part of its energy.

Let's take a look at what velocity does to energy. A 100-grain bullet driven at 2,000 f.p.s. (with roughly the power of the .25/35) turns up 887 foot-pounds of energy. Step it up to 3,000 f.p.s. (about like the .257) and it delivers 1,996. Give it 4,000 f.p.s. and our little 100-grain bullet is hitting with 2,549 foot-pounds, or about like the standard 150-grain load in the .270. Step it up to 5,000 f.p.s. and the energy has more than doubled. Our little 100-grain bullet is striking as hard a blow as the very heaviest double-barreled elephant rifles.

What has fooled the heavy-bullet boys is that, all too often, light, high-speed bullets do not penetrate well enough to deliver the energy in the middle of the animal, and they have considered bullet weight a virtue in itself rather than as a means to get in where it does some good.

I once autopsied the carcass of a 600-pound grizzly shot with a

41-grain bullet at about 4,200 f.p.s. fired from a .22/.250. The first bullet blew up on the shoulder blade and made a superficial wound (the .22/.250 is no good on large game); the second bullet slipped between two ribs and killed the bear instantly (the .22/.250 is a deadly grizzly cartridge). Two answers, so take your pick.

Modern high-speed photography showing bullets striking gelatine, and other substitutes for tissue, tell us a lot about wounding effect that before we have had to guess at. For instance, few of us would have dreamed of the enormous cavities opened up within tissue by high-speed bullets, in spite of the fact that we have seen chucks and jacks literally explode when hit.

Too many of us have judged the severity of the wound simply by the size of the permanent cavity created. Some of us have judged wound severity by the size of the hole on the far side. We have neglected the killing effect of the bloodshot tissue around the permanent wound channel and the effect of the opening of the temporary cavity.

Once the bullet gets inside the animal, the faster it loses its energy, the quicker it apparently kills, and that is why observant hunters have noticed that on some animals and in some calibers the new controlled expanding bullets kill less quickly than old-fashioned, thin-jacketed soft points with pure lead cores. In the fall of 1950 I shot a very large Dall ram with a certain make of 150-grain bullet in the .30/06. Both shots were in the rump as he ran away. The first shot deflected a bit and came out through the ribs after penetrating two-thirds of the big ram's body; the second shot went through from stem to stern and came out the front of the chest. The guide said he saw the ram hump up at the first shot, but I couldn't tell it was hit. Even after the second shot he ran twenty feet or so before he went down. The bullets didn't shed their energy fast enough.

But the bullet has to get inside the animal. I once saw an antelope shot with a 100-grain bullet in the .270 at about 150 yards. The animal was quartering away. The bullet blew up on

KILLING POWER

the ribs, making a shallow but wicked-looking wound, and damaging the lobe of the right lung. The antelope wobbled around and went down, but kill was not instantaneous, as the bullet did not get inside.

As long as the bullet gets inside, then, velocity contributes more to killing power than bullet weight. In the .30/06, the 150-grain bullet at close to 3,000 f.p.s., *and if it gets well into the chest cavity*, will give a higher percentage of quick kills than the 180-grain bullet, and the 180-grain will give a higher percentage than the 220-grain. The only two grizzlies I have ever seen killed instantly in their tracks were shot with bullets traveling at high velocity—one a 130-grain .270 bullet, the other a 180-grain bullet from a .300 Weatherby Magnum.

The difference in killing power between the .30/30 and the .30/06 lies in the velocity. At short ranges, the .220 Swift has stiffened big stuff like elk and even moose with one shot. The 48-grain Swift bullet is only slightly heavier than the 46-grain Hornet bullet and, for that matter, not much heavier than the 40-grain, .22 Long Rifle bullet. But, brother, there is a lot of difference in the size of the cavities those .22 bullets open up, and in the killing power!

Killing the Heaviest Game

Compared to genuinely large game, the animals we shoot in North America are relatively small. A big Alaska brown bear (the very biggest), may weigh 1,500 pounds, but a lot of them weigh a good deal less than 1,000. A big Alaska bull moose, whether he is shot in northern British Columbia, the Yukon, or in Alaska itself, will weigh in the neighborhood of 1,500. Both the bear and the moose, though large from American standards, are soft skinned, and thin skinned. They cannot compare for a moment to the really big thick-skinned animals of the Old World—to the Indian or African elephants, to the tough and ferocious wild cattle like the African Cape buffalo or its Asiatic relatives, to that animated tank known as the rhino, or even to the timid and non-dangerous but enormous giraffe.

Those large animals are hard to kill. For one thing, their hides are thick and tough and a bullet which will give adequate penetration on any North American big game will fly to pieces prematurely when shot at one of the big fellows. For another, their bones, in order to carry their great weight, are tremendously massive and will turn or break up anything but the most rugged of bullets. For still another, they are so large that a wound of a size which would be comparatively large even on a large grizzly will be small on one of the big fellows.

Bullets used on them should be of such a nature that, come hell or high water, they will drive on in a straight line through hide and bone into vital areas. Expanding bullets should be of such mass and construction that they will not, under any circumstances, go to pieces and inflict a superficial wound. Rhino and elephants are usually hunted with full-metal cased bullets, or "solids," as the British call them. They should have very thick jackets, heavily reinforced at the forward portion and almost flat at the nose, so there will be no chance for them to deflect on a bone and go astray. The usual British jacket material is cupronickel, but many experienced African hunters prefer jackets of mild steel. For elephants, such bullets will weigh, as we have seen in the chapter on rifles for heavy, dangerous game, from 450 to 700 grains and be of from .45 to .60 caliber. Their great mass and heavy construction give them power to plow right through bone, gristle, and hide into vital areas.

The only way the largest animals can be killed quickly with any missile fired from a shoulder weapon is by the destruction of tissue immediately necessary to life. For this reason, the seasoned elephant hunter tries to get close enough so that he can be sure of driving his bullet into the relatively small brain, by aiming, I understand, at a point between the eye and the orifice of the ear. In case the animal is screened by brush, or standing in such a position that aim there is impossible, the enormous momentum of those great elephant bullets will still knock the beast down, stunned for the moment, so that the hunter can get in another shot. Even a shot in the chest with a .465 or a .470, those who have shot in Africa tell me, will smash an elephant back on his haunches for a moment, or turn a charge. Such a rifle is no doubt a lifesaver and the safest thing to use, yet some professional hunters in Africa have shot literally hundreds of elephants using full-metal cased bullets in the .256 Mannlicher (160 grains) or in the 7 x 57 (175 grains). They claim that their mild recoil enables them to drive the bullet home more surely, since they have no tendency to flinch. In rebuttal, though, other hunters say that at the time professional ivory hunters were using these light rifles the great game was found more often in the open than it is today, and that now one simply must have the knock-down power of the Big Berthas to turn a charge, even when the bullet does not strike right on the button.

This ability to drive right on through to a vital area from any angle, through hide, bone, and muscle, is an absolute must on any dangerous game. Even the comparatively small African lion calls for a bullet that will drive through heavy chest muscles if he is facing the hunter or charging. He does not need a "solid," but he needs a bullet that expands or "sets up" slowly so that a head-on shot will drive back into the vital heart-lung area. The late Stewart Edward White, who did about as much African hunting as any American ever did, used for his lion rifle a .30/06 with the 220-grain Remington delayed expanding mushroom, which was a bullet with a full jacket over a hollow point, and with the Western 220-grain boat-tail with only a pin-point of lead exposed at the tip. Neither bullet is now made, but their place has been taken by the Remington 220-grain soft-point Core-lokt and the Western-Winchester Silvertip of like weight.

The relatively light, high-speed, fast-expanding bullets give the quickest kills on soft-skinned game of moderate size, even with broadside shots on animals as large as moose and grizzly.

THE BIG-GAME RIFLE

There is, however, always the chance that such a bullet will fly to pieces prematurely on heavy bone or muscle. Just prior to the first World War, when the .280 Ross was in its glory, a titled Englishman was mauled and killed by a charging lion because the 145-grain Ross bullet at its very high velocity went to pieces on the massive chest muscles and allowed the lion to close on him.

With big, dangerous animals, the brain shot is the thing. If that is impossible, the shoulder shot, which will break down an animal and render him helpless for a finishing shot, should be taken. The heart shot will kill quickly, but not instantly, and when the hunter is in heavy bush and the animal he is after has to be taken literally at feet, he has to kill or disable with his first shot. If he tries to whittle an elephant down by shooting at the whole elephant he, sooner or later, is going to come to grief!

CHAPTER XVIII

Reloading Ammunition for Big-Game Rifles

HANDLOADING center-fire rifle cartridges is one of the fastest growing of all hobbies related to the rifle. Back in the black-powder days, almost all riflemen were handloaders, and it was common for great manufacturers like Winchester to furnish tools along with the rifle. The enormous herds of buffalo that were killed off in the 1870's and very early 80's were largely shot with handloaded ammunition. Priming their fired cases, casting and patching their bullets with paper, then reloading with special British black powder, were jobs that the expert buffalo hunter had to perform, not only to save ammunition but to get the finest accuracy and the flattest trajectory.

With the adoption of smokeless powder, handloading dropped off, because cartridge cases would not stand up. At the time, it was felt that the trouble lay in the properties of the mysterious new propellant, and the manufacturers warned against attempting to reload with smokeless powder ammunition. One of the troubles was that handloaders were working with much higher pressures than they had used in the old days. The real seat of the trouble, though, was that in those days primers employed mercury in their composition. When the harmful mercury was combined with large amounts of black powder, the trouble was not noticed, but with the smaller amounts of smokeless powder and the higher pressures, the trouble developed. I have an old

THE BIG-GAME RIFLE

Winchester broadside published in the early 1900's warning against any reloading of Winchester cases that had been used with smokeless powder.

By 1920, the handloading of center-fire rifle ammunition was just about a thing of the past. Probably what gave rise to new interest in home-cooked ammunition was the sale of cheap components to members of the National Rifle Association through the Director of Civilian Marksmanship along in the early 1920's. In those days, government primers, powder, and bullets could be purchased, almost literally, for a song. The handloader was almost entirely a .30/06 user and a target shot. It was now safe enough, since most center-fire rifle primers were made on formulas that did not incorporate brass-destroying mercury, since they were similar to the famous Frankfort Arsenal No. 70 mixture. They used potassium chlorate, and although they were moisture-attracting and rust-causing, they did not ruin cases. Good DuPont and Hercules powders were available, so were either military or commercial primers, plenty of military and commercial bullets.

The depression gave handloading a second shot in the arm. The price of factory ammunition went down, but it did not go down as fast as wages, and many a man who liked to shoot found that he simply could not afford to unless he rolled his own. I found myself in exactly that position along in the early 1930's. My income fell by about one-third and my young wife started presenting me with bouncing boys. For a time it looked as if father was going to have to quit popping caps if the young O'Connors were going to wear shoes. Instead, I took up handloading—and I have been at it ever since.

Interest in handloading increased throughout the 1930's, as better tools became available, new and better powders came on the market, and the interest in wildcat cartridges increased. It was the wartime shortage of ammunition, however, that really made it jump. Riflemen who did not handload found themselves without ammunition, whereas the handloaders could usually cobble up some kind of a load. Many a man bought himself a tool and swore that never again would he be caught without a supply of components.

Since the end of the war in 1945, many new tools have come on the market, and the demand for components is so strong that literally dozens of firms have sprung up to furnish bullets, cases, and items of equipment. When, not too long after the outbreak of the Korean war, Western-Winchester and Remington stopped furnishing primers, Federal Cartridge Company started making a new and excellent one.

The attitude of the big loading companies toward the handloader is what can only be called mixed. Many sales executives feel that the reloading of ammunition costs them sales, and the technical men shudder when they read about some of the concoctions the screwier reloaders cook up.

Actually the handloader is the best customer that the big companies have. I am convinced that he actually spends far more money with them than the non-reloader. He buys his cases from them, usually in the form of loaded ammunition. If he can get them, he is also a customer for bullets and primers. The average handloader probably fires 1,000 shots a year. The non-handloader probably does not fire 40. Furthermore, our handloader is a sort of an oracle, a local authority. He loves guns and shooting and infects others, and every one he infects becomes a better customer for Remington and Winchester. If I were big brass in any of the loading companies, I'd cherish the handloader like a rare and precious plant. I'd seduce him with information, woo him with components. He is the real rifle enthusiast and the more rifle enthusiasts there are, the better the arms and ammunition business.

Let's take a look at the advantages of handloading:

1. First, perhaps, is this little matter of cost. Roughly, a centerfire big-game cartridge costs, over the counter, about 20 cents, at this writing. If the rifle enthusiast is going to shoot the 1,000 rounds a year which is usually considered necessary to turn out

a first-rate shot, the cost with store-bought ammunition will be around $200. Our handloader can do as much shooting for less than half of that, or for around $85. His ammunition will shoot just as hard, kick just as much.

2. The handloader has a more versatile rifle. He can load home-cast, lubricated, gas-check bullets very cheaply for short- and mid-range target practice, and if he wishes he can turn out ammunition suitable for potting small game like grouse and rabbits. He can load light jacketed bullets at very high velocity for use on varmints, or he can brew up loads more powerful, in many cases, than anything the factories regularly load. With the .30/06, for instance, he can load a 125-grain bullet at 3,200 f.p.s. for jackrabbits or chucks, or he can use a 250-grain bullet at 2,200 in case he has to shoot through a Kodiak bear from end to end.

3. Chances are that he can load more accurate ammunition. His fired cases have expanded to fit the chamber and present the bullet in line with the bore. He can seat his bullets to touch the lands in their present state of decay, or almost to touch the lands, or any other way his heart desires, that he finds gives him the best accuracy in his particular barrel, and he can find out what kind and how much powder to put behind it.

4. In many cases he can load more useful ammunition, better on particular game than anything he can get from the factory. If he owns a 7-mm. Mauser, for instance, he cannot begin to get full value out of it without reloading. Fine cartridge though it is, the 7 mm. is not particularly popular, and the big loading companies have discontinued the 139-grain bullet that was formerly loaded to 2,900 f.p.s., and the 150-grain bullet loaded to 2,750. Only the load of the 175-grain bullet, at 2,450, is now available over the counter. If the 7-mm. owner is a handloader, this sad state of affairs should not bother him one bit. He can duplicate the old 139-grain load and also the 150-grain load, and in addition he can obtain and load bullets the big companies never dreamed of—110, 120, 130, 160, and 180. The fancier of the .257 has, with factory ammunition, a sort of superior .250/3000,

RELOADING AMMUNITION FOR BIG-GAME RIFLES

but if he handloads, he can make that little cartridge step right on the heels of the .270.

5. The owner of a rifle of wildcat (or unstandard) caliber has to be a handloader or submit to no end of inconvenience and indignity, as he who has a wildcat rifle, and no set of reloading tools to go with it, is like the owner of an automobile that runs only on the milk of wild two-humped lady camels. In other words it isn't of much use to him.

6. Handloading leads its practitioners into many interesting highways and byways—into interior and exterior ballistics, accuracy testing. No one really knows his rifle unless he loads for it. Handloading is an exceedingly interesting hobby in itself.

Actually, the process of handloading is a simple one. When a factory cartridge is fired, the primer, the bullet, and the powder charge are expended, leaving the case as good as new, which represents over half the cost of the cartridge. The handloader simply replaces the components that have been used up.

To do so he must perform the following steps:

Decap (remove the fired primer); recap (seat a new primer); neck size (reduce diameter of neck so the bullet will be held friction tight); neck expand (part of the necking operation, necessary in order that necks be uniform and give uniform tension); put in powder charge; seat bullet. When this has been done the cartridge is as good as new.

The handloader needs some kind of a tool or tools to perform these operations. He also needs something with which to measure his powder charge. If he loads full-power ammunition, his first purchase should be a scale and his second, a powder measure.

The cheapest tool that will perform the operations is the Ideal tong tool, often called the Nutcracker. It is inexpensive. It does not need to be attached to a bench. It is small and can be stored in a drawer. It is, however, very slow, since every one of the operations of preparing the case is entirely separate.

A better bet, faster, but more cumbersome and much more expensive, is a tool of the straight-line bench type like the Pacific

THE BIG-GAME RIFLE

or the Hollywood Universal. Such a tool must be attached to a heavy bench, but it will decap, recap, neck size and neck expand with two strokes of the handle—up and down.

In time, the serious handloader will pick up case gauges, neck trimmers and various other gimmicks to make his hobby easier and more precise, but it need not be very expensive, at the beginning anyway.

Anyone beginning to itch from a bite of the handloading bug should first of all send 75 cents to the Lyman Gun Sight Co., Middlefield, Conn., for the latest edition of the "Ideal Handbook." It describes the Ideal tong and bench-type tools, gives powder charges for most standard and many wildcat calibers, tells how to go about the whole business. Another good investment is the "Belding & Mull Handbook" obtainable for a like amount from Belding & Mull, Box 428, 830 Osceola Road, Philipsburg, Pa. Two booklets entitled, "Handloading Information, Vols. 1 and 2," can be purchased from the National Rifle Association, 1600 Rhode Island Avenue, Washington, D. C., for 75 cents each. They contain a lot of excellent reloading and background material and give pressure data, something which the other manuals do not list. For information on the Pacific tool, the prospective handloader should write the Pacific Gun Sight Co., 355 Hayes St., San Francisco 2, California; and for dope on the Hollywood Universal tool he should write the Hollywood Gun Shop, 6116 Hollywood Blvd., Hollywood 28, California.

Loads below are some I have used myself and which are for the more popular calibers. The recommended loads should be o.k. in good rifles with normal chambers. Many other loads for these, and all other standard American calibers, are to be found in the Ideal and Belding & Mull Handbooks and in the two reloading handbooks put out by the National Rifle Association. The man who shoots a rifle in the Weatherby Magnum Series is all fixed up for reloading dope since in his book "Tomorrow's Rifles Today," Roy Weatherby gives extensive reloading data for all calibers.

RELOADING AMMUNITION FOR BIG-GAME RIFLES

TESTED BIG GAME LOADS FOR POPULAR CALIBERS

BULLET WEIGHT	POWDER CHARGE	VELOCITY	REMARKS
.250/3000			
100	40.5—No. 4350	2920	Equals factory .257 loads. Pressure below 45,000 p.s.i.
100	36.5—No. 4064	2969	Good load.
100	39 —No. 4350	2747	Mild pressure. Good load for lever actions.
.257			
100	46 —No. 4350	3034	Mild pressure. Good load.
100	39 —No. 4064	2900	Very accurate; excellent deer load.
100	39 —No. 4895	3025	A bit hot for varmint use, but O.K. for big game.
117	45 —No. 4350	2925	Reasonable pressure. Excellent deer, antelope or sheep load.
120	45 —No. 4350	2925	Excellent 300-yard load for mountain game.
125	44 —No. 4350	2875	If the .257 can be made into an elk rifle, here is the load that will do it.
.270 W.C.F.			
130	49.5—No. 4064	3025	Usually a very accurate load in any good .270 with any good bullet. Pressure is 47,500 pounds; case life is long.
130	51.5—No. 4320	3100	Pressure about 51,000. Good load, but one which has not given me quite the accuracy of 49.5 grains of No. 4064.
130	57 —No. 4350	3160	Pressures right up there, probably 55,000 in a tight-chambered rifle. Often quoted load of 60 grains. No. 4350 with this bullet is bad business. Even 58 grains is too hot. Load of 56 grains is better.

THE BIG-GAME RIFLE

TESTED BIG GAME LOADS FOR POPULAR CALIBERS

BULLET WEIGHT	POWDER CHARGE	VELOCITY	REMARKS
130	60 —No. 4831	3220	Maximum velocity and killing power with 52,000 pounds pressure.
150	53.5 to 55 grains No. 4350	2900– 2960	The spitzer 150-grain bullets with stiff charges of No. 4350 make probably the best medicine for heavy game in the .270. Pressures run from 52,000 to 55,000 p.s.i.
160	52 —No. 4350	2750	An accurate, powerful deep-penetrating load for heavy game, but needs a 1–10 twist.
180	50 —No. 4350	2700	No good. Accuracy poor even with 1–10 twist; lousy with 1–12.
	7 x 57 Mauser		
130	42 —No. 4895 Lot 27277	2756	Mild. 40,000 p.s.i.
130	44 —No. 4895 Lot 27277	2900	Pressures apparently around 50,000 p.s.i., maximum in my rifle.
130	44 —No. 3031	2950	About the same as load above.
130	50 —No. 4350	2900	Mild. Any of these loads with 130-grain bullets excellent for sheep, deer, antelope.
140	45 —No. 4064	2850	Duplicated old Western factory load.
145	42 —No. 3031	2820	Maximum.
145	45.5—No. 4320	2800	About maximum.
160	49 —No. 4350	2700	For the big stuff. About maximum.
175	47.5—No. 4350	2600	Maximum. Elk and grizzly load.
	.30/06		
150	55 —No. 4320	2925	My favorite hunting load for mountain game in the .30/06. Accurate. Cases last forever.
150	51.5—No. 3031	3000	Too hot in my .30/06 rifles.
150	53 —No. 4676	2935	Very accurate.
180	57 —No. 4350	2800	Pressures maximum. I like 56 grains.
180	49.5—No. 4320	2700	Good load for all-around use.
200	56 —No. 4350	2650	Powerful, flat-shooting load.

RELOADING AMMUNITION FOR BIG-GAME RIFLES
TESTED BIG GAME LOADS FOR POPULAR CALIBERS

BULLET WEIGHT	POWDER CHARGE	VELOCITY	REMARKS
.300 Magnum			
220	52 —No. 4064	2300	*Very accurate. Good woods load.*
220	54 —No. 4064	2500	*Medicine for the heaviest game.*
150	73 —No. 4831	3200	
150	68 —No. 4350	3200	*O.K. for sheep, deer, antelope.*
180	67 —No. 4350	2930	*Poison on any mountain game including grizzly.*
220	65 —No. 4350	2650	*Brown bear or African load.*

LOADING HUNTING AMMUNITION

If ammunition is to be loaded for practice shooting, it does not make much difference if the cases are somewhat hard to extract, as speed of fire is not essential. With cartridges to be fired at game, it is, however, another story. Such ammunition should be loaded in cases fired *once* or full-length resized *once* as, above all, hunting cartridges should be easy to seat and extract. No one is going to shoot any vast number of cartridges at big game, in North America anyway, during any one season, so the supply of ammunition that is to be taken on a hunt should be run through the chamber individually to see that they chamber easily. The supply of handloaded *hunting* ammunition should be put up separately and so marked so it will not get mixed up with practice ammunition.

Bullets for hunting cartridges should never be seated so they contact the lands. If bullets are so seated, sooner or later a bullet will stick in the throat when a cartridge is removed from the chamber. Then getting the bullet out may be difficult, and powder will probably be spilled in the magazine. Bullets should be seated deep enough so there is no possibility of a magazine jam when the magazine is hastily filled, and so they will never stick in the throat.

I do not think it is wise ever to full-length resize a case that is to be used in hunting more than once. If a case that has been resized once becomes difficult to extract it should either be discarded or used for practice loads. Full-length resizing works the brass, particularly if a chamber is a bit sloppy at the rear end, and with resized cases one will get head separations, even in rifles with normal headspace.

Cases used in high-intensity rifles, particularly in .270 and .300 Magnum calibers, should be neck-trimmed back to the original length after they have been fired three or four times. They should always be neck-trimmed after full-length resizing. Cases should be discarded as soon as the primer seats with light pressure, as the pockets have expanded and primer leaks may result. Cases should also be discarded if they show a bright ring about one-fourth inch forward of the extraction groove. They have stretched and are thin at that point. A rupture may result, and if this happens in the field, the rifle is usually out of commission.

CHAPTER XIX

Slings, Scabbards, Cleaning Kits

THE SKEET and trap shot has to carry his scattergun only from his car into the clubhouse and from the clubhouse to the field. Likewise, the wild fowl hunter can sit by the hour in his duck boat or blind, while ice crystals slowly form in his veins. The target rifleman lugs his pet cannon only between firing points, and the tiger hunter perches in a machan in a tree, or in a howdaw on the back of an elephant.

But the average big-game hunter usually has to carry his rifle for great distances. Even when he does a good deal of hunting from horseback he will find that, at least part of the time, he'll have to tie his nag up, pull his rifle out of the saddle scabbard, and hunt the heads of draws and canyons on foot if he is going to have any luck. He may walk many miles in still hunting through forested terrain or he may climb around through high, rough mountains.

He will carry his rifle a lot more than he will shoot it, and it is a sad fact that most rifles are clumsy and awkward burdens that have a tendency to weigh three or four times as much at 5 o'clock in the afternoon as they did at 5 o'clock in the morning.

The big-game hunter can carry his rifle over his shoulder like a soldier on parade. He can lug it in his arms as if it were a baby. He can carry it at the ready like the upland gunner walking up game. None of those ways is, alas, a very comforting way to transport a funny looking instrument made of wood and steel and noted for its projections and angles.

THE BIG-GAME RIFLE

The answer is a sling, something which European sportsmen have used for generations on shotguns as well as on sporting rifles, but which American big-game hunters have adopted in any numbers only since the middle 1920's.

There are two schools of thought in this sling business. The members of the first, like the Europeans, use the sling strictly for carrying, apparently with no realization that the sling is also a great aid in shooting. Their slings are merely straps from $5/8-3/4$ inch in width. The other type of sling originated with American military rifle shots and is designed for both shooting and carrying. For the serious big-game hunting rifleman, particularly the one trained in military shooting or willing to learn, this shooting gun sling should be the choice.

Until comparatively recently no American sporting rifles had any provision whatsoever for the attachment of slings. Except for recent models, like the Model 71 and the Winchester Model 64 Deer, the old Winchester lever-action rifles were not equipped for slings at all. Neither were the Remington slide-action or automatic rifles. Even a good many bolt-action rifles have come out with no provision for a sling. As this is written I have, for examination and report, a pilot model of the new Remington Model 640 slide-action rifle in .30/06. It is completely innocent of any provision for the attachment of a sling, but if I ever own one it is certainly going to get swivels of some kind put on.

The American shooting gun sling evolved from the military sling, which for rough military use is excellent. It is $1\frac{1}{4}$ inches wide, fine for lugging a heavy rifle on long hikes and marches, excellent for steady holding, but a bit on the clumsy and heavy side for the sporting rifle.

The best slings for the hunter rifleman available in this country are narrower and lighter than the military sling but for hunting they do just as well. They measure from $7/8$ to 1 inch in width. They would not be particularly good for target shooting because, adjusted for a tight loop, a sling so narrow would be

SLINGS, SCABBARDS, CLEANING KITS

wearing in a long rifle match. Such a sling might also bruise the shoulder a bit if it were used to lug a 10½-pound rifle on a 30-mile march. The hunting rifle, however, is not ordinarily used on 30-mile marches, nor to fire long strings.

There are two types of shooting gun slings in use in this country—the two-piece and the one-piece. The two-piece sling is simply a narrow version of the big military sling. The front portion forms the loop into which the upper arm is inserted. It consists of a strip of leather 47 inches long with two keepers and a claw hook. The rear portion of the sling is known as the tail or tail piece. It, likewise, has a claw hook for adjustment and it is attached to the loop portion with a metal loop which forms a part of it.

The one-piece, or "Whelen," sling is a single strip of leather usually about 52 inches in length with a claw hook at one end and with holes punched in the strap for the hook. The sling has two leather keepers and a leather lacing.

The fact that in Europe some slings are attached to military rifles on the side shows how little Europeans know about the use of the sling for shooting as well as carrying. In the United States, however, the slings are attached to the rifles by swivels on the forend and at the butt stock. Many factory rifles come equipped with permanently attached swivel bows. This is satisfactory except that it makes removal of the sling difficult—and under certain circumstances, such as carrying the rifle in a saddle scabbard, the sling should be removed. With swivels of the quick detachable type such as those furnished with the Winchester Model 70 Super Grade sporters, the Winchester Model 52 sporter, and on the better custom made rifles, the sling can be quickly removed so that the rifle can be carried in the saddle scabbard with no chance of the sling catching on a snag and yanking the rifle out. It is also convenient when the sling is to be removed so the rifle can be put away in a gun case. Still another advantage is the fact that if a man has his rifles equipped with swivel bases the same distance apart, he can use the same sling with the same adjustment and with the same detachable swivels on more than one rifle.

European rifle makers almost always attach the front swivel directly to the barrel, forward of the forend tip, either with a band or by sweating a base to the barrel. Back in the 1920's when custom rifle making was just getting under way in this country, many of the American custom makers also employed this method. Early Owen, Griffin & Howe, and Sukalle sporters almost always had the swivels so attached. Such method of attachment has no advantages and many disadvantages. The worst disadvantage is, perhaps, that with the sling so attached it is impossible to jam the left hand up hard against the base of the swivel as one should do in using a tight gun sling for shooting. Another disadvantage is that if any pressure is put upon the sling in shooting, the tendency is to pull the barrel down and make the rifle shoot low. This method of attachment may look quite exotic, but it isn't practical.

Swivels or swivel bases should be from 26–27½ inches apart on a sporting rifle, the front swivel from 2–4 inches behind the forend tip, depending on the length of the customer's arms and on the length of the forend. The rear swivels should be 2½–3 inches forward of the toe of the stock.

Rear swivels or swivel bases are put in with a long wood screw. In fact, the bases for quick detachable swivels are attached to such screws. There is plenty of wood to bite in to. The front swivel is at times also attached by this method, but usually the front swivel screws into a nut that is countersunk into the stock below the barrel channel. Often the front swivel screws into a threaded stud attached to the barrel band. The late Alvin Linden used to tie the forend to the barrel by a separate barrel band, then put the swivel base forward of that. His theory was that the left hand against the swivel would not transfer the tension to the barrel that way. I am inclined to believe he was correct, and with an old .270 Linden sporter of mine with a swivel so attached, a tight sling does not change the point of impact at all.

I like to adjust a sling so that it is right for carrying and also for shooting in the sitting position, which in open country and in mountain hunting is the most useful position, as we have seen. This means that when so adjusted to be right for carrying, the sling is, for me, 33 to 36 inches long depending on how far the swivels are apart. This length is for the sling strap itself in case of permanent swivels, or the strap and the detachable swivels in case of the quick detachable outfit. The sling can quickly be made longer, of course, by casting loose a claw hook and putting it in another set of holes. It can likewise be made shorter. The length, however, is about right for carrying.

How far the end of the loop should be from the forward swivel base depends on the build of the shooter. The loop should be adjusted exactly right. If it is too loose, it is of very little help in firm holding. If it is too tight, it is difficult to get into and clumsy to use. With my own rifles I adjust the sling so that the rear of the loop is exactly 17½ inches from the base of the forward swivel. A shorter loop is difficult to get into and it introduces a tremor when I shoot. A longer loop is likewise awkward.

Some experimenting will show the shooter just how much loop he needs. Adjustment should be made so that in the sitting position it is almost necessary, when the upper arm is in the loop, to seat the butt plate at the right shoulder with the right hand. For target shooting, where there is more time, this is the correct adjustment, but for sporting use the sling should be just a shade looser for the sake of speed.

In the two-piece sling the loop is adjusted by putting the claw hook in the proper hole until the length is about right. Sometimes it is necessary to punch new holes for absolute comfort and perfection. For sporting use, it is also a pious idea to lace the loop portion of the sling together, as sometimes claw hooks have a way of falling out. Over-all length is obtained by placement of the claw hook in the holes in the tail piece of the sling.

The one-piece sling is something else again. The over-all length of the sling is obtained, of course, by the position of the claw hook. The loop itself is made by the placement of the leather lacing and the lacing itself forms the rear portion of the loop. If you want the loop to be shorter you put the lacings through a set of holes farther forward. If you want the loop to be longer you use a set of holes farther to the rear. I have found it best to put both leather keepers over the loop portion because then one serves as a keeper and the other is sort of a "keeper's keeper." Not only is a good sling an aid in carrying, but it is a great aid in shooting, particularly from the sitting position. The man who has time to get into a tight loop and settle into a good, firm position can, from the sitting position, do shooting that is comparable to that which can be done from prone. A good, well-adjusted sling is indeed handy on a rifle when the shot has to be taken from the sit because of rocks, long grass, topography, etc. The sling is also exceedingly handy when the man is heaving from a long climb, and has to steady down quickly in order to get off a shot. I would not be without one under any circumstances.

Scabbards and Carrying Cases

Until recently it was absolutely impossible to walk into a sporting goods store and get a saddle scabbard suitable for a scope-mounted bolt-action rifle. Those that were for sale were very small, suitable only for a short, lever-action carbine. Some old U. S. cavalry scabbards were for sale at army surplus stores, but they were worthless for scope-sighted rifles since they were not only too short but too skimpy all the way around. If a man wanted to have a decent saddle scabbard for a scope-sighted rifle he had to have it made by a saddle maker to his order. Today, a fair number of good saddle scabbards are for sale. Many of them are advertised as "fitting any scope-sighted rifle." Actually, that

SLINGS, SCABBARDS, CLEANING KITS

is taking in too much territory. The advertisements should read "many scope-sighted rifles." Then they would be more nearly correct.

A good rifle scabbard should be long enough so that leather will come up well over the comb—about halfway back between the butt and the comb. It should be generously enough built so that the rifle can go into the scabbard with no binding, and so that most of the weight of the rifle will rest on the muzzle. With many mounts, particularly those that use aluminum in the construction, some bending will take place if the scabbard is too short and the weight of the rifle rests on the front end of the scope. No matter what position the rifle is carried in on the horse, the sight should always be up, never down. The movement and jouncing of a heavy rifle carried on a horse with the scope sight down, does the sights and the sighting no good, even with the strongest mounts and the strongest steel-tube scopes.

Some years ago, I hunted mule deer on the Salmon River of Idaho with a fine .30/06 with a side mount with aluminum arms. Before I left I had paid no particular attention to the scabbard. When the fireworks began, I found, much to my embarrassment, that my rifle was shooting high enough at 200 yards to cause me to miss three well-squeezed shots at a big buck standing between 200 and 225 yards away. As a usual thing a man who misses three set-up shots like that won't get another shot during the same day. At least that has been my luck. However, later that afternoon I saw a nice fat buck lying in the snow in a basin below me. Calling for my companion to take my binoculars and observe the shot carefully, I squeezed one off with a hold right in the middle of the buck's chest. The snow flew about 4 or 5 inches above his back. I quickly worked the bolt, held about 6 inches below the bottom of the buck's chest, squeezed off a shot and killed the buck. When I got back home I checked the rifle carefully by visual inspection and on the target. What happened was that the scabbard was not wide enough, and the rifle had been carrying all its weight on the forward end of the scope tube. The

THE BIG-GAME RIFLE

scope was a Lyman Alaskan with a steel tube and was not bent in the slightest, but the arm of the mount was slightly bent down and the rifle, of course, was shooting high, since in relation to the scope the barrel was pointing up. One of the best scabbards I have ever seen, represents a combination of my ideas with those of the late Capt. A. H. Hardy, the famous leather worker and old-time exhibition shot who was living in Beverly Hills at the time of his death. The scabbard is 36½ inches long and it covers all but the last 7 inches of the butt stock. It is constructed of heavy, stiff, sole leather and was constructed to be an exact fit for a nice little scope-sighted 7-mm. sporter with a 22-inch barrel. To protect the butt for shipping, it has a sort of a boot of flexible leather in two pieces which are zipped together with a heavy zipper. These two pieces can be completely removed from the scabbard by a zipper running around the scabbard, or they can be folded back and tied down to the body of the scabbard with leather thongs. Besides the leather straps for attaching the scabbard to the saddle, the scabbard has a handle for carrying. When the leather straps are wrapped around the body of the scabbard and buckled and when the protecting hood, or boot, is zipped up, the scabbard forms a most excellent carrying case for shipment of a rifle in the baggage compartment of an airplane or for carrying in the luggage compartment of a car, or in the stateroom of a ship or train. When one is hunting from horseback, as is done in many parts of the West, the fact that the two parts of the hood can be tied back with a leather thong so that the butt of the rifle is instantly available makes the scabbard as convenient as any. In hunting areas such as the Canadian North, where a horse is simply used to get to the foot of a mountain where the climb is begun and there is plenty of time for the shot, the hood can be zipped up to protect the butt stock of the rifle on the trail from being gouged and scraped by brush and limbs. It is a good deal. This particular scabbard has been used both as a scabbard and as a carrying case for two long trips—one into the Yukon and the other into the Atlin district of far northwestern

SLINGS, SCABBARDS, CLEANING KITS

British Columbia—and in many thousands of miles of travel it has protected the rifle perfectly.

Another excellent case is one I had made by the Schoellkopf Company of Dallas, Texas. It, too, is a stiff leather case with a handle for carrying and it protects the rifle as well as does the Hardy job. Dimensions of the case are similar, but instead of employing the flexible leather boot zipped to the body of the scabbard, the Schoellkopf case employs a stiff leather removable boot which is attached to the body of the case by snaps. A light leather thong is attached to the stiff boot and can be tied to the scabbard so that if the hunter wants to jerk the boot off and grab his rifle he will not lose it. It, too, is an excellent and sturdy job and serves well as both a carrying case and a scabbard.

Hoods or boots to protect the butt stocks of rifles are very useful. In some areas of stiff, thorny brush a few days out on horseback will ruin the finish of a fine custom stock if it is not protected.

In addition to scabbards which I have described the standard fleece-lined carrying case with straps comes in handy, particularly for transporting a rifle by car, because such a case will protect the finish of a rifle. Such cases are available at most stores. A word of warning, however; the rifle should not be *stored* in a case of that sort because in time the fleece will attract dampness and cause rust.

Another exceedingly useful piece of leather goods for the big-game hunter is a stout leather cartridge box made of a size to take the inner portion of an ammunition box, and fitted with belt loops. One simply throws the outer portion of the ammunition box away, slips the inner part with the cartridges into the little cartridge case, then fits it on his belt. Of course, different size cartridges take different size leather boxes. One would have no luck trying to use a leather cartridge box designed for the .250/3000 with .30/06 cartridges, nor would he be successful in employing a box for the .30/06 with the .300 Magnum. However, to a considerable extent one can use cartridges of more than one caliber in the same box. For instance, .270 cartridges go well in a .30/06 box and so do 7 mm. and .257 cartridges. One can use .250/3000 cartridges in a box designed for the .30/30. The .300 and .375 Magnum cartridges will fit the same box.

Cleaning Equipment

Unless the big-game rifle has extraordinarily hard use, it is not difficult to keep one in excellent condition if it is cared for regularly with only a few minutes of labor. I have an old .270 on a Mauser action which was stocked by Alvin Linden. No one would take it for a brand-new rifle but in spite of the fact that it has traveled many thousands of miles and has been used, and used hard, from Mexico to the Alaska border, it still bears a presentable appearance. It is now on its third barrel and it has probably been fired at least 10,000 times.

Prior to the advent of non-corrosive priming and the universal use of gilding metal jackets along in the very early 1930's, keeping the bore of a rifle clean was quite a tiresome chore, since the harmful residue of potassium chlorate primers had to be removed by pumping hot water through the bore, or by using some kind of an aqueous solution as a cleaner. Often barrels metal fouled and the fouling had to be removed by messy and smelly ammonia dope. Those sad days are over. Modern commercial priming causes no rust and the fouling deposited by gilding metal jackets does not build up in lumps and is so microscopically thin it does not interfere with accuracy.

The foundation for any cleaning kit is a good one-piece steel rod as made by Belding & Mull or the Marble Arms Company. One should also have a supply of Canton flannel patches of the proper size. At this point I might also add that if a man has several rifles he will probably need two or three sizes of rods, as one cannot very well use a .30 caliber rod on a .25 caliber. One can obtain cut patches of various sizes or he can buy Canton flannel at a dry goods store and cut up his own supply. As this is written, there is a considerable supply of flannel patches being sold as surplus from World War II. They can be picked up cheaply and are excellent.

Even the most casual rifleman should have a set of bristle brushes to fit his cleaning rod, and of proper size for the rifles he owns. He should also have brass brushes of correct caliber for the removal of the occasional metal fouling which pops up even today. An old toothbrush can be used for cleaning out dirt in the checking or in the knurling on the butt plate or pistol grip cap.

Another handy piece of equipment for the rifleman is a bristle brush on a short handle to clean out a rifle chamber, and also a short pistol cleaning rod to be used for the same purpose.

If a rifle is to be used shortly I ordinarily dip a bristle brush of the proper size in some good solvent, or a light oil, put them on the end of the rod and push them through the bore. I then set the rifle away, muzzle down, so the surplus solvent will drain out instead of running back into the action and chamber. The next day when I take the rifle out to shoot it, I run a dry patch through the bore.

If the rifle is to be set away for a longer time, I remove the light oil or solvent with a dry patch, usually use a second patch with oil or solvent followed by another dry patch. I then run a patch through which is saturated with some preservative oil with more body. I have found Field Oil excellent. I have also used a good deal of Fulcrum oil which is a sperm base oil and good for lubricating as well as preserving the bore. In a dry house, and particularly in a heated house, there is little danger of the bore rusting with ordinary care, but if a gun is to be set away for a long period of time it should be thoroughly protected by a good, heavy gun grease preferably put in hot.

Before a rifle is set away, even overnight, all metal parts should be gone over with an oily rag to protect them from moisture and to wipe away the salty sweat of finger prints.

On a hunting trip, a little cleaning kit should be taken along. I ordinarily take with me a jointed rod, a couple of dozen cut

THE BIG-GAME RIFLE

patches of the proper size and a couple of small bottles or cans of some oil with a good body like Fulcrum or Field Oil. When I have fired the rifle I run an oily patch through the bore, usually as soon as I get to camp. Before I set the rifle away I will use the same patch to go over all metal parts to cover them with a very thin coat of oil and to wipe away dampness and finger prints. If I should get caught in the rain and the rifle gets wet, I dry and oil it very thoroughly both inside and out. On these trips I usually take with me a small bottle of linseed oil and once or twice during the trip I will put two or three drops in my hand, rub it on the stock, taking care to avoid the checking, then wipe off all surplus with a flannel patch. Such simple and elementary care will keep a rifle looking like new.

As part of the kit, I also take along a small file, a pair of long-nosed pliers, and screwdrivers to fit the guard screws of the rifle and the smaller screws on the scope mount, etc.

Most factory stocks have lacquer finishes. The lacquer looks very lovely when the guns are new, but a little use soon chips off the finish, leaving the bare wood beneath showing. Good custom rifles have various types of more durable finishes—the straight linseed oil finish known as the London oil finish, linseed oil over some kind of a filler, linseed oil over a couple of coats of Spar varnish mixed with oil, French polish, straight spar varnish, etc. A lacquer finish usually means a refinishing job sooner or later, but the other finishes can be cared for and kept looking new by the application of an occasional two or three drops of linseed oil rubbed on evenly, then rubbed off with a dry rag, followed by some more rubbing by the hand.

It is not difficult to keep a gun in good condition if only the slight chore is attended to regularly, something which no real lover of fine rifles begrudges. In time, of course, the bluing will wear off and a reblue job will become necessary. There is no excuse for letting the finish of the stock wear off to the bare wood or for letting rust develop in the bore or on the outside metal parts.

CHAPTER XX

The Selection of the Battery

IN THE middle of the twentieth century many different influences are operating on the big-game rifle and its further development, through magazine articles, the hot stove league, and by word of mouth. On one hand the backward-lookers tell us that no modern cartridge has the killing power of the old .50/110, and on the other, experimenters are attempting to push velocities with hunting-weight bullets up toward 4,000 f.p.s. The rifle nut, who is interested not particularly in big-game hunting itself but only in rifles, has his say. So does the varmint shooter, the target shot, and the bench rest expert. Hobby-riders jump on the merry-go-round. Members of the long-range school do not bat an eye at knocking off game at 700 yards, and the shoot-them-in-the-eye boys say that anyone who does not stalk his game to within 100 yards or closer is a fumbling fellow and probably a panty-waist. A small, but very vocal, clique of big-bore lovers wouldn't be caught dead shooting any animal larger than a coyote with a rifle of less than .33 caliber and throwing a bullet weighing less than 250 grains, and those in the small-bore school are willing to take on Alaska brown bear with the .220 Swift. Those who lay their money on heavy bullets at moderate velocity are at the throats of those who want light bullets at very high velocity, and both are at the throats of the conservatives.

The bench rest shots sneer at any rifle that won't group in a minute of angle, even if it is to be used on moose, and when some of the varmint hunters go after big game they want 12 pound rifles with 8-x scopes. One group thinks all progress in cartridge design stopped with the .30/06, and another swears that the .30/06 is no better than a pea-shooter and is as obsolete as the .45/75.

Some writers on rifles and some exceedingly vocal critics of rifles have had no great amount of experience in big-game hunting. One gun editor, who is now no longer with us, was a most interesting and excellent writer with very definite ideas on all manner of subjects, but he was a ballistician and a target shot and by no means a big-game hunter. He had shot a few mule deer and, I believe, one caribou, but when I knew him he had quit hunting even for deer. It bored him. It was always my feeling that he was not much better qualified to make pronouncements on big-game rifles than Jim Jones, the trapper, who lives on game the year around, is to be an oracle on the subject of 1,000-yard target shooting.

One rifle nut, with an engineering background, dug out his slide rule, went into a trance, and when he recovered consciousness, he announced to the world that the .270 W.C.F. with the 130-grain bullet was completely inadequate for any animal weighing more than 275 pounds. That must have made very strange reading to a man like Russell Anabell, the Alaskan guide and writer, who used a .270 on big Alaska moose and even on brown bear. Before I had hunted moose I read up on the subject and was pretty well convinced that the bullet fired by a moose rifle ought to weigh no less than 250 grains. I got my first shot at a big bull when I had a .270 in my hands. The little 130-grain bullet went up through his paunch and into the lungs as he quartered away. The moose ran about 40 yards and fell. I had to shoot him again, but that first bullet surely did him no good.

Testimonial evidence is very queer stuff indeed, and much of it has to be greeted with a lifted eyebrow. In my mail, the day before I wrote this, was, among others, a letter from a guide who belongs to the big-bore, heavy-bullet school and who hunts the

THE SELECTION OF THE BATTERY

Middle Fork of the Salmon River in Idaho. He had read a piece I had written on the .30/06 rifle and he told me that the blood of a lot of elk that would escape to die because they had been shot at with .30/06 and .270 rifles would be on my head. Both calibers were, he said, no better than deer and antelope rifles. I had another letter from a Texas business man, who had, with friends, only recently returned from a Wyoming hunt. Between them they had killed seven elk and moose with nine shots with .30/06 and .270 rifles. Take your pick!

As we look back on the evolution of the big-game rifle in the past several decades, I believe most of us will decide that nothing too astoundingly revolutionary has happened. Developments are more in the nature of refinements.

The excellent little 7 x 57 Mauser cartridge was designed back in the early Nineties, the .30/06 in 1906 on a case that had been put into production three years earlier. Even the .300 and .375 H. & H. Magnum cartridges, which are today pretty hot numbers and just achieving some popularity in the United States, were in use by British hunters in Africa prior to the first World War. So was the 7 x 64 Brenneke, a cartridge considered superior to the .270 W.C.F. by some—and the .270, incidentally, came out in 1925. The latest 7 mm. and .30 caliber super-wildcats do not have much on the cartridges developed by Charles Newton before the first World War, or on the .280 Ross cartridge.

The world's standard action for high intensity big-game cartridges is the Mauser that was developed in 1898, and newer actions like the Winchester Model 70 and the Remington Model 721 are simply modifications of the basic Mauser design. Even today, the Weatherby Magnum rifles for the high performing line of Weatherby semi-wildcat Magnums are built on Mauser actions made in Belgium. Except for very minor modifications to facilitate scope mounting they are basically the old Model 98.

Refinements that have helped bring the modern big-game rifle to its present state of near-perfection are myriads of minor, though important, developments. In the ammunition itself, new

THE BIG-GAME RIFLE

powders, particularly the I.M.R. line by DuPont, have enabled the loading companies to step up the velocity of old cartridges. New powders are stable, clean-burning, progressive in action. The United States currently leads the world in powder development, but I doubt if we have anything much on the Germans. Non-corrosive, non-mercuric priming has lengthened the life of big-game rifles and has made cleaning easier. Bullet design has improved and the use of gilding metal rather than cupro-nickel jackets has taken another headache out of owning a high-velocity rifle.

Barrel steels have been greatly improved, and barrels themselves are bored, reamed, rifled, and chambered to smaller tolerances than prevailed twenty years ago. Whereas many big-game rifles in use before the first World War would not group into six minutes of angle from a rest, most such rifles on the market today will shoot into two minutes and many into less.

The perfection of the hunting scope and mount has enabled the big-game hunter to see better, hold better, and shoot better, and better modern stocks make the rifle faster to handle, steadier to hold. However, no development within the past half century can begin to compare in importance to the invention of smokeless powder, the brass center-fire cartridge case, or even to the invention of the Mauser and other repeating actions.

Somewhat higher velocity has increased killing range, so has better accuracy, better stocks, and the use of telescopic sights. But the man behind the rifle is still a human being full of wobbly joints and a beating heart, subject to short wind, buck fever, bum eyesight, and delusions of persecution. He has a better rifle than he had fifty years ago, but he isn't a better man.

He is, however, a better informed man. Actually, he probably shoots more than his city-dwelling father. He reads more and has more theory. He probably does some varmint shooting. He knows how to sight his rifle in as a rule, and he knows something about trajectory.

THE SELECTION OF THE BATTERY

The modern big-game hunter is usually smart enough to laugh at some of the things his less sophisticated father wrote. When he sees a statement such as I culled out of a magazine article written prior to the first World War, he snickers. "I thought the ram was about 1,000 yards away, so I put up the highest backsight and killed it with the first shot." He knows that the hunter was either drawing a long bow, that he flinched just right, or that the ram wasn't a thousand yards from the muzzle.

The best contemporary big-game rifles are better sighted, better stocked, more accurate, and use better ammunition than the rifles of thirty and forty years ago. They are more deadly and have an enormously greater sure hitting range than the old black-powder rifles of the 70's and 80's.

In selecting a battery of rifles, the big-game hunter will do well to evaluate the advice on rifles he gets and the articles he reads in the light of the prejudice, experience, and crotchets of those holding forth on big-game rifles. The target shooters will always demand large, thick, heavy forends so they won't get their fingers burned during a string of rapid fire. How often, though, does the big-game hunter sit down and fire ten shots as fast as he can aim and let them go? The bench rest shooter demands hair-splitting accuracy, but how often does the rifleman carry a bench rest around with him. Because the accuracy nuts insist on heavy rifles, many a hunter has gone on a mountain hunt with a rifle that was so heavy it wore him out. The big-game hunter is usually better off with a reasonably light, portable rifle that he can carry around without undue fatigue, even at some sacrifice in bench rest accuracy. The varmint hunting enthusiast without much big-game experience would send the novice out on a sheep hunt with an 11-pound rifle with a 6- or 8-x scope. The old sheep hunter will tell the same man that he should keep the weight of his rifle down to 9 or even 8 pounds, and that it is not once in several blue moons that he'll need a scope of more than 4-x. How does he know that? Experience!

THE BIG-GAME RIFLE

The All-Around Battery

I am often asked what rifle I would select if I had to hunt all North American big game and also do some varmint hunting with one weapon. I am just as aware as anyone else that there is no such thing as an all-around rifle. There are only makeshift all-around rifles. If the unfortunate fate of being a one-rifle man actually did overtake me, I believe I'd pick a good .270 which weighed around 8½–9 pounds and which was equipped with a good 4-x scope. I have an old .270 in the rack. I have been shooting it around 20 years and it is now on its third barrel. It began life in the shop of Bill Sukalle, the Arizona barrel maker. I bought from him a 24-inch .270 barrel fitted to a Model 98 Mauser action with a butter-knife bolt handle for, if I remember correctly, $30. I had the late Alvin Linden fit a stock of European walnut to it for $75, and Frank Pachmayr fit a Noske scope (later replaced with a Lyman Alaskan) on Noske mount. With that rifle, I have shot literally hundreds of jackrabbits, many coyotes, a couple of javelinas, mule and whitetail deer, elk, moose, desert, bighorn, Stone, and Dall sheep, grizzly, and black bear, antelope, Rocky Mountain goat, timber wolves, and caribou. Curious thing is that most of the shooting was done with the 130-grain bullet, which did a good job on Arizona jackrabbits and Yukon moose. I wouldn't call it an ideal all-around rifle, but I got by with it.

The man who lives east of the Rockies and who does not plan to hunt anything larger than deer and black bear is pretty well off with a one-rifle battery consisting of either a .250/3000 or a .257 Roberts. For woodchuck shooting alone I'd prefer a rifle of the .220 Swift class, and for most Eastern deer hunting a slide- or lever-action rifle in .300 Savage, .348 Winchester, .35 Remington is to be preferred. But the man who doesn't want to have his apartment cluttered up with deer or a problematical black bear

THE SELECTION OF THE BATTERY

in the fall, can get by very nicely with the 100-grain .25 caliber bullet as used in either the .250/3000 or the .257.

I have never shot an Alaska brown bear, and as far as my personal experience goes, 130-grain .270 bullets may bounce off of the big brownies like raindrops off a tin roof. I do know, however, again not from personal experience but from a lot of testimonial evidence, that 220-grain .30/06 bullets do not bounce off of Alaska brown bears. The .30/06, with the great variety of bullet weights available for it, is an excellent all-around cartridge for North American big game—probably not quite as good as the .270 on the smaller animals but possibly better with the heavier bullets on the big stuff.

Minimum Complete Battery

Theoretically at least, the big-game hunter can do a pretty good job on all North American big game with two rifles—a woods rifle and a long-range mountain rifle. If I were confining myself to two rifles, one of them would be a pump- or lever-action rifle for a fairly powerful cartridge—a Marlin Model 336 in .35 Remington, a Winchester Model 71 in .348, a Remington Model 760 in .300 Savage, .35 Remington, or .30/06. I would equip that rifle either with a peep sight or a 2½-x scope on a quick detachable side mount so that in case of rain, snow, or wet brush the scope could be taken off and iron sights used. The second rifle would be a .30/06 or .270 or possibly one of the hot-shot .270 or 7 mm. wildcats on a bolt-action and with a 4-x scope.

Battery for the Rockies

Anyone planning an expensive pack trip into the Rocky Mountain area of the Western states or Canada, should take two rifles

THE BIG-GAME RIFLE

with him, or if there are two men in the party, there should be an extra rifle. The hunter will carry one of his rifles on his horse in a saddle scabbard. The other can be lashed to the top pack of a good reliable pack-horse or it can be carried on the saddle of the cook or one of the guides. With a good stiff leather scabbard carrying case, such as I have described in a previous chapter, this extra rifle should be safe enough.

Some of the more crotchety outfitters hate to be bothered with extra rifles taken by the dudes and advise the hunter against more than one. I cannot agree with this, and I consider an extra rifle good insurance against disappointment. In 1945, when Myles Brown and I hunted around the head of the White River in the Yukon, I had with me a .270 and a .30/06. Along toward the middle of the trip, the elevation adjustments in the scope on the .270 went to the bad and my trip would have been a failure if I hadn't gone to the trouble of taking the .30/06 along. On a trip into Sonora in 1941, my wife and I had a .257 and a .270, but no spare. The ejector broke on her .257 and she got her game with my .270. I had previously shot a fine desert mule deer and hence did not get skunked, but while she used the .270 I had to content myself with quail shooting. In 1943, when Jack Holliday and I hunted north of Jasper Park in British Columbia and Alberta, the head blew off a .270 case and my .270 was out of commission for three days until I worked out a method of removing the stuck case. In the meantime I fell back on my spare rifle and shot the largest grizzly I have ever seen, before or since. In 1946 when Doc Du Comb and I hunted Stone sheep, moose, grizzly, and caribou and went clear from the Alaska highway to the heads of the Prophet and Muskwa Rivers in northern British Columbia, I got caught in a heavy rainstorm on the top of a very high mountain 3,000 feet above and miles away from camp. My guide and I fought our way back through miles of soaking "shintangle." The permanently mounted scope on the rifle I was carrying got moisture between the elements of the ocular lens and, for four or five days, it would fog up every time the temperature changed.

THE SELECTION OF THE BATTERY

Until the scope dried out I was very glad that I had a spare with me.

I have hunted in the Rockies with 7 mm., .270, .30/06, .300 Weatherby Magnum, and 7 mm. Weatherby Magnum rifles. Any of them is satisfactory. Choice should depend on how much recoil the hunter can handle and how much weight, as a .300 Weatherby Magnum will naturally kick harder than a 7 mm. and it will also weigh more.

If two rifles are taken, I am convinced that one of them should have a quick detachable scope mount, with a good receiver sight like the Lyman 48 available. Not only is a rifle so equipped handy for hunting in rain or wet brush, but the extra sight may save the hunter's bacon if something should happen to the scope. The *sensible* thing to do on the long pack trip is to take two rifles of the same caliber, as this simplifies the ammunition problem. Most big-game hunters and rifle enthusiasts are not sensible men, however.

An addition to the battery (or at least to the combined outfit of the party) should be something to shoot grouse and ptarmigan with. I like to eat grouse, particularly blue grouse, a big juicy white-meated bird that is superior even to pheasant and so far ahead of chicken that there is no comparison. On various trips into the North I have shot their heads off with full-power loads in the .30/06 and .270, with reduced loads in the .270, with .22 rifles, and with a .410 shotgun.

In case handloaders may be interested, a full-metal cased 100-grain .270 bullet in front of 25 grains of No. 4198 shoots to exactly the same point of aim at 25 yards as the factory .270 130-grain load, in my rifles anyway, which means that with a scope-sighted rifle putting the bullet to point of aim at 275 yards, either the full-power or reduced load first crosses the line of aim at 25 yards. I have shot many grouse through the head with full-power loads at 25 yards, or thereabouts, and also with the reduced load.

In 1951 my son, our guide, and I lost the outfit and had to lie out all night. The next morning we breakfasted on broiled grouse, all with their heads shot off with full-power loads in the .270.

If a .22 is the grouse rifle, ammunition with hollow-point bullets should be taken. Solid bullets do not kill grouse reliably with body shots.

In many areas, grouse are plentiful enough so that the big-game hunter can take a day off and have some excellent upland gunning if there is a shotgun in the party. Birds often are a welcome change from red meat and upland gunning from the hunting of big game. Any shotgun will do, but the ideal one is, I believe, a .410. The last couple of trips I have taken a Winchester Model 42 pump bored modified, and I have had a lot of fun with it. The gun is light and the ammunition is easy to carry. One of the best meals I have ever eaten came because my son, Bradford, had the little pump along when we were on a jackcamp for Fannin sheep. We cut up four big grouse, floured them and fried them in deep fat. With green beans, mashed potatoes, milk gravy, and hot bannocks, they made a wonderful meal.

Rifles for Alaska Browns

I wouldn't run away from an Alaska brown bear if I had a .270 using 160- or even 150-grain bullets, or a .30/06 with 180- or 220-grain bullets, but the brownie is a large, potentially dangerous animal mostly shot in brush and forest. He needs to be stopped and stopped right now. There is no doubt that the best medicine for brownies is a heavy bullet of large diameter. Professional brown bear guides nearly all use big bores.

Since a hunt for Alaska browns is expensive, anyone taking a trip can well afford a special rifle. Probably the stand-out is the Winchester Model 70 in .375 Magnum, this country's most powerful factory produced rifle. Because the islands of southeast Alaska, Kodiak, and the Alaska peninsula are foggy, rainy, and

THE SELECTION OF THE BATTERY

generally drip with moisture, the scope on the .375 should be mounted with a quick detachable mount like the Griffin & Howe or Mykrom. A favorite among the guides in Alaska is the Pachmayr Lo-Swing mount, which can instantly be swung up out of the way of iron sights.

Besides the .375, various wildcat calibers are suitable. The .333 OKH with its long, mean 250-grain bullet driven at a velocity of about 2,750 f.p.s. should be excellent. The .35 Whelen with a 250-grain bullet at 2,700, or a 275-grain at 2,400, also has its admirers, as has the stepped-up, blown-out .375 Weatherby Magnum.

The African Battery

I have never hunted in Africa but many of my friends have. Consensus is that the most universally useful of African rifles is the .375 Magnum, sighted for about 150 yards with the 300-grain Winchester Silvertip or full-metal cased (solid) bullet. With the expanding bullet, the .375 is excellent medicine for lion and large antelope and with the solid it does well on buffalo and rhino and in a pinch can be used on elephant.

There seems to be no particular place in the African battery for a rifle like the .270 W.C.F., and most of those who have hunted there recommend a .30 caliber with 180- and 220-grain bullets like the .30/06 and the .300 Magnum. In the past few years a surprising number of .300 Weatherby Magnums have been taken to British East Africa and those who have used them like them enormously.

The American hunting in Africa could take a .30 and a .375 with him. Each should, I believe, be equipped both with scope and iron sights, some such combination as a Lyman 48 in conjunction with a 2½-x scope on a quick detachable side mount.

Not only does Africa offer what to an American seems a fantastic amount of big game, but it also offers varmint shooting in

THE BIG-GAME RIFLE

incredible variety—predatory hawks, wild dogs, jackals, and so on. For this, a scope-sighted .22 Hornet or .220 Swift might well be taken along. Such a rifle would be useful on small antelope as well as on varmints.

To complete the weapons to be taken from this country, a shotgun is a good addition since ducks, geese, francolin, sand grouse, and bustard are plentiful, offer a variety of sport, and a change in diet. Col. Sandy McNabb told me once that when he went to Africa again he would take a .410 shotgun, but some friends who took 20 gauge guns told me they found African game difficult to kill with a small-bore and the light British loads and that if they went again they would take 12-bores.

The big stopping rifle can be a bolt-action or a double. It can be purchased in England or rented for the season in Nairobi or some other outfitting point. There is not much point in buying a $1,000 double for a three or four months' safari which is taken once in a lifetime. If the double is selected, it should be one of the powerful ones like the .465, .470, or .475 No. 2. Magazine rifles like the .404 or .416 have also been used successfully on elephants.

Some Americans do not like to shoot borrowed or rented rifles and will want to own all the weapons in their battery. Double rifles in good condition can often be bought at good prices at Abercrombie & Fitch in New York or in London. Bolt-action big-game rifles more powerful than the .375 can be made up in this country. Griffin & Howe turns out rifles for the .404 and also, I believe, the .416 Magnum. Anderson's Gun Shop of Yakima, Washington builds rifles for an interesting cartridge called the .450 Watts Magnum. It uses the .375 case necked to .45 and a line of special 400- and 500-grain bullets made by Fred N. Barnes, the bullet maker. Ballistics are very similar to those of cartridges used in the big British doubles. The cartridge is worth an investigation by any potential African hunter who wants to own his stopping rifle.

THE SELECTION OF THE BATTERY

Conclusions

For the average hunting of whitetail deer and black bear in the wooded East, cartridges of the .30/30 class are entirely adequate in the hands of a competent shot; but under public hunting conditions where some other hunter is apt to put his tag on a buck unless it drops in its tracks, a somewhat more powerful cartridge will give a higher proportion of one-shot kills. For mountain hunting for anything from mule deer to moose above timberline, rifles of the .30/06–.270 class are entirely adequate, but for shots at Alaska brown bear in brush and timber and at any of the other of the world's dangerous game, a rifle approximating the .375 Magnum is to be preferred.

At any rate, though, the man behind the rifle is far more important than the rifle he shoots. The hunter becomes deadly through skill acquired by practice, not by money spent at the sporting goods store or at the custom gun makers.

Index

Abercrombie & Fitch, 82, 370
accuracy, 13, 23, 36–8, 117, 118, 137, 142, 145, 147, 150, 151, 175, 192, 204, 356, 362, 363; for antelope shooting, 112; of black-powder rifles, 27; of British sportsmen, 139, 238; from different positions, 279–296; of double-barreled rifles, 54, 211–15; of hand-loaded ammunition, 340; for jungle hunting, 18; of Kentucky rifles, 23; of Mauser-type bolt-action rifles, 51; of Remington rifles, 63, 64, 73; due to rifling, 91; of saddle rifles, 176; of Savage Model 99, 64–5, 116; of semi-automatic rifles, 56; sights a factor in, 235, 240–2, 249, 250; of smokeless powder rifles, 30; due to stocks, 99, 101; of Weatherby Magnum cartridges, 48, 163; for whitetail shooting, 112
Ackley, P. O., 83, 162, 171
Ackley Magnum cartridges, 165; .270, 162; 7 mm., 162
actions: advantages and disadvantages of different types of, 50–73; metal work on, 88–93; weight figures of, 92; *see also* rifles and specific names
Adolph, Fred, 39
Adolph Express cartridge .30, 39
African Rifles and Cartridges, 221
American Hi-Vel No. 2, 28
American Rifle, The, 35, 39
American Rifleman, 157
Anabell, Russell, 360

Anderson Gun Shop, 90, 370
Anderson, H. B., 222–3
antelope, 3; bullets for, 225, 230, 328; cartridges and rifles for, 12, 18, 25, 38, 44, 112, 125, 145, 150–1, 153, 168, 194–5, 203, 205, 209, 215, 305, 364, 369, 370; habitats of, 13–14; size of, 192–3
Arizona Bullet Company, 145
Askins, Major Charles, 162
Automatic Colt pistol cartridge .32, 66

Baker cheek pieces, 102
ballistics, 39, 40, 45–8, 79, 125, 139, 160, 175, 219, 341; of the .30/30, 124; of the 7 x 64, 158–9; of the .318, 197; of cartridges for dangerous, thick-skinned game, 222; of cartridges for forest game, 134; of cartridges for heavy, soft-skinned game, 207–8; of cartridges for mountain game, 166; of early, high velocity cartridges, 49; of Holland & Holland rifles, 182, 223; of Watts Magnum cartridge, 370; of Weatherby rifles, 47
Barnes, Fred N., 198, 370
Barnes bullets, 130, 145, 147–8, 159, 198, 370
barrels: alignment of, 53, 143, 212–14; contour of, 74, 88, 91–3; of custom-made rifles, 74–8, 80, 82–4, 86, 165; diameter of, 36, 59; fouling of, 42, 356–7; of Kentucky rifles, 23; length of, 22, 24, 39, 51, 59–61,

[i]

INDEX

barrels (*continued*)
64, 67–8, 70, 86–8, 90–1, 116, 121, 135–7, 141–2, 145, 164, 171, 175–6, 179, 180, 184, 354, 364; makers of, 83–6, 91–2; Remington, 63, 73, rifling of, 49, 91; steels of, 28, 30, 49, 58, 362; weight of, 59–61, 64, 71, 86, 87, 116, 154, 164, 176; Winchester, 58, 171

battery: for African use, 205–9, 215, 369–70; all-around, 364–5; minimum, 365; for the Rocky Mountains, 365–8; selection of, 359–71

Bausch & Lomb mounts, 253

Bausch & Lomb scope-sights: 4-x, 247; variable power, 247

bear, Alaskan brown: 186; bullets for, 132, 231, 365; cartridges and rifles for, 61, 151–3, 156, 164, 172, 191, 197, 201, 202, 360, 368–9, 371; danger from, 4, 9; weight of, 4, 186, 190–1, 333

bear, black: 3; cartridges and rifles for, 22, 111, 124, 135, 149, 364, 371; habitats of, 110–11; hunting on horseback, 176; weight of, 111

bear, grizzly, 4, 9–10, 186; bullets for, 229, 231, 233, 317, 328, 333, 335; cartridges and rifles for, 9, 10, 24, 25, 38, 43, 61, 130–2, 143, 145, 149, 151, 152, 156, 164, 172, 190–2, 197, 201, 202, 221, 305, 364; danger from, 186, 189; hunting on horseback, 174; weight of, 186, 191

Bearcat bullet, 42

Belding & Mull, 342, 356

Belding & Mull Handbook, 342

Belgian Browning rifles, 71

Berdan primers, 157

Biesen, Alvin, 83–84, 89, 105

big-game hunting: in Africa, 3; in different types of country, 12–18; habits of different nationalities, 19–22, 136–9; on horseback, 173–185, 354; popularity of began, 19–22

Birmingham Small Arms Co., 44, 72, 75

Bishop, E. C. and Sons, 94

bore, 27, 33, 49, 232; axes of, 211–14; cleaning of, 356–8; diameter of, 38; of German custom rifles, 77–8; large, 22, 26, 58, 200, 217, 218, 225, 238, 329–30, 360, 368, 370; lining of with bullet, 258–268, 340; medium, 216; small, 22, 58, 202, 216, 224, 370

Boxer-type primer, 157

Braddock, Dr. E. G., 187, 286

Brenneke 7 x 64 cartridge, 157–9, 234, 361

Brenneke, Wilhelm, 48, 157

British cartridges: .303, 62, 75, 138, 160, 267; .366, 199; .450, 217; Super .30, 195–6; for double-barreled rifles, 210–19; table of factory-loaded, 168

British rifles, 72; magazine, 75–6; short model, 75

British Textbook of Small Arms, 330

Brown, Myles, 187–9, 303, 366

Browning cartridge: 7.65 mm. short, 66

Buehler mount, 142–3, 184, 251, 253

buffalo: in Africa, 3; bullets for, 225, 232; cartridges and rifles for, 18, 23, 25, 151, 193, 194, 197, 201, 224, 369; danger from, 11, 18, 193; habitats of, 194; hunting conditions for, 14; size of, 193

Buhmiller, J. R., 83

bull eland, *see* antelope

bullets: caliber of, 328, 329; conical, 218; construction of, 17, 124, 155, 225–34, 328–30, 334, 362; for dangerous, thick-skinned game, 210–24, 333–6; for double-barreled rifles, 212–24; expansion of, 43, 124, 133, 135, 154, 225–28, 230–33, 329, 330, 332, 334, 335, 369; for forest game, 17, 110–35; full-metal cased (solid), 33, 34, 146, 193, 194, 201–3, 229, 231, 232, 334, 335, 367–9; for heavy, soft-skinned game, 187–209, 226; hollow point, 125, 195, 335, 368; for horseback hunting, 175–184; jacketed, 30, 42, 195, 199, 215–17, 226, 229, 230, 231, 329,

INDEX

bullets (*continued*)
332, 334, 335; jacket materials for, 226, 334, 362; killing power of, 327–33; lead, 23, 30, 225, 226, 228, 329, 332; for mountain game, 136–72; open point, 147, 230, 233; penetration of, 123, 124, 156, 175, 194, 203, 204, 224–9, 231, 233, 329–31, 334; round nose, 113, 226, 227, 229, 262; sectional density of, 44, 147, 152, 158, 165, 193, 198, 231, 262, 328, 330; soft nose, 125, 226; soft point, 38, 113, 124, 190, 193, 201, 202, 203, 218, 226–9, 231, 233, 332; spherical, 225; spitzer (sharp-pointed), 33, 34, 45, 49, 112, 113, 149, 154, 176, 226–8, 232, 233, 262; velocity of, 10, 18, 23, 25, 26, 29, 30, 32–49, 65, 112–13, 118, 122–3, 125, 130–1, 135, 137, 139–172, 175–184, 192, 193, 195–204, 213, 216–24, 226–9, 231–3, 261–9, 328, 330, 331, 333, 340, 359, 362, 369; weight of, 17, 18, 31, 33, 34, 36, 37, 43, 44, 46–8, 53, 65, 112, 113, 147, 192–5, 198–201, 203–4, 210, 213, 215–16, 218–19, 221, 223–5, 229, 230, 328, 331–3, 359, 360, 364, 368; *see also* specific names

Bullseye powder, 28
Burbank Rifle Range, 197
Burgess, Tom, 89, 142
Burrard, Major Gerald, 138–9

caribou: bullets for, 231, 328; cartridges and rifles for, 149, 151, 152, 155, 156, 168, 364; hunting on horseback, 174
carrying cases, 354–5, 366
cartridge boxes, 355–6
cartridge cases, 28, 35, 37–40, 42, 46–8, 51, 52, 55, 61, 65, 66, 159, 161, 162, 165, 196, 215, 216, 221, 222, 337, 339, 340, 341, 345, 346, 355, 362
cartridges: .30/06, 32–5, 37, 39, 40–1, 43–5, 47–9, 55–7, 59, 62–3, 67–8, 70–3, 76, 79, 90–1, 98, 113, 118, 130–3, 141–2, 147–8, 151–7, 161, 164–5, 170–2, 176, 178, 184, 186–9,

cartridges (*continued*)
190–2, 194–9, 200, 202, 205, 208, 226, 233, 253, 260–2, 266–7, 305, 308, 318–19, 324, 328, 331, 333, 335, 338, 340, 348, 353, 355–6, 360–1, 365–9, 371; 8 mm. short (8 x 51), 67; 6.5 mm. short (6.5 x 54), 67, 68; .75 x 68, 68; .38/55, 122; .25/20, 123; 7 mm./06, 157; .32/40, 160; 8 mm./06 (8 x 63), 161; .50/110, 359; .45/75, 360; .410, 368, 370; black-powder, 25, 26, 29, 31, 57, 217–18, 222; for bolt-action rifles, 51, 113; center-fire, 57, 58, 62, 65, 112, 146, 151, 152, 159, 160, 219, 337–9, 362; changes in design of, 33–49; choice of depends on, 5; for dangerous thick-skinned game, 210–24; for different types of country, 12–18; for forest game, 110–35; for heavy game in Africa, 186, 192–200, 202–9; for heavy game in North America, 186–92, 197; for hunting on horseback, 175–84; for mountain game, 136–72; rim-fire, 57, 62; rimless, 31, 197, 198, 210, 221; shape of, 30, 33–49; smokeless powder, 28–32, 159, 160; table of American factory-loaded, 167; table of British factory-loaded, 168; wildcat, 38, 39, 46, 47, 82, 135, 157, 161, 162, 166, 184, 196, 198, 200, 202, 221, 222, 338, 361, 365, 369; *see also* specific names

chamois: cartridges for, 13, 18, 137, 138
cleaning equipment, 356–8
cordite, *see* powder
Core-Lokt bullet, 42, 124, 125, 130, 155, 190, 195, 229, 231, 260, 335
Crossman, Capt. E. C., 34, 97, 242
Curtis, Paul, 242
Czechoslovakian actions and rifles: Brno, 72, 158, 166; carbine, 180; G-.33/40, 67; VZ-24, 142; VZ-33, 67, 72
Czechoslovakian Brno, 72

[iii]

INDEX

Dayton-Traister Company, 89
Dayton-Traister trigger, 142
deer, 4; bullets for, 226, 329; cartridges and rifles for, 23, 25, 37, 38, 44, 52, 60, 65, 72, 176, 187, 226, 233, 305; habitats of, 15–17; hunting on horseback, 176, 178, 180, 181
deer, Asian: rifles for, 133
deer, mule: 192, bullets for, 230, 328; cartridges and rifles for, 140, 141, 143, 145, 146, 155, 172, 177, 364, 371; danger from, 10–11; habitats of, 173; hunting on horseback, 176
deer, roe: cartridges for, 13, 137, 138
deer, whitetail, 3, 192; bullets for, 228, 328; cartridges and rifles for, 4, 5, 12, 22, 38, 111–126, 130–1, 133, 138, 140, 143, 145, 151, 308, 364, 371; habitats of, 110–11, 173, 177; hunting on horseback, 16, 176–9; weight of, 111
Dubiel cartridge, 46; .280, 163
Dubiel, John, 82
DuComb, Doc, 366
Dunlap, Roy, 89

Early, Red, 191
Eddystone Arsenal, 153
elephant: in Africa, 3; bullets for, 225, 229, 231, 232, 329, 334, 335; cartridges and rifles for, 46, 146, 194, 197, 201, 202, 203, 205, 210, 215, 216, 218, 220–4, 369, 370; danger from, 11, 18; habitats of, 194
Eley cartridge .404, 204, 205
elk, 186; bullets for, 225, 231, 328, 329; cartridges and rifles for, 18, 62, 132, 140, 146, 149–52, 155, 164, 168, 187, 197, 221, 226, 305, 333, 364; habitats of, 17, 132, 140, 173; hunting on horseback, 176, 180; weight of, 132, 193
Ellinwood, Tom, 299–300
Enfield actions and rifles, 44, 62, 72, 75, 80, 92, 138, 153, 166, 223; *see also* Lee actions, Pattern 14, and U. S. Model 1917

Everhart, Bill, 300
Express .425 Magnum cartridge, 221
Express .45 black-powder rifle, 31, 218

Fabrique Nationale, 44, 70–71, 154; rifles, 70–1
Farquharson actions, 57, 75
Federal Cartridge Company, 339
Field oil, 357–8
Firearms International Company, 71, 144
Forsythe, developer of percussion cap, 24
Frankfort Arsenal, 338
Frontier Model Colt revolver, 25
Fulcrum oil, 357–8

Garand, *see* M-1
George, John, 132
Gerlich, H., 45
German cartridges: 7 x 57, 211, 226; 7 x 64, 48–9, 70; 7.6 U. S., 153; 7 x 62 x 63, 153–4; 7.9 military, 33; 8 x 60 "Magnum," 67, 72, 161; 9.3 x 74-R, 204
Germania Waffenfabrik, 157; *see also* Waffenfabrik Mauser
Gewehr rifles: Model 41, 55; Model 43, 55
Gibbs cartridges: .404, 254; .505, 220–2, 254
Gibbs, George, 220
goats, *see* sheep and goats
Golata, Frank, 174
Griffin & Howe, 44, 67–69, 82, 83, 85, 86, 89, 94, 98, 102, 105, 109, 126, 144–5, 171, 200, 204, 206, 221, 254, 350, 370; *see also* Griffin, Seymour; Howe, James; Johnstone, Phil
Griffin & Howe .350 Magnum cartridge, 82, 193
Griffin & Howe mount, 242, 243, 250, 369
Griffin, Seymour, 44, 82, 206
grouse: rifles for, 367–8

H & H Magnum cartridges, 35; .375, 40, 45, 48, 59, 68, 82, 87, 91, 113,

[iv]

INDEX

H & H Magnum cartridges (*cont.*) 133, 138, 156, 191, 192, 197, 200–5, 247, 254, 305, 356, 361, 368–71; .300 (Super .30), 46–8, 58–9, 63, 68, 82, 87, 91, 138, 152, 162, 164, 165, 168, 170, 171, 191, 195, 196, 205, 305, 317, 355, 356, 361, 369; .270, 46, 47, 161; 7 mm., 46, 47, 161, 162, 165; .275, 48, 82; .404, 68, 370; .465 "India," 205, 208, 219, 335, 370; .416, 370
Halger cartridges and rifles, 45, 46, 68; .335, 45; .280, 46; *see also* Halger-Gerlich
Halger-Gerlich .280, 45
Hammer, Ralph, 197, 223–4
Hammett, Dr. John, 9
handloading: advantages of, 339–41; of hunting ammunition, 345–6; process of, 341–2; of target and varmint ammunition, 337–45, 367; tested loads for, 343–5; tools for, 338–42
Handloading Information, Vols. 1 and 2, 342
Hardy, Capt. A. H., 354–5
Hargreaves, Roy, 297
Hawken Brothers, 24
Henry and Spencer repeating rifles in Civil War, 24
Hensoldt scope-sights, 43, 241
Hercules Powder Company, 28, 338
Hoffman Arms Company, 43, 67, 68, 82, 98, 171, 200, 204, 221
Hoffman, Frank, 82; *see also* Hoffman Arms Co.
Holland & Holland, 48, 68, 75, 88, 170, 182, 200, 201, 211, 219
Holland & Holland rifles: No. 2 grade, 211; Model de Luxe, 211; *see also* H & H Magnum cartridges
Holliday, Jack, 229, 366
Hollywood Gun Shop, 47, 196, 200, 342
Hollywood Universal handloading tool, 342
Holmes, Morgan, 105

Hornet .22 cartridge, 58, 59, 60, 64, 123, 152, 209, 333, 370
Howe, James, 82

Ideal Handbook, 342
Ideal (Nutcracker) tong tool, 341–2
Imperial Chemical Industries, 204, 221

Jacquot, Gene, 38
Jaeger rifle, 22–4
javelina (peccary): bullets for, 228; cartridges and rifles for, 18, 43, 118, 145, 364; danger from, 10; weight of, 4
Jeffery cartridges: .333, 198, (*see also* Nitro-Express .333); .500, 221
Jeffery, W. J. & Co., 198, 221
Johnson Automatic, Inc., 56, 153
Johnson, Eric, 82
Johnson, Field, 9, 287
Johnstone, Phil, 206, 254
Jones, Jim, 360

Kentucky rifle, 19, 22–4, 96, 97, 111
Kerr Sporting Goods, 86
Klein, Herb, 192, 231
Kollmorgen Optical Corporation, 244
Kosholleck, Emil, 86, 107
Krag .30/40, 24, 29, 30, 32, 34, 80, 132, 160, 196, 226, 267
Kreighoff, 153
Krippner, William, 157

Lebel 8 mm. cartridge, 28
Lee actions and rifles, 50, 75, 138; *see also* Enfield
Lee, Capt. T. K., 256
Lemon, Carroll, 317, 326
Leonard, Russ, 143
Leupold scope-sights, 247
Leupold-Stevens Instrument Co., 244, 253
Linden, Alvin, 81, 84, 86, 95, 96, 98, 104, 108, 350–1, 356, 364
lion: in Africa, 3; bullets for, 132, 231, 335; cartridges and rifles for, 151, 153, 156, 194, 197, 198, 201, 203, 216, 335, 369; danger from, 11, 193; weight of, 193

INDEX

Lo-Swing scope mounts, 84, 369
Luger 9 mm. cartridge, 66
Lyman Gun Sight Company, 239, 243, 342
Lyman sights, 30; "1-A," 117; "48," 98, 120, 206, 240, 241, 250, 367, 369; "57," 241; Alaskan, 208, 243, 245, 250, 254, 354, 364; Challenger, 141, 244, 246, 247

M-1, 55, 118, 153
M.G.S. bullets, 130, 159, 165
Magnum cartridges, see H & H Magnum cartridges
Magnum Mauser actions, see Mauser
makers, of custom-made rifles, 74-109
Mannlicher actions and rifles, 50, 64, 69, 70, 75, 78, 151, 180; 6.5, 29, 175, 194, 231; "Haenel," 159; Model 88, 69, 159; Model 1895, 50; Model 1897, 194; Model 1903, 13, 69, 70, 136-7; Model 1905, 70; Model 1908, 70; Model 1910, 70; Model 1924, 70, 153; Model 1950, 153
Mannlicher cartridges: 6.5 x 54 rimless, 13, 69, 136, 137, 139; 8 mm., 152; 7 x 64, 158; 9 mm., 203; 9.5, 203; .256, 335; for Model 1893, 29; for various rifle models, 69-70
Mannlicher stocks, 67, 72
Mannlicher-Schoenauer, see Mannlicher
manufacturers: of factory-made rifles, 50-73
Marble Arms Company, 356
Marlin Arms Company, 65, 175
Marlin rifles: lever-action, 27, 52, 65-6, 97, 126, 175-6; Model 336, 65-6, 365
Mashburn Arms Co., 162, 196
Mashburn Magnum cartridges, 165; 7 mm. short, 162; 7 mm. long, 162, 163; .300 long, 196
Mauser actions and rifles, 13, 30-1, 36, 44-6, 50-2, 55, 62-3, 66-9, 71-2, 75-8, 80-2, 87, 89, 92, 138, 144, 147, 151, 153, 154, 165, 170, 171, 184, 196, 197, 199, 200, 210, 215,

Mauser actions and rifles (*continued*) 220, 356; "Mexican," 154; Model 88, 159, 160; Model 93, 146, 166; Model 95, 146, 166; Model 98, 58, 66, 67, 71, 74, 76, 83, 87, 90, 92, 147, 159, 160, 165, 166, 198, 361, 364; Model 1888, 159; Model 1905, 159, 160, 226; Model 1912, 67, 68; particulars of, 183; "Schilling," 159
Mauser cartridges: 7 x 57 (7 mm.), 29, 30, 32, 49, 59, 67, 68, 70, 71, 76, 90, 91, 117, 132, 142, 145-8, 154, 156, 157, 164, 166, 176, 177, 184, 194, 226, 231, 267, 319, 327, 335, 340, 354, 356, 361, 367; 8 x 57 (8 mm.), 29, 30, 67, 68, 152, 154, 159-61, 198, 226; 11 mm., 29; 9 mm., 59, 68, 203; 7.65, 59; 7.63, 66; 9.3, 68, 70, 199, 200; 10.75 x 68 (.443), 204; for magazine rifles, 220-4
Mauser Werke, 66, 67, 70, 76, 82, 153, 161, 199, 203; see also Waffenfabrik Mauser
McNab, Colonel Sandy, 208-9, 370
Mews, Leonard, 84
Miller, Ralph Waldo, 47
Miller Single Trigger Company, 89
Minar, Adolph, 81
moose, 186, 187; bullets for, 228, 233, 328, 329, 335, 360; cartridges and rifles for, 4, 5, 12, 38, 43, 61, 62, 72, 127-33, 146, 149, 151, 152, 164, 168, 188, 189, 192, 197, 221, 305, 333, 360, 364, 371; habitats of, 17, 127-8; hunting on horseback, 174; weight of, 4, 127, 186, 333
mounts: bridge, 249-53, 366; cost of, 243; custom-made, 252; German, 241-2; for scope-sights, 184, 206, 243, 249-55, 362; side, 238, 241-3, 250-2, 254, 353, 365, 367, 369; special, 247; see also specific names
muzzle energy, 23, 25, 26, 39, 40, 46, 122-6, 131, 134, 143, 146, 149, 163, 164, 195, 196, 198, 199, 201-4, 217-19, 221-3, 331-2
muzzle velocity, see bullets, velocity of

[vi]

INDEX

Mykrom mount, 250, 369

N.R.A. Sporter, 98; *see also* Springfield Model 1903
National Rifle Association, 79, 98, 338, 342
Neidner Arms Corporation, 43, 67, 81–3, 98, 200, 222
Neidner .400 cartridge, 222
Neidner mount, 243
Newton cartridges: .256, 39, 42–3, 227; .30, 39, 46, 162; .35, 40, 227
Newton, Charles, 37, 38, 39–44, 48, 153, 227, 361
Niles, Ken, 141
Nitro-Express cartridges, 218, 267; .577, 31, 219; .240, 48; .242 rimless Vickers, 48; .600, 54, 219; .318 rimless, 197, 198; .333 flanged, 198; .333 rimless, 198; .404 rimless, 203–4, 222; .470, 205, 208, 218, 335, 370; .45, 218; .475 No. 2, 218–19, 370
Nitro-Express rifles, 46, 217; .45, 31; .465, 18; double-barrel, 219; Model 30, 62
Norman-Ford & Co., 244
Noske mount, 184, 242, 364
Noske, R., 184, 242
Noske scope-sight, 364
Nosler bullet, 192, 231
Notes on Sporting Rifles, 138

O.K.H. .333 cartridge, 135, 198–9, 369
O'Connor, Bradford, 368
Owen, R. G., 80–81, 98, 105, 350

P.M.V.F. cartridges, 47, 196
Pachmayr, August, 81
Pachmayr, Frank, 81, 84, 364
Pachmayr Gun Works, 86, 106
Pachmayr Recoil Pads, 84
Pacific Gunsight Co., 157, 200, 342
Pacific handloading tool, 341–2
Pattern 14 action and rifles, 44, 50, 62, 72, 87, 151; *see also* Enfield actions
percussion cap: development of, 24, 26

Pfeffer, George, 286
Pfeifer .300 Improved Magnum cartridge, 196
Pfeifer Rifle Co., 171, 196
pistols, *see* rifles
position: with bench rest, 36, 150, 201, 240, 259, 276, 288, 312, 363; kneeling, 279, 280, 287, 304; offhand, 97, 112, 126, 189, 193, 197, 275, 279–82, 287–96, 300, 304, 306; prone, 36, 272, 276, 278, 279, 285–7, 295, 304, 311; sitting, 190, 201, 240, 279–88, 290, 291, 295, 300, 304, 312, 351, 352
powder: No. 10, 39; No. 13, 40; No. 15, 39; No. 3031, 147; No. 4064, 147, 203; No. 4198, 367; No. 4320, 156, 160, 161; No. 4350, 42, 147, 149, 156, 158, 159, 162–5, 196–8, 203; No. 4895, 146, 222–3; cordite, 27–8, 31, 171, 195, 202, 210, 214, 217–19; for double-barreled rifles, 213–15, 217–19, 222–3; double-base, 27–8; nitro-cellulose, 45, 195, 202, 213; Rottweil, 49, 158; single-base, 28; *see also* powder, black *and* powder, smokeless
powder, black, 23; composition of, 27; disadvantage of, 27; handloading with, 337; killing power of bullets using, 329; rifles using, 24–6, 217–18, 363; speed of, 27; trajectory of bullets using, 264
powder, smokeless: advantages of, 28, 30; bullets for, 226, 330; color of, 27; composition of, 27; development of, 27, 28, 33, 362; disadvantages of, 28; form of, 27; handloading with, 337–8
Powell, E. Baden, 47, 171
Power-Pac choke, 84
primer, 27, 53, 337–9, 341, 346, 362; *see also* specific names
Purdey .246 cartridge, 48
Purdey rifles, 211; .465, 220

R.W.S. Torpedo jacket bullet, 234
Redfield Gun Sight Company, 241
Redfield, Lyman, Williams, 61

[vii]

INDEX

Redfield mounts, 184, 251–2
Redfield sights: Series 70, 241; Series 102, 241
Remington Arms Co., 44, 62, 79, 98, 153, 339
Remington bullets: bronze-point, 10, 154, 178, 233, 318, 324; mushroom, 156, 194–5, 335; *see also* Core-Lokt
Remington cartridges: .25 rimless, 62, 123, 124; .30 rimless, 55, 62, 125, 267, 314, 369; .32 rimless, 62, 125; .35 rimless, 55, 59, 62, 65, 68, 73, 113, 126, 175, 267, 364, 365; .222 varmint, 63; .257, 63, 176, 319, 340, 356, 365, 366
Remington rifles: Model 8, 56, 118; Model 14, 55, 314; Model 30, 44, 80, 98, 126, 147, 153, 166, 184; Model 37, 58; Model 81, 56, 118, 126; Model 141, 55, 116, 226; Model 640, 348; Model 720, 44, 62, 153; Model 721, 44, 50, 62–4, 87, 142, 151, 153, 361; Model 722, 50, 63, 87, 146; Model 760, 55, 73, 126, 365; Mauser-type bolt-action, 62; Rider rolling block, 27
Remington-Hepburn single-shot actions, 57
Rheinisch-Westfalische Sprengstoff-Actien-Gesellschaft, 234
rhinoceros: in Africa, 3; bullets for, 225, 229, 232, 329, 334; cartridges and rifles for, 151, 193, 201, 215, 220, 224, 369; danger from, 11–12
Rigby, 75, 211, 214
Rigby cartridges: .350 Magnum, 204; .416, 204, 222
rifles: bolt-action, 41, 43, 44, 50–3, 55–8, 62–3, 65, 72–3, 77, 80, 84, 86, 97, 99, 101, 103, 113, 116–17, 126, 132–3, 141, 175, 179, 181, 196, 211, 215–16, 240, 348, 352, 365, 370; box-lock action, 52; breechloading, 24–6, 53, 79; caplock, 24, 79; changes in caliber of, 23–4; for dangerous game, 5, 12–18, 210–24; development of in America, 19–32, 361–3; for different types of

rifles (*continued*)
country, 12–18; double-barrel, 26, 50, 52–4, 57–8, 75–8, 80, 138–9, 160, 193, 196–8, 202, 204–5, 208, 210–24, 254, 331, 370; factory-made, 50–73, 141, 144; flintlock, 24, 79; for forest game, 5, 17, 110–35; for heavy, soft-skinned game in Africa, 186, 192–200, 202–9; for heavy, soft-skinned game in North America, 186–92, 197; lever-action, 25, 27, 41, 50, 52, 54, 57, 61, 64, 65, 73, 97, 116, 117, 126, 130, 133, 143, 175, 348, 352, 364, 365; for mountain game, 5, 15–17, 136–72, 365; muzzle-loading, 19, 24, 79, 96, 111, 225; for non-dangerous game, 5, 12–18; in pioneer days, 19–32, 111; for plains game, 5, 13–14, 24, 221; range of various, 307–8; remodeling of, 34–5; repeater, 24, 27, 57, 79; saddle, 51, 52, 60, 65, 173–85; semi-automatic or self-loading, 55–6, 116, 118, 153, 348; side-lock action, 52; single-shot, 50, 53, 56–7, 78, 138, 147, 160, 210, 215; slide-, or pump-action, 50, 57–8, 73, 116–17, 126, 314, 348, 364–5; three-barrel, 77, 211; *see also* rifles, custom-made, *and* specific names
rifles, custom-made, 74–109, 142, 349, 350, 358; cheek pieces on, 102–3, 105; how to choose, 85–109; makers of, 74–109
Roberts .257 cartridge, 48, 59, 71, 91, 133, 145–6, 187, 364
Rock Island arsenal, 153
Roosevelt, Theodore, 34
Ross actions and rifles: .280 sporting, 35, 336; Model 1910, 35, 36, 50
Ross .280 cartridges, 35, 36, 45, 68, 138, 226, 361
Ross, Sir Charles, 35
Ross scope-sights, 206

Sarber, Hosea, 156
Sauer, J. P., 153

INDEX

Savage Arms Corp., 64, 98, 153; *see also* Savage-Stevens Company
Savage cartridges: .303, 31; .250/3000, 37–9, 43, 48, 58, 64, 65, 67–8, 71, 87, 91, 116, 133, 143–5, 175, 226, 319, 340, 355–6, 364–5; .22 High Power, 37–9, 48, 54, 211, 226; .300, 55, 59, 63–5, 71, 73, 118, 133, 267, 319, 364–5
Savage rifles: .22, 65; .30/30 carbine, 65; lever-action, 52, 64, 97; Model 40, 153; Model 45, 153; Model 99, 64–5, 69, 116, 121, 143–4, 175
Savage-Stevens Company, 65; *see also* Savage Arms Corp.
scabbards, 180–1, 184, 347, 349, 352–5, 366; mounts for, 250–1
Scheutzen cheek pieces, 102–3
Schielke, George, 89
Schoellkopf Company, 355
scope mounts, *see* mounts
Sempert and Kreighoff, 69, 76
Sequoia Importing Company, 70
Sergel, Kristen, 220
Sharps actions and rifles, 25, 79; breechloader, 26; in Civil War, 24; single-shot, 57
Sharps cartridges: .40/90, 25; "Buffalo," 218
Sharps-Borchard single-shot actions, 57
sheep and goats, 192; bullets for, 230, 328; cartridges and rifles for, 12, 13, 25, 38, 137–41, 143, 146, 151, 155, 172, 187, 191, 197, 201, 364; habitats of wild, 14–15; hunting on horseback, 174, 176
Shelhamer, Tom, 82, 86, 98, 105, 107
shotguns, *see* rifles
shots: long-range, 305–13; placement of, 313–22; types of, 298–322
sighting in, 119, 121, 125–6, 154, 164, 198, 205, 237–40, 255, 258–69, 271–2, 274–5, 277, 287–9, 353, 362; ranges for, 268–9, 308–11
sights: adjustment of, 235, 258–69; on British rifles, 205, 206, 208, 237–8; on custom-made rifles, 74–109; development of, 30, 245; for dif-

sights (*continued*)
ferent types of country, 12–18; for different types of rifles, 53–4, 58, 68, 109, 175–6, 181, 184, 214, 216, 235–49; on factory-made rifles, 235, 237; for woods rifles, 55, 116, 118–21, 135, 245–6; *see also* sights, iron; sights, open; sights, peep; sights, scope, *and* specific names
sights, iron, 23, 59, 61, 68, 73, 92, 98, 101, 116, 120, 136, 142–4, 146, 171, 184, 206, 236, 239, 242, 244–5, 249, 259, 264, 266–8, 303, 365, 369; adjustment of, 259–60
sights, open, 59, 116, 118, 119, 121, 139, 142, 175, 235, 236, 304; adjustment of, 237–8, 241, 259–60; disadvantages of, 236–9
sights, peep (receiver), 54, 61, 71, 119–21, 135, 206, 208, 236, 239, 240–1, 244, 250, 254, 304, 365, 367; adjustment of, 240–1, 259–60; how to use, 239
sights, scope, 30, 36, 54, 57, 59, 60, 64, 68, 76–7, 90, 98–9, 101, 116, 135, 176, 181, 184, 206, 208, 238, 241–57, 259–60, 264, 266–7, 303–4, 352–4, 362, 364–7, 369, 370; adjustment of, 243–4, 249, 253–4, 259; advantages of, 244, 248; cost of, 243–4, 246–7; on custom-made rifles, 74–109; for different types of big game, 12–18, 245–9; disadvantages of, 244–5, 254; how to choose, 245–9; for hunting on horseback, 177, 179, 184, 250–1; for mountain game rifles, 141–72, 246; reticules for, 255–7, 304; suitability of various rifles for, 58–73; target, 36, 248; variable power, 247–8
Silvertop bullet, 124, 129, 131, 154, 195, 202, 229, 233, 266, 317, 335, 369
Simson, 76
Simpson, Leslie, 193
Sisk bullets, 229
sling, 348–52; types of, 284–5, 349, 351–2; use of, 284–7

INDEX

Speer bullet, 145–7, 158, 160, 165, 200
Speer Products, 47, 145
Speer, Vernon D., 200
Springfield actions and rifles, 90, 100, 144, 166, 198; .45/70, 24, 226; .50/70, 24; breechloader, 26; 1903, 32, 34, 50, 58, 79, 80, 87, 90, 92, 97–9, 120, 154; .30, 92
Springfield Arsenal, 98, 153
Stark Mantel bullet, 199
Stegall, Keith, 86
Steyr Werke, 69, 78, 158
Stith Bear Cub scope-sights, 141, 143, 179, 244–8, 250, 253
Stith-Kollmorgen scope-sights, 247
Stith Mounts, 244, 252
Stith mounts: Master, 253; Streamline, 184, 252
stocks: for custom-made rifles, 74–109; design of, 96–106, 362; for factory-made rifles, 59–73, 358; finishes for, 107–8, 358; one-piece, 51, 211; ornamentation of, 108–9; two-piece, 52; woods for, 93–6
Stoeger Arms Corporation, 68, 70, 144, 180
Sukalle safety, 142
Sukalle, W. A., 43–44, 83, 86, 89, 90, 145, 350, 364
Swedish Husqvarna, 44, 71
Swedish Husqvarna Mausers, 71, 151, 154
Swift .220 cartridge, 46, 58–60, 71, 112, 171, 253, 299, 319, 333, 364, 370

Tate, R. D., 81
Taylor, John, 221
Texan 4-x scope-sights, 247
Thalson Company, 180
tiger: bullets for, 132; cartridges and rifles for, 201; danger from, 12, 18; weight of, 12
Tilden Manufacturing Co., 251
Tilden mount, 184, 251
Tomorrow's Rifles Today, 342
trajectory, 25, 26, 29, 30, 32, 33, 42, 43, 44, 46, 48, 79, 112, 113, 126, 137, 141, 145, 146, 152, 158, 161, 164, 165, 168, 175, 178, 192, 194, 197,

trajectory (*continued*)
198, 201, 203, 260–9; effected by cartridge development, 33, 42, 43, 46, 48; kind needed in different types of country, 12–18; knowledge of, 260, 362; with use of black powder, 25–6; with use of smokeless powder, 29–30, 32; of various bullets, 268–9
trigger guard, *see* triggers
triggers: on custom-made rifles, 74–109; on factory-made rifles, 58–73
turkey: habitats of, 173; hunting on horseback, 176
twist, 34, 91, 147, 164

Unertl Optical Co., 247
Unertl scope-sights: 2¾-X, 247; 4-X Hawk, 247; 6-X Condor, 143, 247; 10-X, 286
U. S. Model 1917 action and rifle, 50, 62, 72, 80, 87, 92, 153, 166, 184, 223

varmint, 52; bullets for, 44, 165, 225, 228, 232; cartridges and rifles for, 46, 57, 64, 116, 133, 145, 151, 152, 186, 209, 223, 364, 370; classification of, 4
velocity: of bullets used by pioneer American hunters, 22–3, 25–6; development of increase in, 33–49; of first smokeless powder cartridges, 29, 31–2; needed in different types of country, 12–18; of sporting and military cartridges, 29, 32; *see also* bullets: velocity of

W.C.F. cartridges: .270, 18, 33, 42–5, 48, 56–60, 63, 69–72, 90, 91, 113, 128, 130–3, 141–2, 145–152, 154–9, 162–5, 172, 176, 178, 180, 184, 186–91, 194, 226, 233, 253, 261, 265, 305, 308, 317, 319, 328, 331, 333, 341, 356, 360–1, 364–9, 371; .35, 31, 131; .405, 31; .38/40, 122; *see also* Winchester cartridges
Waffenfabrik Mauser actions and rifles, 36, 40, 66, 67, 126, 144, 158; *see also* Mauser

[x]

INDEX

Watts .450 Magnum cartridge, 222-4, 370
Weatherby Magnum cartridges, 47-8, 84, 342, 361; .300, 10, 13, 87, 171-2, 191-2, 196-7, 202, 205, 231, 233, 247, 305, 308, 333, 346, 367, 369; .270, 161, 162, 346; 7 mm., 163-5, 172, 361, 365, 367; .375, 202-3, 238, 369; data on, 169-70
Weatherby, Roy E., 47, 48, 84, 96, 104, 105, 197, 202, 232, 342; *see also* Weatherby's, Inc.
Weatherby's, Inc., 84, 86, 87, 165, 196
Weaver, Bill, 243, 244
Weaver scope-sights: K-4, 141, 142, 244, 246-8; K-6, 143, 179, 244; K-8, 244; K-2.5, 244-5, 248, 261; Model 330, 243; Model 440, 243; variable power, 247
Wesley Richards, 197, 221
Wesley Richards cartridges: .318, 68, 156; .333, 156
Western bullets: boat-tail, 156, 195, 335; open-point, 154, 233, 319, 327; *see also* Silvertip
Western Cartridge Co., 39, 40, 147
Western Tool and Copper Works, 156
Whelen cartridges: .35, 82, 135, 200, 204, 369; .400, 82, 221, 222
Whelen cheek pieces, 102
Whelen sling, 284, 349
Whelen, Townsend, 35, 39, 242
White, Stewart Edward, 34, 156, 194, 335
Wilkinson, Jim, 162
Williams Foolproof sights, 241
Winchester actions and rifles, 79; lever-action, 27, 35, 52, 97, 176; Model 12 pump-action, 58; Model

Winchester actions and rifles (*cont.*) 21, 54, 58; Model 42, 368; Model 52, 58, 349; Model 54, 43, 46, 58, 80, 98, 147, 153, 165, 243; Model 64, 61, 116, 125, 348; Model 70, 42-4, 50, 57-60, 63, 86-7, 92, 126, 128, 141, 142, 144, 145, 147, 151, 153, 165, 166, 171, 179-80, 200, 201, 205, 243, 254, 349, 361, 368; Model 71, 61-2, 130-1, 348, 365; Model 79 single-shot, 57; Model 92, 314; Model 94 carbine, 60-1, 116, 175; Model 95, 35, 97, 131-2; Model 1873, 25; Model 1879 breechloader, 26-7; Model 1886, 61, 122; Model 1892, 122; Model 1894, 29; Model 1895, 26, 35, 153; semi-automatic sporting, 56
Winchester bullets, 230, 233; *see also* Silvertip
Winchester cartridges: .50/100, 26; .40/72, 26; .30/30, 29, 31, 35, 60-1, 65, 123-7, 133, 137, 139, 175, 226, 333, 356, 361, 371; .25/35, 39, 60, 123-4, 175, 267; .405, 54, 97, 131, 132, 156; .32 Special, 60, 65, 125, 175, 267; .348, 61, 130-1, 133, 165, 267, 364-5; .44/40, 122; .45/70, 122-3; .32/20, 123, 314; .35, 131; *see also* W.C.F. cartridges
Winchester Repeating Arms Co., 35, 46, 57, 98, 153, 337-9
Wright, John, 82
Wundhammer, Hans, 97, 100

zebra: cartridges and rifles for, 194; size of, 192
Zeiss scope-sights, 143, 241; Zeilklein, 243; Zielvier, 243

[xi]